# PRENTICE-HALL FOUNDATIONS OF FINANCE SERIES

# PRENTICE-HALL FOUNDATIONS OF FINANCE SERIES

**Ezra Solomon,** *Editor*

# Portfolio Analysis
## Second Edition

**Jack Clark Francis**

*Bernard M. Baruch College*
*The City University of New York*
*New York City*

**Stephen H. Archer**

*Willamette University*
*Salem, Oregon*

PRENTICE-HALL, INC. Englewood Cliffs, New Jersey 07632

*Library of Congress Cataloging in Publication Data*

Francis, Jack Clark.
    Portfolio analysis.

    Includes bibliographies and index.
    1. Investment analysis.  I. Archer, Stephen Hunt,
joint author.  II. Title.
HG4521.F69  1979        332.6′7        78-10568
ISBN  0-13-686675-1

Editorial/production supervision by Marian Hartstein
Manufacturing buyer: Trudy Pisciotti

Printed in the United States of America

10  9  8  7  6  5  4  3

Prentice-Hall International, Inc., *London*
Prentice-Hall of Australia Pty. Limited, *Sydney*
Prentice-Hall of Canada, Ltd., *Toronto*
Prentice-Hall of India Private Limited, *New Delhi*
Prentice-Hall of Japan, Inc., *Tokyo*
Prentice-Hall of Southeast Asia Pte. Ltd., *Singapore*
Whitehall Books Limited,*Wellington, New Zealand*

TO

Our Children

# Contents

## SECTION FOUR: UTILITY ANALYSIS

## SECTION FIVE: ASSET AND LIABILITY MANAGEMENT BY MEANS OF PORTFOLIO ANALYSIS

# SECTION SEVEN: OTHER ISSUES

# Preface

THE purpose of this monograph is to summarize the major parts of portfolio theory between two covers and under one consistent set of notations, to organize the material in a readable fasion, to articulate some relationships that seem to go unsaid in spite of their importance, and to inject a few of our own new insights (see especially Chapter 13 for new material). As the title of this Series implies, you should be near frontiers of finance in the portfolio analysis area after you've finished this book.

This book stresses economic rationale, mathematical definitions, numerical examples, and "how to do it yourself" math pointers to the exclusion of institutional and descriptive material. It will be clear at several points in the text that we believe it is more important to stress the tools with which the answers may be found than to "give the answers." We believe this is true for both research-oriented students and students who are training to be line managers. The analytical tools are as useful in solving cases as they are in research.

The amount of math and econometrics used in this book exceeds that which is found in most finance books. This represents a compromise. We tended toward less discussion and more analysis. Our students and reviewers, however, persuaded us to decrease the level of mathematics. What mathematics remains has been expanded with subjective discussion and numerical examples. This was done in hopes that the book may be read on several levels. Most business people and undergraduates may read the chapters and omit the appendices. More advanced students and professional analysts can read the appendices and track down the references that are most relevant to their work.

The only part of this monograph which was undeniably created by its authors are the errors. Many students, reviewers, colleagues, former students, reviewers, colleagues, former students, and friends helped us to develop whatever good parts the book may possess. Dr. Harry Markowitz provided the intellectual foundation. John Bildersee at Wharton, Andrew Chen at Ohio State University, Ed Elton at New York University, Frank Fabozzi at

Hofstra University, Donald Farrar at the University of Utah, Bob Haugen at the University of Wisconsin, Charles Haley at the University of Washington, Gabriel Hawawini at New York University, Cheng Few Lee at the University of Illinois, James Morris at the University of Houston, Timothy J. Nantell at the University of Michigan, George Oldfield at Dartmouth University, Herbert Phillips at Temple University, Gordon Alexander at the University of Minnesota, and Donald Thompson at Georgia State University are among the professors and research associates at other colleges and universities who contributed valuable comments on the manuscript. Professor Francis's colleagues at Baruch—Saman Hong, Gerald Pogue, and Stavros Thomadakis—similarly contributed significantly in developing this book. Each of these people read chapters and offered valuable advice. Barbara Gutman, Thelma Dixon, Sandy Kahn, Luise Webber, Roberta Chapey, Rosemary Alino, Christine Sherman, Marianne Mele, Roz May, Surachanee Pukdewong, Karen Reynolds, and Mary Wilkinson all helped with typing, debugging computer programs, drawing graphs, and other essentials. We are grateful to the Literary Executor of the late Sir Ronald A. Fisher, F.R.S., to Dr. Frank Yates, F.R.S., and to Longman Group Ltd., London, for permission to reprint Table 4.4 from their book Statistical Tables for Biological, Agricultural and Medical Research (6th edition, 1974). We are indebted to all these and others for help with this book.

Jack Clark Francis       *New York*
Stephen H. Archer        *Salem, Oregon*

```
1111111111111111111111111111111111111111111111111111111111111111111111111111111111
1111111111111111111111111111111111111111111111111111111111111111111111111111111111
111111111111111111111111111111111111111111    11111111111111111111111111111111111111
111111111111111111111111111111111111111111    11111111111111111111111111111111111111
111111111111111111111111111111111111111111    11111111111111111111111111111111111111
111111111111111111111111111111111111111111    11111111111111111111111111111111111111
111111111111111111111111111111111111111111    11111111111111111111111111111111111111
111111111111111111111111111111111111111111    11111111111111111111111111111111111111
111111111111111111111111111111111111111111    11111111111111111111111111111111111111
111111111111111111111111111111111111111111    11111111111111111111111111111111111111
111111111111111111111111111111111111111111    11111111111111111111111111111111111111
1111111111111111111111111111111111111111111111111111111111111111111111111111111111
1111111111111111111111111111111111111111111111111111111111111111111111111111111111
```

# Introduction

Sᴇᴄᴜʀɪᴛɪᴇs markets have long captured most people's curiosity and imagination. The mysteries and stories of sudden wealth are tantalizing—so much so that many people are moved to "play" the market.[1] Although investing is a complex subject, the potential rewards are great and an investor's interest usually grows. Recently, academicians and businesspersons, whose credentials suggest they seek to satisfy their intellectual curiosity as well as to supplement their incomes, have become interested in investments. Some of the relationships and facts that these people have uncovered are reported in this book.

## 1.1  Investments as a Subject of Study Is Changing

In 1952, Harry M. Markowitz published a now-classic paper which marked the beginning of a new type of investments research and analysis.[2] The report was practically unintelligible to most investments professors and practitioners when it was published because it used algebra and statistics. Rigorous scientific analysis was almost unknown on Wall Street and in college finance classes in the 1950s. The paper was misunderstood, viewed with

---

[1]For a discussion of "playing" the stock market, read *The Money Game* by "Adam Smith" (New York: Random House, Inc., 1967). The book puts rigorous analysis into an entertaining perspective.

[2]Harry M. Markowitz, "Portfolio Selection," *Journal of Finance*, March 1952, pp. 77–91.

some alarm, but largely ignored. However, Markowitz's paper, the monograph he wrote to expand the idea introduced in his paper,[3] and articles that can trace their foundations to Markowitz's work have ushered in a new era of investment teaching and methodology. However, these changes have affected the college classroom more than they have affected the way businesspeople invest.

In college-level investments courses, lectures about what happens on the floor of a stock exchange, the tax status of different sources of income, the needs of various investing institutions, and other descriptive and institutional matters are giving way to deeper analysis. The newer courses treat problems on a more abstract and general level. They seek more efficient methods of achieving investment objectives. They are more concerned with the "why" and less with the "who" and "where" questions.

More instructors and researchers are attempting to reduce the portion of the study of investments that previously had been left to judgment. Models of investor and market behavior have been constructed and a new body of conceptual relationships and principles has evolved. It is felt that this approach has more applications in more different areas and can be retained by students better than the descriptive and institutional material.

### 1.2 Characteristics of New Developments in Investments

The new developments that are reshaping investments courses have some common elements. First, the important new developments are all *mathematical* to some extent.[4] To those uninitiated in mathematics, this is a source of frustration. Those who are able to use mathematics recognize the following advantages of such theorizing:

1. All hypothesized relationships are explicit.
2. Definitions are clearer and in measurable terms.
3. The model readily yields to numerous forms of analysis that may result in subtle and revealing discoveries.
4. The model may be well suited for prediction.
5. Mathematics permits more succinct, and at the same time more complete, statements than verbal language.

A second element common to the newly developing models is their *simplicity*. They all abstract from reality. Rather than become bogged down in numerous real and imagined eventualities, the theories sometimes assume

---

[3]Harry M. Markowitz, *Portfolio Selection*, Cowles Foundation Monograph 16 (New York: John Wiley & Sons, Inc., 1959).

[4]The first Nobel prize ever awarded to economics or business scholars was awarded for econometric model building in November 1969. The second, given a year later, was also for mathematical economics. Since then, economic model builders have continued to win Nobel prizes while the other "social sciences" have won none.

ambiguities away. Then, on the basis of their assumptions, they deduce conclusions. There is nothing wrong with such model building. After all, if a theory indulged every eventuality, it would not be a theory—it would be description. Models are by definition abstractions of reality.

A third common element is the background of the theorists. In addition to being mathematically proficient, these men are either *economists* or have strong backgrounds in the discipline. Economics has a tractable model that can often be useful in financial analysis. The large amount of new financial literature being written by economists attests to the usefulness of such training.

Fourth, the theories are often very *general*. The perceptive student of these theories can readily adapt them to purposes unrelated to finance. Unfortunately, space does not permit a pursuit of the wide application of the theories discussed. Even the Markowitz model of portfolio analysis, to which this book is primarily directed, will not be extended into other fields. But a little imagination will allow the reader to see that Markowitz's analysis is adaptable for any decision involving risk, such as selecting an automobile, a home, a career, or even a spouse!

Fifth, the new models use *mathematical statistics*, which can be related to observable economic values. That is, the theories use real numbers and have "real-world" implications. This realism makes the models more interesting to two particular groups: (1) econometricians, and (2) business investment executives. The econometricians have found a wealth of mathematical models about investor behavior which they can formulate for empirical testing. And investments managers have been faced with an important and growing body of new knowledge to aid them in their work.

Finally, the processing of empirical data to test and apply the new theories must frequently be done with the aid of an *electronic digital computer*. The computer is the workhorse of the modern financial analyst. It surely and rapidly performs hundreds of thousands of calculations per second to test and implement the models developed by the economic theorists and formulated by the econometricians.

Considering all the characteristics of the new investments material suggests that the ideal modern investments student should be a mathematical economist who could readily formulate and test various econometric hypotheses with massive empirical data using a large computer. Fortunately, however, the student need not be expert in all these skills to perform well on the job. The work tends to be organized to carry out portfolio management employing specialists in each area.

### 1.3 Topics to Be Discussed

The general topic of this monograph is portfolio management. *Portfolio management* is a broad investments topic that includes the following three activities:

1. *Security analysis*—this work focuses on the probability distributions of the different investment alternatives rates of return.

2. *Portfolio analysis*—this phase of portfolio management mathematically delineates the optimum portfolio possibilities that can be constructed from the various investment opportunities which are avilable.

3. *Portfolio selection*—this final part of the portfolio management process deals with selecting and maintaining the one "best" portfolio from the menu of all good portfolios that are delineated by means of portfolio analysis.

Each of these three tasks is discussed briefly below.

### A.  The Security Analyst's Job

The demands on the security analyst are not as stringent as they may sound. For example, the forecaster need not forecast a security's returns for many periods into the future. In fact, he need only forecast "one period" into the future, since portfolio analysis deals with only one time period. The length of that time period can vary within wide limits. It definitely may not be a short-run period (portfolio analysis is not designed for speculative trading) or a very long-run period. But between, say, three months and ten years, the portfolio managers can select any planning horizons that fit the portfolio owner's needs.

The security analyst's forecast should be in terms of rates of return:

$$\text{rate of return} = \frac{(\text{ending price} - \text{beginning price}) + \text{dividends}}{\text{beginning price}}. \quad (1.1)$$

Equation (1.1) defines the rate of return on a common stock investment for "one period." Other definitions for the rate of return are given in Appendix 1A, the appendix to this chapter.

The security analyst need not make point estimates. Rather, it is necessary that he furnish the portfolio analyst with an estimated *probability distribution of returns* for each security. These may be estimated using historical data. The distribution may then need to be adjusted to reflect anticipated factors that were not present historically. Consider Fig. 1.1, an example of a probability distribution of rates of return for some security.[5]

The security analyst must also estimate correlation coefficients or covariances between all securities under consideration. His task will be discussed more extensively in Chapter IV. Given these pieces of information (input data), portfolio analysis can determine the optimal portfolio for any investor who is adequately described by the assumptions listed next.

---

[5]This probability distribution is a finite distribution, since the outcomes (rates of return) do not assume all possible values in the relevant range.

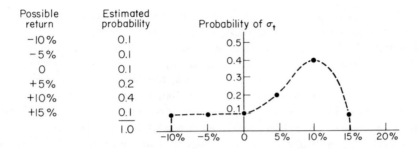

| Possible return | Estimated probability |
|---|---|
| −10% | 0.1 |
| −5% | 0.1 |
| 0 | 0.1 |
| +5% | 0.2 |
| +10% | 0.4 |
| +15% | 0.1 |
| | 1.0 |

Figure 1.1. Finite Probability Distribution of Rates of Return

## B. Portfolio Analysis

Portfolio analysis is all based on *four basic assumptions*.

1. All investors maximize one-period expected utility and exhibit diminishing marginal utility of wealth. This implies that investors visualize each investment opportunity as being represented by a probability distribution of additions to their terminal wealth. Equivalently, all investors visualize assets as probability distributions of expected returns over some holding period.

2. Investors' risk estimates are proportional to the variability of the expected returns.

3. Investors are willing to base their decisions solely in terms of expected return and risk. That is, utility $(U)$ is a function of variability of return $(\sigma)$ and expected return $[E(r)]$. Symbolically, $U = f(\sigma, E(r))$.

4. For any given level of risk, investors prefer higher returns to lower returns. Symbolically, $\partial U/\partial E(r) > 0$. Conversely, for any given level of rate of return, investors prefer less risk over more risk. Symbolically, $\partial U/\partial \sigma < 0$.

These assumptions will be maintained throughout the discussion of portfolio analysis and capital market theory. Investors described by these assumptions will prefer "Markowitz-efficient assets."

In essence, portfolio analysis is based on the premise that the most desirable assets are those which have:

1. The minimum expected risk at any given expected rate of return, or, conversely,
2. The maximum expected rate of return at any given level of expected risk.

Such assets are usually portfolios rather than individual assets. These assets are called "efficient portfolios" whether they contain one or many assets.

In the "real world" many investors are observed holding nonefficient portfolios. Furthermore, portfolio analysis is based on some simplified assumptions about reality. This raises questions as to the efficacy of the analysis. Before proceeding, it might be wise to examine the validity of these assumptions underlying portfolio analysis.

The first assumption about probability distributions of terminal wealth or rates of return may be violated in several respects. First, many investors simply do not forecast assets prices or know how to define the rate of return from an investment. Second, investors are frequently heard discussing the "growth potential," the "glamor" of a stock, the "ability of management," and numerous other considerations other than terminal wealth or rates of return. Third, investors often base their decisions on estimates of the "most likely" outcome rather than considering a probability distribution.

These seeming disparities with assumption 1 are not serious. If investors are interested in a security's "glamor" or "growth," it is probably because they (consciously or subconsciously) believe that these factors affect the asset's rate of return or terminal value. And, even if investors cannot define rate of return they may still try to maximize it merely by trying to maximize additions to their terminal wealth: the two objectives are equivalent. Furthermore, visualizing probability distributions need not be explicit. "Most likely" estimates are prepared either explicitly or implicitly from a subjective probability distribution.

The risk definition given in assumption 2 does not conform to the risk measures compiled by some popular financial services. The published quality ratings seem implicitly to define risk to be the probability of default. However, firms' probability of default is correlated with their variability of return so assumption 3 is invalid.[6]

As pointed out above, investors sometimes discuss concepts such as the "glamor" or "image" of a security. This may seem to indicate that the third assumption is an oversimplification. However, if these factors affect the expected value and variability of a security's rate of return, this assumption is not violated either.

The fourth assumption may also seem inadequate. Behavioralists have pointed out to economists that businesspersons infrequently, if ever, maximize or minimize. The behavioralists explain that businesspeople usually strive only to do a satisfactory or sufficient job. Rarely, if ever, do they work to attain the optimum of complete maximization or minimization, whichever may be the appropriate objective. However, if some highly competitive business managers attain near-optimization of their objective and other business managers follow these leaders, then this assumption also turns out to be not unrealistic.

In any event, all the assumptions underlying portfolio analysis have been shown to be inadequate to at least some extent. This raises questions as to the validity of portfolio analysis.

Although it would clearly be better if none of the assumptions underlying the analysis were ever violated, this condition is not necessary to establish the

---

[6]F. J. Fabozzi, "The Association between Common Stock Systematic Risk and Common Stock Rankings," *Review of Business and Economic Research*, Vol. XII, No. 3, Spring 1977, pp. 66–77.

value of the analysis. If the analysis rationalizes complex behavior that is observed (such as diversification), or, if the analysis yields worthwhile predictions, then it can be valuable in spite of fallacious assumptions. Furthermore, if the assumptions are only slight oversimplifications, as are the four above, they are no cause for alarm. People need only behave *as if* they were described by the assumptions for a theory to be valid.

Presuming that all investors behave *as if* they were described by the four basic assumptions discussed above means that the portfolio analysts can proceed to delineate the set of efficient portfolios. The set of efficient portfolios is called the *efficient frontier* and is illustrated in Fig. 1.2. The *efficient portfolios* along the curve between points $E$ and $F$ have the maximum rate of return at each level of risk. The efficient frontier is the menu from which the portfolio selection is made.

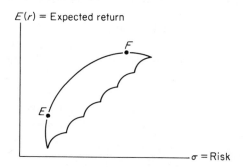

Figure 1.2. The Efficient Frontier

C. Portfolio Selection

The final phase of the portfolio management process is to select one "best" portfolio from the efficient frontier (that is, the curve between points $E$ and $F$ in Fig. 1.2) and then maintain the desirability of that portfolio. Of course, as security prices change, newer information becomes available, and cash dividends and/or coupon interest payments from bonds are acquired, the selected portfolio must be revised to maintain its superiority over alternative investment opportunities. Thus, portfolio selection leads, in turn, to additional security analysis and portfolio analysis work. The process of portfolio management is never-ending, if done properly.

## 1.4 Mathematics Segregated to Appendices

What follows will be partially mathematical. However, the reader who is uninitiated in mathematics can master the basic material. All that is needed is a remembrance of freshman college algebra, one course in classical statistics, and patience—mostly patience. The material is presented at the simplest possible level that a fair coverage of the model will allow. The basic material is presented completely in terms of elementary finite probability theory and algebra supplemented with graphs, explanation, and references where more complete explanations may be found.

Differential calculus and matrix algebra are used in some of the appendices. The reader is hereby forewarned and may avoid this material if he wishes. The book is written so its continuity will not be disturbed by skipping these appendices. Little, if any, of the vocabulary or basic concepts necessary for an acquaintance with the subject is found in these parts of the book. Most of the appendices contain practical solution techniques for large problems, proofs, derivations, and other material of interest only to the devout.

### Appendix 1A
### Various Single-Period Rates of Return Defined

#### 1A.1   Definitions

Rate of return may be defined in several ways. Consider the following three possible definitions of rates of return:

$$\text{market return} = \frac{\text{capital gains or loss plus dividend income}}{\text{purchase price}},$$

$$\text{earnings return} = \frac{\text{earnings per share}}{\text{market value per share}},$$

$$\text{accounting return} = \frac{\text{earnings per share}}{\text{book value per share}}.$$

The three different rates of return above are typically not even highly correlated with each other for the same firm and over the same periods. Thus, it makes a big difference how rate of return is defined. The vagaries of the accounting procedure and an investigation of how income should be defined will not be undertaken here. Suffice it to say, for investment decisions the investor is primarily concerned with the rate at which wealth or value increases. Since the market rate of return measures the rate at which the investor's wealth or the investment's value grows (or shrinks), this is the definition used throughout this book.

#### 1A.2   Calculating the Market Rate of Return Per Period

If an investor pays the price $p_0$ at the beginning of some period (say, a year) and gets back dividends $(d)$ or interest plus the price $p_1$ at the end of the period, the rate of return $(r)$ for that period is the discount rate that equates the present value of all cash flows to the cost of the investment. Symbolically,

$$p_0 = \frac{p_1 + d}{1 + r},$$
$$p_0(1 + r) = p_1 + d,$$
$$p_0 r = (p_1 - p_0) + d,$$
$$r = \frac{(p_1 - p_0) + d}{p_0}$$
$$= \frac{\text{capital gains plus dividends for the period}}{\text{beginning price}}. \quad (1.1)$$

Thus, if $100 is invested for one year and returns the principal plus $7 capital gains, plus $8 dividends, the return $r_1 = 15$ percent is found as follows:

$$p_0 = \$100 = \frac{107 + 8}{1 + r} = \frac{115}{1 + r},$$
$$r_1 = \frac{7 + 8}{\$100} = \frac{\$15}{\$100} = 15 \text{ percent} = \text{annual rate of return}$$

by equation (1.1). And, if the $115 is invested and returns the $115 principal plus $-$13.75 capital loss plus $8 dividend, the annual return is $r_2 = -5$ percent.

$$\$115 = p_0 = \frac{115 - 13.75 + 8.00}{1 + r} = \frac{109.25}{1 + r},$$
$$r_2 = \frac{-13.75 + 8}{115} = \frac{-5.75}{115} = -5 \text{ percent annual rate of return.}$$

The rate of return defined by equation (1.1) is thus seen to be identical to the internal rate of return, the holding-period yield, or the marginal efficiency of capital for investments of "one-period" duration.

Equation (1.1) is defined in terms of the income sources from common stock investment, since this analysis is primarily concerned with portfolios of common stocks. However, the rate of return on other forms of investment is easily defined, and this analysis is general enough so that assets other than merely common stocks may be considered. For example, the rate of return on a real estate investment could be defined as

$$r = \frac{V_1 - V_0}{V_0}, \quad (1A.1)$$

where $V_1$ is the investor's end-of-period value for a real estate holding and $V_0$ is the beginning-of-period value or cost.

### 1A.3 Taxes

The analysis presented here can be conducted to fit the needs of an investor in a given tax situation. That is, equation (1.1) may be adapted to treat any tax differential between dividends and capital gains that the analyst considers appropriate. This would require restating equation (1.1) in the form

$$r_t = \frac{(\text{ending price} - \text{beginning price})(1 - T_G) + \text{dividends}(1 - T_O)}{\text{beginning price}},$$

(1.1a)

where $T_G$ is the relevant capital gains tax rate and $T_O$ the relevant ordinary income tax rate to the particular investor. To conduct the analysis in this manner will obviously require additional calculation. To avoid this calculation, tax considerations will not be incorporated explicitly throughout the analysis. However, the effects of taxes, brokerage commissions, and other transactions costs that are relevant to a given investment situation can readily be included in the computations. Equation (1.1b) defines a common stock's one-period return after commissions and taxes for a stock purchased on margin.

$$r_t = \frac{(p_1 - p_0 - \text{commissions})(1 - T_G) + d_t(1 - T_O)}{p_0(1 - m)},$$

(1.1b)

where $m$ is the proportion of $p_0$ borrowed to buy the security on margin, $0 \leq m \leq 1.0$.

### 1A.4 Continuous Compounding

Equations (1.1) and (1A.1) define a holding-period yield that is compounded once per period. These equations must be restated if continuous compounding is assumed. The continuous analog to equation (1.1) is

$$r_t = \ln\left(\frac{p_{t+1} + d_t}{p_t}\right) = \ln(p_{t+1} + d_t) - \ln p_t,$$

(1A.2)

where ln denotes the natural or naperian logarithm.[1] The continuous analog to equation (1A.1) is

$$r = \ln\left(\frac{V_1}{V_0}\right) = \ln V_1 - \ln V_0.$$

(1A.3)

---

[1]Natural logarithms are used because they offer advantages over common logarithms. First, the natural logarithm of the value relatives is a good estimate of the rate of return for returns below 15 percent—for example, ln ($110/$100) = 0.095. Second, the differentiation rule for natural logarithms is simple.

The rate of return computed with continuous compounding is smaller than the return calculated with less frequent compounding.[2] For example, $1 invested at the beginning of some period that returns $1.10 at the end of the period would have a rate of return of 10 percent by equation (1A.1)—namely

$$\frac{V_1 - V_0}{V_0} = \frac{1.10 - 1.00}{1.00} = \frac{0.10}{1.00} = 10 \text{ percent.}$$

But, by equation (1A.3), the return on this same investment is 9.5 percent, calculated as follows:

$$\ln \left(\frac{V_1}{V_0}\right) = \ln \left(\frac{1.10}{1.00}\right)$$
$$= \ln (1.1) - \ln (1.00) = 0.095 - 0 = 0.095 = 9.5 \text{ percent.}$$

The advantage of using equations (1A.2) and (1A.3) is that they are adapted to calculation of the geometric mean return.[3]

---

[2]For an insightful comment about measuring continuously compounded single-period returns, see Norman E. Mains, "Risk, the Pricing of Capital Assets, and the Evaluation of Investment Portfolios: Comment," *Journal of Business*, Vol. 50, No. 3, 1977, pp. 371–384.

[3]The geometric mean rate of return (or compounded average rate of return, or time-weighted rate of return) is discussed in Chapter 12 of this monograph.

# Section One

# RISK ESTIMATES

CHAPTER II lays the foundation for the remainder of this monograph by defining risk analytically—in terms of the finite-probability model. Chapter III discusses risk more intuitively and redefines some old financial words, such as *portfolio* and *diversification,* to give them new dimensions of meaning. Chapter IV shows several ways to obtain empirical esmates of the financial statistics introduced in Chapters II and III.

```
2222222222222222222222222222222222222222222222222222222222222222222222222222222222222
2222222222222222222222222222222222222222222222222222222222222222222222222222222222222
22222222222222222222222222222222222     222     2222222222222222222222222222222222222
22222222222222222222222222222222222     222     2222222222222222222222222222222222222
22222222222222222222222222222222222     222     2222222222222222222222222222222222222
22222222222222222222222222222222222     222     2222222222222222222222222222222222222
22222222222222222222222222222222222     222     2222222222222222222222222222222222222
22222222222222222222222222222222222     222     2222222222222222222222222222222222222
22222222222222222222222222222222222     222     2222222222222222222222222222222222222
22222222222222222222222222222222222     222     2222222222222222222222222222222222222
22222222222222222222222222222222222     222     2222222222222222222222222222222222222
2222222222222222222222222222222222222222222222222222222222222222222222222222222222222
2222222222222222222222222222222222222222222222222222222222222222222222222222222222222
```

# Finite-Probability Foundations

Most people are surprised when they first see how mathematical the modern scientific investments analysis appears. This is because many people have weak backgrounds in mathematics and are therefore unfamiliar with its symbols and definitions. The purpose of this chapter is to calm those who are surprised and explain to those who are unfamiliar with mathematics what they need to know to master modern investments analysis.

Essentially, this chapter explains the tools with which risk may be analyzed. More specifically, the chapter reviews the parts of freshman college algebra and elementary finite probability courses which are relevant to investments analysis. This is simple undergraduate mathematics. But the rigor of the explicit definitions used in mathematics "turns some people off." Allowing yourself to be "turned off" and "dropping out" rather than perservering is short-sighted. If you will "bite the bullet" and master this topic, it will not only teach you how to scientifically analyze investment opportunities, it will also raise your level of consciousness in other academic and nonacademic areas. That is, mathematics applied to real-world problems is powerful stuff that can make your life sweeter. It sounds corny but it is true. Words such as *expectation* and *risk* will be given new rigorous definitions that may fascinate you.

## 2.1 Mathematical Expectation

For a $1 bet on the flip of a coin, the expected value of the outcome is the probability of heads times the $1 loss plus the probability of tails times the $1 gain. Symbolically,

$$\text{expected value} = p(\text{heads})(-\$1) + p(\text{tails})(+\$1)$$
$$= 0.5(-1) + 0.5(+1) = 0,$$

where $p(\text{heads})$ represents the probability that heads occurs. The symbols above are a very definitive statement of what is meant by the phrase, "we expect that gamblers will break even." Writing this expression for expected value in even more general and compact form,

$$E(x) \equiv \sum_{t=1}^{T} p_t x_t$$
$$\equiv (p_1)(x_1) + (p_2)(x_2) + \cdots + (p_T)(x_T). \tag{2.1}$$

It is assumed that the probabilities sum to 1, $\sum_{t=1}^{T} p_t = 1.0$. In words, equation (2.1) says that the expected value of the random variable $x$ (for example, $x$ might be the dollar outcome of the gamble or any other number resulting from an experiment involving chance) equals the sum of all $T$ different products of $(p_t)$ and $(x_t)$, where $p_t$ is the probability of the $t$th outcome [for example, $p$ (heads) $= p_t = \frac{1}{2}$ when flipping coins] and $x_t$ is the $t$th outcome (for example, $x_t = -\$1$ or $+\$1$ might represent heads or tails).

Mathematicians say that the letter $E$ as used in equation (2.1) is an *operator*. They mean that the letter $E$ specifies the operation of multiplying all outcomes times their probabilities and summing those products to get the expected value. Finding the expected values of a set of numbers is roughly analogous to finding the *weighted average* of the numbers—using probabilities for weights. Do not be confused, however; although the arithmetic is the same, an average is conceptually different from an expectation. An expectation is determined by its probabilities and it represents a hypothesis about an unknown outcome. An average, however, is a summarizing measure. There is some connection between the average and the expectation—the mechanical similarity of the calculations. And, both the average and the expected value measure what physicists call the *center of gravity*.

The operator $E$ will be used to derive several important formulas. Therefore, consider several elementary properties of expected values, which will be used later:

(i) The expected value of a constant number is that constant. Symbolically, if $c$ is any constant number (for example, $c = 2$ or 99 or 1064),

$$E(c) = p_1c + p_2c + \cdots + p_Tc = c.$$

This simple statement is almost a tautology.

(ii) The expected value of a constant times a random variable[1] equals the constant times the expected value of the random variable. Thus, if $x$ is a random variable where $x = -1$ represents a loss and $x = +1$ represents a win in a coin flip and $c$ is the constant number of dollars bet on each toss, this situation may be restated as follows:

$$E(cx) = cE(x).$$

The proof follows:

$$E(cx) = \sum_{t=1}^{T} p_t(cx_t) = p_1(cx_1) + \cdots + p_T(cx_T)$$

$$= p_1cx_1 + \cdots + p_Tcx_T$$

$$= c(p_1x_1 + \cdots + p_Tx_T) = c\sum_{t=1}^{T} p_tx_t = cE(x).$$

(iii) The expected value of the sum of $n$ independent random variables is simply the sum of their expected values. For example, if $n = 2$ for random variables called $x$ and $y$,

$$E(x + y) = E(x) + E(y).$$

The proof follows:

$$E(x + y) = \sum_{t=1}^{T} p_t(x_t + y_t)$$

$$= p_1(x_1 + y_1) + p_2(x_2 + y_2) + \cdots + p_T(x_T + y_T)$$

$$= p_1x_1 + p_1y_1 + p_2x_2 + p_2y_2 + \cdots + p_Tx_T + p_Ty_T$$

$$= (p_1x_1 + p_2x_2 + \cdots + p_Tx_T) + (p_1y_1 + p_2y_2 + \cdots + p_Ty_T)$$

$$= \sum_{t=1}^{T} p_tx_t + \sum_{t=1}^{T} p_ty_t = E(x) + E(y),$$

where $p_t$ is the *joint* probability of $x_t$ and $y_t$ occurring jointly.

(iv) The expected value of a constant times a random variable plus a constant equals the constant times the expected value of the random variable

---

[1]A random variable is a rule or function that assigns a value to each outcome of an experiment. For example, in the coin toss, the random variable is $x$ and it can assume two values, $-1$ for $x_1$ and $+1$ for $x_2$.

plus the constant. Symbolically, if $b$ and $c$ are constants and $x$ is a random variable,

$$E(bx + c) = bE(x) + c.$$

The proof is a combination of the proofs for (i), (ii), and (iii).

The reader who has trouble with this brief development of expected-value operator is encouraged to consult an elementary text on finite probability theory.[2]

## 2.2   Risk

The phrase "dispersion of outcomes around the expected value" could be substituted for the word "risk" as used here. The word "riskier" simply means "*more* dispersion of expected outcomes around the expected value." The "dispersion-of-outcomes" definition of risk squares with the common but less precise use of the word in everyday conversation. Consider a more formal version of this definition, which lends itself well to analysis.

The mathematics terms *variance* and *standard deviation* measure dispersion of outcome about the expected value. Symbolically, the variance of the random variable $x$ is

$$\sigma_x^2 = \sigma_{xx} = \sum_{t=1}^{T} p_t[x_t - E(x)]^2 = E[x - E(x)]^2$$

$$= p_1[x_1 - E(x)]^2 + p_2[x_2 - E(x)]^2 + \cdots + p_T[x_T - E(x)]^2. \qquad (2.2)$$

In words, the variance $(\sigma_x^2)$ is the sum of the products of the squared deviations times their probabilities. If all $T$ outcomes are equally likely, $p_i = 1/T$. If a coin-flipping gamble is fair [that is, $E(x) = 0$] and the stakes are \$5, the variance is computed as follows:

$$\begin{aligned} \text{var (\$5 gamble)} &= p_1[x_1 - E(x)]^2 + p_2[x_2 - E(x)]^2 \\ &= (\tfrac{1}{2})(-5 - 0)^2 + (\tfrac{1}{2})(+5 - 0)^2 \\ &= 12.50 + 12.50 = 25. \end{aligned}$$

The variance of the \$5 gamble is 25 "dollars squared." To convert this measure of risk into more intuitively appealing terms, the standard deviation $(\sigma)$, which is simply the square root of the variance, will be used.

$$\sigma = \sqrt{\sum_{t=1}^{T} p_t[x_t - E(x)]^2} = \sqrt{\sigma_{xx}} = \sqrt{E[x - E(x)]^2} = \sqrt{\sigma^2}. \qquad (2.3)$$

---

[2]A book such as F. Mosteller, R. E. K. Rourke, and G. B. Thomas, *Probability with Statistical Applications* (Reading, Mass.: Addison-Wesley Publishing Co., Inc., 1961), would be an excellent source for self-taught finite probability theory and a handy reference for readable definitions.

Thus, $\sqrt{25}$ "dollars squared" = \$5 = standard deviation of the \$5 gamble.

Notice in equations (2.2) and (2.3) that the variance and standard deviations are both defined two ways. First, they are defined using the summation sign $(\Sigma)$ and probabilities. Second, they are defined using the expected-value operator $(E)$, which equation (2.1) showed means the same thing as the summation sign and probabilities. The definitions will be used interchangeably. Consider another example—one more appropriate for portfolio analysis.

*Example 2.1*     Two securities' annual rates of return for a 10-year period are shown below. Assume that these are historical data.

| Year | American Telephone Works (ATW) (%) | General Auto Corp. (GAC) (%) | Joint Probability |
|------|------|------|------|
| 1 | 7 | 5 | 0.1 |
| 2 | 4 | 0 | 0.1 |
| 3 | 0 | −5 | 0.1 |
| 4 | 7 | 5 | 0.1 |
| 5 | 10 | 10 | 0.1 |
| 6 | 14 | 16 | 0.1 |
| 7 | 7 | 16 | 0.1 |
| 8 | 4 | 10 | 0.1 |
| 9 | 10 | 10 | 0.1 |
| T = 10 | 7 | 10 | 0.1 |
| | | | 1.0 |

From the data a security analyst computes the following relative frequencies —or, in our usage, probability distributions.

| American Telephone Works (ATW) | | General Auto Corp. (GAC) | |
|------|------|------|------|
| Forecasted Return (%) | Marginal Probabilities | Forecasted Return (%) | Marginal Probabilities |
| 0 | 0.1 | −5 | 0.1 |
| 4 | 0.2 | 0 | 0.1 |
| 7 | 0.4 | 5 | 0.2 |
| 10 | 0.2 | 10 | 0.4 |
| 14 | 0.1 | 16 | 0.2 |
| | 1.0 | | 1.0 |

To derive the probability distributions above, the security analyst could have ignored the historical data or paid little attention to them. He could have made a subjective probability distribution based on his experience and intuition. The security analyst's tools are examined in Chapter IV. However, assuming that the processes determining the historical returns will not change in the future, the expected probability distribution is derived directly from the historical data.

### 2.3  Expected Return

The expected return of ATW is calculated using equation (2.1) and substituting the random variable $r$ for the random variable $x$ in the equation as follows:

$$E(x) = \sum_{t=1}^{T} p_t x_t, \tag{2.1}$$

$$E(r_{\text{ATW}}) = \sum_{t=1}^{10} p_t r_t. \tag{2.1a}$$

Or, using the marginal probabilities instead of the joint probabilities, equation (2.1a) may be written as

$$E(r_{\text{ATW}}) = \sum_{1}^{5} pr$$

$$= (0.1)(0) + (0.2)(0.04) + (0.4)(0.07) + (0.2)(0.1) + (0.1)(0.14)$$

$$= 0 + 0.008 + 0.028 + 0.02 + 0.014 = 0.07 = 7 \text{ percent.}$$

The reader may check his or her understanding of formula (2.1a) by verifying $E(r_{\text{GAC}}) = 0.077 = 7.7$ percent $=$ the expected return for GAC.

### 2.4  Risk in a Security

Risk was generally defined as the expected dispersion of the outcomes. In discussing securities it will be assumed that the rate of return is the single most meaningful outcome associated with the securities' performance. Thus, discussion of the risk of a security will focus on dispersion of the security's rate of return around its expected return. That is, one might equate a security's risk with its "variability of return."[3] The standard deviation of rates of return (or variance of rates of return) is a possible measure of the phenomenon defined above as the risk of a security. Symbolically, this can be written by substituting $r_i$'s in the place of $x$'s in equation (2.2).

$$\sigma_i^2 = \sigma_{ii} = \sum_{t=1}^{T} p_{it}[r_{it} - E(r_i)]^2 = E[r_i - E(r_i)]^2. \tag{2.2a}$$

---

[3]Harry M. Markowitz, *Portfolio Selection*, Cowles Foundation Monograph 16 (New York: John Wiley & Sons, Inc., 1959), p. 14.

Equation (2.2a) defines the variance of returns for security $i$. The value of $\sigma_{ii}$ is in terms of a "rate of return squared." The standard deviation of returns is the square root of the variance.

$$\sigma \text{ or } \sigma_i = \sqrt{\sum_{t=1}^{T} p_{it}[r_{it} - E(r_i)]^2} = \sqrt{E[r - E(r)]^2} = \sqrt{\sigma_{ii}}. \qquad (2.3a)$$

Thus, for the returns on ATW in Example 2.1, using the marginal probabilities, the variance and standard deviation of returns are found as follows:

$$\begin{aligned}
\sigma_{\text{ATW}}^2 &= (0.1)(0 - 0.07)^2 + (0.2)(0.04 - 0.07)^2 + (0.4)(0.07 - 0.07)^2 \\
&\quad + (0.2)(0.1 - 0.07)^2 + (0.1)(0.14 - 0.07)^2 \\
&= (0.1)(0.0049) + (0.2)(0.0009) + (0.4)(0) + (0.2)(0.0009) \\
&\quad + (0.1)(0.0049) \\
&= 0.00049 + 0.00018 + 0 + 0.00018 + 0.00049 = 0.00134 \\
\sigma_{\text{ATW}} &= \sqrt{0.00134} = 0.0368 = 3.68 \text{ percent.}
\end{aligned}$$

It is left as an exercise for the reader to verify that the standard deviation of returns from GAC is 6.28 percent.

### 2.5  Covariance of Returns

The covariance of returns on securities $i$ and $j$ will be denoted by $\sigma_{ij}$ or $\text{cov}\,(r_i, r_j)$.

$$\begin{aligned}
\sigma_{ij} &= E\{[r_i - E(r_i)][r_j - E(r_j)]\} \\
&= \sum_{t=1}^{T} p_t\{[r_{it} - E(r_i)][r_{jt} - E(r_j)]\}, \qquad (2.4)
\end{aligned}$$

where $r_{it}$ is the $t$th rate of return for the $i$th firm. The 10 ordered pairs of rates of return $(r_{\text{ATW}}, r_{\text{GAC}})$ from Example 2.1 have been graphed in Fig. 2.1, and a numerical example follows.

By making the assumption that all 10 returns are equally likely to occur, $p_t = 1/T = \frac{1}{10}$ can be substituted for the probabilities in the formula for covariance. Thus, the formula can be rewritten

$$\sigma_{ij} = \sum_{t=1}^{10} \tfrac{1}{10}[r_{\text{ATC}_t} - E(r_{\text{ATC}})][r_{\text{GAC}_t} - E(r_{\text{GAC}})].$$

The calculations are shown below. Notice that in Fig. 2.1 all but one of the ordered pairs $(r_{\text{ATW}}, r_{\text{GAC}})$ are plotted in the first quadrant, the northeast quadrant.

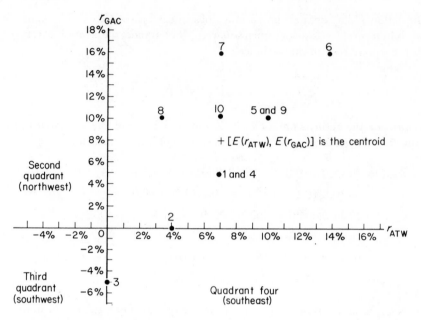

Figure 2.1. Ten Ordered Pairs ($r_{ATW}$, $r_{GAC}$) of Rates of Return from ATW and GAC Data in Example 2.1

| Obser-vation, $t$ | ATW | | GAC | | Prob-abilities, $p_t = 1/r$ | Products Column, $(p_t)[r_{it} - E(r_i)][r_{jt} - E(r_j)]$ |
|---|---|---|---|---|---|---|
| | $r_{it}$ | $r_{it} - E(r_i)$ | $r_{jt}$ | $r_{jt} - E(r_j)$ | | |
| 1 | 0.07 | 0 | 0.05 | −0.027 | 0.1 | 0 |
| 2 | 0.04 | −0.03 | 0 | −0.077 | 0.1 | +0.000231 |
| 3 | 0 | −0.07 | −0.05 | −0.127 | 0.1 | +0.000889 |
| 4 | 0.07 | 0 | 0.05 | −0.027 | 0.1 | 0 |
| 5 | 0.1 | 0.03 | 0.1 | 0.023 | 0.1 | +0.000069 |
| 6 | 0.14 | 0.07 | 0.16 | 0.083 | 0.1 | +0.000581 |
| 7 | 0.07 | 0 | 0.16 | 0.083 | 0.1 | 0 |
| 8 | 0.04 | −0.03 | 0.1 | 0.023 | 0.1 | −0.000069 |
| 9 | 0.1 | 0.03 | 0.1 | 0.023 | 0.1 | +0.000069 |
| 10 | 0.07 | 0 | 0.1 | 0.023 | 0.1 | 0 |
| | | | | | 1.0 | 0.001770 |

$$E(r_{ATW}) = 0.07 \qquad E(r_{GAC}) = 0.077 \qquad \sum_{t=1}^{T=10} p_t[r_{it} - E(r_i)][r_{jt} - E(r_j)]$$

The first and third quadrants of Fig. 2.1 contain the ordered pairs whose products (that is, $r_{ATW}$ times $r_{GAC}$) are positive. The second and fourth quadrants contain the ordered pairs whose products are negative. However, in calculating the covariance the origin (the point where $r_{ATW} = 0$ and $r_{GAC} = 0$) is not used to determine whether the 10 observed values of $r_{ATW}$

22

and $r_{GAC}$ are high (positive) or low (negative) deviations. The covariance uses deviations of the random variable from its expected value [that is, the $t$th deviation is $(r_t - E(r))$], which, in effect, shifts the point of reference from the origin to the *centroid*, the "center of gravity" for the 10 points.[4]

Thus, points northeast and southwest of the centroid will have positive products [that is, $(p_t) \cdot (r_{it} - E(r_i)) \cdot (r_{jt} - E(r_j))$] in the products column of the computations shown. Since only the eighth ordered pair lies either northwest or southeast, it is the only negative product in the products column of the computation. Obviously, the positive products exceed the negative products; that is, there are more points southwest and northeast of the centroid. Thus, the sum of these products, which is the covariance of returns, is positive. The sign of the net total of these products determines the sign of the covariance.

If the 10 ordered pairs had been further northeast and southwest of the centroid, the covariance would have been a larger positive number. If the majority of the plotted points were southeast and northwest of their centroid, their covariance would be negative because the two variables moved inversely (were negatively correlated).

The covariance of some variable with itself equals the variance of that variable: compare formulas (2.2) and (2.4). The covariance of returns on securities $i$ and $j$ is

$$\sigma_{ij} = E[(r_i - E(r_i)) \cdot (r_j - E(r_j))]. \qquad (2.4)$$

Note that when $i = j$, equation (2.4) becomes equation (2.2a).

$$\sigma_{ij} = \sigma_{ii} = \sigma_{jj} = E[r_i - E(r_i)]^2 = E[(r_j - E(r_j))]^2, \qquad (2.2a)$$

which shows that the covariance of $i$ or $j$ with themselves or with identical securities (that is, when $i = j$) equals the variance.

In calculating covariances it makes no difference which variable comes first. Thus, $\sigma_{ij} = \sigma_{ji}$ for any variables $i$ and $j$.

If the reader is unsure of these assertations, he should take real numbers such as given in the numerical examples and calculate the values by hand.

## 2.6   Correlation of Returns

Within the context of portfolio analysis *diversification* can be defined as *combining securities with less than perfectly positively correlated* returns. In order for the portfolio analyst to construct a diversified portfolio, the analyst must know correlation coefficients between all securities under consideration. Denote the correlation coefficient between securities $i$ and $j$ as $\rho_{ij}$.

---

[4]The centroid is the point where the expected values of all variables occur. In $(r_{ATW}, r_{GAC})$ space $[E(r_{ATW}), E(r_{GAC})]$ is the centroid.

A correlation coefficient can vary as follows: $-1 \leq \rho \leq +1$. If $\rho_{ij} = +1$, the returns on securities $i$ and $j$ are perfectly positively correlated; they move in the same direction at the same time. If $\rho_{ij} = 0$, the returns of $i$ and $j$ are uncorrelated; they show no tendency to follow each other. If $\rho_{ij} = -1$, securities $i$ and $j$ vary inversely; they are perfectly negatively correlated. The definition of $\rho_{ij}$ is

$$\rho_{ij} = \frac{\text{cov}\ (r_i, r_j)}{\sigma_i \sigma_j} = \frac{E[(r_i - E(r_i))(r_j - E(r_j))]}{\sigma_i \sigma_j}$$

$$= \frac{\sum p_t[(r_{it} - E(r_i))(r_{jt} - E(r_j))]}{\sigma_i \sigma_j}, \tag{2.5}$$

where $\sigma_i$ is defined by equation (2.3a) and cov $(r_i, r_j)$ is the covariance of returns of the two securities $i$ and $j$ defined in equation (2.4).

The covariance measures how the random variables vary together—how they covary. Thus, the covariance always has the same sign as the correlation coefficient. Using equation (2.5), the correlation of returns for $i = \text{ATW}$ and $j = \text{GAC}$ can be computed as follows:

$$\rho_{ij} = \frac{\sigma_{ij}}{\sigma_i \sigma_j} = \frac{0.00177}{(0.0368)(0.0628)} = \frac{0.00177}{0.00231} = +0.77 = \rho_{\text{ATW,GAC}}.$$

Using circular definitions, the covariance can be defined in terms of the correlation coefficient and the standard deviations,

$$\sigma_{ij} = (\rho_{ij})(\sigma_i)(\sigma_j). \tag{2.6}$$

Equation (2.6) is derived by simple algebraic manipulation of equation (2.5).

### 2.7   Data Required for Portfolio Analysis

Portfolio analysis requires that the security analyst furnish the following estimates for every security to be considered:

1. The expected return.
2. The variance of returns.
3. The covariances between all securities.[5]

The security analyst could obtain these inputs from historical data; or he can subjectively estimate these inputs. If the historical data are accurate and conditions in the future are expected to resemble those from the period in

---

[5]Using Sharpe's simplified model, covariances based on some market index may be used instead of covariances between all possible combinations of securities. These simplified models are examined in Chapter VII.

which the data were derived, the historical data may be the best estimate of the future. But if the security analyst is "expert" or the market is changing, subjective estimates may be preferable to historical data.

Since the security analyst can consider each security separately, he deals primarily with single random variables. The tools and concepts developed so far in this chapter are appropriate for such work.

The portfolio analyst must consider many securities at once when constructing the optimum portfolio. That is, he must be concerned with the expected return and risk of the weighted *sum* of many random variables. In the next few pages the statistical tools the portfolio analyst uses will be developed.

### 2.8  Weights Within the Portfolio

The portfolio analysis technique that follows does not directly indicate the dollar amount that should be invested in each security. Rather, it yields the optimum *proportions* each security in the optimum portfolio should assume. These proportions, weights, or participation levels, as they are variously called, will be denoted by $x_i$'s. Thus, $x_i$ is the fraction of the total value of the portfolio that should be placed in security $i$. Assuming that all funds allocated for portfolio use are to be accounted for, the following constraint is placed on all portfolios:

$$\sum_{i=1}^{n} x_i = 1. \tag{2.7}$$

In words, the $n$ fractions of the total portfolio invested in $n$ different assets sum up to 1. This constraint cannot be violated in portfolio analysis or the analysis has no rational economic interpretation. Equation (2.7) is simply the well-known balance sheet identity where equity is defined as 100 percent $= 1.0$ and the total assets have a total weight equal to the sum of the $n$ different $x_i$ decision variables. Assuming that the portfolio has no liabilities means that total assets equals equity—as shown in equation (2.7). Portfolios with liabilities will be considered in Chapters III, VIII, and XIII.

### 2.9  Expected Return from a Portfolio

Letting $r_p$ denote some actual return from portfolios and $E(r_p)$ its expected return, $E(r_p)$ may be defined as in equation (2.8):

$$E(r_p) = \sum_{i=1}^{n} x_i E(r_i) = \sum_{i=1}^{n} x_i \left( \sum_{t=1}^{T} p_{it} r_{it} \right)$$
$$= x_1 E(r_1) + x_2 E(r_2) + \cdots + x_n E(r_n). \tag{2.8}$$

In words, the expected return on a portfolio is the weighted average of the expected returns from the $n$ assets in the portfolio.

Thus, the expected return of the portfolio with $x_{ATW} = 0.4$ and $x_{GAC} = 0.6$ is

$$E(r_p) = (0.4)E(r_{ATW}) + (0.6)E(r_{GAC}) = (0.4)(0.07) + (0.6)(0.077)$$
$$= 0.028 + 0.0462 = 0.0742 = 7.42 \text{ percent.}$$

Note that $\sum_{i=1}^{2} x_i = 1$, this is the balance sheet identity.

### 2.10  Portfolio Risk

It is necessary to expand the mathematical definition of risk used for single securities into a form describing the returns of all securities in the portfolio. Following the "dispersion of outcome" or "variability of return" definitions of risk, the risk of a portfolio is defined as the variability of its return—that is, the variability of $r_p$. Denoting the variance of $r_p$ by var $(r_p)$, it is possible to derive an analytical expression for var $(r_p)$ in terms of the $r_i$'s of all securities in the portfolio. This is the form of the expression suitable for portfolio analysis.

Substituting $r_p$ for $r_i$ in equation (2.2a) yields equation (2.2b), which will be denoted by var $(r_p)$.

$$\sigma_{ii} = E[r_i - E(r_i)]^2 = \sigma_i^2, \tag{2.2a}$$
$$\sigma_{r_p}^2 = \text{var } (r_p) = E[r_p - E(r_p)]^2. \tag{2.2b}$$

A simple two-security portfolio will be used to analyze equation (2.2b). However, the results are perfectly general and follow for an $n$-security portfolio, where $n$ is any positive integer. Substituting the quantity $(x_1 r_1 + x_2 r_2)$ for the equivalent $r_p$ into equation (2.2b) yields equation (2.2c).

$$\text{var } (r_p) = E[(x_1 r_1 + x_2 r_2) - E(x_1 r_1 + x_2 r_2)]^2. \tag{2.2c}$$

Removing the parentheses and using property (i) of the expectation (since the $x_i$'s can be treated as constants) results in an equivalent form:

$$= E[x_1 r_1 + x_2 r_2 - x_1 E(r_1) - x_2 E(r_2)]^2.$$

Collecting terms with like subscripts and factoring out the $x_i$'s gives

$$= E(x_1[r_1 - E(r_1)] + x_2[r_2 - E(r_2)])^2.$$

Since $(ab + cd)^2 = (a^2 b^2 + c^2 d^2 + 2abcd)$, the squared quantity above can likewise be expanded by letting $ab = x_1[r_1 - E(r_1)]$ and $cd = x_2[r_2 - E(r_2)]$, which gives

$$E(x_1^2[r_1 - E(r_1)]^2 + x_2^2[r_2 - E(r_2)]^2 + 2x_1x_2[r_1 - E(r_1)] \cdot [(r_2 - E(r_2)]).$$

Using property (ii) of the $E$ operator yields

$$x_1^2 E[r_1 - E(r_1)]^2 + x_2^2 E[r_2 - E(r_2)]^2$$
$$+ 2x_1x_2 E([r_1 - E(r_1)] \cdot [r_2 - E(r_2)]),$$

and, recalling equations (2.3a) and (2.4), which define $\sigma_{ii}$ and $\sigma_{ij}$, we recognize the expression above as

$$= x_1^2 \sigma_{11} + x_2^2 \sigma_{22} + 2x_1x_2\sigma_{12}$$
$$= x_1^2 \, \text{var} \, (r_1) + x_2^2 \, \text{var} \, (r_2) + 2x_1x_2 \, \text{cov} \, (r_1r_2). \tag{2.9}$$

In words, equation (2.9) shows that the variance of a weighted sum is not always simply the sum of the weighted variances. The covariance term may increase or decrease the variance of the sum, depending on its sign.

The derivation of equation (2.9) is repeated in a more coherent manner as follows:

$$\begin{aligned}
\sigma_{r_p}^2 = \text{var} \, (r_p) &= E(r_p - E(r_p))^2 \\
&= E[x_1r_1 + x_2r_2 - E(x_1r_1 + x_2r_2)]^2 \\
&= E[x_1r_1 + x_2r_2 - x_1E(r_1) - x_2E(r_2)]^2 \\
&= E[x_1(r_1 - E(r_1)) + x_2(r_2 - E(r_2))]^2 \\
&= E[x_1^2(r_1 - E(r_1))^2 + x_2^2(r_2 - E(r_2))^2 \\
&\quad + 2x_1x_2(r_1 - E(r_1))(r_2 - E(r_2))] \\
&= x_1^2 E(r_1 - E(r_1))^2 + x_2^2 E(r_2 - E(r_2))^2 \\
&\quad + 2x_1x_2 E[(r_1 - E(r_1))(r_2 - E(r_2))] \\
&= x_1^2 \, \text{var} \, (r_1) + x_2^2 \, \text{var} \, (r_2) + 2x_1x_2 \, \text{cov} \, (r_1r_2). \tag{2.9}
\end{aligned}$$

The derivation of equation (2.9) is one of the main teaching points of this chapter. An understanding of equation (2.9) is essential to understanding diversification and portfolio analysis. Next, equation (2.9) will be expanded (without proof) to measure the risk of more realistic portfolios (portfolios with more than two securities). However, even in its more elaborate versions, equation (2.9) is still simply the sum of the weighted variances and covariances.

Equation (2.9) is sometimes written more compactly as

$$\text{var} \, (r_p) = \sum_i^n x_i^2 \sigma_{ii} + \sum_i^n \sum_{\substack{j \\ \text{for } i \neq j}}^n x_i x_j \sigma_{ij},$$

where $n = 2$ or any other positive integer. To clarify this notation, consider the following table of terms. The subscript $i$ is the row number and $j$ is the column number.

| | Column 1 | Column 2 | |
|---|---|---|---|
| var $(r_p) =$ | $+x_1x_1\sigma_{11}$ | $+x_1x_2\sigma_{12}$ | Row 1 |
| | $+x_2x_1\sigma_{21}$ | $+x_2x_2\sigma_{22} =$ | Row 2 |

$$= x_1x_1\sigma_{11} + x_1x_2\sigma_{12} + x_2x_1\sigma_{21} + x_2x_2\sigma_{22}$$

$$= x_1^2\sigma_{11} + 2x_1x_2\sigma_{12} + x_2^2\sigma_{22} \qquad \text{since } x_1x_2\sigma_{12} = x_2x_1\sigma_{21}$$

$$= \sum_{i=1}^{2} x_i^2\sigma_{ii} + \sum_{\substack{j=1}}^{2}\sum_{\substack{i=1 \\ \text{for } i \neq j}}^{2} x_ix_j\sigma_{ij} \tag{2.9a}$$

$$= \sum_{j}^{2}\sum_{i}^{2} x_ix_j\sigma_{ij} \qquad \text{since cov } (r_i, r_i) = \text{var } (r_i) \text{ for } i = j \tag{2.9b}$$

$$= \sum_{i=1}^{2} x_i^2\sigma_{ii} + \sum_{\substack{i=1 \\ \text{for } i \neq j}}^{2}\sum_{j=1}^{2} x_ix_j\rho_{ij}\sigma_i\sigma_j \qquad \text{since } \sigma_{ij} = \rho_{ij}\sigma_i\sigma_j. \tag{2.9c}$$

The three factors that determine the risk of a portfolio are the weights of the securities, the standard deviation (or variance) of each security, and the correlation coefficient (or covariance) between the securities.

Expressions of var $(r_p)$ for a large number of securities take the following form.

| | Col. 1 | Col. 2 | Col. 3 | | Col. $n - 1$ | Col. $n$ | |
|---|---|---|---|---|---|---|---|
| | $x_1x_1\sigma_{11} +$ | $x_1x_2\sigma_{12} +$ | $x_1x_3\sigma_{13} +$ | $\cdots +$ | $x_1x_{n-1}\sigma_{1,n-1} +$ | $x_1x_n\sigma_{1n} +$ | Row 1 |
| | $x_2x_1\sigma_{21} +$ | $x_2x_2\sigma_{22} +$ | $x_2x_3\sigma_{23} +$ | $\cdots +$ | $x_2x_{n-1}\sigma_{2,n-1} +$ | $x_2x_n\sigma_{2n} +$ | Row 2 |
| var $(r_p) =$ | $x_3x_1\sigma_{31} +$ | $x_3x_2\sigma_{32} +$ | $x_3x_3\sigma_{33} +$ | $\cdots +$ | $x_3x_{n-1}\sigma_{3,n-1} +$ | $x_3x_n\sigma_{3n}$ | Row 3 |
| | . | . | . | | . | . | . |
| | . | . | . | | . | . | . |
| | . | . | . | | . | . | . |
| | $x_nx_1\sigma_{n1} +$ | $x_nx_2\sigma_{n2} +$ | $x_nx_3\sigma_{n3} +$ | $\cdots +$ | $x_nx_{n-1}\sigma_{n,n-1} +$ | $x_nx_n\sigma_{nn}$ | Row $n$ |

The data above comprise a matrix. The matrix can be represented more compactly using the succinct summation symbols shown:

$$\text{var } (r_p) = \sum_{i=1}^{n} x_i^2\sigma_{ii} + \sum_{\substack{i=1 \\ \text{for } i \neq j}}^{n}\sum_{j=1}^{n} x_ix_j\sigma_{ij} = \sum_{i=1}^{n}\sum_{j=1}^{n} x_ix_j\sigma_{ij}.$$

A matrix can be thought of as an array of numbers or a table of numbers.[6] The matrix above represents the weighted sum of all $n$ variances plus all

[6]The matrix above is a special type of matrix called the *variance–covariance matrix*.

$(n^2 - n)$ covariances. Thus, in a portfolio of 100 securities ($n = 100$), there will be 100 variances and $(100^2 - 100 =)9900$ covariances. The security analyst must supply all of these plus 100 expected returns for the 100 assets being considered. Later, a simplified method will be shown to ease the securities analyst's work.[7]

Notice that the spaces in the matrix containing terms with identical subscripts form a diagonal pattern from the upper left-hand corner of the matrix to the lower right-hand corner. These are the $n$ weighted variance terms (for example, $x_i x_i \sigma_{ii}$). All the other boxes contain the $(n^2 - n)$ weighted covariance terms (for example, $x_i x_j \sigma_{ij}$). Since $x_i x_j \sigma_{ij} = x_j x_i \sigma_{ji}$, the variance–covariance matrix is *symmetric*. Each covariance is repeated twice in the matrix. The covariances above the diagonal are the mirror image of the covariances below the diagonal. Thus, the security analyst must actually estimate only $(\frac{1}{2})(n^2 - n)$ unique covariances.

If the two securities from Example 2.1 are combined into a portfolio, the expected return $E(r_p)$ is found with equation (2.8). To calculate the variance of such a portfolio, recall that $\sigma_{12} = \sigma_{21} = 0.00177$, $\sigma_{11} = (\sigma_{ATW})^2 = (0.0368)^2 = 0.00134$, $\sigma_{22} = (\sigma_{GAC})^2 = (0.0628)^2 = 0.00393$. Assuming that half the portfolio's funds were invested in ATW and half in GAC, then $x_1 = x_2 = \frac{1}{2}$. Equation (2.9) is evaluated as follows:

$$
\begin{aligned}
\text{var}(r_p) &= x_1^2 \sigma_{11} + x_2^2 \sigma_{22} + 2x_1 x_2 \sigma_{12} \\
&= (0.5)^2(0.00134) + (0.5)^2(0.00393) + 2(0.5)(0.5)(0.00177) \\
&= (0.25)(0.00134) + (0.25)(0.00393) + 2(0.25)(0.00177) \\
&= (0.25)(0.00134) + (0.25)(0.00393) + (0.5)(0.00177) \\
&= 0.000335 + 0.000982 + 0.000885 = 0.002202.
\end{aligned}
$$

The standard deviation of this security portfolio is

$$
\sigma_{r_p} = \sqrt{\text{var}(r_p)} = \sqrt{0.0022} = 0.047 = 4.7 \text{ percent.} \qquad (2.10)
$$

### 2.11  Summary of Notation and Formulas

A summary of notation and important equations concludes this chapter. The simple single-period rate-of-return from a share of stock is

$$
r = \frac{(\text{ending price} - \text{beginning price}) + \text{dividends}}{\text{beginning price}} \qquad (1.1)
$$

The following notation will be used throughout the analysis:

$$
p_i = \text{probability of the } i\text{th outcome, } 0 \le p_i \le 1
$$

---

[7]See Chapter VII about a simplified method.

$x_i$ = weight of $i$th security in portfolio, or the participation level of the $i$th security

$\sigma_{ii}$ = variance of $i$th random variable—for example, the variance of the $i$th security or the covariance of the $i$th random variable with itself

$\sigma_i$ = standard deviation of $i$th random variable

$\sigma_{ij}$ = cov $(i,j)$ = covariance of $i$th and $j$th random variables

$r_i$ = rate of return on $i$th security

$\rho_{ij}$ = correlation coefficient between $i$th and $j$th random variables

$R$ = pure or riskless rate of interest

$\sigma_p$ = SD$(r_p)$ = standard deviation of portfolio = $\sqrt{\text{var }(r_p)}$.

The expected rate of return is

$$E(r) = \sum_{t=1}^{T} p_t r_t = p_1 r_1 + p_2 r_2 + \cdots + p_T r_T = \sum_{i=1}^{T} p_i r_i. \quad (2.1a)$$

The variance of returns for a single random variable is

$$\sigma_{ii} = \sum_{t=1}^{T} p_{it}[r_{it} - E(r_i)]^2 = E[r - E(r)]^2$$

$$= p_1[r_1 - E(r)]^2 + p_2[r_2 - E(r)]^2 + \cdots + p_T[r_T - E(r)]^2. \quad (2.2a)$$

The standard deviation of returns is

$$\sigma = \sqrt{\sum_{t=1}^{T} p_{it}[r_{it} - E(r)]^2} = \sqrt{E[r - E(r)]^2}. \quad (2.3a)$$

The covariance of returns of the $i$th and $j$th securities is denoted cov $(r_i, r_j)$ and also as

$$\sigma_{ij} = E[(r_i - E(r_i)) \cdot (r_j - E(r_j))] = \sum_{t=1}^{T} (p_t)[r_{it} - E(r_i)][r_{jt} - E(r_j)] \quad (2.4)$$

$$= (\rho_{ij})(\sigma_i)(\sigma_j). \quad (2.6)$$

The correlation coefficient between the $i$th and $j$th securities rates of return is

$$\rho_{ij} = \frac{\text{cov }(i,j)}{\sigma_i \sigma_j} = \frac{E[(r_i - E(r_i)) \cdot (r_j - E(r_j))]}{\sigma_i \sigma_j}. \quad (2.5)$$

The sum of all $n$ weights in the portfolio must be 1:

$$\sum_{i=1}^{n} x_i = 1. \quad (2.7)$$

The expected return of the portfolio is the weighted average of the expected returns of the assets comprising the portfolio:

$$E(r_p) = \sum_{i=1}^{n} x_i E(r_i) = \sum_{i=1}^{n} x_i \left( \sum_{t=1}^{T} p_{it} r_{it} \right) \qquad (2.8)$$

$$= x_1 E(r_1) + x_2 E(r_2) + \cdots + x_n E(r_n). \qquad (2.8a)$$

The variance of the portfolio can be defined simply for the two-security portfolio:

$$\text{var } (r_p) = x_1^2 \sigma_{11} + x_2^2 \sigma_{22} + 2x_1 x_2 \sigma_{12}. \qquad (2.9)$$

For the $n$-security portfolio, the variance of the portfolio's returns can be denoted several ways, all of which are equivalent.[8]

$$\text{var } (r_p) = \sum_{i=1}^{n} x_i^2 \sigma_{ii} + \sum_{j=1}^{n} \sum_{i=1}^{n} x_i x_j \sigma_{ij} \qquad \text{for } i \neq j \qquad (2.9a)$$

$$= \sum_{j=1}^{n} \sum_{i=1}^{n} x_i x_j \sigma_{ij} \qquad (2.9b)$$

$$= \sum_{i=1}^{n} x_i^2 \sigma_{ii} + \sum_{j=1}^{n} \sum_{i=1}^{n} x_i x_j \rho_{ij} \sigma_i \sigma_j \qquad \text{for } i \neq j. \qquad (2.9c)$$

The standard deviation of the $n$-security portfolio is

$$\sigma_{r_p} = \text{SD}(r_p) = \sqrt{\text{var } (r_p)}. \qquad (2.10)$$

The formulas above comprise the skeleton of the investment analysis model, the subject of this book. Chapter III begins to flesh in this skeleton by using graphs and realistic numerical examples to explicate a few applications-oriented examples.

---

[8]Different derivations of these same essential formulas may be found elsewhere: namely, Markowitz, *Portfolio Selection*, Chaps. 3 and 4.

## Selected Reference

Markowitz, Harry M., *Portfolio Selection*. New York: John Wiley & Sons, Inc., 1959. This classic is the sixteenth book in the Cowles Foundation Monographs, an invitational series of scholarly economics books. Chapters 3, 4, and 5 present an explanation of the finite probability model, which is easy to read and presumes zero mathematics background.

## Questions and Problems

1. A die is a small cube that is rolled across gambling tables in games of chance. The six sides of a die are numbered with the integers from 1 through 6. If the die is fair, all six sides are equally likely to be up when the rolled die comes to rest. Make a probability distribution for all possibilities that might turn up when a fair die is rolled. What is the mathematical expected value of the outcome for each roll of a fair die? Is this expected value actually a possible numerical outcome from any one roll of a die? If not, then what is the value of the expected value in this die-rolling application?

2. When two fair dice are rolled simultaneously and then come to rest, the numbers that are facing upward on the two dice are added together to find a score on that particular roll of the dice. Make a probability distribution for all possible scores when two fair dice are rolled. What is the mathematical expected value of the score everytime two fair dice are rolled? What is the variance of all possible scores when two fair dice are rolled? What is the expected correlation coefficient between the two separate scores turned up on the two dice when they are rolled?

3. Find a rigorous mathematical statistics book and look up the definition of "random variable." Is one number in a series of randomly fluctuating outcomes from an experiment involving chance (for example, dice scores) a random variable? Explain. (*Hint:* It isn't.)

4. Draw a scatter diagram on a two-dimensional graph showing what you expect to be the relationship between the following pairs of variables:

   (a) Storks flying over Texas and babies born in Texas in each of 25 different years. Plot 25 points. Do you think storks bring babies?
   
   (b) The sales of left shoes and the sales of right shoes in the borough of Brooklyn every month for two years. Plot 24 points. Are these two variables directly or inversely related?
   
   (c) The temperature outside the White House in Washington, D.C., and the amount of heating oil needed to heat the White House every month for three years. Plot 36 points. Why do you expect that this relationship is not perfectly inverse?

Make an "eyeball" estimate of the correlations between the two variables plotted in each of the three scatter diagrams. Then, calculate the actual correlation coefficients and compare them.

```
33333333333333333333333333333333333333333333333333333333333333333333333333333333333
33333333333333333333333333333333333333333333333333333333333333333333333333333333333
333333333333333333333333333333333333   333   333   33333333333333333333333333333333
333333333333333333333333333333333333   333   333   33333333333333333333333333333333
333333333333333333333333333333333333   333   333   33333333333333333333333333333333
333333333333333333333333333333333333   333   333   33333333333333333333333333333333
333333333333333333333333333333333333   333   333   33333333333333333333333333333333
333333333333333333333333333333333333   333   333   33333333333333333333333333333333
333333333333333333333333333333333333   333   333   33333333333333333333333333333333
333333333333333333333333333333333333   333   333   33333333333333333333333333333333
333333333333333333333333333333333333   333   333   33333333333333333333333333333333
33333333333333333333333333333333333333333333333333333333333333333333333333333333333
33333333333333333333333333333333333333333333333333333333333333333333333333333333333
```

# Risk, Efficiency, and Diversification

CHAPTER III presents some key investments concepts. Terms such as risk, dominant, efficient, opportunity set, capital market line (CML), naive diversification, efficient Markowitz diversification, and others will be discussed in an intuitive fashion. Later, they will be examined in more depth.

### 3.1   What Is Risk?

A common dictionary definition of *risk* is that it is the chance of injury, damage, or loss. Although this definition is certainly good and correct, it is unsuitable for *scientific* analysis. The topic of this study is portfolio *analysis*. Analysis cannot proceed very far using verbal definitions, for several reasons. (1) Verbal definitions are not exact; different people interpret them in different ways. (2) Verbal definitions do not yield to analysis; they can only be broken down into more verbose verbal definitions and examples. (3) Verbal definitions do not facilitate ranking or comparison because they are usually not explicit enough to allow measurement of the item defined.[1] Suffice it to say that a quantitative risk surrogate is needed to replace the verbal definition of risk if portfolio analysis is to proceed very far.

The model used here for analyzing risk focuses on probability distributions

---

[1]Most physical and social sciences are moving to refine and quantify their studies. For example, biometrics, econometrics, and psychometrics are focusing on quantification of the studies of biology, economics, and psychology, respectively.

of some quantifiable outcome. Since the rate of return on an investment is the relevant outcome of an investment, financial risk analysis will focus on probability distributions of rates of return such as the one shown in Fig. 3.1.

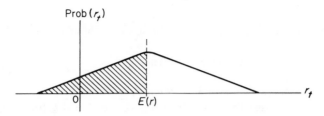

Figure 3.1. Probability Distribution of Rates of Return

The mean or expected value of the probability distribution of returns, $E(r)$, represents the mathematical expectation of the various possible rates of return. The expected return was defined in Chapter II as

$$E(r) = \sum_{t}^{T} p_t r_t, \qquad (2.1)$$

where $p_t$ is the probability of the $t$th rate of return.[2]

Rates of return below $E(r)$ represent disappointing outcomes to the investor studying the asset's probability distribution of returns. The area within the probability distribution that lies to the left of $E(r)$ graphically represents the investor's chance of injury, loss, or damage—that is, risk. The *semivariance of returns* $(s)$, defined in equation (3.1), is a quantitative risk surrogate that measures the area below $E(r)$ in the probability distribution of returns:

$$s = \sum_{i} p_i [\dot{r}_i - E(r)]^2, \qquad (3.1)$$

where $\dot{r}_i$'s are rates of return that are less than $E(r)$. The $\dot{r}_i$'s are below-average rates of return. The square root of (3.1) is called the *semideviation of returns* and is an equivalent financial risk surrogate that may be more intuitively pleasing.[3]

The semivariance and semideviation of returns are special cases of the variance and standard deviation of returns. The variance of returns, defined

---

[2]Continuous probability distributions will be ignored here. The estimated returns will assume only finite values and finite variances.

[3]Harry M. Markowitz, *Portfolio Selection* (New York: John Wiley & Sons, Inc., 1959), Chap. 9. For a comparison of different quantitative risk surrogates, see P. L. Cooley, R. L. Roenfeldt, and N. K. Modani, "Interdependence of Market Returns," *Journal of Business*, Vol. 50, No. 3, 1977. pp. 356–363.

in equation (2.2a), measures the dispersion or width of the entire probability distribution, rather than merely the portion of it lying below $E(r)$.

$$\sigma^2 = \sum_{t}^{T} p_t[r_t - E(r)]^2 \tag{3.2}$$

The standard deviation of returns is the square root of (3.2).

### A. Symmetric Probability Distributions of Returns

Consider Figs. 3.2, 3.3, and 3.4, which show three different types of skewness in probability distributions of returns. If assets' probability distributions

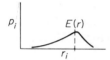

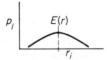

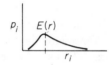

Figure 3.2. Probability
Distribution Skewed Left

Figure 3.3. Symmetric
Probability Distribution

Figure 3.4. Probability
Distribution Skewed Right

of rates of return are symmetric, as shown in Fig. 3.3, rather than skewed to the left or right, "an analysis based on (expected return) and (standard deviation) would consider these . . . (assets) as equally desirable" relative to an analysis based on expected return and semideviation.[4] Since most studies published thus far indicate the distributions of returns are approximately symmetric,[5] the semideviation will be abandoned here in favor of the standard deviation of returns. As Markowitz points out, the standard deviation (or variance) "is superior with respect to cost, convenience, and familiarity" and "will produce the same set of efficient portfolios" as the semideviation (or semivariance) if the probability distributions are symmetric.[6]

Thus, the variance or standard deviation of returns is the risk surrogate that will be employed throughout the remainder of this book. This is equivalent to defining financial risk as variability of return.

---

[4]Markowitz, *Portfolio Selection*, p. 190.

[5]M. G. Kendall, "The Analysis of Economic Time Series, I: Prices," *Journal of the Royal Statistical Society*, Ser. A, 1953, pp. 11–25; M. F. M. Osborne, "Brownian Motion in the Stock Market," *Operations Research*, Vol. 7, 1959, pp. 173–195; H. V. Roberts, "Stock Market 'Patterns' and Financial Analysis: Methodological Suggestions," *Journal of Finance*, Vol. 14, 1951, pp. 1–10. *Foundations of Finance* by E. F. Fama (New York: Basic Books, Inc., 1976), Chaps. 1 and 2, discuss and give empirical statistics for the symmetry of the distributions of one-period rates of return.

[6]Markowitz, *Portfolio Selection*, pp. 193–194.

### B.  Fundamental Security Analysis

The logic of analyzing only a firm's rate of return may seem oversimplified compared with more fundamental security analysis techniques that stress ratio analysis of financial statements, management interviews, industry forecasts, the economic outlook, and so on. However, there is no contradiction in these two approaches. After the fundamental security analyst completes his task, he need only to convert his estimates into several possible rates of return and attach probability estimates to each. The security analyst's consideration of such matters as how highly the firm is levered (that is, how much debt is used relative to the equity), its ability to meet fixed obligations, instability within the industry, the possibility of product obsolescence, the aggressiveness of competitors, the productivity of research and development, management depth and ability, and macroeconomic conditions are all duly reflected in the forecasted rates of return and their probabilities. Thus, the variability of the expected returns is a measure of risk grounded in fundamental analysis of the firm, its industry, and the economic outlook.[7]

### 3.2  Utility Foundations of Portfolio Analysis

In economic analysis the ultimate objective of human behavior is assumed to be utility maximization. Of course, utility is considered to be a function of many things. But, since consumption embraces those variables determining utility over which man has some control, utility is typically assumed to be a function of consumption goods (such as food, leisure, health care, and education). Because the consumption goods that man can control to some extent have a cost, consumption is assumed to be a function of wealth. Thus, utility can be restated as a function of wealth.

Investment activity affects utility through its effects on wealth. Since the rate of return is a measure of the rate at which wealth is accumulated, the utility from investment activity can be restated as a function of the rate of return on invested wealth. This can all be summarized symbolically as follows, where $U$ denotes utility and $g$, $h$, and $j$ are some positive functions.

---

[7]Studies showing how financial statement data relate to market-determined risk measures include the following:

W. H. Beaver, P. Kettler, and M. Scholes, "The Association between Market-Determined and Accounting-Determined Risk Measures," *The Accounting Review*, October 1970, pp. 654–682.

J. S. Bildersee, "Market-Determined and Alternative Measures of Risk," *The Accounting Review*, January 1975, pp. 81–98.

George Foster, *Financial Statement Analysis*, Prentice-Hall, Englewood Cliffs, N.J., 1978, see especially Chapter Nine.

Also see Appendix A to Chapter 4 of this monograph about the study by Dr. Thompson.

$$U = g(\text{consumption}) \tag{3.3}$$

$$= g[h(\text{wealth})] \qquad \text{since consumption} = h(\text{wealth}) \tag{3.3a}$$

$$= g\{h[\,j(\text{rate of return})]\} \qquad \text{since wealth} = j(\text{rate of return}) \tag{3.3b}$$

In a world of certainty where all outcomes were known in advance, a utility maximizer would simply invest his wealth in the one asset with the highest rate of return. However, in an *uncertain* world, investors can only maximize what they *expect* utility to be—not what it will actually turn out to be, since this is an unknown. Thus, with the advent of uncertainty, risk considerations enter the picture. Symbolically, equation (3.4) summarizes the relation between an investor's utility and his investments in a world of uncertainty.

$$E(U) = f(E(r), \text{ risk}). \tag{3.4}$$

Consider the following example of how rational investment decisions can be made within the context of the two-parameter model (that is, considering only risk and return of the securities).

## A. Numerical Example

Assume that an investor is trying to select one security from among five securities. The securities and their estimated return and risk are:

| Name of Security | Expected Return, $E(r)$ (%) | Risk, $\sigma$ (%) |
|---|---|---|
| American Telephone Works (ATW) | 7 | 4 |
| General Auto Corp. (GAC) | 8 | 5 |
| Yellow Tractor Co. (YTC) | 15 | 15 |
| Fairyear Tire & Rubber (FTR) | 3 | 4 |
| Hotstone Tire Corp. (HTC) | 8 | 12 |

The five securities are compared in the two-dimensional Fig. 3.5 with expected return on the vertical axis and risk on the horizontal axis. Clearly, GAC *dominates* HTC, since they both offer the same expected return but GAC is less risky. And FTR is dominated by ATW, since they are both in the same risk class (that is, $\sigma = 4$ percent) but ATW offers a higher expected return. Thus, FTR and HTC can be eliminated from consideration: they would not make good purchases individually.

*Dominance definition*    A *dominant* security has one of the following: (1) the lowest risk ($\sigma$) in its $E(r)$ class, or (2) the highest $E(r)$ in its risk class, or (3) both an $E(r)$ that is above another security's $E(r)$ and a $\sigma$ that is below the other security's risk.

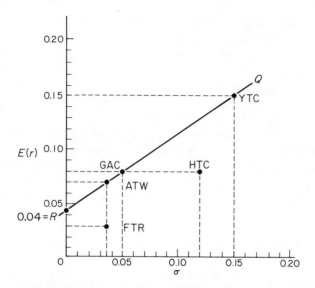

Figure 3.5. Investment Opportunities in Risk-Return Space

It appears that the number of choices has been narrowed from five to three. This is not true. Portfolios of the three dominant securities create an infinite number of choices which lie *approximately* along the line $RQ$, or left of it—depending on the correlation coefficients between the securities.[8]

For example, a portfolio composed of 50 percent ATW and 50 percent GAC has an expected return of 7.5 percent [by equation (2.8)] and a standard deviation of 4.5 percent [by equation (2.9) and assuming perfect positive correlation]. The expected return on this portfolio is calculated as follows:

$$E(r_p) = x_{\text{ATW}}E(r_{\text{ATW}}) + x_{\text{GAC}}E(r_{\text{GAC}})$$

$$= \tfrac{1}{2}(7\%) + \tfrac{1}{2}(8\%) = 7.5 \text{ percent.} \qquad (2.8)$$

The standard deviation of returns is calculated as follows:

$$\sigma_p = \sqrt{x_{\text{ATW}}^2\sigma_{\text{ATW}}^2 + x_{\text{GAC}}^2\sigma_{\text{GAC}}^2 + 2x_{\text{ATW}}x_{\text{GAC}}(\rho_{\text{ATW, GAC}})\sigma_{\text{ATW}}\sigma_{\text{GAC}}}$$

$$= \sqrt{(\tfrac{1}{2})^2(4\%)^2 + (\tfrac{1}{2})^2(5\%)^2 + 2(\tfrac{1}{2})(\tfrac{1}{2})(1)(4\%)(5\%)} \qquad (2.9)$$

$$= \sqrt{0.002025} = 0.045 = 4.5 \text{ percent.}$$

---

[8]Actually, correlation coefficients between securities in a given portfolio that are below $+1$ will produce points that dominate the line $RQ$ and may even represent portfolios containing the two dominated securities, HTC and FTR. These and other possibilities will be discussed later in this chapter.

Plotting this portfolio on Fig. 3.5 would produce a point about halfway between ATW and GAC. Likewise, letting the point $R$ denote investing in risk-free assets at 4 percent return (for example, short-term government bonds), the points between points $R$ and ATW represent portfolios of varying proportions of government bonds and ATW shares. By borrowing at rate $R$ and investing in ATW, GAC, or FTC, the investor creates points on $RQ$ that lie out past FTC (that is, by using leverage).

By elimination of dominated securities, the choice has been limited to points ATW, GAC, FTC, and the *infinite* number of portfolios containing some combination of securities, which is assumed, to keep things simple, to lie along the line $RQ$ in Fig. 3.5. Exactly which point along $RQ$ an investor selects depends on the personal preferences in the trade-off between risk and return.

### B. Investor Preferences and Indifference Curves

*Indifference curves* can be used to represent investors' preferences for risk, $\sigma$, and return, $E(r)$. Indifference curves are drawn such that investors' satisfaction is equal all along their length; they are sometimes called *utility isoquants*. Assuming that investors dislike risk and like larger expected returns, the indifference curves are positively sloped. The amount of slope depends on the investors' particular preferences for a safe return versus a larger and more risky return. The indifference map of a timid, risk-fearing investor is shown in Fig. 3.6. Figure 3.7 depicts an aggressive, risk-averting investor who will accept large risks for a small increase in return. Both the timid and aggressive investors dislike risk. However, the timid investor in Fig. 3.6 dislikes risk more than the aggressive investor in Fig. 3.7. A risk lover (such as an inveterate gambler) would have indifference curves concave to the origin.

The higher-numbered utility isoquants represent higher levels of satisfaction. These curves grow more vertical as they rise, reflecting a diminishing willingness to assume risk.

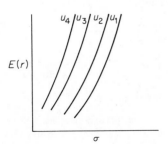

Figure 3.6. Timid Risk-Averter's Indifference Map

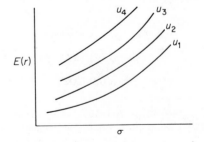

Figure 3.7. Aggressive-Risk Averter's Indifference Map

Reproducing line *RQ* from Fig. 3.5, the analysis can be made determinate with the addition of an indifference map as in Fig. 3.8. The investor will seek the highest indifference curve tangent to the dominant opportunity locus, *RQ*, and thus reach a point such as *M* where his satisfaction is maximum.

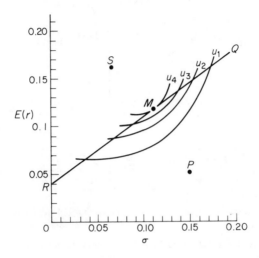

Figure 3.8. A Risk-Return Preference Ordering

Assets such as *P* in Fig. 3.8, which are dominated, will suffer from lack of demand, and their price will fall.[9] The rate of return is the ratio of dividends plus capital gains or losses, all over the purchase price. After a price fall, the denominator of the ratio will be reduced enough to increase the value of the rate of return. This means that the equilibrium return on *P* will move toward *RQ* after the temporary capital losses cease. Points above the line *RQ* (like *S*) represent undervalued assets whose prices will be bid up. The resulting higher equilibrium price (that is, higher denominator in rate-of-return ratio) will lower the expected rate of return on the previously under-valued asset, and it will tend to be relocated on *RQ*.

An equilibrium rate of return is a rate of return on the ray *RQ*. Equilibrium returns have no tendency to change. Note however, that price changes may be necessary to maintain equilibrium rates of return.

### 3.3  Opportunity Set

Plotting all investments' $E(r)$ and $\sigma$ in Fig. 3.9 and connecting these pos-sible investments with lines representing possible combinations (that is, port-folios) of the individual assets generates an *opportunity set* that might take on

---

[9]Technically, *P* could represent an individual security in equilibrium if that security were held in an efficient portfolio.

the escalloped quarter-moon shape shown. Within the opportunity set are all individual securities as well as all portfolios not containing $R$. Thus, all points within this space are feasible investments. The left side of the opportunity set between points $E$ and $F$ is the *efficient frontier* of the opportunity set. It is comprised of all "efficient investments."

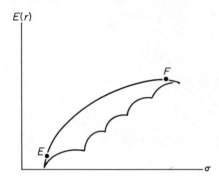

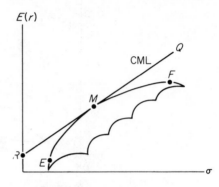

Figure 3.9A. Without Borrowing and Lending

Figure 3.9B. With Borrowing and Lending at Riskless Rate

Figure 3.9. Two Sets of Investment Opportunities

*Efficient investment definition:*     An *efficient investment* has either (1) more return than any other investment in its risk class (that is, any other security with the same variability of returns), or (2) less risk than any other security with the same return. The efficient frontier of the opportunity set *dominates* all other investments in the opportunity set. These investments are sometimes said to be *Markowitz efficient*, referring to Harry Markowitz, the originator of two-parameter portfolio analysis.

Hirschleifer expressed the reason for the particular shape of the efficient frontier of the opportunity set as follows:

> The curvature shown for the efficient frontier—opposite to that of the $(E(r), \sigma)$ indifference curves—follows also from the covariance effect, since moving to higher values of portfolio $E(r)$ progressively reduces the number of securities that can be held in combination so as to lower $\sigma$.[10]

Adding the possibility of borrowing or lending at rate $R$ a new opportunity set, the line $RMQ$ is created. The line $RMQ$ represents the continuum of possible portfolios an investor could construct from $R$ and $M$ by borrowing and lending at rate $R$. $RMQ$ is called the *capital market line* (CML). As

---

[10]Jack Hirschleifer, "Efficient Allocation of Capital in an Uncertain World," *American Economic Review*, May 1964, p. 79.

graphed in Fig. 3.9, the CML is the true efficient frontier—it dominates all other investment opportunities. The CML can be viewed as the locus of the maximum rates of returns for each risk class. The CML represents the opportunity foregone by investing in less efficient investments.

Each point on the CML is determined by values for $E(r)$ and $\sigma$. The $\sigma$ determines the *risk class* of the investment. The $E(r)$ is the *cost of capital*, or *capitalization rate*, appropriate for that particular risk class.

### 3.4  Diversification

Markowitz diversification is the particular form of diversification activity implied by portfolio analysis. This type of diversification differs from *naive diversification*, used widely by security salesmen and traditional investments texts. These sources define diversification as "not putting all your eggs in one basket" or "spreading your risks." The possible benefits of naive diversification will be discussed later. Naive diversification ignores the covariance between securities and results in superfluous diversification.

*Markowitz diversification definition:*    *Markowitz diversification* involves combining investments with less than perfect positive correlation in order to reduce risk in the portfolio without sacrificing any of the portfolio's return. In general, the lower the correlation of the assets in a portfolio, the less risky the portfolio will be. This is true regardless of how risky the assets of the portfolio are when analyzed in isolation.

Markowitz puts it this way[11]:

> Not only does [portfolio analysis] imply diversification, it implies the "right kind" of diversification for the "right reason." The adequacy of diversification is not thought by investors to depend on the number of different securities held. A portfolio with sixty different railway securities, for example, would not be as well diversified as the same size portfolio with some railroad, some public utility, mining, various sorts of manufacturing, etc. The reason is that it is generally more likely for firms within the same industry to do poorly at the same time than for firms in dissimilar industries.

> Similarly, in trying to make variance [of returns] small it is not enough to invest in many securities. It is necessary to avoid investing in securities with high covariances among themselves.

---

[11]Harry M. Markowitz, "Portfolio Selection," *Journal of Finance*, Vol. 7, No. 1, 1952, p. 89. Reprinted in S. H. Archer and C. A. D'Ambrosio, *The Theory of Business Finance: A Book of Readings* (New York: Macmillan Publishing Co., Inc., 1967), p. 599; E. B. Frederickson, *Frontiers of Investment Analysis* (Scranton, Pa.: International Textbook Co., 1966), p. 364; H. Wu and A. J. Zakon, *Elements of Investments* (New York: Holt, Rinehart and Winston, Inc., 1965), p. 310. Parenthetical phrase added.

A.  Diversification Illustrated

Consider the following two securities:

| Investments | $E(r)$ (%) | $\sigma$ (%) |
|:-----------:|:----------:|:------------:|
| A | 5 | 20 |
| B | 15 | 40 |

Combining securities $A$ and $B$, the expected return of the resulting portfolio is as follows:

$$E(r_p) = \sum_{i=1}^{2} x_i E(r_i) = x_A E(r_A) + x_B E(r_B) \tag{2.8}$$

$$= (x_A)0.05 + (x_B)0.15$$

$$= (\tfrac{2}{3})0.05 + (\tfrac{1}{3})0.15 = 0.083 = 8.3 \text{ percent,}$$

if $x_A = \tfrac{2}{3}$ and $x_B = \tfrac{1}{3}$.[12] The risk of the portfolio is given by the following function:

$$\sigma_{r_p} = \sqrt{x_A^2 \sigma_{AA} + x_B^2 \sigma_{BB} + 2x_A x_B \sigma_{AB}}$$

$$= \sqrt{x_A^2 \sigma_{AA} + x_B^2 \sigma_{BB} + 2x_A x_B \rho_{AB}\sigma_A\sigma_B} \quad \text{since } \sigma_{AB} = \rho_{AB}\sigma_A\sigma_B. \tag{2.10}$$

Using the values for assets $A$ and $B$ in equation (2.10) yields the following calculations:

$$\sigma_p = \sqrt{(\tfrac{2}{3})^2(20\%)^2 + (\tfrac{1}{3})^2(40\%)^2 + 2(\rho_{AB})(\tfrac{2}{3})(\tfrac{1}{3})(20\%)(40\%)}$$

$$= \sqrt{0.0175 + 0.0175 + 0.035(\rho_{AB})} = \sqrt{0.035 + 0.035(\rho_{AB})}.$$

---

[12]The minimum variance weights may be found by trial and error. However, the standard calculus optimization techniques are much more efficient. The variance of the portfolio of $A$ and $B$ is given by the following equation:

$$V = \text{var } (r_{A+B}) = x_A^2 \sigma_{AA} + x_B^2 \sigma_{BB} + 2x_A x_B \sigma_{AB}$$

$$= 0.04x_A^2 + 0.16x_B^2 + 2(-1)(0.2)(0.4)x_A x_B \quad \text{where } \rho_{AB} = -1$$

$$= 0.04x_A^2 + 0.16(1 - x_A)^2 - 0.16x_A(1 - x_A) \quad \text{since } x_B = (1 - x_A) \text{ in this two-asset}$$

portfolio

$$= 0.04x_A^2 + 0.16 - 0.32x_A + 0.16x_A^2 - 0.16x_A + 0.16x_A^2.$$

To minimize this variance, set $dV/dx_A = 0$ and solve for $x_A$.

$$\frac{dV}{dx_A} = 2(0.04)x_A - 0.32 + (2)(0.16)x_A - 0.16 + (0.16)2x_A = 0$$

$$= 0.08x_A - 0.48 + 0.64x_A = 0$$

$$= 0.72x_A - 0.48 = 0$$

$$x_A = \frac{0.48}{0.72} = \frac{2}{3}.$$

Thus, $x_B$ must equal $\tfrac{1}{3}$ to minimize this portfolio's variance (that is, risk).

Although the expected return of this portfolio is fixed at 8.3 percent for these proportions of $A$ and $B$ the risk of the portfolio varies with $\rho_{AB}$, the correlation coefficient. Thus, if $\rho_{AB} = +1$, then $\sigma_p = \sqrt{0.07} = 26.7$ percent. If $\rho_{AB} = 0$, then $\sigma_p = \sqrt{0.035} = 18.7$ percent. And, if $\rho_{AB} = -1$, then $\sigma_p = \sqrt{0} = 0$. The locus of all possible proportions ($x_A$ and $x_B$) for investments $A$ and $B$ are plotted in Fig. 3.10 for $\rho_{AB} = 1, 0$, and $-1$.

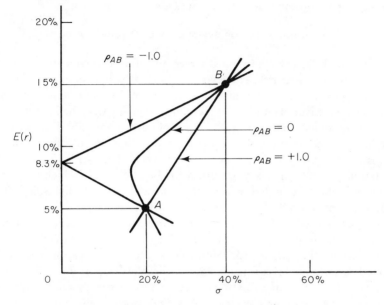

Figure 3.10. The Effects of Markowitz Diversification

### B. Graphical Diversification Analysis

Figure 3.10 graphically depicts how Markowitz diversification affects risk in the portfolio.[13] Figure 3.10 shows that the lower the $\rho_{AB}$, the more risk is reduced by combining $A$ and $B$ into a portfolio. The straight line between $A$ and $B$ defines the locus of $E(r)$ and $\sigma$ combinations for all possible portfolios of $A$ and $B$ when $\rho_{AB} = +1$. Considering the effects of diversification as depicted in Fig. 3.10, the reader is invited to reexamine Fig. 3.9. The particular shape [that is, curves convex to the $E(r)$ axis] given the opportunity set in Fig. 3.9 is the result of diversification.

Figure 3.10 also illustrates graphically that Markowitz diversification reduces the risk (that is, the variability of return) only on the owner's equity. The risk and expected return of the individual assets, $A$ and $B$, is not affected by the formation of a diversified portfolio of which they happen to be a

---

[13]Fig. 3.10 was first published in W. F. Sharpe's article, "Capital Asset Prices: A Theory of Market Equilibrium Under Conditions of Risk," *Journal of Finance*, September 1964.

part. Throughout this monograph on portfolio analysis the focus is ultimately on (1) the expected rate of return *on the owner's equity*, and (2) the
variability of return (that is, the risk) of *the owner's equity*. The individual
assets are merely the objects of choice that portfolio analysis endeavors to
form into dominant investment portfolios. The risk and return statistics on
the individual assets being considered for possible inclusion in the portfolio
are exogeneous constants in portfolio analysis.

### 3.5  Preliminary Conclusions About Diversification

People who have invested typically recognize that diversification is a useful way to reduce their risk. However, few of these people have ever thought
about risk scientifically. If an investor's concept of risk is not sufficiently well
defined to be measured empirically, it follows logically that the investor must
also be working with only a vague concept of how to diversify. Furthermore,
some investors erroneously develop perverted notions about diversification.
For instance, some people erroneously believe that low-risk (for example,
public utility) stocks and (say, government) bonds, both of which may have
low returns, must be added to a portfolio to make it well diversified. This
chapter has introduced ideas about better ways to diversify.

Risk can be reduced by means of Markowitz diversification without
decreasing return at all—such diversification is optimal.[14] Of course, naive
diversification will reduce risk. However, naive diversification cannot be
expected to minimize risk since it ignores the most important variable, the
correlation (or covariance) between assets. Naive diversification only con-
centrates on owning many assets—that is, "not putting all your eggs in one
basket." In contrast, Markowitz diversification is a scientific form of diversification.

---

[14]The authors have found that their students sometimes misinterpret Fig. 3.10 and think
that the correlation between securities also affects the portfolio's *return*. The error of this conclusion is easily seen by noting that the correlation coefficient is not to be found in the formula
for the portfolio's return, equation (2.8). Thus, $E(r_p)$ is independent of the benefits of
Markowitz diversification.

## Selected References

Latane, H. A., D. L. Tuttle, and C. P. Jones, *Security Analysis and Portfolio Management,* 2nd ed. New York: The Ronald Press Company, 1975.

This comprehensive investments textbook uses mathematics moderately. Chapters 18 through 21 inclusive show how diversification helps to maximize the value of an investment portfolio over a long-run period of investing, liquidating, and reinvesting.

Modigliani, F., and G. A. Pogue, "An Introduction to Risk and Return: Concepts and Evidence," *Financial Analysts Journal,* Part I, March/April 1974, Part II, May/June 1974.

This lengthy article provides a fine review of some of the best diversification studies that have been executed within the risk–return orientation. Moderate use of mathematics and statistics, combined with an ample number of well-explained graphs, makes this article well worth reading.

## Questions and Problems

1. Consider the following statements. "A portfolio of 100 different assets is five times better diversified than a portfolio of only 20 different assets." Is this statement true, false, or uncertain? Explain why.

2. Does defining risk as "variability of return" and measuring it with the standard deviation (or variance) of returns ignore facts about the individual investment common stocks' (a) earnings growth, (b) "glamor" in the eyes of other investors, (c) listing (for example, over-the-counter or on the NYSE), and (d) the expertise of the firms' managers? Explain.

3. Consider a hypothetical company named the Red Ink Company of America, Incorporated (RICA hereafter), which manufactures only red ink. Suppose that RICA's sales and profits were counter cyclical because during recessions when most firms were reporting losses RICA's product sold unusually well. The accountants of the many firms whose profits become losses during the recessions use red ink to report negative earnings, and this makes RICA a countercyclical firm. Should the countercyclical nature of RICA affect in any way its desirability as an investment? Explain.

4. Standard and Poor's assigns the following quality ratings to common stocks:

AAA—highest quality; insignificant chance of going bankrupt

AA —very high quality

A —high quality

BBB very good quality; bankruptcy is conceivable as a result of a long run of unforeseen bad luck; but bankruptcy not likely in the shortrun

BB good quality

B —a quality stock

CCC—a speculative stock, but one that is not likely to go bankrupt this year

CC a very speculative stock

C a highly speculative stock; a real gamble

Do you suspect that the stocks Standard and Poor's give high quality ratings have low levels of variability of return? Explain.

```
44444444444444444444444444444444444444444444444444444444444444444444444444444444
44444444444444444444444444444444444444444444444444444444444444444444444444444444
4444444444444444444444444444444   444  444444444444   44444444444444444444444444
4444444444444444444444444444444   4444  4444444444   44444444444444444444444444
4444444444444444444444444444444   44444  444444444   44444444444444444444444444
4444444444444444444444444444444   444444  4444444   44444444444444444444444444
4444444444444444444444444444444   4444444  44444   44444444444444444444444444
4444444444444444444444444444444   4444444  444   44444444444444444444444444
4444444444444444444444444444444   44444444  4   44444444444444444444444444
4444444444444444444444444444444   444444444   44444444444444444444444444
4444444444444444444444444444444   4444444444   44444444444444444444444444
4444444444444444444444444444444   4444444444   44444444444444444444444444
44444444444444444444444444444444444444444444444444444444444444444444444444444444
44444444444444444444444444444444444444444444444444444444444444444444444444444444
```

# Generating the Statistical Inputs

$C$HAPTERS V, VI, and VII explain various methods of performing Markowitz portfolio analysis, and later chapters explain other phases of investment
analysis which are derived from Markowitz's portfolio theory. In each case
it will be assumed that a security analyst has furnished the portfolio analyst
with the statistical inputs required for portfolio analysis. The purpose of this
chapter is to show approaches to security analysis that will yield the statistics
needed for portfolio analysis.

### 4.1  The Required Statistical Inputs

If a portfolio analyst is going to derive the efficient frontier from a group
of $n$ assets (where $n$ is any positive interger), the following statistics are
required:

1. Expected return estimates for all $n$ assets under consideration.
2. Expected standard deviation (or variance) of the rate of return for all $n$ assets.
3. All the expected covariances between these various $n$-asset rates of return. It can
   be shown that $\frac{1}{2}(n^2 - n)$ different covariances are required for an $n$-asset analysis.

The formulas for the expected rate of return, $E(r)$; standard deviation, $\sigma$;
and the covariance, cov $(r_i, r_j)$, were derived and discussed in Chapter II.

The efficient portfolios generated by portfolio analysis are no better than
the statistical inputs on which they are based. Thus, it is imperative that
attention be devoted to this phase of portfolio management. In this chapter

three different approaches will be suggested for generating the statistical inputs: (1) ex post data may be tabulated and projected into the future with or without being subjectively adjusted, (2) ex ante probability distributions which are entirely subjective can be compiled, or (c) a simple econometric relationship may be used to forecast returns. Ideally, all three approaches should be pursued independently for each of the $n$ assets. These independent forcasts could then be compared and contrasted by a committee of security analysts, and a consensus reached as a final step in security analysis. This final consensus would represent the best attainable statistics and could be given to the portfolio analyst.

## 4.2  Ex Post Data

Gathering historical (that is, ex post) empirical data on a firm's expected return, standard deviation, and covariance is a good place to begin security analysis. Although these statistics may change with the passage of time, they can give the security analyst an objective point of reference from which he may proceed. The historical data needed are the market prices and dividends for each firm being considered.

### A.  Sources for Historical Data

Data on a security's market prices and dividends may be found in several different places, including the following[1]:

1. *Moody's Handbook of Widely Held Common Stocks* is a quarterly paperback publication covering about 1000 companies. It contains stock prices, cash dividends, earnings per share, stock dividend or split information, and selected items from each firm's financial statements.

2. *ISL Daily Stock Price* is published quarterly and lists over 2000 securities from the NYSE and AMEX. These books contain stock prices, the volume of shares traded daily, and quarterly earnings and dividend data.

Data about stock and bond market averages can be found in Standard and Poor's *Trade and Securities Statistics*. This is an annual paperback book containing decades of past data that are updated with monthly pamphlets. There are many satisfactory sources for historical data on market prices and dividends. The sources above are suggested only because they contain both price and dividend data and they are easy to read. Forms such as the one in Fig. 4.1 may expedite the data gathering.[2]

---

[1]See Chapter 6 of J. C. Francis, *Investments: Analysis and Management*, 2nd ed. (New York: McGraw-Hill Book Company, 1976), for more detail on data sources.

[2]Electronic computers may be advantageously employed in tabulating historical statistics. The necessary data are available on magnetic tapes designed for use with computers. The University of Chicago has prepared the CRSP tape, which is sold by Standard and Poor's Corporation. The Standard and Poor's quarterly Compustat tapes and the ISL tapes are also useful.

Name of firm researched_____ Researcher_____

Type of security_____ Source of data_____

Industry_____

| Quarter Years | Reported Data | | | Changes in Unit of Account | Adjusted Data | | | Rate of Return [1] | Growth in E.P.S. [2] |
|---|---|---|---|---|---|---|---|---|---|
| | Begin. Mkt. Price | Qtrly. Div. | Qtrly. E.P.S. | | Begin. Mkt. Price | Qtrly. Div. | Qtrly. E.P.S. | | |
| 1976–IV | ___ | ___ | ___ | ___ | ___ | ___ | ___ | ___ | ___ |
| 1976–III | ___ | ___ | ___ | ___ | ___ | ___ | ___ | ___ | ___ |
| 1976–II | ___ | ___ | ___ | ___ | ___ | ___ | ___ | ___ | ___ |
| 1976–I | ___ | ___ | ___ | ___ | ___ | ___ | ___ | ___ | ___ |
| 1975–IV | ___ | ___ | ___ | ___ | ___ | ___ | ___ | ___ | ___ |
| 1975–III | ___ | ___ | ___ | ___ | ___ | ___ | ___ | ___ | ___ |
| 1975–II | ___ | ___ | ___ | ___ | ___ | ___ | ___ | ___ | ___ |
| 1975–I | ___ | ___ | ___ | ___ | ___ | ___ | ___ | ___ | ___ |
| 1974–IV | ___ | ___ | ___ | ___ | ___ | ___ | ___ | ___ | ___ |
| 1974–III | ___ | ___ | ___ | ___ | ___ | ___ | ___ | ___ | ___ |
| 1974–II | ___ | ___ | ___ | ___ | ___ | ___ | ___ | ___ | ___ |
| 1974–I | ___ | ___ | ___ | ___ | ___ | ___ | ___ | ___ | ___ |
| 1973–IV | ___ | ___ | ___ | ___ | ___ | ___ | ___ | ___ | ___ |
| 1973–III | ___ | ___ | ___ | ___ | ___ | ___ | ___ | ___ | ___ |
| 1973–II | ___ | ___ | ___ | ___ | ___ | ___ | ___ | ___ | ___ |
| 1973–I | ___ | ___ | ___ | ___ | ___ | ___ | ___ | ___ | ___ |
| 1972–IV | ___ | ___ | ___ | ___ | ___ | ___ | ___ | ___ | ___ |
| 1972–III | ___ | ___ | ___ | ___ | ___ | ___ | ___ | ___ | ___ |
| 1972–II | ___ | ___ | ___ | ___ | ___ | ___ | ___ | ___ | ___ |
| 1972–I | ___ | ___ | ___ | ___ | ___ | ___ | ___ | ___ | ___ |
| 1971–IV | ___ | ___ | ___ | ___ | ___ | ___ | ___ | ___ | ___ |
| 1971–III | ___ | ___ | ___ | ___ | ___ | ___ | ___ | ___ | ___ |
| 1971–II | ___ | ___ | ___ | ___ | ___ | ___ | ___ | ___ | ___ |
| 1971–I | ___ | ___ | ___ | ___ | ___ | ___ | ___ | ___ | ___ |
| 1970–IV | ___ | ___ | ___ | ___ | ___ | ___ | ___ | ___ | ___ |
| 1970–III | ___ | ___ | ___ | ___ | ___ | ___ | ___ | ___ | ___ |
| 1970–II | ___ | ___ | ___ | ___ | ___ | ___ | ___ | ___ | ___ |
| 1970–I | ___ | ___ | ___ | ___ | ___ | ___ | ___ | ___ | ___ |
| 1969–IV | ___ | ___ | ___ | ___ | ___ | ___ | ___ | ___ | ___ |
| 1969–III | ___ | ___ | ___ | ___ | ___ | ___ | ___ | ___ | ___ |
| 1969–II | ___ | ___ | ___ | ___ | ___ | ___ | ___ | ___ | ___ |
| 1969–I | ___ | ___ | ___ | ___ | ___ | ___ | ___ | ___ | ___ |
| 1968–IV | ___ | ___ | ___ | ___ | ___ | ___ | ___ | ___ | ___ |
| 1968–III | ___ | ___ | ___ | ___ | ___ | ___ | ___ | ___ | ___ |
| 1968–II | ___ | ___ | ___ | ___ | ___ | ___ | ___ | ___ | ___ |
| 1968–I | ___ | ___ | ___ | ___ | ___ | ___ | ___ | ___ | ___ |
| 1967–IV | ___ | ___ | ___ | ___ | ___ | ___ | ___ | ___ | ___ |
| 1967–III | ___ | ___ | ___ | ___ | ___ | ___ | ___ | ___ | ___ |
| 1967–II | ___ | ___ | ___ | ___ | ___ | ___ | ___ | ___ | ___ |
| 1967–I | ___ | ___ | ___ | ___ | ___ | ___ | ___ | ___ | ___ |

Variance in rates of return_____ Standard deviation_____

Average rate of return_____

Regression coefficients for characteristic line $A$_____ $B$_____ $Q$_____

[1] $r_t = (P_{t+1} - P_t + D_t)/P_t$ = rate of return in period $t$.

[2] $g_t = (\text{EPS}_t - \text{EPS}_{t-1})/\text{EPS}_{t-1}$ = earnings growth in period $t$.

Average growth in EPS_____

Figure 4.1. Form for Gathering Common Stock Data

## B.   Changes in the Unit of Account

For reasons that are dubious in many cases, corporations frequently declare stock dividends and/or stock splits. Although such paper shuffling does not change the market value of the firm, it does require the security analyst to make adjustments for these changes in the per share unit of account. Consider the hypothetical data in Table 4.1.

TABLE 4.1   Hypothetical Market Data on a Per-Share Basis

|                            | Time Period |          |          |          |          |
|----------------------------|-------------|----------|----------|----------|----------|
|                            | *1*         | *2*      | *3*      | *4*      | *5*      |
| Beginning market price     | $100        | $100     | 50       | 25       | 25       |
| Earnings per share         | 10          | 10       | 5        | 2.50     | 2.50     |
| Dividends per share        | 5           | 5        | 2.50     | 1.25     | 1.25     |
| Par value per share        | 1           | 1        | 0.50     | 0.25     | 0.25     |
| Book value per share       | 20          | 20       | 10       | 5        | 5        |
| Multiplication adjustment  | × 1         | × 1      | × 2      | × 4      | × 4      |
| Division adjustment        | × (1/4)     | × (1/4)  | × (1/2)  | × 1      | × 1      |
| True rate of return        | 5%          | 5%       | 5%       | 5%       | 5%       |

Assume that the firm represented in Table 4.1 had no fluctuations in the market price of its stock except those caused by a 2-for-1 stock split (or equivalently, a 100 percent stock dividend) between periods 2 and 3 and again between periods 3 and 4.[3] Realistically, this hypothetical firm had no capital gains or losses; the 5 percent dividend yield each period thus equals the true rate of return calculated by equation (1.1). The decrease in the market price per share between periods 2 and 3 and again between periods 3 and 4 reflects changes in the unit of accounts, not capital losses. To adjust for changes in the unit of account, either the multiplication or the division adjustment factors (but not both) shown in Table 4.1 may be used. This converts the market data to comparable levels. The rate of return for each period may then be calculated with equation (1.1).

---

[3]Accountants and attorneys maintain the fiction that a 2-for-1 stock split is not equivalent to a 100 percent stock dividend. However, economists and experienced financial analysts ignore the bookkeeping entries that form the basis for any difference and focus instead on the effect of the transaction on market prices and the investors' wealth. An in-depth empirical analysis of the effects of stock splits and stock dividends is provided in E. F. Fama, L. Fisher, M. D. Jensen, and R. Roll, "The Adjustment of Stock Prices to New Information," *International Economic Review*, February 1969, pp. 1–21. This study suggested that changes in the unit of account (that is, stock dividends and splits) generated no new wealth for the investors. This study did not allow for changes in the risk of the firms (namely, the betas). A more recent study which tended to overcome the flaw in the earlier study also analyzed massive empirical data and reached somewhat similar conclusions—that changes in the unit of account do not benefit investors. In fact, the later study found that under certain circumstances, a change in the unit of account could be harmful to investors, because it increased their risk exposure. See S. Bar-Yosef and L. D. Brown, "A Reexamination of Stock Splits Using Moving Betas," *Journal of Finance*, September 1977, pp. 1069–1080.

## C.  Formulas for Ex Post Data

When estimating the ex ante input statistics for an asset from ex post data, each historical observation is treated as being equally likely. Assume that historical data are gathered for $T$ time periods. The probability of each observation is $p = (1/T)$. Substituting this probability into equations (2.1), (2.3), and (2.4) yields the formulas below.

The historical average return ($\bar{r}$), calculated as shown in equation (4.1), may be used as an estimate of the expected return, $E(r)$.

$$\bar{r}_i = \left(\frac{1}{T}\right) \sum_{t=1}^{T} r_{it}. \tag{4.1}$$

The historical standard deviation, $\hat{\sigma}$, may be used as an estimate of expected risk,

$$\hat{\sigma}_i = \left[\left(\frac{1}{T}\right) \sum_{t=1}^{T} (r_{it} - \bar{r}_i)^2\right]^{1/2}. \tag{4.2}$$

The historical covariance, $\hat{\sigma}_{ij}$, may be used as an estimate of the expected covariance, $\sigma_{ij}$.

$$\hat{\sigma}_{ij} = \left[\left(\frac{1}{T}\right) \sum_{t=1}^{T} (r_{it} - \bar{r}_i)(r_{jt} - \bar{r}_j)\right]. \tag{4.3}$$

## D.  Subjective Adjustments for Historical Statistics

After historical data are tabulated and $\bar{r}_j$, $\hat{\sigma}_i$, and $\hat{\sigma}_{ij}$ are calculated, it may be desirable to adjust these statistics for some companies. If the firm under consideration has added or dropped product lines; entered large new sales territories or left old ones; had a complete management shake-up; experienced a significant technological breakthrough; been faced with tough, new competitors; obtained important new government permits, sanctions, or subsidies; won or lost important legal battles that set new precedents for the future; or experienced other changes that are expected to alter the firm's future average return, risk, and/or covariance, then the security analyst should make subjective adjustments in $\bar{r}_i$, $\hat{\sigma}_i$, and/or $\hat{\sigma}_{ij}$ for the firm. Consider a numerical example.

Imagine an (hypothetical) airline named West Coast Lines (WCL), which has been in operation for many years. Assume that WCL has been flying between Seattle, Los Angeles, and San Francisco and that its operating statistics over the past decade have been tabulated. Further imagine another airline, say, Trans Continental Airlines (TCA), about the same size, which flies everyplace that WCL flies. But TCA also flies to Las Vegas and Hawaii. Table 4.2 shows historical statistics gathered for the two hypothetical airlines over the past decade.

TABLE 4.2  Operating Statistics for Past Decade

| Ex Post Statistic | WCL | TCA |
|---|---|---|
| $\bar{r}_i$ | 0.15 = 15.0% | 0.2 = 20.0% |
| $\hat{\sigma}_i$ | 0.4  = 40.0% | 0.5 = 50.0% |
| $\hat{\sigma}_{ij}$ | 0.25 | 0.4 |

Now, assume that WCL obtains permission from the Civil Aeronautics Board to make passenger flights to Las Vegas and Hawaii. How will this change in WCL's product line and sales territory be expected to affect its average return, risk, and covariance in the next five years?

Flying affluent passengers on champagne flights and vacations to Hawaii and Las Vegas will likely increase WCL's sales, profits, and average return in the future. However, since champagne flights and vacations are luxury items that many people cancel during recession periods, it seems probable that WCL will experience more variability of return (that is, risk) in future years than it has in the past.

Nearly all stock prices are highly positively correlated with the national economy.[4] Since WCL's new flights will increase the correlation of its sales, profits, and returns with the national economy, it is likely that WCL's covariance of returns with most other stocks will also rise. Thus, WCL's average return, risk, and covariance can all be expected to rise as a result of the Civil Aeronautics Board's ruling.

The exact values forecasted for WCL's average return, risk, and covariance may be estimated subjectively by the security analyst. WCL's historical figures, shown in Table 4.2, furnish the minimum estimates. The figures for TCA furnish good guidelines to follow when reevaluating WCL's return, risk, and covariance statistics. The forecasted statistics may not prove to be perfect. However, a qualified security analyst should be able to generate estimates to use as inputs for portfolio analysis.[5]

---

[4]B. J. King, "Market and Industry Factors in Stock Price Behavior," *Journal of Business*, Vol. 39, No. 1, 1966, pp. 139–190.

[5]M. E. Blume, "Betas and Their Regression Tendencies," *Journal of Finance*, June 1975, pp. 785–795; F. J. Fabozzi and J. C. Francis, "Stability Tests for Alplas and Betas Over Bull and Bear Market Conditions," *Journal of Finance*, September 1977; F. J. Fabozzi and J. C. Francis, "Beta as a Random Coefficient," *Journal of Financial and Quantitative Analysis*, March 1978; N. L. Jacob, "The Measurement of Systematic Risk for Securities and Portfolios: Some Empirical Results," *Journal of Financial and Quantitative Analysis*, March 1971, pp. 815–834; R. C. Klemkosky and J. D. Martin, "The Adjustment of Beta Factors," *Journal of Finance*, September 1975, pp. 1123–1128; R. S. Levy, "On the Short-Term Stationarity of Beta Coefficients," *Financial Analysts Journal*, November–December 1971; B. Rosenberg and J. Guy, "Beta and Investment Fundamentals," *Financial Analysts Journal*, Part I, May–June 1976; Part II, July–August 1976; W. F. Sharpe and G. M. Cooper, "Risk–Return Classes of NYSE Common Stocks, 1931–67," *Financial Analysts Journal*, March–April 1972, pp. 413–446.

J. C. Francis and F. J. Fabozzi, "The Effects of Changing Macroeconomic Conditions on the Parameters of the Single-Index Market Model," *Journal of Financial and Quantitative Analysis*, June 1979.

### 4.3 Establishing Ex Ante Probability Distributions

A second approach to forecasting return, risk, and covariance statistics is to develop subjective probability distributions of returns for each firm over the states of nature (economic conditions) that may pertain. This second approach is similar to the first, since historical experience and subjective hunches may be used. However, the second approach is different in that it focuses on developing a probability distribution from which the needed statistics are tabulated. The first approach concentrated directly on the needed statistics and tended to ignore the underlying probability distribution.

#### A. The States of Nature and Their Probabilities

The states of nature that have the largest effect on securities rates of return are economic conditions such as boom and recession. These states of nature may be meaningfully separated into, say, four categories, as shown in Fig. 4.2.

---

The security analyst should fill in the estimated rate of return which will occur for_____company during the future period from_____ to_____for each of the four possible economic conditions. The economist should fill in the probabilities associated with each economic condition.

| Economic Condition | Probability | Forecasted Rate of Return |
|---|---|---|
| Boom | —— | —— |
| Slow growth | —— | —— |
| Zero growth | —— | —— |
| Recession | —— | —— |
| | 1.0 | |

---

Figure 4.2. Form for Tabulating Probability Distribution of Rates of Return for a Security

More or less than four economic conditions may be used for the form suggested in Fig. 4.2. In any event, an information sheet should accompany the form explaining in detail the nature of the various economic conditions.[6] This information would aid the security analyst in forecasting the rate of return that might occur under each state of nature. Using equations (2.1a),

---

[6]Harry M. Markowitz, *Portfolio Selection* (New York: John Wiley & Sons, Inc., 1959), pp. 28–32.

(2.3a), and (2.4), the data from Fig. 4.2 can be converted into the statistical inputs needed for portfolio analysis.[7]

## B. Conditional Estimates of the Rates of Return

The security analyst's task is to estimate the rates of return that may be expected to prevail over the planning horizon for each of the economic conditions the firm may experience. Historical data and/or subjective estimates may be used to derive these conditional estimates of the firm's various rates of return. The simplified models suggested by Markowitz[8] and Sharpe[9] are also quite useful in this work, and they will be explained next.

### 4.4  A Simple Econometric Forecasting Model

A third approach to generating the statistical inputs uses a regression line of the form shown in equation (4.4).

$$r_{it} = a + b(r_{It}) + e_{it}, \qquad (4.4)$$

where $r_i$ is the rate of return on asset $i$ during some time period, $r_I$ is the rate of change in some market index during the same period, the $e$'s are random errors above and below the regression line, and $a$ and $b$ are the intercept and slope coefficient of the regression line. Equation (4.4) is sometimes called the *characteristic line* for the $i$th asset because it measures certain investment characteristics of the $i$th asset. Equation (4.4) is also called the *single-index market model* because it has a single explanatory variable which is a market index and the equation is a model of the way the $i$th asset interacts with stock market movements.[10]

One form that equation (4.4) may assume is represented graphically in Fig. 4.3. Assuming that the errors average out to zero, the conditional expectation is shown in equation (4.5).

$$E(r_i \mid r_I) = a + b(r_I). \qquad (4.5)$$

[7]To calculate the covariances using equation (2.4) the states of nature and their probabilities must be the same for all assets under consideration. However, this should present no problem—only one economic forecast need be prepared for all securities.

[8]Markowitz, *Portfolio Selection*, p. 100.

[9]W. F. Sharpe, "A Simplified Model for Portfolio Analysis," *Management Science*, Vol. 9, No. 2, 1963, pp. 277–293.

[10]The characteristic regression line can be decomposed into an earnings-generating model and an earnings-multiplier model for those who prefer to analyze securities in terms of earnings and price–earnings ratios. See J. C. Francis, "Analysis of Equity Returns: A Survey with Extensions," *Journal of Economics and Business*, Spring/Summer 1977. This article shows that the characteristic line may be viewed as a reduced-form model of a more complex process.

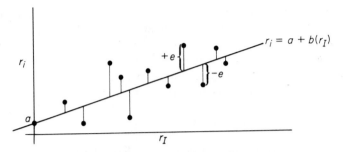

Figure 4.3. One Possible Form for Equation (4.4)

Using this conditional expectation facilitates prediction. For example, if the economist predicts that the market index $(r_I)$ assumes the value $r_{I0}$, then equation (4.5) implies that $r_{i0}$ is the expected value of the $i$th asset's rate of return. Figure 4.4 graphically depicts this process. Note, however, that this form of forecasting is dependent upon the constancy over time of the underlying regression model of equation (4.4).

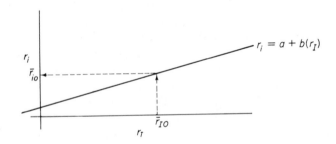

Figure 4.4. One Possible Form of Equation (4.5)

Regression models such as (4.4) are stationary, unbiased, and efficient estimators only if the assumptions listed below are not violated:

1. $e$ is a random variable with a mean of zero [that is, $E(e) = 0$].
2. $e$ has a constant variance (that is, homoscedasticity).
3. $e_t$ and $e_{t+1}$ are not correlated [that is, cov $(e_t, e_{t+1}) \doteq 0$.]
4. $e_t$ and $r_{It}$ are not correlated [that is, cov $(r_{It}, e_t) = 0$.]

If probability statements are to be made, $e$ must also conform to a known probability distribution and be stochastically independent. Fama has shown that these assumptions may be violated.[11] Blume has conducted an investiga-

---

[11]E. F. Fama, "The Behavior of Stock-Market Prices," *Journal of Business,* Vol. 38, No. 1, 1965, pp. 34–100.

tion of models (4.4) and (4.5) to determine their adequacy and see if the assumptions are violated.[12] Blume concludes that the assumptions are not significantly violated in the post-World War II period. Thus, models (4.4) and (4.5) are useful.[13] Particularly when the other independent estimates of return, risk, and covariance suggested earlier in this chapter are also used, the econometric models suggested here are appropriate.

## A. Formulas for Simplified Predictions

In Chapter VII the following formulas are derived from equation (4.4):

$$E(r_i) = a_i + b_i[E(r_I)], \tag{4.5}$$

$$\text{var}(r_i) = b_i^2[\text{var}(r_I)] + \sigma_i^2, \tag{4.6}$$

$$\text{cov}(r_i, r_j) = b_i b_j[\text{var}(r_I)], \tag{4.7}$$

where $E(r_i)$ is the expected return for asset $i$, $a_i$ and $b_i$ are the regression parameters from equation (4.4) for the $i$th asset, $E(r_I)$ is the expected return on the market index, $\text{var}(r_I)$ is the variance of returns for the market index, $\sigma_i^2$ is the residual variance for regressing $r_i$ onto $r_I$, and $b_j$ is the regression slope coefficient for asset $j$. The three formulas above may be used to estimate returns, risk, and covariances for various assets.[14] The regression parameters, $a$ and $b$, for each asset could be generated from historical data and perhaps adjusted subjectively. Then, an economist could predict the needed values of $E(r_I)$ and $\text{var}(r_I)$. It would then be a simple computation to generate all the statistical inputs needed for portfolio analysis by using equations (4.5), (4.6), and (4.7).

Using this technique greatly simplifies forecasting the needed inputs. If $n$ assets are under consideration, $n$ expected returns, $n$ variances, and $[\frac{1}{2}(n^2 - n)]$ covariances are required for portfolio analysis. By using equa-

---

[12]M. E. Blume, "The Assessment of Portfolio Performance: An Application of Portfolio Theory," unpublished Ph. D. dissertation, University of Chicago, March 1968.

[13]It has been shown that stock price returns are normally distributed in terms of transaction time (that is, per transaction) rather than per unit of calendar time (for example, per day). C. W. J. Granger and O. Morgenstern, *Predictability of Stock Market Prices* (Lexington, Mass.: D. C. Heath & Co., 1970) appear to be the first to present this evidence. Also see P. K. Clark, "A Subordinated Stochastic Process Model with Finite Variance for Speculative Prices," *Econometrica*, January 1973, pp. 135–155; R. Westerfield, "The Distribution of Common Stock Price Changes: An Application of Transactions Time and Subordinated Stochastic Models," *Journal of Financial and Quantitative Analysis*, December 1977; and I. G. Morgan, "Stock Prices and Heteroscedasticity," *Journal of Business*, October 1976, pp. 496–508.

[14]K. J. Cohen and J. A. Pogue, "An Empirical Evaluation of Alternative Portfolio-Selection Models," *Journal of Business*, Vol. 40, No. 2, 1967, pp. 166–193. Cohen and Pogue generate portfolios using unadjusted historical data. They also suggest more sophisticated econometric models which can be used to generate the input data.

tions (4.5), (4.6), and (4.7), all these statistics may be generated from only the two economic estimates, $E(r_I)$ and var $(r_I)$, and the $n$ values of $a$ and $b$.

## B. Beta Stability

The regression statistics $a$ and $b$ in equation (4.4) may be generated by a computer program. A regression program can be used to process historical data widely available on magnetic tapes. Some of these statistics are sufficiently stationary over time that they need not be reestimated frequently for most securities. For example, consider the data in Table 4.3; regression slope

TABLE 4.3 Intertemporal Beta Coefficients

| Firm | Time Period* | Beta | $R^2$† |
|------|------|------|------|
| Union Oil of California | 1/27– 6/35 | 0.55 | 0.58 |
| | 7/35–12/43 | 0.57 | 0.49 |
| | 1/44– 6/51 | 0.97 | 0.45 |
| | 7/51–12/60 | 0.98 | 0.32 |
| IBM | 1/27– 6/35 | 0.49 | 0.49 |
| | 7/35–12/43 | 0.25 | 0.26 |
| | 1/44– 6/51 | 0.56 | 0.29 |
| | 7/51–12/60 | 0.86 | 0.23 |
| May Dept. Stores | 1/27– 6/35 | 0.83 | 0.74 |
| | 7/35–12/43 | 0.64 | 0.49 |
| | 1/44– 6/51 | 0.72 | 0.35 |
| | 7/51–12/60 | 0.82 | 0.32 |
| Atlantic Coast Line RR | 1/27– 6/35 | 1.2 | 0.73 |
| | 7/35–12/43 | 1.26 | 0.70 |
| | 1/44– 6/51 | 1.17 | 0.43 |
| | 7/51–12/60 | 1.63 | 0.57 |

*Date: month/year.
†$R^2$ = coefficient of determination
   = (correlation coefficient)$^2$
   = percent of variation explained.

coefficients (that is, the beta coefficients) are shown. Over the 33 years covered by the data, the May Department Store's betas appear to be fairly consistent period after period.[15] The precentage of variation explained by the regressions ($R^2$) is significantly above zero. Clearly, these econometric relationships are useful. A procedure for detecting beta regression slope statistics in equation (4.4) that change and thus need to be adjusted is explained in the remainder of this chapter. This is work for the security analyst.

---

[15]Blume, "The Assessment of Portfolio Performance." For a more recent study of beta stability, see Sharpe and Cooper, "Risk–Return Classes of NYSE Common Stocks, 1931–67;" Fabozzi and Francis, "Beta as a Random Coefficient."

## 4.5 Beta Estimates

The regression slope coefficient in time-series equation (4.4) for the $i$th asset is called the *beta coefficient*, or simply the *beta*. The beta statistic is like an *elasticity estimate* for the percentage price change in the $i$th asset which accompanies the concurrent percentage change in the market index.[16] Most stocks' betas lie between 0.5 and 1.5 (that is, $0.5 < b_i < 1.5$), with an average value of unity. A beta of, say, 1.1 means that the asset tends to rise 10 percent more than the market average (for example, the Standard and Poor's 500 Stock Composite Index) in a bull market and fall 10 percent more than the market average in a bear market. A beta of 0.65 implies that the asset for which the beta was estimated tends to rise and fall proportionally only 65 percent as much as the market average.

Since assets' betas furnish estimates of how much each asset tends to move with the market, the betas are measures of *undiversifiable* or *systematic risk*. Chapters VIII, IX, and X explore in detail the market implications of the beta coefficient. Suffice it to say for now that the beta is useful for much more than applying equations (4.5), (4.6), and (4.7) to predicting expected return, variance, and covariance statistics. The point being developed here is that some betas are good elasticity estimates and some betas are worthless elasticity estimates.

### A. Good and Bad Betas

It is important to be able to tell the good beta coefficients from the bad ones, since the betas are useful in several different investment analysis applications. It may be easy to tell good beta undiversfiable risk estimates from worthless betas merely by observing the correlation coefficient (or, equivatently, the coefficient or determination, or the beta's $t$-statistic) associated with regression equation (4.4).

The good beta elasticity estimates will have high correlation coefficients (or, in general, goodness-of-fit statistics). The ideal beta would be from a regression that had high positive correlation with the market, since assets that are negatively correlated with the market are rare. The worthless betas would be from regressions that had correlations near zero or below.

When regression equation (4.4) is estimated for all of the approximately 1300 stocks on the New York Stock Exchange (NYSE), most of the regressions have correlation coefficients between one-half and seven-tenths (that is, $0.5 < \rho_{iI} < 0.70$). The correlation coefficient ($\rho$) squared is called the *coefficient of determination* (denoted $\rho^2$ or $R^2$) and measures the percentage of variation in the regression's dependent variable (namely, the asset's returns, $r_{it}$) explained by the independent variable (that is, the market's rate of

---

[16]Strictly speaking, the elasticity for the $i$th stock estimated with equation (4.4) is defined as $[b_i(\bar{r}_m/\bar{r}_i)]$. But the beta itself is a first approximation of this elasticity, since $(\bar{r}_m/\bar{r}_i) \cong 1.0$.

change, $r_{It}$). For most NYSE stocks, equation (4.4) explains between one-quarter ($= 0.25 = 0.5^2 = \rho^2$) to one-half ($\cong 0.49 = 0.70^2 = \rho^2$) of the variance in the stock's percentage price changes. Since most stocks regression intercept terms (called their *alphas*) are equal to approximately zero and are statistically insignificant (as measured by the alphas' *t*-statistics), practically all of equation (4.4)'s explanatory power may be attributed to its beta coefficient. Thus, the explanatory power of equation (4.4) is usually used as an indicator of whether the beta is valuable for investment analysis work, or is worthless.

Table 4.4 will be useful in discriminating between the good and bad betas. In fact, the table can also be used to tell whether the whole characteristic line model for a given stock has a significant amount of explanatory power. Table 4.4 shows the absolute values of the simple correlation coefficients from a regression model such as equation (4.4). The table classifies the level of statistical significance of the correlation coefficients for different sample sizes. Essentially, the table of values can be used to tell if a given beta or a given characteristic line has explanatory power that is significantly more than zero.

### B. Econometric Analysis of Betas

The two main problems that limit regression equation (4.4) and its beta undiversifiable risk coefficient in various investment analysis applications are: (1) the betas for some individual securities may be intertemporally unstable —as shown, for example, in Table 4.3; and (2) although equation (4.4) has significant explanatory power for most NYSE stocks, its usefulness is limited because it typically explains less than half of the variability of the stock's returns.[17] Econometric analysis into these two related problems has yielded insights that are so numerous they could fill several volumes.[18] Essentially, the root of the problem appears to be that some beta coefficients change through time.

*Random coefficients* Equation (4.4) may be rewritten to include random coefficients as shown in equation (4.8).[19]

$$r_{it} = a_i + b_i r_{It} + w_{it}. \tag{4.8}$$

---

[17]An empirical study of betas for NYSE stocks and portfolios of stocks using different differencing intervals for calculating the returns, and, other interesting devices was done by N. L. Jacob, "The Measurement of Systematic Risk for Securities and Portfolios: Some Empirical Results."

[18]For a summary of empirical research related to equation (4.4) that was done prior to 1972, see M. C. Jensen, "Capital Markets: Theory and Evidence," *Bell Journal of Economics and Management Science*, Autumn 1972, pp. 357–398.

[19]This discussion of random coefficients is tangential to pages 622–627 of *Principles of Econometrics* by Henri Theil (New York: John Wiley & Sons, Inc., 1971).

TABLE 4.4 Absolute Values of Significant Simple Correlation
Coefficients for Different Levels of Significance
and Different Sample Sizes

| | *Different Levels of Significance* | | | |
|---|---|---|---|---|
| $T^*$ | 0.1 | 0.05 | 0.01 | 0.001 |
| 6 | 0.6215 | 0.7067 | 0.8343 | 0.92493 |
| 7 | 0.5822 | 0.6664 | 0.7977 | 0.8982 |
| 8 | 0.5494 | 0.6319 | 0.7646 | 0.8721 |
| 9 | 0.5214 | 0.6021 | 0.7348 | 0.8471 |
| 10 | 0.4973 | 0.5760 | 0.7079 | 0.8233 |
| 11 | 0.4762 | 0.5529 | 0.6835 | 0.8010 |
| 12 | 0.4575 | 0.5324 | 0.6614 | 0.7800 |
| 13 | 0.4409 | 0.5139 | 0.6411 | 0.7603 |
| 14 | 0.4259 | 0.4973 | 0.6226 | 0.7420 |
| 15 | 0.4124 | 0.4821 | 0.6055 | 0.7246 |
| 16 | 0.4000 | 0.4683 | 0.5897 | 0.7084 |
| 17 | 0.3887 | 0.4555 | 0.5741 | 0.6932 |
| 18 | 0.3783 | 0.4438 | 0.5614 | 0.6787 |
| 19 | 0.3687 | 0.4329 | 0.5487 | 0.6652 |
| 20 | 0.3598 | 0.4227 | 0.5368 | 0.6524 |
| 25 | 0.3233 | 0.3809 | 0.4869 | 0.5974 |
| 30 | 0.2960 | 0.3494 | 0.4487 | 0.5541 |
| 35 | 0.2746 | 0.3246 | 0.4182 | 0.5189 |
| 40 | 0.2573 | 0.3044 | 0.3932 | 0.4896 |
| 45 | 0.2428 | 0.2875 | 0.3721 | 0.4648 |
| 50 | 0.2306 | 0.2732 | 0.3541 | 0.4433 |
| 60 | 0.2108 | 0.2500 | 0.3248 | 0.4078 |
| 70 | 0.1954 | 0.2319 | 0.3017 | 0.3799 |
| 80 | 0.1829 | 0.2172 | 0.2830 | 0.3568 |
| 90 | 0.1726 | 0.2050 | 0.2673 | 0.3375 |
| 100 | 0.1638 | 0.1946 | 0.2540 | 0.3211 |

$^*T$ represents the number of observations used to estimate equation (4.4), that is, the number of time periods.

*Source:* This table is taken from Table VII of Fisher and Yates: *Statistical Tables for Biological, Agricultural and Medical Research*, published by Longman Group Ltd., London (previously published by Oliver and Boyd, Edinburgh), and by permission of the authors and publishers.

where the symbol $a_i$ is the population parameter alpha, which is estimated by the sample statistic from equation (4.4); $b_i$ is the mean beta coefficient averaged over the intertemporally changing short-term betas, denoted $b_{it}$ for the $i$th asset in period $t$; and $w_{it}$ is a residual error term that is not serially correlated; $E(w_{it}, w_{i,t-1}) = 0$ is uncorrelated with the market, $E(w_{it}, r_{It}) = 0$, and is uncorrelated with the coefficient changes, $E(w_{it}, b_{it}) = 0$.

To see how the beta in equation (4.4) is affected by the random coefficient changes, the error term $w_{it}$ is analyzed in equation (4.9).

$$w_{it} = (b_{it} - b_i)r_{It} + e_{it}, \tag{4.9}$$

where $b_{it}$ is the beta coefficient for the $i$th asset at time $t$, $b_i$ is the mean beta coefficient for asset $i$—that is, $E(b_{it}) = b_i$ over the time period under consideration.

It can be easily shown that the ordinary least squares (OLS) estimate used to estimate (4.4) provides an unbiased estimate for the mean beta, $b_i$. However, the OLS estimate for the mean beta is flawed because it is not a minimum-variance estimator.

What is the implication for the security analyst if the true model is a random coefficient model?[20] Systematic risk will vary from period to period around the mean beta. As a result, beta risk statistics must be updated often.

*Adjusted betas*    Published research has shown that some of the factors that cause the regression coefficients in equation (4.4) to change randomly are fundamental characteristics of the firm, such as changes in the firm's leverage, cash dividend yield, earnings growth, and so on. Rosenberg and Guy (RG hereafter) have suggested a prediction rule for developing beta estimates for assets.[21]

Essentially, the analyst may begin with the industry average betas shown in Table 4.5 and modify them by adding on appropriate adjustment factors from Table 4.6 to obtain a beta prediction for an individual firm's stock. For example, if a steel firm had a cash dividend yield that was 1 standard deviation above the means for all firms, then the $-0.044$ adjustment factor from Table 4.6 would be added to the steel industry beta of 1.02 from the Table 4.5 to obtain $(1.02 - 0.0444) = 0.9756$ as a beta estimate. If any characteristics of this steel firm besides its cash dividend yield differed from the average for all firms, then additional adjustments would be needed.

Since the beta coefficient does not rise and fall over bull and bear market conditions,[22] the adjusted beta estimates are better estimates than the firm's own historical beta estimates.[23] The problem with this procedure, of course, is that the proper adjustments for all possible changes and combinations of changes must be estimated econometrically.

---

[20]The author has found that the beta appears to be a random coefficient: Fabozzi and Francis, "Beta as a Random Coefficient."

[21]Rosenberg and Guy, "Beta and Investment Fundamentals—Part II."

[22]F. J. Fabozzi and J. C. Francis, "Stability Tests for Alphas and Betas Over Bull and Bear Market Conditions," *Journal of Finance*, September 1977.

[23]Rosenberg and Guy, "Beta and Investment Fundamentals, Part II," p. 68.

TABLE 4.5 Industry Differentials in Beta Coefficients

| Industry | Average Industry Values of Beta | Industry Risk Differences Not Explained by Other Fundamental Firm Characteristics†<br>Adjustment to Beta |
|---|---|---|
| Nonferrous metals | 0.99 | −0.142*** |
| Energy raw materials | 1.22 | −0.030 |
| Construction | 1.27 | 0.062 |
| Agriculture, food | 0.99 | −0.140*** |
| Liquor | 0.89 | −0.165*** |
| Tobacco | 0.80 | −0.279*** |
| Apparel | 1.27 | 0.019 |
| Forest products, paper | 1.16 | −0.016 |
| Containers | 1.01 | −0.140** |
| Media | 1.39 | 0.124* |
| Chemicals | 1.22 | 0.011 |
| Drugs, medicine | 1.14 | −0.099*** |
| Soaps, cosmetics | 1.09 | −0.067* |
| Domestic oil | 1.12 | −0.103* |
| International oil | 0.85 | −0.143* |
| Tires, rubber goods | 1.21 | 0.050 |
| Steel | 1.02 | −0.086* |
| Producer goods | 1.30 | 0.043 |
| Business machines | 1.43 | 0.065 |
| Consumer durables | 1.44 | 0.132* |
| Motor vehicles | 1.27 | 0.045 |
| Aerospace | 1.30 | 0.020 |
| Electronics | 1.60 | 0.155** |
| Photographic, optical | 1.24 | 0.026 |
| Nondurables, entertainment | 1.47 | 0.042 |
| Trucking, freight | 1.30 | 0.098 |
| Railroads, shipping | 1.19 | 0.030 |
| Air transport | 1.80 | 0.348*** |
| Telephone | 0.75 | −0.288*** |
| Energy utilities | 0.60 | 0.237*** |
| Retail, general | 1.43 | 0.073 |
| Banks | 0.81 | −0.242*** |
| Miscellaneous finance | 1.60 | 0.210** |
| Insurance | 1.34 | 0.103 |
| Real property | 1.70 | 0.339*** |
| Business services | 1.28 | 0.029 |
| Travel, outdoor recreation | 1.66 | 0.186** |
| Gold | 0.36 | 0.827*** |
| Miscellaneous conglomerate | 1.14 | 0.089* |

†One asterisk indicates significance at the 95 percent level of confidence; two asterisks, significance at the 99 percent level; and three asterisks, significance at the 99.9 percent level.

Source: Barr Rosenberg and Vinay Marathe, "The Prediction of Investment Risk Systematic and Residual Risk," in Proceedings: Seminar on the Analysis of Security Prices, Center for Research in Security Prices, Graduate School of Business, The University of Chicago, November 1975.

TABLE 4.6 Optimal Adjustments for Short-Term Beta Forecasts
for Selected Fundamental Changes in the Firm

| Descriptor | Adjustment in Betas for a Difference of 1 Standard Deviation from the Mean of All Firms† |
|---|---|
| Variance of cash flow | 0.022*** |
| Variance of earnings | 0.023* |
| Growth in earnings per share | −0.004*** |
| Market capitalization | −0.043*** |
| Current dividend yield | −0.044*** |
| Total debt to assets | 0.041*** |

†These figures are standardized so as to be comparable with one another. For example, the coefficient of 0.022 for the variance of cash flow, VFLO, indicates that if the VFLO for a firm lies 1 standard deviation from the mean VFLO of all firms, the predicted beta for that firm is increased by 0.022. Roughly 17 percent of all firms will lie more than 1 standard deviation above the mean, and these will experience upward adjustments of 0.044 or more as a result of this descriptor. Of course, equally as many firms will lie below the mean and receive negative adjustments of the same amount.

The significance of estimated coefficients is as follows: * indicates significance at the 95 percent level of confidence; **, at the 99 percent level of confidence; and ***, at the 99.9 percent level of confidence.

*Source:* Barr Rosenberg and Vinay Marathe, "The Prediction of Investment Risk. Systematic and Residual Risk," in *Proceedings Seminar on the Analysis of Security Prices,* Center for Research in Security Prices, Graduate School of Business, The University of Chicago, November 1975.

## 4.6 Conclusion—A Consensus

It has been suggested that the ex ante statistical inputs necessary for portfolio analysis be estimated independently by three procedures. First, historical statistics may be tabulated and perhaps adjusted subjectively. Second, economic forecasters and fundamental security analysts can work together to generate subjective probability distributions of expected returns over various conditions. Finally, econometric relationships were suggested that can be useful in generating the input statistics needed for portfolio analysis.

These three procedures can be used to generate three independent estimates of return, risk, and covariance for each asset under consideration.[24] The analysts compiling these different estimates can meet together after their estimates are finished. Then, these different estimates can be compared, argued, adjusted, and finalized. In this manner the portfolio analyst will

---

[24]Unfortunately, the first technique is not useful for new issues.

be assured of receiving a consensus of opinion about each asset's expected return, risk, and covariance. Thus, the foundation is laid for portfolio analysis.[25]

**Appendix 4A**
**The Determinants of Beta**

Every common stock, bond, preferred stock, piece of real estate, art object, and every other market asset has a beta coefficient that can be estimated with the characteristic regression line. These beta coefficients are quite important in the overall portfolio theory because they are a risk measure for each asset. And, since risk is the primary determinant of what makes some assets yield higher returns than other assets, it is worthwhile to consider what factors underlie the beta risk measure.

Security analysts traditionally calculated financial ratios to obtain estimates of the risk inherent in an investment. A few of the more popular financial ratios are listed below.

1. The current ratio, $cr$, measures liquidity and thus the risk of insolvency:

$$cr_t = \frac{\text{current assets}_t}{\text{current liabilities}_t}.$$

2. The debt-to-total assets ratio, $da$, is a financial leverage measure useful in gauging indebtedness.

$$da_t = \frac{\text{total debt}_t}{\text{total assets}_t}.$$

3. The range of earnings per share (eps) is a measure of the stability of the earning power that underlies a share of common stock and thus affects its ability to pay cash dividends and to avoid bankruptcy. This range is usually measured over a recent number of years:

$$\text{eps range} = (\text{highest recent eps}) - (\text{lowest recent eps})$$

The security analyst would traditionally calculate a number of different ratios over a period of years in order to evaluate the investment potential of an asset. Then these ratios would be compared with competitors' ratios

---

[25]Estimating the return statistics and, in particular, the risk statistics necessary for portfolio analysis requires significant knowledge of applied econometrics. Furthermore, the econometric work requires (1) a large digital computer, (2) large data bases of stock prices and related financial information from past years, (3) sophisticated computer programs and/or programming skills, and (4) the ability to handle and manage these various resources efficiently. Some investment managers retain external consultants to do this work—especially in the early stages of developing their own quantitative investment management techniques.

(that is, cross-sectionally) and the firm's own historical ratios (namely, time series) to obtain different perspectives to aid in their interpretation.

In contrast to the traditional practice of pondering over numerous financial ratios for each potential investment, modern risk–return-oriented financial analysts focus their attention on only one statistic for each potential investment—the beta coefficient. This practice is based on the belief that the beta coefficient subsumes the information contained in all the traditional financial ratios and summarizes it into one simple number.

The beta is viewed as an index of systematic or undiversifiable risk—the most undesirable kind of risk to have in a portfolio. The average of all different assets' beta values is unity. Most betas lie between zero and $+2$. The betas from completely different and unrelated firms may be readily compared, and thus the beta is a handy tool. Furthermore, the beta is not supposed to be biased by financial statements which unethical financial managers have manipulated because the sophisticated financial analysts will see through the deceptive accounting. Thus, modern portfolio theory redefines the role of the investment analyst (as suggested by Lev,[1] for example) to include somewhat different duties than had been traditional (as described by Graham, Dodd, and Cottle,[2] for example).

Some traditional investment analysts find the modern risk–return analysis offensive because it seems to disregard their traditional forms of financial ratio analysis. This is an oversimplified and erroneous interpretation of modern analysts concern over betas. The beta is the focal point of risk–return investment analysis, because the beta handily includes all the information gathered more slowly and laboriously by the traditional ratio analysts.[3] That is, betas are studied because (1) betas are easier to calculate and interpret than financial ratios, (2) betas summarize the information contained in numerous financial ratios, and (3) betas are a part of the theory of asset pricing (which is presented in Chapter VIII).

Some traditional ratio analysts doubt that the beta risk measure is able to give simultaneous consideration to numerous different ratios. Thompson has correlated the betas of a large sample of common stocks and portfolios with their own financial ratios to delineate the determinants of betas. Thompson's results in Table 4A.1 show scientific evidence that the assets' betas are simultaneously influenced by the same financial ratios and fundamental facts with which the traditional ratio analysts work.[4]

[1]Baruch Lev, *Financial Statement Analysis*, Prentice-Hall Contemporary Topics in Accounting Series (Englewood Cliffs, N. J.: Prentice-Hall, Inc., 1974).

[2]Benjamin Graham, David Dodd, and Sidney Cottle, *Security Analysis*, 4th ed. (New York: McGraw-Hill Book Company, 1962).

[3]Barr Rosenberg and James Guy, "Beta and Investment Fundamentals," *Financial Analysts Journal*, July–August 1976, pp. 62–70.

[4]D. J. Thompson II, "Sources of Systematic Risk in Common Stocks," *Journal of Business*, Vol. 49, No. 2, 1976, pp. 173–188.

To obtain the linear correlation coefficients shown in Table 4A.1, Thompson ran the cross-sectional regression shown in equation (4A.1):

$$b_i = a_0 + a_1 \cdot x_i + w_i, \qquad\qquad (4A.1)$$

where $a_0$ is a regression intercept term, $a_1$ is the regression slope coefficient, $x_i$ is ratio or variable $x$ for the $i$th firm or portfolio, $b_i$ denotes the beta coefficient for the $i$th market asset, and $w_i$ is the residual portion of the beta left unexplained by regression equation (4A.1)—it has an expected value of zero. Equation (4A.1) was estimated over a sample 211 firms' ratios observed during the 1951–1959 sample period, 193 firms from the 1960–1968 sample, and a sample of small portfolios formed from these stocks (ranked and grouped on their ratios). The correlation coefficient is a goodness-of-fit statistic for regression equation (4A.1).

TABLE 4A.1   Correlation Coefficients Between Common Stock Betas and Explanatory Variables

| Corporate Risk Factors and Corporate Explanatory Variables | Single Securities | | Portfolios |
|---|---|---|---|
| | *1951–59* | *1960–68* | *1960–68* |
| Dividends, earnings multiple, and earnings stability factors simultaneously | | | |
| Model | 0.53** | 0.36** | 0.88** |
| Dividends stability factor | | | |
| Dividend beta | 0.17** | 0.15** | 0.12 |
| Dividend variance | 0.21** | 0.05 | — |
| Mean dividend payout ratio | −0.44** | −0.37** | −0.76** |
| Sum of dividends to sum of earnings | −0.41** | −0.15** | — |
| Earnings multiple stability factor | | | |
| Earnings multiple beta | 0.51** | 0.29** | 0.69** |
| Earnings multiple variance beta | 0.40** | 0.50** | 0.74** |
| Earnings yield beta | 0.39** | 0.24** | — |
| Earnings yield variance | 0.17** | 0.20** | — |
| Earnings stability factor | | | |
| Earnings beta | 0.37** | 0.24** | 0.62** |
| Earnings variance | 0.30** | 0.27** | 0.75** |
| Operating income stability factor | | | |
| Operating income beta | 0.42** | 0.21** | 0.72** |
| Operating income variance | 0.36** | 0.29** | 0.87** |
| Sales stability factor | | | |
| Sales beta | 0.42** | 0.07 | — |
| Sales variance | 0.31** | 0.11* | — |
| Growth factor | | | |
| Asset growth | 0.11* | 0.21** | 0.56* |
| Earnings growth | −0.06 | 0.13* | — |
| Sales growth | 0.01 | 0.13* | — |
| Asset, earnings, and sales growth | 0.01 | 0.19** | — |
| Ratio of investment to earnings | 0.15** | −0.02 | — |
| Return on investment | 0.05 | −0.01 | — |

| Corporate Risk Factors and Corporate Explanator Variables | Correlation Coefficient | | |
|---|---|---|---|
| | Single Securities | | Portfolios |
| | *1951–59* | *1960–68* | *1960–68* |
| Common stock marketability factor | | | |
| Market volume | 0.39** | 0.15** | 0.32 |
| Financial leverage factor | | | |
| Total debt to total assets beta | 0.18** | −0.14* | — |
| Total debt to total assets variance | 0.17** | 0.02 | — |
| Mean total debt to total assets | 0.02 | 0.24** | 0.53* |
| Cash flow to total debt beta | 0.27** | 0.12* | — |
| Cash flow to total debt variance | 0.23** | 0.24** | — |
| Mean cash flow to total debt | 0.00 | −0.22** | — |
| Pretax interest coverage beta | 0.30** | 0.34** | — |
| Pretax interest coverage variance | 0.27** | 0.28** | — |
| Mean pretax interest coverage | −0.02 | −0.23** | −0.41 |
| Liquidity factor | | | |
| Current ratio beta | 0.38** | −0.07 | — |
| Current ratio variance | 0.24** | 0.21** | — |
| Mean current ratio | −0.14* | −0.05 | — |
| Working capital to total assets beta | 0.34** | −0.11* | — |
| Working capital to total assets variance | 0.26** | 0.19** | — |
| Mean working capital to total assets | −0.28** | −0.03 | — |
| Quick assets to operating expense beta | 0.30** | 0.05 | — |
| Quick assets to operating expense variance | 0.21** | 0.18** | — |
| Mean quick assets to operating expense | −0.04 | −0.06 | — |
| Size factor | | | |
| Asset size | 0.21** | −0.11* | — |
| Earnings size | 0.21** | −0.19** | — |
| Sales size | 0.16** | −0.11* | — |

†One asterisk, significantly different from zero at the 5 percent level; two asterisks, the 1 percent level.

*Source:* D. J. Thompson II, "Sources of Systematic Risk in Common Stocks," *Journal of Business*, Vol. 49, No. 2, 1976, p. 184.

## Appendix 4B
## Characteristic Line in Risk Premium Form

The *risk premium, $rp_{it}$*, or *excess return* for the $i$th market asset in the $t$th time period is defined as the nominal rate of return, $r_{it}$, in excess of the riskless rate of return, $R_t$, as defined in equation (4B.1).

$$rp_{it} = (r_{it} - R_t) = \text{risk premium}_{it}. \qquad (4B.1)$$

The risk premium measures that portion of the period's return over and above the return that could have been earned in a riskless asset (such as U.S. Treasury bills).

### 4B.1 The Riskless Rate of Return

The one-period yield on riskless assets (such as Treasury bills or commercial paper) rises and falls with rate of inflation so that they earn a real rate of return that is positive.[1] More explicitly, if $i_t$ denotes the rate of inflation during time period $t$ and $R_t$ is the nominal (that is, measured in dollar values current in period $t$ rather than inflation-adjusted values) rate of return from some riskless asset, then the *real rate of return* from the riskless asset is defined in equation (4B.2):

$$\text{real return in period } t = (R_t - i_t) \qquad (4B.2)$$

The real or inflation adjusted rate of return for a riskless asset measured by equation (4B.2) must be positive or else the riskless asset's investors will suffer a loss in *purchasing power* from their investment. Economists rationalize the level of riskless interest rates by pointing out that they must contain an *inflation premium* to compensate for purchasing power lost to inflation by holding a monetary asset which cannot inflate in value, plus another premium, called a *time value of money premium*, for delaying their consumption opportunities in order to make the investment. The time value of money premium is unobservable and is presumed to remain constant and positive. The inflation premium estimates suggest that it equals the rate of inflation. This is all summarized in equation (4B.3), which shows that if the rate of inflation rises, say, two percentage points, the riskless rate will rise by approximately the same amount simultaneously.[2]

$$R_t \cong \text{(time value of money premium)} + \text{(inflation premium)} \qquad (4B.3)$$

$$\cong \text{(positive constant)} + i_t. \qquad (4B.3a)$$

### 4B.2 Returns Involving Bankruptcy Risk

The nominal rate of one-period return on risky assets such as common stocks and corporation bonds typically exceeds the riskless rate—that is, $E(r_i) > E(R)$—because investors require a default risk premium to induce them to take their savings out of riskless assets and invest them in a risky asset that might go bankrupt. This is summarized in equation (4B.4).

$$r_{it} = [R_t] + \text{(risk premium}_t). \qquad (4B.4)$$

Sometimes however, risky assets can depreciate in value rapidly because of

---

[1] W. E. Gibson, "Interest Rates and Inflationary Expectations: New Evidence," *American Economic Review*, December 1972, pp. 854–865.
[2] Ibid.

recession economics, bear-market conditions, or other prospects of financial disaster. This means the risk premium can become negative so that $r_{it} < R_t$ in some periods. The risk premiums from investing are particularly interesting because they are what can make poor men become rich. The classic characteristic regression-line model ignores this explicit distinction between nominal risky returns and the returns from risk premiums, however.

### 4B.3  Classic Characteristic Line

The original characteristic regression line[3] for the $i$th market asset was defined in equation (4.4):

$$r_{it} = a_i + b_i r_{It} + e_{it}, \qquad E(e_{it}) = 0, \qquad (4.4)$$

where the regression intercept is called alpha and denoted $a_i$; the beta slope coefficient, $b_i$, is a systematic risk coefficient; the residual error, $e_{it}$, has a mathematical expected value of zero and is econometrically well behaved; the dependent variable is the single-period rate of return for security $i$, as defined in equation (1.1) for common stocks; and the independent variable, $r_{It}$, is the one-period rate of return from some market index. This important econometric model may be reformulated in terms of risk premiums instead of returns.

### 4B.4  Reformulated Characteristic Line

Equations (4B.5) and (4B.5a) redefine the characteristic regression line in terms of risk premiums.

$$r_{it} - R_t = A_i + B_i(r_{It} - R_t) + u_{it}, \qquad E(u_{it}) = 0, \qquad (4B.5)$$

$$rp_{it} = A_i + B_i(rp_{It}) + u_{it}, \qquad (4B.5a)$$

where the regression intercept, $A_i$, measures any excess returns the $i$th asset earns over the periods used to estimate this time-series regression; the regression slope, $B_i$, is conceptually identical to the beta systematic risk coefficient in equation (4.4); and $u_{it}$ is a residual error with zero expected value. Graphically speaking, Figs. 4B.1 and 4B.2 illustrate the similarity between equations (4.4) and (4B.5).

---

[3]Harry M. Markowitz, *Portfolio Selection* (New York: J. Wiley & Sons, Inc. 1959), p. 100; W. F. Sharpe, "A Simplified Model for Portfolio Analysis," *Management Science*, January 1963; J. L. Treynor, "How to Rate the Management of Investment Funds," *Harvard Business Review*, January–February 1965.

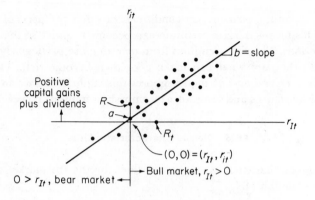

Figure 4B.1. Traditional Characteristic Line

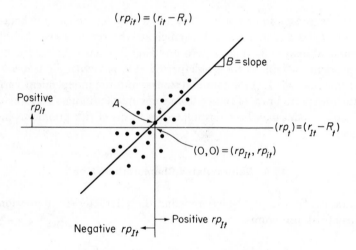

Figure 4B.2. Reformulated Characteristic Line

### 4B.5   Differences in the Two Models

The beta measure of undiversifiable risk is defined in equation (4B.6) for the $i$th market asset:

$$b_i = \frac{\text{cov}\,(r_{it}, r_{It})}{\text{var}\,(r_{It})}. \qquad (4B.6)$$

This beta coefficient can be derived mathematically from Markowitz's portfolio theory[4] (see Appendix 8A) and it is estimated empirically with the

---

[4]W. F. Sharpe, "Capital Asset Prices: A Theory of Equilibrium Under Conditions of Risk," *Journal of Finance*, Vol. 19, September 1964.

traditional characteristic line of equation (4.4). The slope coefficient from equation (4B.5) is similar to the beta coefficient, but not identical.

Equation (4B.7) defines the $B_i$ slope coefficient from the characteristic line reformulated in terms of risk premiums.

$$B_i = \frac{\text{cov}\,[(r_{it} - R_t),\,(r_{It} - R_t)]}{\text{var}\,(r_{It} - R_t)} \qquad\qquad (4B.7)$$

$$= \frac{\text{cov}\,(r_{it},\,r_{It})}{\text{var}\,(r_{It} - R_t)}. \qquad\qquad (4B.7a)$$

Equation (4B.7a) follows from (4B.7) because $\text{cov}\,[(r_{it} - R_t)(r_{It} - R_t)]$ $= \text{cov}\,(r_{it},\,r_{It})$. Equation (4B.7a) shows mathematically that the slope coefficients from the two formulations of the characteristic line will differ slightly (that is, $b_i \neq B_i$) because $\text{var}\,(r_{It}) \neq \text{var}\,(r_{It} - R_t)$. Since $B_i$ is not identical to the beta derived from portfolio theory $(b_i)$, it will not be discussed as much as the beta from equilibrium theory in this monograph.[5] However, equation (4B.5) is nevertheless useful in its own right (as a portfolio performance measure, which is explained in Chapter X).[6]

As a practical matter it makes little or no difference whether the $B_i$ from equation (4B.5) or the $b_i$ from equation (4.4) is used for teaching or econometric purposes. Equation (4B.5) is useful in instruction, where equilibrium theory definitions of beta are not important, because it shows how an asset's risk premium, $(r_{it} - R_t)$, relates to its undiversifiable risk as measured by $B_i$.[7] In econometric work the numerical difference between $b_i$ and $B_i$ is statistically insignificant.[8] But it is impossible to discern whether equation (4.4) or (4B.5) is more descriptive of reality because of ambiguities about the riskless rate in equation (4B.5)—there is no consensus about which empirical interest rate is the best estimate of the theoretical riskless rate, $R_t$.

---

[5]In the case that the riskless rate is constant (that is, in static equilibrium theory) the following equality will prevail:

$$\text{var}\,(r_{It}) = \text{var}\,(r_{It} - R).$$

In this case $B_i = b_i$. However, this situation is not likely to occur in empirical time-series applications because $R_t$ varies from period to period when observed empirically.

[6]M. C. Jensen, "Risk, the Pricing of Capital Assets, and the Evaluation of Investment Portfolios," *Journal of Business*, Vol. 42, 1969.

[7]It is also possible to completely reformulate Markowitz's portfolio analysis in risk-premium terms, that is, in {var $(r - R)$, $[E(r) - R]$} space, to rationalize using equation (4B.5) on theoretical grounds.

[8]Jensen discusses the empirical difference between $b_i$ and $B_i$ after acknowledging that $b_i$ is theoretically correct based on the classic capital market theory model. See M. C. Jensen, "Capital Markets: Theory and Evidence," *Bell Journal of Economics and Management Science*, Autumn 1972, pp. 363–367, especially footnote 23.

### 4B.6   A Caveat

In conclusion, a caveat about equation (4B.5) may be in order. Equation (4B.5) uses "difference risk premia," that is, the risk premia are derived by means of subtraction. However, a "ratio risk premia," such as shown in equation (4B.8), for example, may be more appropriate:

$$\text{ratio } rp_{it} = \frac{1 + r_{it}}{1 + R_t}. \tag{4B.8}$$

Inflation-risk premium theory was originally formulated in the ratio fashion.[9] Research by one of the authors tends to support the superiority of the ratio measure over the difference measure.[10] Use of the ratio form of risk measure by other financial analysts in their common stock research also attests implicitly to their preference for the concept of risk premiums as a multiplicative process rather than as an additive process.[11] Further research is needed on this topic, however.

---

[9]Irving Fisher, *The Theory of Interest* (New York: Macmillan Publishing Co., Inc., 1930).

[10]J. C. Francis, "Bond Risk Premia," a paper presented at the Western Finance Association Meetings in San Francisco in 1976. Abstracted in *Journal of Financial and Quantitative Analysis*, November 1976.

[11]A. Kraus and R. H. Litzenberger, "Skewness Preference and the Valuation of Risk Assets," *Journal of Finance*, September 1976.

## Selected References

Fabozzi, F. J., and J. C. Francis, "Beta as a Random Coefficient," *Journal of Financial and Quantitative Analysis*, March 1978, pp. 101–116.
This empirical study of individual NYSE stocks suggests that their beta coefficients change significantly over time and that the beta may be a random coefficient. Several regression models are discussed. This article concludes with an informative discussion of the implications of time-varying beta systematic risk statistics.

Francis, J. C., and F. J. Fabozzi, "The Effects of Changing Macro-Economic Conditions on the Parameters of the Single-Index Market Model," *Journal of Financial and Quantitiative Analysis*, June 1979.
This empirical study uses a binary variable multiple-regression model to delineate a cause for significant shifts in alpha intercepts and beta systematic risk statistics.

Jacob, N. L., "The Measurement of Systematic Risk for Securities and Portfolios: Some Empirical Results," *Journal of Financial and Quantitative Analysis*, March 1971, pp. 815–834.
This empirical study uses regression analysis to test various aspects of the characteristic line. The characteristic line is estimated with returns and also in risk-premium form. Both individual securities and portfolios are studied using monthly, quarterly, and annual returns.

## Questions and Problems

Select some security, calculate 30 returns for the asset and some market average, and then estimate various characteristic regression lines for the asset as suggested below.

1. Estimate the characteristic line with continuously compounded returns, $r_{it} = \ln \left[ (p_{i,t+1} + d_t)/p_t \right]$, and also, with noncompounded returns, $r_{it} = (p_{i,t+1} - p_{it} + d_{it})/p_{it}$. Are the regression statistics changed much by changing the type of returns used?

2. Estimate the characteristic line in its classic form using returns, $r_{it} = a_i + b_i r_{mt} + e_{it}$. Also, estimate it using risk premiums, $r_{it} - R_t = a_i + b_i(r_{mt} - R_t) + e_{it}$. Are the betas from these two different models similar?

3. Estimate the characteristic line using 30 monthly returns, and also estimate it with 10 quarterly returns gathered from the same period as the 30 monthly returns. Are the regression statistics affected merely by these changes in the length of the differencing interval?

4. Partition your sample of 30 observations into two mutually exclusive subsamples which each have 15 observations. Then estimate the characteristic line twice for the same stock—once using the first subsample, and again, using the second subsample. Do the regression statistics appear to be stable over time (that is, from the first 15 periods to the second 15 periods)?

5. Calculate the standard error of the beta slope coefficient for one of the characteristic lines which you estimated. Then construct confidence intervals around the beta you estimated. Assuming a normal distribution, how much could your beta be expected to vary due purely to normal sampling error? (*Hint:* Two standard errors above and below the original beta includes normal sampling error at the 0.05 level of significance.) Did this exercise increase or diminish your confidence in your point estimate of the beta?

6. Calculate the standard error of the alpha intercept coefficient for one of the characteristic lines you estimated. Then construct confidence intervals around the alpha you estimated. Assuming a normal distribution, how far could this alpha vary solely as a result of normal sampling error? (*Hint:* Three standard errors above and below the alpha you estimated includes normal sampling error at the 0.01 level of significance.) Does this exercise increase or decrease your confidence in your point estimate of alpha?

# Section Two

# PORTFOLIO ANALYSIS

$S$ECTION Two presumes a mastery of the material in Section One. With this background in probabilistic risk analysis, Chapters V, VI, and VII go on to explicate different techniques for delineating the set of efficient portfolios. Chapter V explains the graphical analysis as a learning device for readers who do not wish to pursue the analysis in terms of higher level mathematics. Chapters VI and VII may be omitted with no loss of continuity by readers who are seeking only an introduction to portfolio analysis. However, those who wish to pursue more general solutions to the efficient portfolio problem may find them in Chapters VI and VII. Readers who have studied advanced calculus and matrix algebra may prefer the rigor and generality of the calculus techniques shown in Chapter VI and the simplified computational models presented in Chapter VII.

Section Two

PORTFOLIO ANALYSIS

```
5555555555555555555555555555555555555555555555555555555555555555555555555555555555555
5555555555555555555555555555555555555555555555555555555555555555555555555555555555555
5555555555555555555555555555555555555    5555555555    55555555555555555555555555555555
5555555555555555555555555555555555555    5555555555    55555555555555555555555555555555
555555555555555555555555555555555555555    555555555    5555555555555555555555555555555
55555555555555555555555555555555555555555    5555555    5555555555555555555555555555555
5555555555555555555555555555555555555555555    55555    5555555555555555555555555555555
55555555555555555555555555555555555555555555    555    55555555555555555555555555555555
5555555555555555555555555555555555555555555555    5    555555555555555555555555555555555
55555555555555555555555555555555555555555555555        5555555555555555555555555555555
5555555555555555555555555555555555555555555555555    555555555555555555555555555555555555
555555555555555555555555555555555555555555555555    5555555555555555555555555555555555555
5555555555555555555555555555555555555555555555555555555555555555555555555555555555555555
5555555555555555555555555555555555555555555555555555555555555555555555555555555555555555
```

# Markowitz Portfolio
# Analysis Graphically

MARKOWITZ portfolio analysis is a mathematical procedure to determine how to select the optimum portfolios of assets in which to invest. The procedure was first made public in 1952 by Harry Markowitz.[1] The theory has caused a scientific revolution in finance. Before Markowitz's scientific procedure investment counselors passed off "commonsense guidelines" to their clients and pretended it was valuable expert advice—and unfortunately, many still do.

The objective of portfolio analysis is to determine the set of "efficient portfolios." In terms of Fig. 5.1, the objective is to find the efficient frontier—the heavy dark curve from $E$ to $F$—for some opportunity set generated by a group of assets that are potential investments.

### 5.1  Solution Techniques Available

Three methods of solving for the efficient set (that is, doing portfolio analysis) are available:

1. Graphical.

---

[1]The analysis was originally presented in an article: "Portfolio Selection," *Journal of Finance*, March 1952, pp. 77–91. Later Markowitz expanded his presentation in a book, *Portfolio Selection*, Cowles Foundation Monograph 16 (New York: John Wiley & Sons, Inc., 1959).

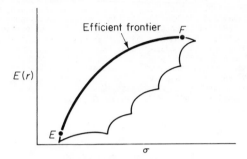

Figure 5.1 The Opportunity Set in $[\sigma, E(r)]$ Space

2. With calculus.
3. By quadratic programming (QP).[2]

For any given set of assets, any of the three algorithms will yield the same efficient set.

The graphical portfolio analysis will be presented in this chapter. The primary advantage of this technique is that it is easier to grasp conceptually. Most students internalize the analysis much more effectively if they have something graphical to which they may refer. Furthermore, leveraged portfolios may be represented graphically. The disadvantage of the graphical analysis is that it cannot handle portfolios containing more than a few securities.

Two calculus algorithms will be presented in Chapter VI. The primary advantage of the calculus methods lies in their ease of manipulation and their ability to handle portfolios containing a more realistic number of securities. Any number of securities may be analyzed, since mathematics can deal in $n$-dimensional space. As a result of these and other advantages, the calculus solution can be useful to researchers. However, the calculus solution technique cannot handle inequality constraints.

Quadratic programming algorithms have been coded for computers. These programs are most useful in handling large-portfolio problems that are solved frequently. Like linear programming, quadratic programming (QP) can accommodate inequality constraints; thus, the portfolio may be optimized within constraints on the proportion of each security. For practical management of mutual funds or other large portfolios, the QP solution method is the most desirable. QP will be discussed further in Chapter VI.

---

[2]Also, Sharpe has written a linear programming algorithm that provides approximate solutions: W. F. Sharpe, "A Linear Programming Algorithm for Mutual Fund Portfolio Selection," *Management Science*, March 1967, pp. 499–510. Furthermore, Sharpe and others have developed simplified solution methods—see Chapter VII.

## 5.2 Inputs for Portfolio Analysis

Portfolio analysis requires certain data as inputs. The inputs to the portfolio analysis of a set of $n$ assets are:

1. $n$ expected returns.
2. $n$ variances of returns.
3. $(n^2 - n)/2$ covariances.

Thus, for a three-security portfolio, the analysis requires the following statistics:

| $E(r)$ | $\sigma_i^2$ | cov $(r_i, r_j)$ |
|--------|--------------|------------------|
| $E(r_1)$ | $\sigma_1^2$ | cov $(r_1, r_2)$ |
| $E(r_2)$ | $\sigma_2^2$ | cov $(r_2, r_3)$ |
| $E(r_3)$ | $\sigma_3^2$ | cov $(r_1, r_3)$ |

In the remainder of this chapter it will be shown how to solve a three-security portfolio graphically. The analysis is conducted upon the graphical plane representing two weights—as shown in Fig. 5.2. Point $A$ represents a portfolio made up of 50 percent (or one-half, or 0.5) each of securities 1 and 2. Point $L$ represents a leveraged portfolio with 150 percent of the original capital invested in security 1 and $-50$ percent of the capital invested in security 2. In other words, a security like security number 2 [for example, a bond with the same $E(r)$ and $\sigma$] is printed and sold in an amount equal to 50 percent of the net value of the portfolio. The (short sale of security 2, or) leverage achieved by issuing a security like number 2 is represented by a negative value for $x_2$.

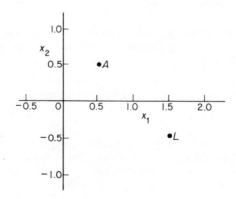

Figure 5.2. Graph of Two Weight Variables—$x_1$ and $x_2$

For example, suppose that the portfolio represented by point $L$ in Fig. 5.2 had $1000 original equity invested. Then, the portfolio manager purchased $1500 of security 1, so $x_1 = 1.5$. To cover the $500 shortage, the portfolio manager issued $500 worth of a security like number 2, so $x_2 = -0.5$. The total of the two weights is 1 (that is, $x_1 + x_2 = 1.5 - 0.5 = 1.0$)—this signifies that the net worth of the portfolio has all been accounted for.

The variables $x_1$ and $x_2$ are weights or percentages of the original capital of the portfolio invested in each security. The sum of the weights must be 1 or the analysis has no meaningful interpretation. Thus, throughout all portfolio analysis, either implicitly or explicitly, the following mathematical condition cannot be violated:

$$\sum_{i=1}^{n} x_i = 1.0 = 100.0\%, \qquad (2.7)$$

where $n$ represents the number of securities being analyzed. This does not mean that all the wealth must be invested. Cash can be one of the $n$ assets.

### 5.3  Three-Security Numerical Example of Graphical Portfolio Analysis

In the interest of realism, real data will be used. Quarterly rates of return were calculated and the following input data derived:

| Company | $i$ | $E(r_i)$ | $\sigma_{ii} = \sigma_i^2$ | cov $(r_i, r_j) = (\rho_{ij})(\sigma_i)(\sigma_j)$ |
|---|---|---|---|---|
| U.S. Steel | 1 | 0.0167 = 1.67% | 0.24 | $\sigma_{12} = 0.1497 = (0.65)(0.49)(0.47)$ |
| Olin-Mathieson | 2 | 0.0534 = 5.34% | 0.22 | $\sigma_{23} = 0.0855 = (0.34)(0.47)(0.52)$ |
| Parke-Davis | 3 | 0.1314 = 13.14% | 0.27 | $\sigma_{13} = 0.1631 = (0.64)(0.49)(0.52)$ |

It would be possible for a good draftsman to find the set of efficient portfolios made from various proportions of three securities with a three-dimensional drawing. However, it is easier for most people to solve the problem in two-dimensional space—that is, the procedure followed here.

To solve the problem in two-dimensional space, the following steps will be performed:

1. Convert the formulas for the portfolio's expected return (that is, the isomean lines) and the portfolio's risk (that is, the isovariance ellipses) from three to two variables.
2. Find the minimum variance portfolio (MVP).
3. Graph the isomean lines.
4. Graph the isovariance ellipses.
5. Delineate the efficient set (that is, the critical line).

6. Calculate the expected return, $E(r_p)$, and risk, $\sigma_p$, for the efficient portfolios.
7. Graph the efficient frontier.

## A.  How to Solve for One Variable Implicitly

Conversion of the three-variable formulas for $E(r_p)$ and var $(r_p)$ to implicit formulas in two variables ($x_1$ and $x_2$) is possible due to the following balance sheet identity:

$$\sum_{i=1}^{3} x_i = 1 = x_1 + x_2 + x_3 \qquad \text{for } n = 3.$$

This relation allows any one weight to be specified in terms of the other weights—for example,

$$x_3 = 1 - x_1 - x_2. \tag{5.1}$$

First, the conversion of $E(r_p)$ will be considered. This conversion is accomplished by substituting equation (5.1) into equation (2.8a) to yield:

$$E(r_p) = \sum_{i=1}^{3} x_i E(r_i) = x_1 E(r_1) + x_2 E(r_2) + x_3 E(r_3) \tag{2.8a}$$

$$= x_1 E(r_1) + x_2 E(r_2) + (1 - x_1 - x_2) E(r_3) \qquad \text{by substitution for } x_3$$

$$= x_1 E(r_1) + x_2 E(r_2) + E(r_3) - x_1 E(r_3) - x_2 E(r_3)$$

$$= [E(r_1) - E(r_3)]x_1 + [E(r_2) - E(r_3)]x_2 + E(r_3). \tag{5.2}$$

Equation (5.2) is a linear equation in two variables ($x_1$ and $x_2$). Substituting the three stocks' numerical values for $E(r_i)$ in equation (5.2) yields equation (5.3).

$$E(r_p) = (0.0167 - 0.1314)x_1 + (0.0534 - 0.1314)x_2 + 0.1314$$

$$= -0.1147x_1 - 0.0780x_2 + 0.1314. \tag{5.3}$$

Equation (5.3) gives the expected return of the three-security portfolio in terms of $x_1$ and $x_2$ explicitly and $x_3$ implicitly—it may be graphed in two variables, $x_1$ and $x_2$.

The three-security portfolio variance formula is similarly converted to two variables by substituting equation (5.1) into equation (2.9b), as follows:

$$\text{var}(r_p) = \sum_{i=1}^{3} \sum_{j=1}^{3} x_i x_j \sigma_{ij} \tag{2.9b}$$

$$= x_1^2 \sigma_{11} + x_2^2 \sigma_{22} + x_3^2 \sigma_{33} + 2x_1 x_2 \sigma_{12} + 2x_1 x_3 \sigma_{13}$$

$$+ 2x_2 x_3 \sigma_{23}$$

$$
\begin{aligned}
&= x_1^2\sigma_{11} + x_2^2\sigma_{22} + (1 - x_1 - x_2)^2\sigma_{33} + 2x_1x_2\sigma_{12} \\
&\quad + 2x_1(1 - x_1 - x_2)\sigma_{13} + 2x_2(1 - x_1 - x_2)\sigma_{23} \\
&= x_1^2\sigma_{11} + x_2^2\sigma_{22} + (1 - 2x_1 - 2x_2 + 2x_1x_2 + x_1^2 \\
&\quad + x_2^2)\sigma_{33} + 2x_1x_2\sigma_{12} \\
&\quad + (2x_1 - 2x_1^2 - 2x_1x_2)\sigma_{13} + (2x_2 - 2x_1x_2 \\
&\quad - 2x_2^2)\sigma_{23} \\
&= x_1^2\sigma_{11} + x_2^2\sigma_{22} + \sigma_{33} - 2x_1\sigma_{33} - 2x_2\sigma_{33} \\
&\quad + 2x_1x_2\sigma_{33} + x_1^2\sigma_{33} + x_2^2\sigma_{33} \\
&\quad + 2x_1x_2\sigma_{12} + 2x_1\sigma_{13} - 2x_1^2\sigma_{13} - 2x_1x_2\sigma_{13} \\
&\quad + 2x_2\sigma_{23} - 2x_1x_2\sigma_{23} - 2x_2^2\sigma_{23} \\
&= (\sigma_{11} + \sigma_{33} - 2\sigma_{13})x_1^2 + (2\sigma_{33} + 2\sigma_{12} - 2\sigma_{13} - 2\sigma_{23})x_1x_2 \\
&\quad + (\sigma_{22} + \sigma_{33} - 2\sigma_{23})x_2^2 + (-2\sigma_{33} + 2\sigma_{13})x_1 \\
&\quad + (-2\sigma_{33} + 2\sigma_{23})x_2 + \sigma_{33}. \quad\quad\quad (5.4)
\end{aligned}
$$

Equation (5.4) is a second-degree equation in two variables. Recall that such equations have the general quadratic form below.

$$Ax^2 + Bxy + Cy^2 + Dx + Ey + F = 0.$$

Inserting the variances and covariances from the numerical example into equation (5.4) yields equation (5.5):

$$
\begin{aligned}
\text{var } (r_p) &= [0.24 + 0.27 - 2(0.1631)]x_1^2 + [2(0.27) + 2(0.1497) \\
&\quad - 2(0.1631) - 2(0.0855)]x_1x_2 + [0.22 + 0.27 \\
&\quad - 2(0.0855)]x_2^2 + [-2(0.27) + 2(0.1631)]x_1 \\
&\quad + [-2(0.27) + 2(0.0855)]x_2 + 0.27 \\
&= 0.1838x_1^2 + 0.3422x_1x_2 + 0.3190x_2^2 - 0.2138x_1 \\
&\quad - 0.3690x_2 + 0.27. \quad\quad\quad\quad\quad\quad\quad\quad\quad (5.5)
\end{aligned}
$$

### B.  Finding the Weights of the Minimum-Variance Portfolio

Before the graphing, it is desirable to find the minimum-variance portfolio (MVP). Standard differential calculus techniques for finding maxima and minima are used on equation (5.4) or its numerical equivalent (5.5). Taking the partial derivatives of (5.4) with respect to $x_1$ and $x_2$ and setting the resulting equations equal to zero yields two linear equations, (5.6) and (5.7):

$$
\begin{aligned}
\frac{\partial V}{\partial x_1} &= 2(\sigma_{11} + \sigma_{33} - 2\sigma_{13})x_1 + (2\sigma_{33} + 2\sigma_{12} - 2\sigma_{13} - 2\sigma_{23})x_2 \\
&\quad + (-2\sigma_{33} + 2\sigma_{13}) = 0, \quad\quad\quad\quad\quad\quad\quad (5.6) \\
\frac{\partial V}{\partial x_2} &= (2\sigma_{33} + 2\sigma_{12} - 2\sigma_{13} - 2\sigma_{23})x_1 + 2(\sigma_{22} + \sigma_{33} - 2\sigma_{23})x_2 \\
&\quad + (2\sigma_{23} - 2\sigma_{33}) = 0 \quad\quad\quad\quad\quad\quad\quad\quad (5.7)
\end{aligned}
$$

Inserting the numerical values for the variances and covariances into equations (5.6) and (5.7) yields equations (5.8) and (5.9):

$$\frac{\partial V}{\partial x_1} = 2[0.24 + 0.27 - 2(0.1631)]x_1$$
$$+ [2(0.27) + 2(0.1497) - 2(0.1631) - 2(0.0855)]x_2$$
$$+ [-2(0.27) + 2(0.1631)]$$
$$= 0.3676x_1 + 0.3422x_2 - 0.2138 = 0. \qquad (5.8)$$

$$\frac{\partial V}{\partial x_2} = [2(0.27) + 2(0.1497) - 2(0.1631) - 2(0.0855)]x_1$$
$$+ 2[0.22 + 0.27 - 2(0.0855)]x_2$$
$$+ [-2(0.27) + 2(0.0855)]$$
$$= 0.3422x_1 + 0.6380x_2 - 0.3690 = 0. \qquad (5.9)$$

To find the minimum-variance portfolio (MVP) equations (5.8) and (5.9) are solved simultaneously. Solving (5.8) and (5.9) yields the weights of the MVP, which are graphed in Fig. 5.3. Equations (5.8) and (5.9) may be solved to obtain equations (5.8a) and (5.9a), as a step toward finding the MVP:

$$x_1 = \frac{-0.3422x_2 + 0.2138}{0.3676}, \qquad (5.8a)$$

$$x_2 = \frac{-0.3422x_1 + 0.3690}{0.6380}. \qquad (5.9a)$$

Substitution yields the following weights for the MVP:

$$x_1 = \left(-0.3422\frac{0.3422x_1 + 0.3690}{0.6380} + 0.2138\right)\bigg/0.3676$$
$$= \frac{0.1836x_1 - 0.1979 + 0.2138}{0.3676}$$
$$= 0.4995x_1 + 0.0433$$
$$= 0.0863,$$

$$x_2 = \left(-0.3422\frac{-0.3422x_2 + 0.2138}{0.3676} + 0.3690\right)\bigg/0.6380$$
$$= \frac{0.3186x_2 - 0.1990 + 0.3690}{0.6380}$$
$$= 0.4994x_2 + 0.2665$$
$$= 0.5321,$$

$$x_3 = 1 - x_1 - x_2$$
$$= 1 - 0.0863 - 0.5321$$
$$= 0.3816.$$

Those who are performing a graphical portfolio analysis but are unfamiliar with the differential calculus may nevertheless find the MVP weights for any

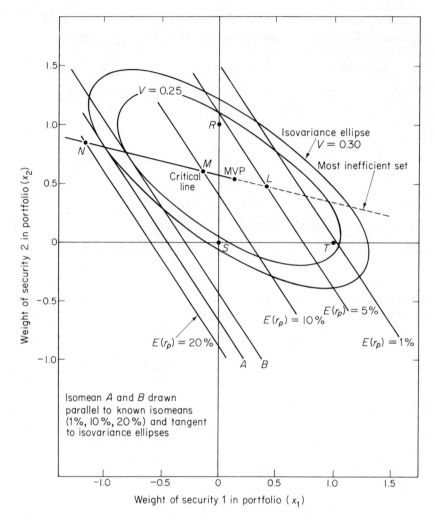

Figure 5.3. Graphical Solution

three-security portfolio by using equations (5.6) and (5.7). By substituting the values for the relevant variances and covariances into these equations and algebraically solving them for $x_1$ and $x_2$, the MVP weights may be determined as above. Thus, the calculus may be avoided.

C. Isomean Lines

After the formulas for the variance and expected return for the portfolio are reduced to two variables and the MVP weights are known, the graphing may begin. It makes little difference whether the graphing begins with the isovariance ellipses or isomean lines. Here the isomeans will be graphed first.

Since the word "iso" means *equal*, it follows that *isomean lines* must be lines that have equal mean returns—that is, equal $E(r_p)$—throughout their length. After arbitrarily selecting a few values of $E(r_p)$ in the neighborhood of the $E(r_i)$'s of the securities in the portfolio, the isomean lines may be determined. By selecting three arbitrary values (5, 10, and 20 percent) of $E(r_p)$ and using equation (5.2), the formulas for three isomean lines are derived:

$$E(r_p) = \phantom{0}5\% = 0.1314 - 0.1147x_1 - 0.078x_2,$$
$$E(r_p) = 10\% = 0.1314 - 0.1147x_1 - 0.078x_2,$$
$$E(r_p) = 20\% = 0.1314 - 0.1147x_1 - 0.078x_2.$$

The easiest way to graph these three linear equations in a cartesian plane as shown in Figs. 5.2 and 5.3 is to set one weight equal to zero and then solve the equation for the other weight. Since the isomean lines intersect the $x_1$ axis when $x_2$ is zero and vice versa, this process will yield points on the two axes. Connecting these points with a line yields the isomean lines.

For example, the 5 percent isomean line must have $x_1 = 0.7097$ when $x_2$ is set equal to zero:

$$0.05 = 0.1314 - 0.1147x_1 - 0.078(0),$$
$$0.1147x_1 = 0.1314 - 0.05 = 0.0814,$$
$$x_1 = \frac{0.0814}{0.1147} = 0.7097.$$

When the 5 percent isomean has $x_1 = 0$, then $x_2 = 1.0436$:

$$0.05 = 0.1314 - 0.1147(0) - 0.078x_2,$$
$$0.078x_2 = 0.1314 - 0.05 = 0.0814,$$
$$x_2 = \frac{0.0814}{0.078} = 1.0436.$$

Similarly, the following points are derived:

| Isomean (%) | $x_1$-Axis Intercept Given $x_2 = 0$ | $x_2$-Axis Intercept When $x_1 = 0$ |
|---|---|---|
| 5 | $x_1 = \phantom{-}0.7097$ | $x_2 = \phantom{-}1.0436$ |
| 10 | $x_1 = \phantom{-}0.2738$ | $x_2 = \phantom{-}0.4026$ |
| 20 | $x_1 = -0.5981$ | $x_2 = -0.8795$ |

Plotting the three isomeans yields the three parallel straight lines in Fig. 5.3.

There are an infinite number of isomeans, but only a few have been graphed. The primary characteristic of the isomeans is that they are all parallel to each other. Knowledge of this characteristic provides a good check when graphing the isomean lines.

### D. Isovariance Ellipses

The next step of the graphical analysis is the graphing of isovariances. Isovariances are ellipses with a common center, orientation, and egg shape. The *isovariance ellipses* are a locus of points that represent portfolios with the same variance. Isovariances are risk isoquants.

Graphing the isovariances should ideally be preceded by finding the minimum-variance portfolio. The *minimum-variance portfolio* (MVP) is the center point for all the isovariances—it represents the portfolio with the least (but not necessarily zero) variance. It is impossible to graph isovariance ellipses for variances less than the variance of the minimum variance portfolio (MVP). Thus, it is desirable to take the weights for the MVP and plug them into equation (5.4) to find the variance of the MVP before plotting any isovariances. In the numerical example, the computation yields:

$$\text{var}\,(r_p) = x_1^2\sigma_{11} + x_2^2\sigma_{22} + x_3^2\sigma_{33} + 2x_1x_2\sigma_{12} + 2x_1x_2\sigma_{13}$$
$$+\ 2x_1x_3\sigma_{13} \tag{2.9}$$
$$= (0.0863)^2(0.24) + (0.5321)^2(0.22) + (0.3816)^2(0.27)$$
$$+\ (2)(0.0863)(0.5324)(0.1497)$$
$$+\ (2)(0.0863)(0.3816)(0.1631)$$
$$+\ (2)(0.5321)(0.3816)(0.0855)$$
$$= 0.0018 + 0.0623 + 0.0392 + 0.0138 + 0.0108 + 0.0347$$
$$= 0.1626 = \text{the variance of the MVP}.$$

This step will save the analyst the frustration of trying to plot isovariances that do not exist (that is, with variances less than that of the MVP).

To graph isovariances, it is necessary to solve equation (5.4) or (5.5) in terms of one of the variables (that is, weights), while treating the remaining variables as constants. Arbitrarily selecting $x_1$ as the variable to be solved for, and treating $x_2$ as a constant, reduces equation (5.4) to a quadratic equation in one variable. The general form of a quadratic equation is: $ax^2 + bx + c = 0$, where the $x$ is a variable and the other symbols are any constant values. Solution of such second-order equations in one variable may be obtained with the quadratic formula

$$x = \frac{-b \pm \sqrt{b^2 - 4ac}}{2a}$$

Let $x = x_1$ in equations (5.4) and (5.5) and treat $x_2$ as a constant. Then, let

$a =$ all coefficients of $x^2$—that is, all coefficients of $x_1^2$ in equations (5.4) and (5.5),

$b =$ all coefficients of $x$—that is, all coefficients of $x_1$ in equations (5.4) and (5.5),

$c =$ all values that are not coefficients of $x_1^2$ or $x_1$ [that is, all constants, which includes the $x_2$'s and the var $(r_p)$] in equations (5.4) and (5.5).

For equation (5.4), set the entire expression equal to zero as follows:

$$0 = (\sigma_{11} + \sigma_{33} - 2\sigma_{13})x_1^2 + (2\sigma_{33} + 2\sigma_{12} - 2\sigma_{13} - 2\sigma_{23})x_1x_2$$
$$+ (\sigma_{22} + \sigma_{33} - 2\sigma_{23})x_2^2 + (-2\sigma_{33} + 2\sigma_{13})x_1$$
$$+ (-2\sigma_{33} + 2\sigma_{23})x_2 + \sigma_{33} - \text{var} (r_p).$$

Then the values of $a$, $b$, and $c$ are

$$a = \sigma_{11} + \sigma_{33} - 2\sigma_{13},$$
$$b = (2\sigma_{33} + 2\sigma_{12} - 2\sigma_{13} - 2\sigma_{23})x_2 - 2\sigma_{33} + 2\sigma_{13},$$
$$c = (\sigma_{22} + \sigma_{33} - 2\sigma_{23})x_2^2 + (-2\sigma_{33} + 2\sigma_{23})x_2 + \sigma_{33} - \text{var} (r_p).$$

The value of $x_1$ can be found by substituting these values of $a$, $b$, and $c$ into the quadratic formula.

Following the procedure outlined above, equation (5.5) yields the following results:

$$\text{var} (r_p) = 0.1838x_1^2 + 0.3422x_1x_2 + 0.3190x_2^2 - 0.2138x_1 - 0.3690x_2$$
$$+ 0.27, \text{ or, in an implicit form,}$$
$$0 = 0.1838x_1^2 + 0.3422x_1x_2 + 0.3190x_2^2 - 0.2138x_1 - 0.3690x_2$$
$$+ 0.27 - \text{var} (r_p),$$
$$a = 0.1838,$$
$$b = 0.3422x_2 - 0.2138,$$
$$c = 0.3190x_2^2 - 0.3690x_2 + 0.27 - \text{var} (r_p).$$

Inserting these values of $a$, $b$, and $c$ into the quadratic formula yields

$$x_1 = \frac{-b \pm \sqrt{b^2 - 4ac}}{2a}$$

$$= \frac{-(0.3422x_2 - 0.2138) \pm \sqrt{\begin{array}{c}(0.3422x_2 - 0.2138)^2 - (4)(0.1838) \\ \times [0.3190x_2^2 - 0.369x_2 + 0.27 - \text{var} (r_p)]\end{array}}}{(2)(0.1838)}.$$

$$(5.10)$$

Equation (5.10) is the solution to equation (5.5) for $x_1$ while treating $x_2$ as a constant. It is necessary to solve the formula to graph the isovariances. To obtain points on the isovariance some arbitrary value for var $(r_p)$ and $x_2$ are selected and equation (5.10) is then solved for two values of $x_1$. It is easiest to select a value for var $(r_p)$ that is slightly larger than the variance of the MVP and select a value of $x_2$ at or near the MVP to get the first two values for $x_1$.

For example, for var $(r_p) = 0.17433$ and $x_2 = 0.3$, equation (5.10) yields the following two values for $x_1$:

$$x_1 = \frac{-[.3422(0.3) - 0.2138] \pm \sqrt{\begin{array}{c}[0.3422(0.3) - 0.2138]^2 - (4)(0.1838) \\ \times [0.3190(0.3)^2 - 0.3690(0.3) + 0.27 - 0.17433]\end{array}}}{(2)(0.1838)}$$

$$= \frac{-0.10266 + 0.2138 \pm \sqrt{0.012352 - 0.010057}}{0.3076}$$

$$= \frac{0.11114 \pm 0.04790}{0.3676} = 0.4326 \text{ and } 0.1720.$$

The variance chosen in this example (0.17433) is the variance of the portfolio when $E(r_p) = 5$ percent. Of course, any value for var $(r_p)$ could have been chosen as long as it exceeded the variance of the MVP (that is, 0.1626).

TABLE 5.1   Isovariance Points in $(x_1, x_2)$ Space

| $w_2$ | Two Values of $x_1$ | | Variance |
|---|---|---|---|
| 0.3 | 0.4326 | 0.1720 | 0.17433 |
| 0.4 | 0.4298 | −0.0113 | 0.17433 |
| 0.6 | 0.2676 | −0.2214 | 0.17433 |
| 0.7 | 0.1282 | −0.2682 | 0.17433 |
| | | | |
| 0.4 | 0.3241 | 0.0944 | 0.16782 |
| 0.6 | 0.1791 | −0.1330 | 0.16782 |
| 0.7 | −0.0080 | −0.1321 | 0.16782 |
| | | | |
| 0.3 | 1.2892 | −0.6845 | 0.35020 |
| 0.4 | 1.2120 | −0.7935 | 0.35020 |
| 0.6 | 1.0314 | −0.9852 | 0.35020 |
| 0.7 | 0.9280 | −1.0681 | 0.35020 |

It is left as an exercise for the reader to verify the points on the isovariance ellipses listed in Table 5.1.[3]

---

[3]It is recommended that a computer program be used to evaluate the points necessary to plot the isovariances. The calculations are very exacting and tedious.

E.   Critical Line

After the isomeans and isovariances are graphed, it is a simple matter to determine the efficient set of portfolios. An efficient portfolio may be defined as the portfolio with the maximum return for any given risk class. Since each isovariance traces out a risk class, the point where the highest-value isomean is just tangent to it is an efficient portfolio. The straight line starting from the MVP and connecting these points is the critical line. This *critical line* is the locus of points in $(x_1, x_2)$ space representing the efficient set. In Fig. 5.3 the set of efficient portfolios starts at the MVP and runs upward to the left along points $M$ and $N$.

Once the critical line is graphed, the efficient frontier may be graphed with ease. Reading weights $(x_1, x_2)$ off the critical line at a few points (such as points $L$, $M$, and $N$ in Fig. 5.3), it is possible to calculate the $E(r)$ and $\sigma$ of portfolios that have the highest rate of return for their risk class. Table 5.2

TABLE 5.2

| Point | $x_1$ | $x_2$ | $x_3$ | $E(r_p)$ (%) | var $(r_p)$ | $\sigma$ |
|-------|-------|-------|-------|-----------|----------|---|
| L | 0.3957 | 0.4617 | 0.1426 | 5 | 0.17433 | 0.41753 |
| M | −0.1200 | 0.5790 | 0.5410 | 10 | 0.16782 | 0.40966 |
| N | −1.1514 | 0.8137 | 1.3377 | 20 | 0.35020 | 0.59178 |

shows these values. The efficient frontier is found by plotting $E(r_p)$ and $(\sigma_p)$ as done in Fig. 5.4. The graphical method is only approximate because of problems in pencil drafting. This completes the graphical portfolio analysis.

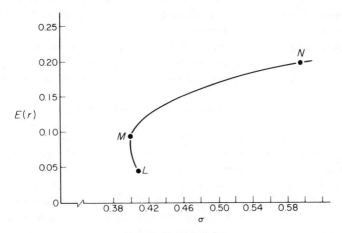

Figure 5.4. Efficient Frontier

### F.  Most Inefficient Set of Portfolios

The inexperienced analyst must take care not to draw the critical line in the wrong direction away from the MVP. Such a line would be the locus of points representing the set of most inefficient portfolios. The dashed line in Fig. 5.3 is such a line; it is the locus of points representing the *minimum* return in each risk class.

Earlier in this chapter the *objective* of portfolio analysis was said to be the determination of the efficient set of portfolios. The efficient set is represented by the infinite number of portfolios whose weights lie along the critical line.

The reader who understands this and the preceding chapters will recognize that portfolio analysis utilizes Markowitz diversification. In fact, it could be said that the objective of portfolio analysis is to maximize the benefits from such diversification at each possible rate of return.

### 5.4  Legitimate Portfolios

Markowitz says an efficient portfolio must meet three conditions:

1. It must have the maximum return in its risk class.
2. It must have the minimum risk in its return class.
3. It must be "legitimate."[4]

The third condition for efficiency has not been imposed in this book. By "legitimate," Markowitz means that the portfolio can contain no negatively weighted securities. Graphically, this means that the critical line may not leave the right triangle with *R*, *S*, and *T* at its corners in Fig. 5.3. Consequently, the "legitimate" efficient portfolios compose only part of the unconstrained critical line. Financially speaking, legitimate means no leverage or short sales are permitted.

Of course, negative weights are possible and have a rational interpretation. In this book the nonnegativity constraint will not be observed. Only public investment funds that are regulated need adhere to the legitimacy condition.

### 5.5  "Unusual" Graphical Solutions Do Not Exist

After performing graphical portfolio analysis, many people are surprised to find that their MVP has negative weights in it, or their isomeans are not tangent to their isovariances, or their entire set of efficient portfolios has negative weights, or their isomeans slope at an angle different than the previous examples they have seen, and so on. These occurrences are not unusual or abnormal. Figure 5.5 is an example containing characteristics that might erroneously surprise beginning analysts.

---

[4]Markowitz, *Portfolio Selection*, p. 140.

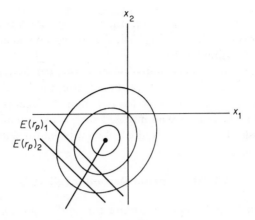

Figure 5.5. "Unusual" Solution

For examples of other graphical solutions, including a four-security portfolio, see Chapter 7 of Markowitz's book.[5]

### 5.6 Graphical Representation of Constraints

Sometimes laws or corporate policies constrain portfolios. For example, law requires that some mutual funds may not borrow money to finance purchases—that is, leveraged portfolios are illegal. This is a portfolio constraint that allows formation of portfolios only within the triangle bounded by $R$, $S$, and $T$ in Fig. 5.3 and 5.6. Further, assume some law made

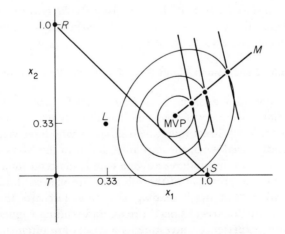

Figure 5.6. Graphical Representation of Diversification Laws

---

[5]Markowitz, *Portfolio Selection.*

it illegal for portfolios to invest more than one-third of their total value in any given security. In terms of Fig. 5.6, the second law means that only the single portfolio at point L is legal.

Laws requiring naive, superfluous diversification can *increase* portfolio risk. With such constraints, the efficient portfolios from the MVP to point M are illegal. These illegal portfolios have *less risk* than the legal portfolio at point L in Fig. 5.6. The legislators who imposed such laws (intended to minimize the financial risk of investment funds) obviously had a naive definition of diversification in mind.

### 5.7   The "Interior Decorator Fallacy"

Brealey explains the "interior decorator concept" of portfolio management as follows:

> It is a commonly held view that the mix of common stocks maintained by an investor should depend on his willingness to bear risk. According to this view, a broker or investment counselor is a kind of financial interior decorator, skillfully designing portfolios to reflect his client's personality.[6]

According to the interior decorator school, an elderly widow should hold government bonds and utilities, for example, while a young aggressive investor should shun these assets.

The portfolio analysis technique developed by Markowitz and explained in this chapter is at odds with the "financial interior decorator" concept of portfolio management. For example, portfolio analysis may indicate that a person desiring to minimize risk should own a portfolio of only *two stocks that are very risky individually*. But, if the two risky stocks covary inversely, the portfolio will most likely have less risk (that is, variability of return) than any portfolio prepared by less analytical techniques.

### 5.8   Conclusions About Graphical Portfolio Analysis

Markowitz portfolio analysis is a new scientific approach to an old problem. Portfolios were never analyzed scientifically until recently. In fact, highly intelligent Wall Street investment advisors who have years of experience are typically awed when they are introduced to the Markowitz model. Of course, the algebra intimidates anyone who is unaccustomed to it. But, more important, the precision of the solutions are viewed dubiously. After years of following "hot tips," reading economic forecasts that are often misleading, studying charts of stocks' prices, and reading vaguely suggestive industry reports, experienced investments advisors are often shocked to see

---

[6]R. A. Brealey, *An Introduction to Risk and Return from Common Stocks* (Cambridge, Mass.: The MIT Press, 1969), p. 115.

investment decisions given with decimal-point exactness. In fact, experience with actual Markowitz portfolios is necessary to understand the strengths and weaknesses of the analysis. This chapter concludes with a discussion of two caveats about portfolio analysis which the successful analyst will bear in mind. Efficient portfolios are derived from input statistics (namely, the expected returns, variances, and covariances) which are supplied to the portfolio analyst by security analysts. Of course, the value of the portfolio analysis is dependent upon the validity of these input statistics. Therefore, considerable attention should be given to the input statistics. Ample resources should be expended on analyzing the individual assets (see Chapter IV) before proceeding to the portfolio analysis and investment portfolio selection. The investment decisions delineated by portfolio analysis can be no better than the input statistics from which the efficient frontier is derived.

After an optimal-efficient portfolio has been selected and the assets purchased, more work remains. Portfolio analysis does not yield permanent solutions—only temporary solutions. As new information arrives continuously, the security analysts must reassess the statistical inputs which they provide to the portfolio analyst. The input statistics change everytime the prospects for a potential investment changes. Furthermore, a change in one security which lowers its covariance with the other securities, reduces its variance, and/or increases its expected return can shift the entire efficient frontier. Thus, the security analysts and the portfolio analysts never finish their work.[7] Valuable investment decisions require continual updating of the input statistics and the efficient frontier.

---

[7]See Chapter IV about shifting input statistics; and Chapter XII delves into portfolio revision.

## Selected References

Markowitz, Harry M., *Portfolio Selection*, Cowles Foundation Monograph 16. New York: John Wiley & Sons, Inc., 1959.
Chapter 7 of this classic book explicates graphical portfolio analysis in an easy-to-read style with ample graphs.

Sharpe, W. F., *Portfolio Theory and Capital Markets*. New York: McGraw-Hill Book Company, 1970.
Chapter 4 explains mathematical portfolio analysis with ample graphical cross references and explanation.

## Questions and Problems

1. Freshman college algebra courses usually study the quadratic function: $y = ax^2 + bx + c$, where $a \neq 0$. Graph this second-degree equation in $(x, y)$ space for the values $a = 1.0$, $b = -5.0$, and $c = 13.0$. Would you call the graph you obtained a parabola or an ellipse, or an egg shape or what?

Now set $y$ equal to some constant, namely, $y = -4.0$, and rewrite the quadratic function above as the quadratic equation: $0.0 = ax^2 + bx + (c - 4.0)$. Graph this quadratic equation in $(x, y)$ space. What shape does it have?

Helpful hint for graphing the quadratic equation: The two roots of any quadratic equation are given by $x_1$ and $x_2$:

$$x_1 = \frac{-b + \sqrt{b^2 - 4ac}}{2a}$$

$$x_2 = \frac{-b - \sqrt{b^2 - 4ac}}{2a}.$$

2. Reconsider the quadratic equation: $0 = ax^2 + bx + c$, where $a \neq 0$. The quality $(b^2 - 4ac)$ is called the *discriminant* of the quadratic equation. In graphing isovariance ellipses, what happens to your solution if the discriminent is

(a) Negative, that is, $(b^2 - 4ac) < 0$?
(b) Zero, that is, $(b^2 - 4ac) = 0$?
(c) Positive, that is, $(b^2 - 4ac) > 0$?

3. Reconsider the quadratic equation from problem 1: $0.0 = ax^2 + bx + (c - y)$, where $a = 1.0$, $b = -5.0$, $c = 13.0$, and $y = -4.0$. Also, consider the linear equation $x - 4y = 1.0$. Show the simultaneous solution to these two equations. (*Hint:* Solve the linear equation for $y$ to obtain $y = (x - 1.0)/4.0$, and then substitute this quantity for $y$ into the quadratic equation and simply factor it.) Next graph these two equations in $(x, y)$ space. What happens at the point where $x = \frac{17}{4}$ and $y = \frac{13}{16}$ in the graph? Could similar algebraic manipulations be useful in handling isovariance ellipses and isomeans expeditiously?

4. Derive the efficient frontier attainable with the three assets below:

| Asset | $E(R)$ (%) | var $(r)$ | cov $(r_i, r_j)$ |
|-------|-----------|-----------|------------------|
| H | $E(r_H) = 5.0$ | $\sigma_{11} = 0.1$ | $\sigma_{12} = -0.1$ |
| K | $E(r_K) = 7.0$ | $\sigma_{22} = 0.4$ | $\sigma_{13} = 0$ |
| T | $E(r_T) = 30.0$ | $\sigma_{33} = 0.7$ | $\sigma_{23} = 0.3$ |

[*Hint:* See Appendix A to Chapter 15 of J. C. Francis, *Investments: Analysis and Management*, 2nd ed. (New York: McGraw-Hill Book Company, 1976), for the details of the solution.]

5. The financial interior decorating approach to portfolio management has been defined as selecting a portfolio of securities which matches the investor's personality as nearly as possible. Thus, an elderly widow (say, Aunt Jane) living on Social Security and the income from a small portfolio should have her funds all invested in bonds or perhaps utility stocks. On the other hand, an aggressive healthy young professional man (say, Dr. Swift) should own a completely different portfolio, containing high-risk common stocks which are expected to yield a high average return. Will this approach to portfolio management maximize the investor's opportunity to select efficient (that is, dominant) investments? Explain.

```
6666666666666666666666666666666666666666666666666666666666666666666666666666666666666666666
6666666666666666666666666666666666666666666666666666666666666666666666666666666666666666666666
666666666666666666666666666666666      6666666666666      666      66666666666666666666666666666666
666666666666666666666666666666666      6666666666      6666      66666666666666666666666666666666
6666666666666666666666666666666666666      66666666      66666      66666666666666666666666666666666
6666666666666666666666666666666666666      6666666      666666      66666666666666666666666666666666
6666666666666666666666666666666666666      66666      6666666      66666666666666666666666666666666
6666666666666666666666666666666666666      666      66666666      66666666666666666666666666666666
6666666666666666666666666666666666666      6      666666666      66666666666666666666666666666666
66666666666666666666666666666666666666      666666666      66666666666666666666666666666666
66666666666666666666666666666666666666      66666666      66666666666666666666666666666666666
6666666666666666666666666666666666666666666666666666666666666666666666666666666666666666666666
6666666666666666666666666666666666666666666666666666666666666666666666666666666666666666666666
```

# Mathematical Portfolio Analysis

$T$HE graphical approach to Markowitz portfolio analysis presented in Chapter V provides a good learning vehicle for people who would rather see things graphically than mathematically. However, for those who wish to be able to solve large portfolio problems involving hundreds of different assets, and/or, become technicians, this chapter shows more sophisticated approaches. These mathematical techniques yield the same answers as the graphical technique. Therefore, some readers may wish to skip this chapter and proceed onto the later chapters. However, the more mathematical techniques explained in this chapter are more general and offer the tools for solving the larger portfolio problems (namely, those involving more than four possible assets) and are provided for the interested readers.

### 6.1  Calculus Minimization of a Lagrangian
### Objective Function

In this section a technique using differential calculus to minimize a Lagrangian objective function will be explained. A review of the basic formulas and symbols used is presented at the end of Chapter II. In presenting the calculus solution, numerical examples are provided in which a two-security problem is solved. Hopefully, the simplicity of the arithmetic will make for easier reading. However, the method can readily be generalized to solve problems with any number of securities. As in Chapter V, a step-by-step "how-to-do-it" approach is followed.

## A. General Formulation

Mathematically, the problem involves finding the minimum portfolio variance—that is, the minimum of

$$\text{var } (r_p) = \sum_{i=1}^{n} \sum_{j=1}^{n} x_i x_j \sigma_{ij} \tag{2.9b}$$

subject to two Lagrangian constraints. The first constraint requires that the desired expected return ($E^*$) be achieved. This is equivalent to requiring the following difference be zero.

$$\sum_{i=1}^{n} x_i E(r_i) - E^* = 0. \tag{6.1}$$

The second constraint requires that the weights sum to 1. Of course, this constraint is equivalent to requiring the following difference be zero.

$$\sum_{i=1}^{n} x_i - 1 = 0. \tag{2.7}$$

Combining these three quantities, the Lagrangian objective function of the risk-minimization problem with a desired return constraint is

$$z = \sum_{i=1}^{n} \sum_{j=1}^{n} x_i x_j \sigma_{ij} + \lambda_1 [\sum_{i=1}^{n} x_i E(r_i) - E^*] + \lambda_2 (\sum_{i=1}^{n} x_i - 1). \tag{6.2}$$

The minimum-risk portfolio is found by setting $\partial z / \partial x_i = \partial z / \partial \lambda_j = 0$ for $i = 1, \ldots, n$ and $j = 1, 2$. The resulting system is composed of the $n + 2$ linear equations shown below.

$$\frac{\partial z}{\partial x_1} = 2x_1 \sigma_{11} + 2x_2 \sigma_{12} + \cdots + 2x_n \sigma_{1n} + \lambda_1 E(r_1) + \lambda_2 = 0,$$

$$\frac{\partial z}{\partial x_2} = 2x_1 \sigma_{21} + 2x_2 \sigma_{22} + \cdots + 2x_n \sigma_{2n} + \lambda_1 E(r_2) + \lambda_2 = 0,$$

$$\cdot$$
$$\cdot$$
$$\cdot \tag{6.3}$$

$$\frac{\partial z}{\partial x_n} = 2x_1 \sigma_{n1} + 2x_2 \sigma_{n2} + \cdots + 2x_n \sigma_{nn} + \lambda_1 E(r_n) + \lambda_2 = 0,$$

$$\frac{\partial z}{\partial \lambda_1} = x_1 E(r_1) + x_2 E(r_2) + \cdots + x_n E(r_n) - E^* = 0,$$

$$\frac{\partial z}{\partial \lambda_2} = x_1 + x_2 + \cdots + x_n - 1 = 0.$$

The last two partial derivatives above are equations (6.1) and (2.7). They were obtained by taking the partial derivatives of the Lagrangian objective function (6.2) with respect to the two respective Lagrangian multipliers, $\lambda_1$ and $\lambda_2$, which were included to provide the two constraints that are necessary for a rational solution.

The first $n$ terms in the first $n$ partial derivatives in equation system (6.3) were obtained by taking partial derivatives of the variance formula shown below with respect to each of the $n$ weight variables.

$$\sum_{i=1}^{n}\sum_{j=1}^{n} x_i x_j \sigma_{ij} = \begin{bmatrix} x_1^2\sigma_{11} + x_1 x_2 \sigma_{12} + x_1 x_3 \sigma_{13} + \cdots + x_1 x_n \sigma_{1n} \\ + x_2 x_1 \sigma_{21} + x_2^2 \sigma_{22} + x_2 x_3 \sigma_{23} + \cdots + x_2 x_n \sigma_{2n} \\ + x_3 x_1 \sigma_{31} + x_3 x_2 \sigma_{32} + x_3^2 \sigma_{33} + \cdots + x_3 x_n \sigma_{3n} \\ \cdot \quad\quad \cdot \quad\quad \cdot \quad\quad \cdot \quad\quad \cdot \\ \cdot \quad\quad \cdot \quad\quad \cdot \quad\quad \cdot \quad\quad \cdot \\ \cdot \quad\quad \cdot \quad\quad \cdot \quad\quad \cdot \quad\quad \cdot \\ + x_n x_1 \sigma_{n1} + x_n x_2 \sigma_{n2} + x_n x_3 \sigma_{n3} + \cdots + x_n^2 \sigma_{nn} \end{bmatrix}.$$

The variance above is the first term in the Lagrangian equation (6.2). The partial derivative of the variance with respect to the $i$th weight variable is shown below in an expanded form.

$$\frac{\partial \, \text{var} \, (r_p)}{\partial x_i} = \begin{bmatrix} + x_1 \sigma_{1i} \\ + x_2 \sigma_{2i} \\ \cdot \\ \cdot \\ \cdot \\ + x_1 \sigma_{i1} + x_2 \sigma_{i2} + \cdots + 2 x_i \sigma_{ii} + \cdots + x_n \sigma_{in} \\ \cdot \\ \cdot \\ \cdot \\ + x_n \sigma_{ni} \end{bmatrix}.$$

The expanded first partial derivative above may be equivalently rewritten in more compact notation.

$$\frac{\partial \, \text{var} \, (r_p)}{\partial x_i} = 2 x_1 \sigma_{i1} + 2 x_2 \sigma_{i2} + \cdots + 2 x_n \sigma_{in} = 0.$$

The preceding equation differs from the $n$ partial derivatives in equation system (6.3) by the last two terms in the $n$ differential equations. These last two terms were obtained by taking the partial derivatives of equations (6.1) and (2.7) with respect to the $i$th weight variable, $x_i$, as the two Lagrangian constraints were encountered in differentiating Lagrangian objective function (6.2). This explains the makeup of the $(n + 2)$ differential equations in equation system (6.3).

The $(n + 2)$ partial derivatives are linear in their weight variables and may be formulated more compactly as Jacobian matrix equation (6.4):

$$
\overset{C}{
\begin{bmatrix}
2\sigma_{11} & 2\sigma_{12} & \cdots & 2\sigma_{1n} & E(r_1) & 1 \\
2\sigma_{21} & 2\sigma_{22} & \cdots & 2\sigma_{2n} & E(r_2) & 1 \\
\cdot & & & & & \\
\cdot & & & & & \\
\cdot & & & & & \\
2\sigma_{n1} & 2\sigma_{n2} & \cdots & 2\sigma_{nn} & E(r_n) & 1 \\
E(r_1) & E(r_2) & \cdots & E(r_n) & 0 & 0 \\
1 & 1 & \cdots & 1 & 0 & 0
\end{bmatrix}}
\overset{x}{
\begin{bmatrix}
x_1 \\ x_2 \\ \cdot \\ \cdot \\ \cdot \\ x_n \\ \lambda_1 \\ \lambda_2
\end{bmatrix}}
\;=\;
\overset{k}{
\begin{bmatrix}
0 \\ 0 \\ \cdot \\ \cdot \\ \cdot \\ E^* \\ 1
\end{bmatrix}},
\qquad (6.4)
$$

where the coefficient matrix is denoted $C$, the weight vector is $x$, and $k$ is the vector of constants. This system may be solved several different ways. Using matrix notation, the inverse of the coefficients matrix $(C^{-1})$ may be used to find the solution (weight) vector $(x)$ as follows:

$$Cx = k,$$
$$C^{-1}Cx = C^{-1}k,$$
$$Ix = C^{-1}k,$$
$$x = C^{-1}k.$$

The solution will give the $n + 2$ variables in the weight vector in terms of $E^*$. The $n$ weights will be in the form shown below.

$$
\begin{aligned}
x_1 &= c_1 + d_1 E^*, \\
x_2 &= c_2 + d_2 E^*, \\
&\;\cdot \\
&\;\cdot \\
&\;\cdot \\
x_n &= c_n + d_n E^*,
\end{aligned}
\qquad (6.5)
$$

where $\sum_{i=1}^{n} x_i = 1$. The $c_i$ and $d_i$ are constants. For any desired value of $E^*$, equations (6.5) give the weights of the minimum-variance portfolio. The weights of the portfolios in the efficient set are generated by varying $E^*$ and evaluating the $x_i$'s. Martin solved this problem and has shown the relationship between the solution and the graphical critical line solution in a readable article which the interested reader is invited to pursue.[1]

---

[1]A. D. Martin, Jr., "Mathematical Programming of Portfolio Selections," *Management Science*, Vol. 1, No. 2, 1955, pp. 152–166. Reprinted in E. B. Fredrickson, ed., *Frontiers of*

## B. Second-Order Conditions

The question may arise as to whether this mathematical analysis delineates portfolios that have the minimum or the maximum risk at each level of expected return. This is a relevant question because the entire opportunity set is bounded by an ellipse,[2] as shown in Fig. 6.1. This ellipse has one global *maximum* and one global *minimum* (namely, point *B*), and the first-order partial derivatives are equal to zero at *both* extremes. Furthermore, at any given level of expected return, there is a minimum-risk portfolio (for example, efficient portfolios *A* and *B* in Fig. 6.1) as well as a maximum-risk portfolio

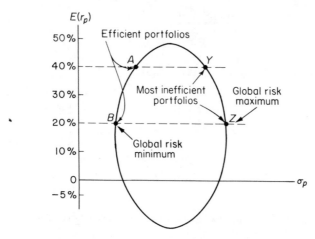

Figure 6.1. Elliptical Opportunity Set with Minimum and Maximum Risk Portfolios

(for example, portfolios *Y* and *Z* are inefficient portfolios) that can be delineated. To determine whether risk is being maximized or minimized, it is necessary to consider the second-order conditions.

Taking the partial differentials of all $(n + 2)$ differential equations in equation system (6.3) with respect to all $(n + 2)$ variables yields a symmetric

*Investment Analysis* (Scranton, Pa.: International Textbook Company, 1965), pp. 367–381. For an interpretation of shadow prices represented by the Lagrangian multipliers, $\lambda_1$ and $\lambda_2$, see Martin's footnote 9. Martin's presentation shows how to delineate legitimate portfolios— that is, portfolios with nonnegative weights.

[2]Elsewhere in this book the investment opportunity set is described and graphically represented as having an escalloped quarter-moon shape—see, for example, Fig. 3.9 on page 42. This is the opportunity set of *viable* investments. However, when *all* nonleveraged risky assets are considered, the opportunity set is an ellipse because risk is measured with a quadratic-form polynomial. When unlimited leverage and/or short selling is introduced, the opportunity set becomes a hyperbola that opens on the right-hand side—see Fig. 8.11 and its discussion on page 166.

bordered Hessian matrix. Equation (6.6) shows this Hessian matrix, denoted
$H$. This Hessian matrix must be either positive definite or positive semidefinite if the extreme point is a minimum-risk point instead of a maximum-
risk point.[3]

$$
\begin{bmatrix}
\dfrac{\partial^2 z}{\partial x_1 \partial x_1} & \dfrac{\partial^2 z}{\partial x_1 \partial x_2} & \cdots & \dfrac{\partial^2 z}{\partial x_1 \partial x_n} & \vdots & \dfrac{\partial^2 z}{\partial x_1 \partial \lambda_1} & \dfrac{\partial^2 z}{\partial x_1 \partial \lambda_2} \\[2mm]
\dfrac{\partial^2 z}{\partial x_2 \partial x_1} & \dfrac{\partial^2 z}{\partial x_2 \partial x_2} & \cdots & \dfrac{\partial^2 z}{\partial x_2 \partial x_n} & \vdots & \dfrac{\partial^2 z}{\partial x_2 \partial \lambda_1} & \dfrac{\partial^2 x}{\partial x_2 \partial \lambda_2} \\[2mm]
\vdots & & & & \vdots & & \\[2mm]
\dfrac{\partial^2 z}{\partial x_n \partial x_1} & \dfrac{\partial^2 z}{\partial x_n \partial x_2} & \cdots & \dfrac{\partial^2 z}{\partial x_n \partial x_n} & \vdots & \dfrac{\partial^2 z}{\partial x_n \partial \lambda_1} & \dfrac{\partial^2 z}{\partial x_n \partial \lambda_2} \\[1mm]
\hdashline
\dfrac{\partial^2 z}{\partial \lambda_1 \partial x_1} & \dfrac{\partial^2 z}{\partial \lambda_1 \partial x_2} & \cdots & \dfrac{\partial^2 z}{\partial \lambda_1 \partial x_n} & \vdots & \dfrac{x^2 z}{\partial \lambda_1 \partial \lambda_1} & \dfrac{\partial^2 z}{\partial \lambda_1 \partial \lambda_2} \\[2mm]
\dfrac{\partial^2 x}{\partial \lambda_2 \partial x_1} & \dfrac{\partial^2 z}{\partial \lambda_2 \partial x_2} & \cdots & \dfrac{\partial^2 z}{\partial \lambda_2 \partial x_n} & \vdots & \dfrac{\partial^2 z}{\partial \lambda_2 \partial \lambda_1} & \dfrac{\partial^2 z}{\partial \lambda_2 \partial \lambda_2}
\end{bmatrix}
=
$$

$$
=
\begin{bmatrix}
2\sigma_{11} & 2\sigma_{12} & \cdots & 2\sigma_{1n} & \vdots & E(r_1) & 1 \\
2\sigma_{21} & 2\sigma_{22} & \cdots & 2\sigma_{2n} & \vdots & E(r_2) & 1 \\
\vdots & & & & \vdots & & \vdots \\
2\sigma_{n1} & 2\sigma_{n2} & \cdots & 2\sigma_{nn} & \vdots & E(r_n) & 1 \\
\hdashline
E(r_1) & E(r_2) & \cdots & E(r_n) & \vdots & 0 & 0 \\
1 & 1 & \cdots & 1 & \vdots & 0 & 0
\end{bmatrix}
= H.
$$

Equation System (6.6). Two Statements of the Same Hessian Matrix

The simplest way to see that the Hessian matrix is positive semidefinite is
to partition the right-hand side (RHS) of equation (6.6). Note that the
RHS of this Hessian is identical to the coefficients matrix denoted $C$ in
equation (6.4). This Hessian is partitioned into the $(n \times n)$ matrix, which
equals the portfolio's variance–covariance matrix multiplied by a scalar of 2.
It is well known that the variance–covariance matrix is positive semidefinite.

In addition to the partitioned variance–covariance matrix, the Hessian
matrix contains three other submatrices with the following dimensions:
$(2 \times n)$, $(n \times 2)$, and $(2 \times 2)$. This partition of the Hessian matrix is
delineated with dashed lines in equation (6.6) for visual inspection. Assuming
that all $n$ assets being considered in the problem have positive expected
returns means that the $(2 \times n)$ and $(n \times 2)$ submatrices both contain only
positive values. By definition, if a matrix $H$ (namely, the Hessian in this case)
is made up of a positive semidefinite quadratic form submatrix (namely, the
variance–covariance matrix in $H$) and other nonnegative elements (that is,

---

[3]For general economics-oriented discussion of Hessian matrices, minimum points constrained by the method of Lagrange, and positive definite matrices, see pp. 41–58 of
*Microeconomic Analysis* by Cliff Lloyd (Homewood, Ill.: Richard D. Irwin, Inc., 1967).

the elements in the three small submatrices in this case), then the matrix $H$ is positive semidefinite.[4] The fact that the Hessian is positive semidefinite precludes it from representing a maximum. And since an ellipse has only one minimum at each level of portfolio return (see Fig. 6.1), the extreme point must be a minimum-risk point.

To add substance to the general discussion above, a simple two-asset portfolio problem will be solved below using real values.

## C. Calculus Minimization of Risk With Two Securities

For a two-security portfolio, the objective function to be minimized is

$$z = x_1^2\sigma_{11} + x_2^2\sigma_{22} + 2x_1x_2\sigma_{12} + \lambda_1(x_1E(r_1)$$
$$+ x_2E(r_2) - E^*) + \lambda_2(x_1 + x_2 - 1). \quad (6.7)$$

The partial derivatives are set equal to zero to yield:

$$\frac{\partial z}{\partial x_1} = 2x_1\sigma_{11} + 2x_2\sigma_{12} + \lambda_1 E(r_1) + \lambda_2 = 0,$$

$$\frac{\partial z}{\partial x_2} = 2x_2\sigma_{22} + 2x_1\sigma_{12} + \lambda_1 E(r_2) + \lambda_2 = 0,$$

$$\frac{\partial z}{\partial \lambda_1} = x_1 E(r_1) + x_2 E(r_2) - E^* = 0, \quad (6.8)$$

$$\frac{\partial z}{\partial \lambda_2} = x_1 + x_2 - 1 = 0.$$

This system is linear, since the weights ($x_i$'s) are the variables and they are all of degree 1. Thus, the system may be solved as a system of linear equations. The matrix representation of this system of linear equations is as follows:

$$\begin{matrix} \begin{bmatrix} 2\sigma_{11} & 2\sigma_{12} & E_1 & 1 \\ 2\sigma_{21} & 2\sigma_{22} & E_2 & 1 \\ E_1 & E_2 & 0 & 0 \\ 1 & 1 & 0 & 0 \end{bmatrix} & \begin{bmatrix} x_1 \\ x_2 \\ \lambda_1 \\ \lambda_2 \end{bmatrix} & = & \begin{bmatrix} 0 \\ 0 \\ E^* \\ 1 \end{bmatrix} \\ C & x & = & k \end{matrix} \quad (6.9)$$

Equation (6.9) is identical in form to equation (6.4); it is merely a specific case of equation (6.4) when $n = 2$. Equation (6.9a) is equivalent to equation (6.9), but not identical. Equations (6.9) and (6.9a) differ in appearance

---

[4]G. Hadley, *Linear Algebra* (Reading, Mass.: Addison-Wesley Publishing Co., Inc., 1961), p. 254, defines positive semidefinite and positive definite. Or, see M. D. Intriligator, *Mathematical Optimization and Economic Theory* (Englewood Cliffs, N.J.: Prentice-Hall, Inc., 1971), pp. 495–497.

because the two bottom rows in equation (6.9) were interchanged to obtain equation (6.9a). Since the rows and/or columns of a system of linear equations can be switched, equations (6.9) and (6.9a) are mathematically equal and will yield identical solutions. However, the coefficients matrix, $C$, in equation (6.9a) is not symmetric, because the last two rows were interchanged.

$$\begin{bmatrix} 2\sigma_{11} & 2\sigma_{12} & E_1 & 1 \\ 2\sigma_{21} & 2\sigma_{22} & E_2 & 1 \\ 1 & 1 & 0 & 0 \\ E_1 & E_2 & 0 & 0 \end{bmatrix} \begin{bmatrix} x_1 \\ x_2 \\ \lambda_2 \\ \lambda_1 \end{bmatrix} = \begin{bmatrix} 0 \\ 0 \\ 1 \\ E^* \end{bmatrix}. \tag{6.9a}$$

$$C \qquad\qquad x \;=\; k$$

To show that the same answers are obtained by solving matrix equations in which the rows have been interchanged, equation (6.9a) will be solved below.[5] This equation system may be solved several different ways. Using matrix notation, the inverse of the coefficients matrix $(C^{-1})$ may be used to find the solution weight vector, $x$.

$$Cx = k, \qquad x = C^{-1}k.$$

The solution will give the $n$ (that is, $n = 2$ in this case) weights in terms of $E^*$.

$$x_1 = c_1 + d_1 E^*, \qquad x_2 = c_2 + d_2 E^*,$$

where the $c_i$ and $d_i$ are constants. For any desired $E^*$, the equations give the weights of the minimum-variance portfolio. A numerical example follows that is solved by means of Cramer's rule.

### D. Numerical Example with Two Assets

Using the values $E(r_1) = 0.05$, $E(r_2) = 0.15$, $\sigma_1 = 0.2$, $\sigma_{11} = 0.04$, $\sigma_2 = 0.4$, $\sigma_{22} = 0.16$, $\rho_{12} = 0$, $\sigma_{12} = 0$ yields the following coefficients' matrix:

$$\begin{bmatrix} 2\sigma_{11} & 2\sigma_{12} & E_1 & 1 \\ 2\sigma_{21} & 2\sigma_{22} & E_2 & 1 \\ 1 & 1 & 0 & 0 \\ E_1 & E_2 & 0 & 0 \end{bmatrix} = \begin{bmatrix} 2(0.04) & 2(0) & 0.05 & 1 \\ 2(0) & 2(0.16) & 0.15 & 1 \\ 1 & 1 & 0 & 0 \\ 0.05 & 0.15 & 0 & 0 \end{bmatrix} = C.$$

Solving this system for the first weight $(x_1)$ using Cramer's rule proceeds as

---

[5]The coefficients matrix, $C$, in equation (6.9a) may be rewritten in a symmetric form merely by interchanging the two bottom rows.

shown below. Using column 1 of the top matrix to expand on yields the following:

$$x_1 = \cfrac{\begin{bmatrix} 0 & 2\sigma_{12} & E_1 & 1 \\ 0 & 2\sigma_{22} & E_2 & 1 \\ 1 & 1 & 0 & 0 \\ E^* & E_2 & 0 & 0 \end{bmatrix} \begin{aligned} &= 0(-1)^{1+1}C_{11} + 0(-1)^{2+1}C_{21} \\ &\quad + 1(-1)^{3+1}C_{31} \\ &\quad + E^*(-1)^{4+1}C_{41} \\ &= -0.015 + 0.1E^*, \end{aligned}}{\begin{bmatrix} 2\sigma_{11} & 2\sigma_{12} & E_1 & 1 \\ 2\sigma_{21} & 2\sigma_{22} & E_2 & 1 \\ 1 & 1 & 0 & 0 \\ E_1 & E_2 & 0 & 0 \end{bmatrix} \begin{aligned} &= 1(-1)^{1+4}C_{14} + 1(-1)^{2+4}C_{24} \\ &\quad + 0(-1)^{3+4}C_{34} \\ &\quad + 0(-1)^{4+4}C_{44} = -0.01, \end{aligned}}$$

where $C_{ij}$ is the minor of the element in the $i$th row and $j$th column. Evaluating $x_1$ yields

$$\begin{aligned} x_1 &= \frac{-[E(r_2)]^2 + E(r_1) \cdot E(r_2) - E^*[E(r_1) - E(r_2)]}{E(r_1) \cdot E(r_2) - [E(r_2)]^2 - [E(r_1)]^2 + E(r_1) \cdot E(r_2)} \\ &= \frac{-0.015 + 0.1E^*}{-0.01} = 1.5 - 10E^*. \end{aligned}$$

Using Cramer's rule to solve for the second weight $(x_2)$ yields the following computations when expanding on column 4 of the top matrix:

$$x_2 = \cfrac{\begin{bmatrix} 2\sigma_{11} & 0 & E_1 & 1 \\ 2\sigma_{21} & 0 & E_2 & 1 \\ 1 & 1 & 0 & 0 \\ E_1 & E^* & 0 & 0 \end{bmatrix} \begin{aligned} &= 1(-1)^{1+4}C_{14} + 1(-1)^{2+4}C_{24} \\ &\quad + 0(-1)^{3+4}C_{34} + 0(-1)^{4+4}C_{44}, \end{aligned}}{\begin{bmatrix} 2\sigma_{11} & 2\sigma_{12} & E_1 & 1 \\ 2\sigma_{21} & 2\sigma_{22} & E_2 & 1 \\ 1 & 1 & 0 & 0 \\ E_1 & E_2 & 0 & 0 \end{bmatrix} = \text{same denominator.}}$$

Evaluating $x_2$ yields

$$\begin{aligned} x_2 &= \frac{-[E(r_1)]^2 + E(r_1) \cdot E(r_2) - E^*[E(r_1) - E(r_2)]}{E(r_1) \cdot E(r_2) - [E(r_2)]^2 - [E(r_1)]^2 + E(r_1) \cdot E(r_2)} \\ &= \frac{-0.1E^* + 0.005}{-0.01} = 10E^* - 0.5. \end{aligned}$$

Thus, the minimum-risk weights are a linear function of $E^*$, which sums to 1:

$$x_1 = 1.5 - 10E^*, \qquad x_2 = -0.5 + 10E^*.$$

When $E^* = 0.07 = 7$ percent is desired, the weights of the minimum variance portfolio are:

$$x_1 = \quad 1.5 - 10(0.07) = \quad 1.5 - 0.7 = 0.8$$
$$x_2 = -0.5 + 10(0.07) = -0.5 + 0.7 = \underline{0.2}$$
$$\phantom{x_2 = -0.5 + 10(0.07) = -0.5 + 0.7 = } 1.0.$$

By varying $E^*$, other portfolios in the efficient set will be generated. Of course, the solutions are identical whether the solution is obtained graphically or with calculus.

This calculus optimization solution may be interpreted as shown in Figs. 6.2 and 6.3. The curve passing through points 1 and 2 in Fig. 6.2 shows that as $E^*$ is increased from $E^* = 5$ percent to $E^* = 20$ percent, the portfolio variance increases from $\sigma_p = 20$ percent to $\sigma_p = 40$ percent, and the efficient frontier is generated.

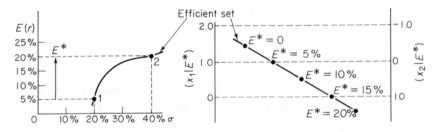

Figure 6.2. Graphical Representation        Figure 6.3. Graphical Representation of Weights
of Portfolio Selected as $E^*$ Varies        as $E^*$ Varies

In Fig. 6.3 the weight of security one, given some $E^*$, that is, $(x_1 \mid E^*)$ is shown on the left vertical axis. On the right vertical axis the weight of security 2 required to achieve the desired $E^*$ is shown. Each dashed horizontal line represents a locus of expected returns for the portfolio [that is, $E(r_p)$]. Thus, Fig. 6.3 shows that for, say, $E(r_p) = 5$ percent, the minimum-risk portfolio would have $x_1 = 1$, and $x_2 = 0$. The diagonal solid line is the locus of all weights for the most efficient portfolio attainable from the two securities for the $E^*$ shown on the horizontal lines. Figure 6.3 covers only the range $0 \leq E^* \leq 20$ percent. However, it could be extended to either negative values of $E^*$ (that is, a portfolio with unfavorable financial leverage) or to values of $E^*$ above 20 percent (that is, a high degree of favorable leverage).

Figure 6.3 shows that the weights change from $x_1 = 1$, $x_2 = 0$ when $E^* = 5$ percent to $x_1 = 0$ and $x_2 = 1$ when $E^* = 15$ percent—these are both simply one-security portfolios. Numerous combinations of weights that sum to 1 may be generated by varying $E^*$. For values of $E^*$ below 5 percent or above 15 percent, one of the weights will be negative, although they will still sum to 1. These negative weights represent the issuance (leverage or short sale) of a security possessing the characteristics (that is, return and risk) of the security to which the negative weights refer.

### E.  Caveat About Negative Weights

As Fig. 6.3 shows, the weights of the efficient portfolio become negative for $E^* < 5$ percent and $E^* > 15$ percent. Such solutions are not always realistic. Some large public portfolios are legally forbidden to use leverage. Also, securities having the same risk and return as the security with the negative weight may not be easy to draw up and issue.

It is possible to extend this algorithm so that it does not produce negative weights. At the point where the first weight reaches zero (before becoming negative), stop the analysis. Remove the row and column in the bordered matrix (6.4) which corresponds to the security that is at zero weight. The solution now has one less asset from which to select. Invert the new, smaller matrix and solve for a new vector of efficient weights. This set of efficient portfolios will intersect the original efficient set where the eliminated asset's weight went to zero. Thus, the analysis proceeds. Each time another asset's weight reaches zero, that asset is eliminated, the new smaller matrix is inverted, and the efficient set is extended further. Martin provides a numerical example and a graphical representation of this process.[6]

For student projects, research, and other work where negative weights are permissible, this calculus solution is recommended. But, for many realistic portfolio problems, either quadratic programming must be used or the process described above must be used to eliminate negative weights.

### 6.2  Calculus Maximization of a Lagrangian Objective Function

In Section 6.2 a solution algorithm using differential calculus to maximize a Lagrangian objective function will be explained. Of course, this technique generates the same set of efficient portfolios as the other calculus technique or the graphical technique. In presenting this calculus solution, a numerical example is provided in which a trivial two-security problem is solved. Hopefully, the simplicity of the arithmetic will make for easier reading.

### A.  Calculus Maximization Solution—General Formulation[7]

The objective of portfolio analysis is to delineate the efficient *set* of portfolios. This problem may be solved mathematically by maximizing a linear

---

[6]A. D. Martin, Jr., "Mathematical Programming of Portfolio Selections."

[7]The authors learned this calculus maximization solution technique from W. F. Sharpe in a seminar presented at the University of Washington during 1968.

combination of the following two equations:

$$E(r_p) = \sum_{i=1}^{n} x_i E(r_i),$$                                          (2.8)

$$-\text{var } (r_p) = -\sum_{i=1}^{n} \sum_{j=1}^{n} x_i x_j \sigma_{ij}, \quad \text{negative of (2.9b)}$$

subject to the following constraint equation:

$$\sum_{i=1}^{n} x_i = 1.$$                                                    (2.7)

Maximizing var $(r_p)$ times $-1$ is equivalent to minimizing var $(r_p)$.

Let $\phi$ represent the portfolio managers' preferences for return relative to risk. The term $\phi$ may be thought of as the reciprocal of the slope of an indifference line in $(E(r), \sigma^2)$ space,[8] where $\phi$ is the weight attached to a unit of $E(r_p)$ relative to a unit of var $(r_p)$. A Lagrangian expression may be formed. As in the graphical portfolio analysis, the weights are variables to be optimized.

$$z = \phi E(r_p) - \text{var } (r_p) + \lambda(1 - \sum_{i=1}^{n} x_i)$$          (6.10)

$$= \phi \left[ \sum_{i=1}^{n} x_i E(r_i) \right] - \sum_{i=1}^{n} \sum_{j=1}^{n} x_i x_j \sigma_{ij} + \lambda(1 - \sum_{i=1}^{n} x_i),$$   (6.10a)

The value of the Lagrangian expression is arbitrarily designated $z$.[9] The value of $z$ is an index of investor satisfaction that has only ordinal significance. Maximizing $z$ subject to the Lagrangian constraint determines the set of weights $(x_i\text{'s})$ that are Markowitz-efficient for some value of $\phi$. Varying $\phi$ delineates the efficient frontier (EF). As shown in Fig. 6.4, when $\phi = 0$, the maximum value of $z$ is $z_2$ and point $A$ represents the appropriate Markowitz-efficient portfolio. When $\phi = 1$, the maximum value of $z$ is $z_3$ and point $B$ is the appropriate Markowitz-efficient portfolio for this investor's preferences.

The Lagrangian expression (6.10a) may be maximized by setting the partial derivative of $z$ with respect to the $x_i$'s and $\lambda$ equal to zero.[10]

---

[8]The use of indifference lines in $(E(r), \sigma^2)$ space is not meant to imply any investor actually has such preferences—it is merely a mathematical convenience. Later, it will be shown that the widely observed phenomena of diversification implies that most investors' indifference curves are concave to the $E(r)$ axis.

[9]For a discussion of similar formulations, see D. E. Farrar, *The Investment Decision Under Uncertainty* (Englewood Cliffs, N.J.: Prentice-Hall, Inc., 1962), Chap. II.

[10]It may be shown that the second-order conditions to ensure a maximum exist. However, such proof will not be given here. See the Hessian matrix equation (6.6) and the accompanying discussion of second-order conditions.

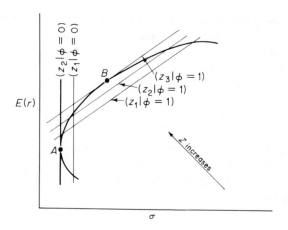

Figure 6.4. Efficient Frontier Traced by Varying $\phi$

$$\frac{\partial z}{\partial x_1} = \phi E(r_1) - 2x_1\sigma_{11} - 2x_2\sigma_{12} - \cdots - \quad 2x_n\sigma_{1n} \quad - \lambda = 0,$$

$$\frac{\partial z}{\partial x_2} = \phi E(r_2) - 2x_1\sigma_{21} - 2x_2\sigma_{22} - \cdots - \quad 2x_n\sigma_{2n} \quad - \lambda = 0,$$

$$\vdots \qquad\qquad\qquad\qquad\qquad\qquad\qquad\qquad\qquad (6.11)$$

$$\frac{\partial z}{\partial x_n} = \phi E(r_n) - 2x_1\sigma_{n1} - 2x_2\sigma_{n2} - \cdots - \quad 2x_n\sigma_{n\cdot n} \quad - \lambda = 0,$$

$$\frac{\partial z}{\partial \lambda} = 1 - x_1 - x_2 - \cdots - x_n = 0.$$

Since the variances, covariances, and the portfolio managers' attitude coefficient ($\phi$) can be treated as constants, the system of equations is linear. Forming the Jacobian matrix (that is, the matrix of first partial derivatives), the system above may be restated as follows:

$$
\begin{matrix} & & C & & & & x & & k \end{matrix}
$$

$$
\begin{bmatrix}
2\sigma_{11} & 2\sigma_{12} & \cdots & 2\sigma_{1n} & 1 \\
2\sigma_{21} & 2\sigma_{22} & \cdots & 2\sigma_{2n} & 1 \\
\vdots & \vdots & & \vdots & \vdots \\
2\sigma_{n1} & 2\sigma_{n2} & \cdots & 2\sigma_{nn} & 1 \\
1 & 1 & \cdots & 1 & 0
\end{bmatrix}
\cdot
\begin{bmatrix}
x_1 \\
x_2 \\
\vdots \\
x_n \\
\lambda
\end{bmatrix}
=
\begin{bmatrix}
\phi E(r_1) \\
\phi E(r_2) \\
\vdots \\
\phi E(r_n) \\
1
\end{bmatrix}.
\qquad (6.12)
$$

Let the coefficient matrix be denoted by $C$, the weight vector by $x$, and the constant vector by $k$. Such simultaneous linear equations may be solved several different ways.

This system of $n + 1$ equations may be represented in matrix notation by writing $Cx = k$. Solving for the vector of $x_i$'s by matrix inversion:

$$Cx = k, \qquad C^{-1}Cx = C^{-1}k, \qquad x = C^{-1}k.$$

In evaluating the weights' vector, $x$, it will be found that the weights are a linear function of the portfolio manager's attitude coefficient ($\phi$). The system of $n + 1$ separate equations with the $x_i$'s as a linear function of $\phi$ is of the following form:

$$
\begin{aligned}
x_1 &= c_1 + d_1\phi \\
x_2 &= c_2 + d_2\phi \\
&\quad \cdot \\
&\quad \cdot \\
&\quad \cdot \\
x_n &= c_n + d_n\phi \\
\lambda &= c_\lambda + d_\lambda\phi,
\end{aligned}
\qquad (6.13)
$$

where the $c$'s and the $d$'s are some constants. By letting $\phi$ vary from zero to infinity, the set of weights that is optimum for each value of $\phi$ is generated.[11]

If the Jacobian matrix is small or a computer program to invert $C$ is not available, the system of equations in matrix form may be solved using Cramer's rule.

Some of the $x_i$'s may be negative for extreme values of $\phi$. These negative $x_i$'s represent short sales or a leveraged portfolio. Consider a simple two-security numerical example of this solution technique which can be represented graphically.

### B. Calculus Maximization—A Numerical Example

For a two-asset portfolio, the Lagrangian objective function is

$$
\begin{aligned}
\text{Max } z = \phi x_1 E(r_1) + \phi x_2 E(r_2) - x_1^2\sigma_{11} \\
- x_2^2\sigma_{22} - 2x_1x_2\sigma_{12} + \lambda(1 - x_1 - x_2),
\end{aligned}
\qquad (6.14)
$$

which is equivalent to equation (6.10). Taking the partial derivative with respect to all variables yields the three linear equations (6.15).

---

[11]Negative values of $\phi$ represent irrational—that is, risk-loving behavior.

$$\frac{\partial z}{\partial x_1} = \phi E(r_1) - 2x_1\sigma_{11} - 2x_2\sigma_{12} - \lambda = 0,$$

$$\frac{\partial z}{\partial x_2} = \phi E(r_2) - 2x_1\sigma_{21} - 2x_2\sigma_{22} - \lambda = 0, \qquad (6.15)$$

$$\frac{\partial z}{\partial \lambda} = 1 - x_1 - x_2 = 0,$$

which is equivalent to the system of equations (6.11). The matrix representation of the above is $Cx = k$.

$$
\begin{matrix}
C & x & k
\end{matrix}
$$

$$
\begin{bmatrix} 2\sigma_{11} & 2\sigma_{12} & 1 \\ 2\sigma_{21} & 2\sigma_{22} & 1 \\ 1 & 1 & 0 \end{bmatrix}
\cdot
\begin{bmatrix} x_1 \\ x_2 \\ \lambda \end{bmatrix}
=
\begin{bmatrix} \phi E(r_1) \\ \phi E(r_2) \\ 1 \end{bmatrix}. \qquad (6.16)
$$

Using the values $E(r_1) = 0.05$, $E(r_2) = 0.15$, $\sigma_1 = 0.2$, $\sigma_{11} = 0.04$, $\sigma_2 = 0.4$, $\sigma_{22} = 0.16$, $\rho_{12} = 0$, $\sigma_{12} = 0$ yields

$$
\begin{matrix}
C & x & k
\end{matrix}
$$

$$
\begin{bmatrix} 0.08 & 0 & 1 \\ 0 & 0.32 & 1 \\ 1 & 1 & 0 \end{bmatrix}
\cdot
\begin{bmatrix} x_1 \\ x_2 \\ \lambda \end{bmatrix}
=
\begin{bmatrix} 0.05\phi \\ 0.15\phi \\ 1.0 \end{bmatrix}, \qquad (6.17)
$$

which is equivalent to the system of equations (6.12). Finding the inverse[12] of $C$, the system may be solved for the weight vector—that is, $x = C^{-1}k$.

$$
\begin{matrix}
x & C^{-1} & k
\end{matrix}
$$

$$
\begin{bmatrix} x_1 \\ x_2 \\ \lambda \end{bmatrix}
=
\begin{bmatrix} 2.5 & -2.5 & 0.8 \\ -2.5 & 2.5 & 0.2 \\ 0.8 & 0.2 & 0.064 \end{bmatrix}
\cdot
\begin{bmatrix} 0.05\phi \\ 0.15\phi \\ 1 \end{bmatrix}. \qquad (6.18)
$$

Writing out the three linear equations in $x_i$ and $\phi$,

$$x_1 = 2.5(0.05\phi) - 2.5(0.15\phi) + 0.8(1.) = 0.8 - 0.25\phi,$$

$$x_2 = -2.5(0.05\phi) + 2.5(0.15\phi) + 0.2(1.) = 0.2 + 0.25\phi, \qquad (6.19)$$

$$\lambda = 0.8(0.05\phi) + 0.2(0.15\phi) + 0.064(1.) = 0.064 + 0.07\phi,$$

---

[12]See T. Yamane, *Mathematics for Economics* (Englewood Cliffs, N.J.: Prentice-Hall, Inc., 1962), pp. 255–275. Or also, Sections 3-18 through 3-22 of G. Hadley, *Linear Algebra* (Reading, Mass.: Addison-Wesley Publishing Co., Inc., 1961).

which is equivalent to the system of equations (6.13). Alternatively, solving the matrix for $x_1$ and $x_2$ using Cramer's rule yields

$$x_1 = \frac{\begin{bmatrix} \phi E(r_1) & 2\sigma_{12} & 1 \\ \phi E(r_2) & 2\sigma_{22} & 1 \\ 1 & 1 & 0 \end{bmatrix}}{\begin{bmatrix} 2\sigma_{11} & 2\sigma_{12} & 1 \\ 2\sigma_{21} & 2\sigma_{22} & 1 \\ 1 & 1 & 0 \end{bmatrix}} = \frac{\phi E(r_2) - \phi E(r_1) + 2\sigma_{12} - 2\sigma_{22}}{4\sigma_{12} - 2\sigma_{11} - 2\sigma_{22}}$$

$$= \frac{0.1\phi - 0.32}{-0.4} = 0.8 - 0.25\phi = x_1. \tag{6.20}$$

Omitting the matrices, the solution for $x_2$ follows.

$$x_2 = \frac{\phi E(r_1) - \phi E(r_2) - 2\sigma_{11} + 2\sigma_{12}}{4\sigma_{12} - 2\sigma_{11} - 2\sigma_{22}} = \frac{-0.1\phi - 0.08}{-0.4}$$

$$= 0.2 + 0.25\phi = x_2. \tag{6.21}$$

Of course, equations (6.21) and (6.22) are identical to the two equations for $x_1$ and $x_2$ in the system of equations (6.19). Obviously, the correct solution does not vary with the technique used to solve the system of linear equations.

Solving for $x_1$ and $x_2$ as $\phi$ varies from zero to 10 yields the following portfolio returns and pairs of weights, which in each case sum to unity.

$$\phi = 0 \begin{cases} x_1 = 0.8 \\ x_2 = 0.2 \end{cases} E(r_p) = 7.0\%,$$

$$\phi = \tfrac{1}{2} \begin{cases} x_1 = 0.675 \\ x_2 = 0.325 \end{cases} E(r_p) = 8.25\%,$$

$$\phi = 1 \begin{cases} x_1 = 0.55 \\ x_2 = 0.45 \end{cases} E(r_p) = 9.5\%,$$

$$\phi = 2 \begin{cases} x_1 = 0.3 \\ x_2 = 0.7 \end{cases} E(r_p) = 11.5\%,$$

$$\phi = 5 \begin{cases} x_1 = -0.45 \\ x_2 = 1.45 \end{cases} E(r_p) = 19.5\%,$$

$$\phi = 10 \begin{cases} x_1 = -1.7 \\ x_2 = 2.7 \end{cases} E(r_p) = 32.0\%.$$

These portfolios may be represented graphically in several different ways. Figure 6.5 shows that as the portfolio manager's attitude coefficient ($\phi$) ranges from $\phi = 0$ to $\phi = 10$, the portfolio's proportion invested in both

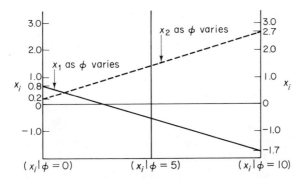

Figure 6.5. Graphical Representation of Weights as $\phi$ Varies

securities varies. The dashed line represents the weights of security 2, $x_2$. The weights for security 2, the more risky security, which offers a higher return, ranges from 0.2 when $\phi = 0$ up to 2.7 when $\phi = 10$ and the portfolio manager is more aggressive. The 2.7 value of $x_2$ may be interpreted as a portfolio with 270 percent of its total amount invested in security 2. To finance this aggressive portfolio, securities with $E(r) = 5$ percent and $\sigma = 20$ percent were issued. That is, the portfolio manager sold securities such as security 1 in an amount equal to 170 percent of the portfolio's equity to form a leveraged portfolio. But the budget constraint is not violated—specifically, $x_1 + x_2 = -1.7 + 2.7 = 1.0$. Figure 6.5 could be extended to cover any values for $\phi$.

Figure 6.6 shows how the indifference line shifts as its slope $\phi$ varies. Higher values of $\phi$ represent more aggressive attitudes for the portfolio manager. Correspondingly, higher values of $\phi$ lead to riskier portfolios—that is, higher tangency points with the efficient frontier. The opportunity

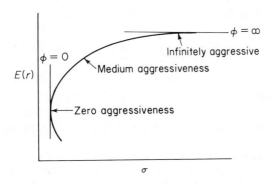

Figure 6.6. Graphical Representation of Portfolio Selected from Efficient Frontier as $\phi$ Varies

115

locus comprised of the $[E(r_p), \sigma_p]$ pairs representing the infinite number of possible efficient portfolios that can be formed from the two securities does not change as $\phi$ is varied. Rather, the indifference line becomes tangent to the opportunity locus at different points as $\phi$ is varied.

## C.  Caveat About Negative Weights

As Fig. 6.5 shows, the weights of some assets in the efficient set can become negative—representing leveraged portfolios. It is against the law for some public portfolios to use leverage. Furthermore, it may not be possible to issue a security with the same risk and return as the security with the negative weight. In such circumstances, the solution generated by this calculus algorithm is inadequate.

It is possible to extend this algorithm so that it will generate efficient port-folios with nonnegative weights. To generate such legitimate portfolios, the analysis begins as described above. However, at the point where the first asset's weight reaches zero (before becoming negative), the analysis stops. The asset whose weight has attained zero is eliminated from the matrix. That is, the row and column in the bordered matrix (6.12) pertaining to this asset are eliminated. This decreases the matrix by one row and one column. This new smaller matrix is inverted, and a new efficient vector of weights is attained. The process repeats again. Where the next asset's weight becomes zero, it is eliminated. Then a new, smaller matrix is inverted and a new efficient vector of weights obtained. The series of successive efficient sets generated by this process are connected at the points where the successive assets go out of solution (that is, weights go to zero).

In the case where the entire efficient set contains negative weights over all ranges of expected return for the portfolio, the first solution is unacceptable. At least one asset (different ones may be tried) must be cast out of the initial matrix until the efficient weights all start with nonnegative values. Then the process outlined in the preceding paragraph is used.

## 6.3  Portfolio Analysis by Means of Quadratic Programming

Markowitz has written an algorithm to solve the mathematical portfolio problem.[13] Markowitz's solution is by quadratic programming rather than calculus. Operational computer codes are available to the public to perform the quadratic programming algorithm.[14] The input data requirements are

---

[13]Harry M. Markowitz, "The Optimization of a Quadratic Function Subject to Linear Constraints," *Naval Research Logistics Quarterly*, Vol. 3, March–June 1956; also see P. Wolfe, "The Simplex Method of Quadratic Programming," *Econometrica*, June 1959, pp. 382–398. Or see Appendix A of Harry M. Markowitz, *Portfolio Selection* (New York: John Wiley & Sons, Inc., 1959).

[14]Programs are available to the general public. The program titled, "Portfolio Selection

the same for either the calculus solution or the quadratic programming technique.

The quadratic programming code lends itself to the solution of problems with upper and/or lower bounds and nonnegativity constraints on the securities weights. For example, suppose that the portfolio manager of a mutual fund is trying to determine his optimum portfolio of securities. But, owing to some regulation he is required to diversify by holding no more than 5 percent of the portfolio in any given security. The portfolio manager can obtain such a constrained optimum solution with the quadratic programming algorithm. By putting an upper bound of 5 percent on any security entering the optimum solution, the portfolio will contain at least 20 securities. The quadratic programming algorithm also handles lower-bound constraints on any or all securities weights. Of course, the unconstrained solution will yield a more efficient portfolio unless none of the constraints are binding.

As a practical matter, one of the advantages of using a quadratic programming computer program to do portfolio analysis instead of one of the mathematical techniques explained above involves the inequality constraints. The mathematical techniques *cannot use inequality constraints*, but the quadratic programming computer codes can employ more inequality constraints than there are securities under analysis if necessary.

## A. The QP Algorithm

The QP algorithm iteratively minimizes the quadratic objective function var $(r_p)$ subject to different values of a linear constraint $E(r_p)$. The tangency points of the minimum values of the quadratic function for each $E(r_p)$, or, what is the same thing, the tangency points of the maximum $E(r_p)$ for each var $(r_p)$ form a straight line—the critical line. The critical line was shown graphically in Fig. 5.3 for the three-security case. The critical line represents the weights of the efficient portfolios in $(x_1, x_2, \ldots, x_n)$ space for an $n$-security portfolio.

In terms of the efficient frontier, the QP algorithm begins by finding the portfolio with maximum $E(r_p)$. This is usually a one-security portfolio. It is located at point $E$ in Fig. 6.7. Point $E$ is the first *corner portfolio*. Corner

Program." For the IBM 1401 computer, program number 1401-F1-04X, described in an IBM manual entitled *Portfolio Selection for the IBM 1401*, is available. For the IBM 7090 the program number is 7090-F1-03X. The Rand Corporation prepared a code titled "Product Form Quadratic Programming Code (RS QPF4)" available in SHARE General Program Library. The latter two programs are quadratic programming algorithms, while the first program uses a simplified model discussed in Chapter 7. See G. J. Alexander, "The Derivation of Efficient Sets," *Journal of Financial and Quantitative Analysis*, December 1976; A. Ravindran, "A Computer Routine for Quadratic and Linear Programming Problems," *Communications of the ACM*, September 1972, pp. 818–820. Many universities' computer centers also have QP codes. Computer codes can also be purchased from Professor Francis, one of the coauthors of the book.

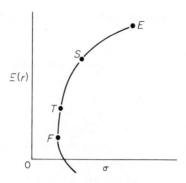

Figure 6.7. Efficient Frontier

portfolios are portfolios where a security either enters or leaves the portfolio. The QP algorithm delineates the set of corner portfolios rather than the infinite number of points along the efficient frontier.

After finding the first corner portfolio at $E$, the algorithm finds the second corner portfolio. The second corner portfolio will lie below $E$ on the efficient frontier (EF) at, say, point $S$ in Fig. 6.7. The second corner portfolio is the efficient portfolio where a second security comes into solution. The computer program calculates the weights in these corner portfolios and prints out their weights and perhaps their $E(r_p)$ and var $(r_p)$, depending on the particular program. The algorithm proceeds down the efficient frontier, finding the corner portfolios. The number of securities in the corner portfolios typically increases at first and reaches a maximum in the neighborhood of point $T$ in Fig. 6.7. Then, as the algorithm moves on down toward point $F$, the number of securities in the successive corner portfolios may or may not change. Point $F$ is the minimum-variance portfolio.

The actual number of assets entering into any given efficient portfolio is largely determined by the upper-bound constraints on the weights of the assets. If the weights are free to assume large values (for example, $x_i = 2.0$), the efficient frontier may contain one- or two-asset portfolios at the low- or high-risk extremes.[15] The slope of the efficient frontier, $\phi = dE(r_p)/d\sigma$, at each point, is the trade-off between risk and return at that point.

Technically, the efficient frontier (ESTF) is not a continuous line like the solid line in Fig. 6.7; rather, it is a series of curves connected at the corner portfolios. A glance at Fig. 3.10 should explain why the efficient frontier assumes this shape.

---

[15]K. J. Cohen and G. A. Pogue, "An Empirical Evaluation of Alternative Portfolio Selection Models," *Journal of Business*, Vol. 40, No. 2, 1967, pp. 166–193. Cohen and Pogue show the number of assets entering efficient portfolios with constraints of $x_i \leq 0.05$ and $x_i \leq 0.025$. See Tables 6 and 7 on pages 183 and 184 of the article.

### B. QP Constraints

Using the quadratic programming algorithm, it is possible to produce a leveraged portfolio. Like linear programming, the quadratic programming algorithm cannot handle negative variables (that is, short sales or leverage), so artificial variables must be used. Gerald Pogue has shown how to formulate the mathematical programming solution to the portfolio problem to incorporate short sales, leverage, transactions costs, and taxes.[16] J. C. Francis has shown an alternative quadratic programming formulation which allows the portfolio to raise capital by issuing liabilities.[17]

The alternative to using quadratic programming to solve the portfolio problem is to use calculus. The optimum solutions with calculus allow negative weights (that is, short sales or leverage) but cannot handle inequality constraints such as upper and lower bounds on the securities weights. However, equality constraints can be included as additional Lagrangian constraints when using one of the calculus methods. The matrix increases one row and one column for each Lagrangian constraint added. The calculus solution seems most advantageous for solving small portfolios without bounds, such as research applications, student projects, and so on.

### 6.4  Conclusions About Mathematical Portfolio Analysis

Portfolio analysis is basically a mathematics problem. The variance–covariance matrix from mathematical statistics is the engine for the analysis. The objective of portfolio analysis is to minimize the quadratic portfolio risk formula (that is, the variance–covariance matrix) subject to two linear constraints. The first linear constraint is that the portfolio earn some linear weighted average rate of return. The second linear constraint is that the weights of all securities in the portfolio sum to unity. This is the portfolio analysis problem.

This chapter presented several different ways to solve the portfolio analysis problem. Differential calculus can be used to delineate the weights of the efficient portfolios. However, the calculus does not permit the solution to contain any inequality constraints. As a result, the calculus solutions may contain negative weights (representing short sales or borrowing) when such solutions are unrealistic, illegal, or otherwise unacceptable.

Quadratic programming (QP) offers an alternative solution to the calculus. The main advantage that can be obtained by use of QP is the use of

---

[16]G. A. Pogue, "An Extension of the Markowitz Portfolio Selection Model to Include Variable Transactions Costs, Short Sales, Leverage Policies and Taxes," *Journal of Finance,* December 1970, pp. 1005–1027.

[17]J. C. Francis, "Portfolio Analysis of Small-, Medium-, and Large-Sized Banks," *Journal of Monetary Economics,* August 1978, Vol. 4, No. 3, pp. 459–480. This paper's results are discussed in Chapter XIII.

inequality constraints. The weights of any or all objects of choice can be constrained to be negative (that is, to be liabilities), to be zero, to be positive, or to be constrained within a bounded range of acceptable values. Or, most simply, the QP problem can be solved without any inequality constraints on the weights. When the latter QP problem is solved, it yields the identical solution as the calculus (when no extra Lagrangian constraints are imposed). The only disadvantage of the QP algorithm is that it must be solved by means of computer if more than a few securities are being considered.

For most portfolio analysis problems the QP algorithm offers the easiest and most flexible method available to solve for the efficient portfolios. The QP solution does require a computer. However, simplified portfolio analysis algorithms, explained in Chapter VII, can be solved on small computers. These simplified solutions achieve approximately the same solutions as the QP algorithm and require fewer computer resources.

## Selected References

Martin, A. D., Jr., "Mathematical Programming of Portfolio Selections," *Management Science*, Vol. 1, No. 2, 1955, pp. 152–166.

This paper uses differential calculus to minimize a Lagrangian objective function and delineate efficient portfolios. Graphs and a numerical example are provided. This article is reprinted in E. B. Fredrickson, ed., *Frontiers of Investment Analysis* (Scranton, Pa.: International Textbook Company, 1965), as reading 23.

Sharpe, W. F., *Portfolio Theory and Capital Markets*. New York: McGraw-Hill Book Company, Inc., 1970.

Mathematical Appendices A, B, and C explain the mathematics of portfolio analysis using differential calculus to optimize a Lagrangian objective function.

## Questions and Problems

1. If you were paid to do a portfolio analysis on 500 different NYSE common stocks in order to determine how much a mutual fund should invest (if any) in each of the 500 stocks under consideration, how would you perform the analysis? Would you use graphical analysis, the calculus minimization technique, the calculus maximization technique, or quadratic programming? Explain why. (*Hint:* Mutual funds are forbidden by law from borrowing or short selling.)

2. Assume that you were going to delineate the Markowitz-efficient portfolios that could be formed from the following four investment assets.
   (a) Preferred stock of National Lead, Inc., with $E(r_N) = 5.06$ percent and var $(r_N) = 71.73$.
   (b) F. W. Woolworth's common stock, with $E(r_W) = 9.58$ percent and var $(r_W) = 414.66$.
   (c) Kennecott Copper common stock, with $E(r_K) = 16.34$ percent and var $(r_K) = 1945.49$.
   (d) A U.S. Savings Bond, with $E(r_U) = 2.0$ percent and var $(r_U) = 0$.
The covariances for these four assets are listed below.

$$\text{cov }(r_N, r_W) = 112.68$$
$$\text{cov }(r_N, r_K) = 153.10$$
$$\text{cov }(r_N, r_U) = 0$$
$$\text{cov }(r_W, r_U) = 0$$
$$\text{cov }(r_W, r_K) = 492.96$$
$$\text{cov }(r_K, r_U) = 0.$$

Find the efficient portfolios that have expected rates of return of 6.0 percent and 9.0 percent with and without borrowing. (*Hint:* See A. D. Martin's article in this chapter's Selected References for the solution.)

3. If you had to analyze several hundred different common stocks to determine efficient portfolios with borrowing or lending at the riskless rate of $R = 5.0$ percent permitted, how would you perform the analysis? (*First clue:* Since QP is the only realistic way to do portfolio analysis when constrained borrowing or lending is permitted, this question boils down to the question: How do you formulate the QP? *Second clue:* The answer can be found in Chapter XIII.)

```
77777777777777777777777777777777777777777777777777777777777777777777777777777777777
77777777777777777777777777777777777777777777777777777777777777777777777777777777777
7777777777777777777777777777  7777777777777  777   777   7777777777777777777777777777
7777777777777777777777777777  7777777777  7777   777   7777777777777777777777777777
77777777777777777777777777777  7777777  77777   777   7777777777777777777777777777
7777777777777777777777777777777  777777  77777   777   7777777777777777777777777777
77777777777777777777777777777777  77777  7777777   777   7777777777777777777777777777
777777777777777777777777777777777  777  7777777   777   7777777777777777777777777777
7777777777777777777777777777777777  7  7777777   777   7777777777777777777777777777
77777777777777777777777777777777777777  7777777   777   7777777777777777777777777777
777777777777777777777777777777777477777  7777777777   777   7777777777777777777777777777
77777777777777777777777777777777777777777777777777777777777777777777777777777777777
77777777777777777777777777777777777777777777777777777777777777777777777777777777777
```

# Simplified Models
# for Portfolio Analysis*

$M$ARKOWITZ's full-covariance model requires a large computer and massive calculations to trace out the efficient frontier when a realistic number of securities are considered. Therefore, Markowitz suggested certain sophistications that may be used to expedite the use of his portfolio analysis model.[1] Following his suggestion, Sharpe developed an ingenious simplified model of portfolio analysis.[2] Sharpe called his model the *diagonal model*. Sharpe's diagonal model, or *single-index model*, will be considered in depth.

The simplified models discussed in this chapter derive their name from the fact that they require fewer input data that can be tabulated more simply, and, the solution process is simplified. As a result, the computer running time for solving the simplified models is a small fraction of the time required to solve the same problem using the full-covariance Markowitz technique. However, as might be expected, the solutions obtained using these simplifications may differ from the solutions obtained with Markowitz's full-covariance model.

---

*This chapter contains mathematics and intricacies that are not essential to grasp the essence of portfolio analysis nor the material in the later chapters.

[1]See Harry M. Markowitz, *Portfolio Selection* (New York: John Wiley & Sons, Inc., 1959), especially pp. 97–101, including footnotes.

[2]W. F. Sharpe, "A Simplified Model for Portfolio Analysis," *Management Science*, January 1963, pp. 277–293.

The simplified models assume that the individual covariances between all securities are zero. Thus, the covariances per se are not used in these models. To allow for interrelationships, the models assume that securities returns are related only through their individual relations with one or more indices of business activity. By reducing the number of covariances needed, both the security analyst's job and the portfolio analysis computations are made easier.

However, some additional inputs are required, too. To use the simplified models, estimates are required of the expected value and variance of the one or more indices of market activity. Markowitz suggested how the forecasts of these indices be tabulated for inputting into the algorithm.[3] The simplified portfolio analysis algorithm is explained next.

### 7.1  Sharpe's Single-Index Model

Sharpe suggests that the return on any security may be related to the performance of some index of business activity. He says[4]:

> The major characteristic of the diagonal model is the assumption that the returns of various securities are related only through common relationships with some basic underlying factor. The return from any security is determined solely by random factors and this single outside element, more explicitly:

$$r_{jt} = a_j + b_j r_{It} + e_{jt}, \qquad (4.4)$$

where $a_j$ and $b_j$ are regression parameters for the $j$th firm, $r_{It}$ is the $t$th return on some market index, $r_{jt}$ is the $t$th return on security $j$, and $e_{jt}$ is the $t$th random-error term for the $j$th firm. This model is based on several assumptions about the random-error term. Assuming:

1. The $e_{jt}$'s average is zero—that is, $E(e) = 0$.
2. The var $(e)$ is constant—that is, homoscedasticity.
3. The $e$'s are uncorrelated with $r_I$—that is, cov $(e, r_I) = 0$.
4. The $e$'s are not serially correlated—that is, cov $(e_{jt}, e_{j,t+n}) = 0$.
5. The $j$th firm's $e$'s are uncorrelated with any other firm's $e$'s; then the regression parameters $a_j$ and $b_j$ are unbiased, minimum-variance linear estimates of the true regression parameters.[5]

Graphically, Sharpe suggests a regression line such as shown in Fig. 7.1.[6] Such a model allows considerable simplifications in portfolio analysis. First, it is possible to estimate the inputs for the regular portfolio analysis—that is,

---

[3]See Markowitz, *Portfolio Selection*, Figs. 6 and 7 (pp. 29, 30).
[4]Sharpe, "A Simplified Model," Sec. IV.
[5]According to the Gauss–Markov theorem.
[6]Equation (4.4), Figs. 4.3 and 4.4, and their discussion in Chapter IV are relevant to equation (7.1) and Fig. 7.1. Some writers refer to equation (4.4) as the *market model*.

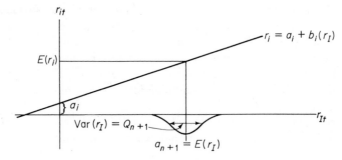

Figure 7.1 Illustration of Single-Index Market Model for One Security

$E(r_i)$, var $(r_i)$, and cov $(r_i, r_j)$—using the following simple formulas:

$$E(r_i) = a_i + b_i E(r_I), \tag{7.1}$$

$$\text{var } (r_i) = (b_{i|I})^2[\text{var } (r_I)] + \sigma^2_{(r_i|r_I)}, \tag{7.2}$$

$$\text{cov } (r_i r_j) = (b_{i|I}) \cdot (b_{j|I}) \cdot [\text{var } (r_I)], \tag{7.3}$$

where $b_{(i|I)}$ is the regression coefficient of $r_i$ onto $r_I$, and $\sigma^2(r_i|r_I) = E(e^2_{jt})$ is the residual variance about the regression line.

Note that the parameters for equations (7.1), (7.2), and (7.3) can be estimated several ways. For example, the regression coefficients can be fitted using historical data, or they can be estimated intuitively. Or, using both approaches, historically derived parameters may be adjusted intuitively. An expected return for the index, $E(r_I)$, and a future variance for the index, var $(r_I)$, may be estimated similarly.

The index statistics are fairly easy to compile for many different possible economic indices which might be used. Therefore, selection of an index should be based on its performance relative to other possible indices that might be used.

Empirical research has suggested that stock market indices yield more desirable efficient portfolios than other economic indices (such as GNP, the money supply, etc.). However, it appears to make little difference which stock market index is used in the index model for portfolio analysis. The well-known stock market indices tend to generate similar portfolios in spite of the fact that their risk and return statistics differ a little bit.[7] Thus,

---

[7]K. V. Smith, "Stock Price and Economic Indexes for Generating Efficient Portfolios," *Journal of Business*, July 1969, pp. 326–336; G. M. Frankfurter, "Ex-Post Performance of the Sharpe Portfolio Selection Model," *Journal of Finance*, June 1976, pp. 949–955; and G. J. Alexander, "Mixed Security Testing of Alternative Portfolio Selection Models," *Journal of Financial and Quantitative Analysis*, December 1977, pp. 817–832. Also, G. J. Alexander, "A Re-Evaluation of Alternative Portfolio Selection Models Applied to Common Stocks," *Journal of Financial and Quantitative Analysis*, March 1978, pp. 71–78. Also N. Paine, "A Case Study in Mathematical Programming of Portfolio Selections," *Applied Statistics*, Vol. 1, 1966, pp. 24–36.

although the different indices may contain unique biases,[8] the portfolios they delineate contain similar proportions of mostly the same securities. Perhaps the approximations resulting from the simplified relationships within the single-index model are the cause of similar results which are obtained from the slightly different stock market indices. The nature of the approximations may be analyzed by studying the mathematical derivations of the simplified portfolio analysis statistics.

The derivation of equations (7.1) and (7.2) and (7.3) follows. The expected value of equation (4.4) is the conditional expectation, equation (7.1):

$$r_i = a_i + b_i r_I + e_i, \qquad (4.4)$$

$$E(r_i) = E(a_i + b_i r_I + e_i)$$

$$= E(a_i) + E(b_i)E(r_I) + E(e_i)$$

$$= a_i + b_i E(r_I) = E[r_i \mid E(r_I)]. \qquad (7.1)$$

Equation (7.2) is derived from the definition of the variance, equation (2.2a), and the assumptions underlying equation (4.4).

$$\text{var } (r_i) = \sigma_{ii} = E[r_i - E(r_i)]^2 \qquad (2.2a)$$

$$= E[(a_i + b_i r_I + e_i) - E(a_i + b_i r_I + e_i)]^2$$

$$\qquad\qquad\qquad\qquad \text{by substitution for } r_i$$

$$= E[a_i + b_i r_I + e_i - E(a_i) - E(b_i)E(r_I) - E(e_i)]^2$$

$$= b_i^2 E[r_I - E(r_I)]^2 + E(e_i^2) + 0$$

$$= b_i^2 \text{ var } (r_I) + \sigma^2(r_i \mid r_I) \qquad (7.2)$$

$$= \text{systematic risk} + \text{unsystematic risk}.$$

In equation (7.2), the first term, that is, $b_i^2 \text{ var } (r_I)$, measures systematic risk. The second term, that is, $\sigma^2_{(r_i \mid r_I)}$, measures unsystematic risk. This relation may clarify the partitioning of the total variance.

Equation (7.3) is derived from the definition of the covariance, as follows:

$$\text{cov } (r_i r_j) = \sigma_{ii} = E[(r_i - E(r_i))(r_j - E(r_j))] \qquad (2.4)$$

$$= E\{([a_i + b_i r_I + e_i] - E[a_i + b_i r_I + e_i])$$

$$\quad \cdot ([a_j + b_j r_I + e_j] - E[a_j + b_j r_I + e_j])\}$$

$$= E\{([b_i r_I - b_i E(r_I)] + e_i)([b_j r_I - b_j E(r_I)] + e_j)\}$$

$$= b_i b_j E[r_I - E(r_I)]^2 + 0 + 0 + 0$$

$$= b_i b_j \text{ var } (r_I). \qquad (7.3)$$

---

[8]P. M. Cootner, "Stock Market Indexes—Illusions and Fallacies," *The Commercial and Financial Chronicle*, September 26, 1966, pp. 18–19; G. M. Frankfurter, H. E. Phillips, and J. P. Seagle, "Bias in Estimating Portfolio Alpha and Beta Scores," *Review of Economics and Statistics*, Vol. 56, August 1974, pp. 412–414.

When using the full-covariance portfolio analysis techniques and $n$ is large, equations (7.1), (7.2), and (7.3) greatly simplify the security analyst's job. For example, if $n = 100$, then $(n^2 - n)/2 = 4950$ covariances are required for the full-covariance Markowitz analysis. Covariances do not readily yield to intuitive estimation as easily as expected return and standard deviation of returns. But, using equation (7.3), only 100 regression coefficients and the var $(r_I)$ must be estimated to derive the 4950 covariances necessary for the full covariance model. The use of the two printed forms suggested by Markowitz[9] and the formulas (7.1), (7.2), and (7.3) is highly recommended for large commercial portfolio applications.

In addition to the three equations presented for deriving the regular input data easily, a second benefit can be obtained by using Sharpe's simplified model. The actual portfolio analysis problem itself may be reformulated in terms of the market index variables, $E(r_I)$ and var $(r_I)$. This simplified model offers computational shortcuts; it is explained in the next section.

## A. Deriving the Single-Index Portfolio Model

The formulation of the simplified model is analogous to the regular Markowitz formulation. The return of the portfolio is defined as before.

$$E(r_p) = \sum_{i=1}^{n} x_i E(r_i). \tag{2.8}$$

However, using equation (4.4), the return on the portfolio is redefined as follows:

$$E(r_p) = \sum_{i=1}^{n} x_i E(r_i) = \sum_{i=1}^{n} x_i E(a_i + b_i r_I + e_i)$$

$$= \sum_{i=1}^{n} x_i(a_i + e_i) + \sum_{i=1}^{n} x_i(b_i r_I).$$

Sharpe suggests that the portion of the portfolio placed in the $i$th security can be viewed as two components:

1. An investment in the "basic characteristics" of the $i$th security—that is, $x_i(a_i + e_i)$.
2. An "investment" in the index—that is, $x_i(b_i r_I)$.

Thus, the portfolio return is a combination of $n$ "basic securities" and an investment in the index, as represented by equation (7.4).

$$r_p = \sum_{i=1}^{n} x_i(a_i + e_i) + \left(\sum_{i=1}^{n} x_i b_i\right) r_I. \tag{7.4}$$

9, 30) of Markowitz's book, *Portfolio Selection*, could be very useful tion to input into the portfolio analysis algorithm.

Sharpe decomposes the rates of change in the market index, denoted $r_{It}$ for the $t$th time period, into two parts in order to formulate the simplified diagonal portfolio analysis model.

$$r_{It} = E(r_I) + e_{n+1,t} \tag{7.5}$$

$$= a_{n+1} + e_{n+1,t}, \tag{7.5a}$$

where $E(r_I) = a_{n+1}$ is essentially a constant that estimates the growth in the market index, and $e_{n+1,t}$ measures the fluctuation around $a_{n+1}$ in time period $t$. In a bullish period, $e_{n+1,t}$ is positive, and it is negative in a bearish period as it fluctuates above and below $a_{n+1}$. Thus, the market index is treated as the $(n + 1)$th security in a portfolio problem involving $n$ securities.

Sharpe also defines a weight for the $(n + 1)$th artificial security (which is, of course, the market index) denoted $x_{n+1}$, as shown in equation (7.6).

$$x_{n+1} = \sum_{i=1}^{n} x_i b_i. \tag{7.6}$$

The variable $x_{n+1}$ simply equals the weighted average of the $n$ beta coefficients—which should equal a number near unity, since all betas in the market average out to unity. The purpose of defining the variables $a_{n+1}$, $e_{n+1,t}$, and $x_{n+1}$ is to simplify equation (7.4) into a form suitable for simplified portfolio analysis. Substituting equations (7.5) and (7.6) into the right-hand side of equation (7.4) yields equations (7.7) and (7.7a).

$$r_p = \sum_{i=1}^{n} x_i(a_i + e_i) + x_{n+1}(a_{n+1} + e_{n+1}) \tag{7.7}$$

$$= \sum_{i=1}^{n+1} x_i(a_i + e_i). \tag{7.7a}$$

Since the expected value of all $(n + 1)$ error terms is zero, the expectations of equations (7.7) and (7.7a) are shown as equations (7.8) and (7.8a), respectively.

$$E(r_p) = \sum_{i=1}^{n} x_i a_i + x_{n+1} E(r_I) \tag{7.8}$$

$$= \sum_{i=1}^{n+1} x_i a_i. \tag{7.8a}$$

Examination of the algebraic simplifications leading to equation (7.8a) wi reveal why the notation $a_{n+1} = E(r_I)$ was used—it facilitates compa notation for deriving the simplified portfolio expected return formulation equation (7.8a). With the aid of a few realistic but simplifying assumptic Sharpe went on to simplify the portfolio risk formula in a correspoi manner.

Portfolio risk may be measured by taking the weighted sum of the variances and covariances for all the assets in the portfolio by using equation (2.9). Or, equivalently, portfolio risk may be measured directly from the portfolio's returns by using equation (2.2b):

$$\text{var}\,(r_p) = E[r_p - E(r_p)]^2. \tag{2.2b}$$

Substituting equation (7.7a) into equation (2.2b) to embody the diagonal model's return-generating process yields equations (7.9) and, ultimately, (7.9c):

$$\text{var}\,(r_p) = E\left\{\left[\sum_{i=1}^{n+1} x_i\,(a_i + e_i)\right] - E\left\{\sum_{i=1}^{n+1} x_i(a_i + e_i)\right\}\right\}^2 \tag{7.9}$$

$$= E\left\{\left[\sum_{i=1}^{n+1} x_i(a_i + e_i)\right] - \sum_{i=1}^{n+1} x_i\{E(a_i) + E(e_i)\}\right\}^2$$

$$= E\left\{\left[\sum_{i=1}^{n+1} x_i(a_i + e_i) - \sum_{i=1}^{n+1} x_i E(a_i)\right]\right\}^2 \quad \text{since } E(e_i) = 0$$

$$= E\left(\sum_{i=1}^{n+1} x_i e_i - 0\right)^2 \quad \text{since } [x_i a_i - E(x_i a_i)] = 0$$

$$= \text{var}\left(\sum_{i=1}^{n+1} x_i e_i\right) \quad \text{since } E\left(\sum_{i=1}^{n+1} x_i e_i\right) = 0. \tag{7.9a}$$

Using the portfolio risk formula, equation (2.9), reveals that equation (7.9a) is equal to equation (7.9b).

$$\text{var}\,(r_p) = \sum_{i=1}^{n+1} x_i^2 \,\text{var}\,(e_i) + \sum_{i=1}^{n+1}\sum_{j=1}^{n+1} x_i x_j \,\text{cov}\,(e_i, e_j) \tag{7.9b}$$

$$= \sum_{i=1}^{n+1} x_i^2 \,\text{var}\,(e_i). \tag{7.9c}$$

Equation (7.9c) follows from (7.9b) because the fifth simplifying assumption on page 124 stipulates that different assets regression error terms, $e_i$, are uncorrelated. The zero correlation implies a zero covariance, since it implies that equation (7.10) equals zero.

$$\rho(e_i, e_j)\sqrt{\text{var}\,(e_i)}\,\sqrt{\text{var}\,(e_j)} = \text{cov}\,(e_i, e_j) = 0. \tag{7.10}$$

As a result, all covariance terms on the right-hand side of equation (7.9b) vanish. Thus, the final simplified portfolio risk formula in equation (7.9c) is derived.

The assumptions that underlie the diagonal model's simplified return-generating process entered into the derivation of equation (7.9c) in two different steps. First, the simplified return-generating process from equation (7.7a) was used to get from equation (2.2b) to equation (7.9). This simplification introduces some small differences between portfolio risk, as measured by Sharpe's simplified equation (7.9c) and as it exists in reality, as measured with equation (2.2b). Second, the assumption about the zero covariances which was used to obtain equation (7.9c) from equation (7.9b) introduces further approximations. However, the approximations are small and may be justified in terms of the computational shortcuts which they permit.

## B.  Simplified Portfolio Analysis

The significance of the name "diagonal model" can be seen from equation (7.9d). The variance–covariance matrix has zeros in all positions other than the diagonal.

$$
[x_1, x_2, \ldots, x_{n+1}]
\begin{bmatrix}
\sigma_{11}^2 & 0 & 0 & \cdots & 0 \\
0 & \sigma_{22}^2 & 0 & \cdots & 0 \\
0 & 0 & \sigma_{33}^2 & \cdots & 0 \\
\cdot & \cdot & \cdot & \cdot & \cdot \\
\cdot & \cdot & \cdot & \cdot & \cdot \\
\cdot & \cdot & \cdot & \cdot \cdot & \cdot \\
0 & 0 & 0 & \cdots & \sigma_I^2
\end{bmatrix}
\begin{bmatrix}
x_1 \\
x_2 \\
x_3 \\
\cdot \\
\cdot \\
\cdot \\
x_{n+1}
\end{bmatrix}
= \text{var}\,(r_p). \quad (7.9d)
$$

The diagonal coefficients in equation (7.9d) matrix can be inverted with less computation than a full covariance matrix. This computational ease leads to considerable savings, particularly in large portfolio problems.

Using the relations above, Sharpe's simplified model may be solved by formulating it as a Lagrangian objective function: Maximize

$$
z = \phi E(r_p) - \text{var}\,(r_p) + \lambda_1 \left(\sum_{i=1}^{n} x_i - 1\right) + \lambda_2 \left(\sum_{i=1}^{n} x_i b_i - x_{n+1}\right), \quad (7.10)
$$

where $E(r_p)$ is defined by equation (7.8a) and $\phi$ is the investor's risk preference coefficient as explained in Section 6.2. Larger values of $\phi$ represent more aggressiveness—that is, a flatter indifference line in Fig. 6.6 on page 115. Var $(r_p)$ is defined by equation (7.9c); the first Lagrangian constraint $(\lambda_1)$ assures that equation (2.7) is not violated; and the second Lagrangian $(\lambda_2)$ constraint assures that equation (7.6) holds. Expanding the objective function (7.10) yields equation (7.10a): Maximize

$$
z = \phi \sum_{i=1}^{n+1} x_i a_i - \sum_{i=1}^{n+1} x_i^2 \,\text{var}\,(r_i) + \lambda_1 \left(\sum_{i=1}^{n} x_i - 1\right)
$$

$$
+ \lambda_2 \left(\sum_{i=1}^{n} x_i b_i - x_{n+1}\right). \quad (7.10a)
$$

Equations (7.10) and (7.10a) are analogous to equations (6.10) and (6.10a) in the full-covariance model solved by the calculus method shown in Section 6.2 on page 110.

## C. Numerical Example for Single-Index Model

Consider a simplified solution to a two-security portfolio problem. Using Sharpe's single-index model for comparison, the objective function for $n = 2$ is shown as equation (7.11): Maximize

$$
\begin{aligned}
z = {} & \phi x_1 a_1 + \phi x_2 a_2 + \phi x_3 a_3 - x_1^2 \operatorname{var}(r_1) - x_2^2 \operatorname{var}(r_2) \\
& - x_3^2 \operatorname{var}(r_3) + \lambda_1 x_1 + \lambda_1 x_2 - \lambda_1 + \lambda_2 x_1 b_1 \\
& + \lambda_2 x_2 b_2 - \lambda_2 x_3.
\end{aligned}
\tag{7.11}
$$

Notice the terms containing $a_3$ and var $(r_3)$ in equation (7.11). The simplified model is able to omit all the covariance terms in the full Markowitz model by substituting the relationship with the index instead. The optimal portfolio using the simplified model depends on the forecasted expected value and variance of the index. As the forecasted index changes, the optimum portfolio will change. This feature provides valuable opportunities for sensitivity analysis, which will be discussed later.[10]

There are five variables in equation (7.11), the three weights and the two Lagrangian multipliers. All other quantities are parameters (that is, constants). Taking the first-order partial derivatives with respect to the five variables in equation (7.11) yields the following five equations, which are linear in the five variables:

$$
\frac{\partial z}{\partial x_1} = \phi a_1 - 2x_1 \operatorname{var}(r_1) + \lambda_1 + \lambda_2 b_1 = 0,
$$

$$
\frac{\partial z}{\partial x_2} = \phi a_2 - 2x_2 \operatorname{var}(r_2) + \lambda_1 + \lambda_2 b_2 = 0,
$$

$$
\frac{\partial z}{\partial x_3} = \phi a_3 - 2x_3 \operatorname{var}(r_3) - \lambda_2 = 0,
\tag{7.12}
$$

$$
\frac{\partial z}{\partial \lambda_1} = x_1 + x_2 - 1 = 0,
$$

$$
\frac{\partial z}{\partial \lambda_2} = x_1 b_1 + x_2 b_2 - x_3 = 0.
$$

---

[10]Later in this chapter it is shown how the optimum weights in the simplified model can be made a function of the index. These formulations allow the portfolio analyst to see how the optimum weights vary with the expectations about the index of market activity. See Table 10.1 on page 134.

The five linear equations (7.12) may be rewritten equivalently in matrix form as equation (7.12a):

$$
\begin{bmatrix}
-2 \operatorname{var}(r_1) & 0 & 0 & 1 & b_1 \\
0 & -2 \operatorname{var}(r_2) & 0 & 1 & b_2 \\
0 & 0 & -2 \operatorname{var}(r_3) & 0 & -1 \\
1 & 1 & 0 & 0 & 0 \\
b_1 & b_2 & -1 & 0 & 0
\end{bmatrix}
\cdot
\begin{bmatrix}
x_1 \\ x_2 \\ x_3 \\ \lambda_1 \\ \lambda_2
\end{bmatrix}
=
\begin{bmatrix}
-\phi a_1 \\ -\phi a_2 \\ -\phi a_3 \\ 1 \\ 0
\end{bmatrix}
\quad (7.12a)
$$

Using Cramer's rule to solve for $x_1$ proceeds.

$$
x_1 = \frac{
\begin{vmatrix}
-\phi a_1 & 0 & 0 & 1 & b_1 \\
-\phi a_2 & -2 \operatorname{var}(r_2) & 0 & 1 & b_2 \\
-\phi a_3 & 0 & -2 \operatorname{var}(r_3) & 0 & -1 \\
1 & 1 & 0 & 0 & 0 \\
0 & b_2 & -1 & 0 & 0
\end{vmatrix}
}{
\begin{vmatrix}
-2 \operatorname{var}(r_1) & 0 & 0 & 1 & b_1 \\
0 & -2 \operatorname{var}(r_2) & 0 & 1 & b_2 \\
0 & 0 & -2 \operatorname{var}(r_3) & 0 & -1 \\
1 & 1 & 0 & 0 & 0 \\
b_1 & b_2 & -1 & 0 & 0
\end{vmatrix}
},
$$

$$
x_1 = \frac{
\begin{aligned}
&-2b_2^2 \operatorname{var}(r_3) - 2 \operatorname{var}(r_2) + \phi a_2 + b_2 \phi a_3 \\
&+ 2b_1 b_2 \operatorname{var}(r_3) - \phi a_1 - b_1 \phi a_3
\end{aligned}
}{
\begin{aligned}
&-2b_2^2 \operatorname{var}(r_3) - 2 \operatorname{var}(r_2) + 4b_1 b_2 \operatorname{var}(r_3) \\
&- 2b_1^2 \operatorname{var}(r_3) - 2 \operatorname{var}(r_1)
\end{aligned}
}. \quad (7.13)
$$

Similarly, $x_2$ is found as shown in equation (7.14).

$$
x_2 = \frac{
\begin{aligned}
&b_1 \phi a_3 - \phi a_2 + \phi a_1 + b_2 \phi a_3 + b_1 b_2^2 \operatorname{var}(r_3) \\
&- b_1^2 2 \operatorname{var}(r_3) - 2 \operatorname{var}(r_1)
\end{aligned}
}{
\begin{aligned}
&-2b_2^2 \operatorname{var}(r_3) - 2 \operatorname{var}(r_2) + 4b_1 b_2 \operatorname{var}(r_3) \\
&- 2b_1^2 \operatorname{var}(r_3) - 2 \operatorname{var}(r_1)
\end{aligned}
}. \quad (7.14)
$$

To compare the solution attained with Sharpe's simplified model and the solution attained in Sections 6.1 and 6.2 using the full variance–covariance matrix, the same data will be used here. Assuming $b_1 = b_2 = 0$ and substituting $a_1 = E(r_1) = 0.05$, $a_2 = E(r_2) = 0.15$, $\sigma_{11} = 0.04$, $\sigma_{22} = 0.16$, $a_3 = E(r_I) = 0.1$, $\operatorname{var}(r_I) = 0.1 = \operatorname{var}(r_3)$, into equations (7.13) and (7.14) yields equations (7.13a) and (7.14a).

$$x_1 = 0.8 - 0.25\phi, \tag{7.13a}$$

$$\frac{x_2 = 0.2 + 0.25\phi}{1.0 + 0.} \tag{7.14a}$$

Equations (7.13a) and (7.14a) are identical to the formulas for the weights found in Section 6.2. As long as $b_1 = b_2 = 0$, equations (7.13a) and (7.14a) will continue to equal the weight formulas attained in equations (6.20) and (6.21). However, if the parameters are changed so that $b_1 \neq b_2$, the weight formulas will differ from those of Section 6.2. For example, if $b_2 = 1$ instead of zero, equations (7.13a) and (7.14a) would change to give more weight to lower-risk asset 1:

$$x_1 = \tfrac{13}{15} - \phi/3, \tag{7.15}$$

$$\frac{x_2 = \tfrac{2}{15} + \phi/3}{1.0 + 0.} \tag{7.16}$$

The weights' formulas in equations (7.13a) and (7.14a) sum to 1, as do the weights in (7.15) and (7.16). The weight of the security with the higher return increases with $\phi$. And, equations (7.13a) and (7.14a) are identical to those attained in Sections 6.1 and 6.2. It appears that Sharpe's simplified model yields identical solutions to the full-covariance model—but this is not true. Only because of the trivial nature of this numerical example did the solutions work out identically. However, the simplified solution does not differ a great deal from the solutions using the full variance–covariance matrix. Comparisons are made later in this chapter.

### D. Sensitivity Analysis with the Index as the Variable

Equations (7.13) and (7.14) or the weights' formulas from the full-covariance model could be solved with $\phi$ set to some value and treating $a_3 = E(r_I)$ and var $(r_3)$ = var $(r_I)$ as variables. Then, by varying the forecasted parameters of the index, it is possible to see precisely how sensitive the optimum portfolio is to these forecasted parameters. If the solution is very sensitive to the index forecast, it might be desirable to devote additional effort to ensure the accuracy of the forecast.

For example, setting $\phi = 1$, $b_1 = 1$, $b_2 = 2$, $a_1 = E(r_1) = 0.05$, $a_2 = E(r_2) = 0.15$, $\sigma_{11} = 0.04$, $\sigma_{22} = 0.16$ in equations (7.13) and (7.14) results in equations (7.17) and (7.18):

$$x_1 = \frac{-4 \text{ var } (r_3) - 0.22 + a_3}{-2 \text{ var } (r_3) - 0.4}, \tag{7.17}$$

$$x_2 = \frac{+2 \text{ var } (r_3) - 0.18 - a_3}{-2 \text{ var } (r_3) - 0.4}. \tag{7.18}$$

Equations (7.17) and (7.18) sum to 1; they are like the other weights' formulas derived above except the expected value, $E(r_I) = a_3$, and the variance of the index, var $(r_3) =$ var $(r_I)$, are treated as variables rather than treating $\phi$ as a variable. If var $(r_3)$ is set at 0.1 and $a_3$ is varied from 0.1 to 0.2, the optimum weights shift toward more of security 2 (that is, $x_2$)—the high-risk, high-return security. The values of equations (7.17) and (7.18) are shown in Table 7.1 as $a_3$ varies. Clearly, when the index is expected to rise, the resulting portfolio will reflect these expectations appropriately.

TABLE 7.1

|  | Bearish $E(r_I) =$ Low $a_{n+1}$ | Bullish $E(r_I) =$ High $a_{n+1}$ |
|---|---|---|
| Given Parameters: | $a_3 = 0.1, V_3 = 0.1$ | $a_3 = 0.2, V_3 = 0.1$ |
| Resulting portfolio: | $x_1 = \frac{26}{30}$ | $x_1 = \frac{21}{30}$ |
|  | $x_2 = \frac{4}{30}$ | $x_2 = \frac{9}{30}$ |
| $x_1 + x_2$ totals: | 1.0 | 1.0 |

## 7.2  Performance Evaluation of the Single-Index Model

The mere existence of Sharpe's single-index portfolio analysis model naturally raises the question as to how the simplified model performs relative to Markowitz's full-covariance model. As a result, in the same paper in which he first published the simplified model, Sharpe compared and contrasted the computational costs and composition of the efficient portfolios generated by his simplified approach and Markowitz's full-covariance model.[11]

Sharpe found that, computationally, the simplified model is extremely economical. Using an IBM 7090 computer, the simplified portfolio model was able to analyze a 100-security portfolio in 30 seconds while it took Markowitz's full-covariance algorithm 33 minutes to solve the same problem. That is, the simplified model did the job in about 1.5 percent of the running time required for the full Markowitz model. This is a rather awesome savings, especially when the security analysis savings involved in using the simplified model are also considerable. However, much faster and larger computers which have much smaller costs per computation are now in widespread use. This technological advancement depreciates the computational savings somewhat—but not completely.

In comparing the composition of the efficient portfolios delineated with the simplified model and the full Markowitz model from a 20-stock universe, Sharpe found the two sets of efficient portfolios to be very much alike. Both algorithms selected the same five out of 20 stocks, and in about the same

[11]W. F. Sharpe, "A Simplified Model," Secs. 7 and 8.

proportions at each level of portfolio return.[12] A somewhat similar study focused on the ability of the two competing portfolio analysis models to generate the dominant and most consistently efficient portfolios.

Frankfurter, Phillips, and Seagle (FPS, hereafter) published a Monte Carlo study of the Sharpe and the Markowitz efficient portfolios based on four common stocks.[13] This small universe of stocks was used to keep the computations from becoming prohibitive. Taking empirical statistics for these four stocks and using them as parameters, FPS simulated the passage of time by generating time-series returns for the stocks from probability distributions of returns having the four stocks' return parameters. From these returns, averages, variances, and covariance statistics were calculated for the Markowitz model inputs. The alpha, beta, and residual variance statistics associated with the single-index market model, equation (4.4), were also calculated for the simplified portfolio analysis. Next, the Markowitz and Sharpe efficient portfolios were derived and recorded for comparison. This simulation was replicated hundreds of times over simulated sample periods 5, 10, and 19 years in length. Figure 7.2 contains summary statistics of the results.

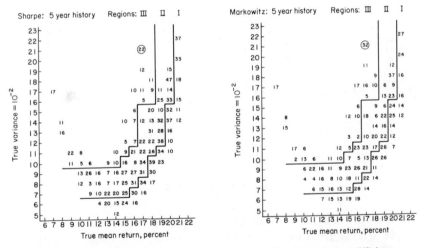

Figure 7.2. Relative Frequency (Percent) with which Portfolios Appear Efficient in Sample Trials

*Source:* G. M. Frankfurter, H. E. Phillips, and J. P. Seagle, "Performance of the Sharpe Portfolio Selection Model," *Journal of Financial and Quantitative Analysis*, June 1976, pp. 195–204, Fig. 1.

---

[12]Ibid., Figs. 6a and 6b.

[13]G. M. Frankfurter, H. E. Phillips, and J. P. Seagle, "Performance of the Sharpe Portfolio Selection Model: A Comparison," *Journal of Financial and Quantitative Analysis*, June 1976, pp. 195–204.

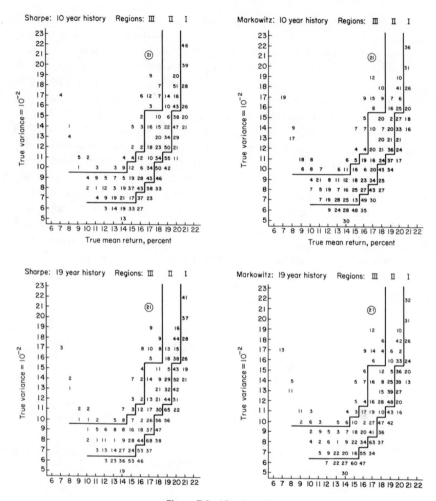

Figure 7.2. (Continued)

The three rows of figures in Fig. 7.2 represent the 5-, 10-, and 19-year sample periods, from top to bottom, respectively, which were simulated by FPS. The column of three figures on the left of Fig. 7.2 shows results from Sharpe's model, while the right-hand three figures summarize the Markowitz results. The circled number in all six small figures represents a portfolio with $E(r) = 17.0$ percent and var $(r_p) = 21.0$ in $[E(r), \sigma]$ space. The circled portfolios are dominated by any portfolios lying to the right and/or below them. For the 5-year simulated sample, the circled portfolio appeared on the efficient frontier 22 percent of the time using Sharpe's model, and 32 percent of the time using the Markowitz model. The other numbers in Fig. 7.2 are interpreted similarly.

The six small figures in Fig. 7.2 are all similarly divided into three regions. The circled portfolios are in Region III; this region contains the least efficient portfolios. Region I is the dominant region—it contains portfolios that are close to or on the efficient frontier attainable with the four stock universe. Region II contains the mediocre portfolios. FPS summarized the findings displayed in Fig. 7.2 as follows:

> For each analytical process, the relative frequency with which the superior portfolios (Region I) appear on the efficient frontier in sample trials increases monotonically with the length of the sample history. For any length of sample history, however, the Sharpe approach, better than the Markowitz approach, demonstrates the ability to identify the superior portfolios of Region I and to discriminate against the inferior portfolios of Region III. But, while the Sharpe approach is nowhere worse than the Markowitz approach, its advantages are most striking for short histories. When as many as 19 annual observations are available, the results obtained by the two analytical processes are not significantly different.[14]

Of course, the FPS conclusions are from only one study. However, their superior performance results for the simplified model combined with the model's computational efficiencies are too appealing for portfolio analysts to ignore.

### 7.3  Multiindex Models

Between the simplicity of Sharpe's single-index model and the comprehensive full-covariance model of Markowitz lies a spectrum of possible models. Two, three, four, or more indices can be used. In effect, the Markowitz model using the full variance–covariance matrix without any simplifications uses each security as an index. Of course, the more indices used, the less simple the model and the less computational savings that can be achieved.

Intuitively, it seems as if a multiindex model should generate a more efficient set of portfolios than a single-index model, since it utilizes more information about the interrelationships. In this case, the loss of computational savings may be more than offset by the gain in the Markowitz efficiency of the solution. The research to date is not clear as to whether or not this balance is, in fact, achieved. One study showed that the single-index model produced more efficient portfolios than a multiindex model.[15]

---

[14]Frankfurter, Phillips, and Seagle, "Performance of the Sharpe Portfolio Selection Model" pp. 201–202.

[15]K. J. Cohen and G. A. Pogue, "An Empirical Evaluation of Alternative Selection Models," *Journal of Business*, Vol. 40, No. 2 1967, pp. 166–193. Cohen and Pogue concluded that their result was due to the homogeneity of their sample—that is, all common stocks. For more heterogeneous samples they suggested multiindex models.

Although multiindex models use several indices, the performance of each security in the portfolio is assumed to be related to only *one of the indices*. The index that is most highly correlated with an asset is usually the best index with which to functionally relate that security to the rest of the portfolio. Thus, in portfolios considering different types of assets (such as common stocks, bonds, commodities, real estate, and others) that are not all highly correlated with each other or with a common index the multiindex models are particularly appropriate.

To reveal the construction of a multiindex model, a two-index model is presented below. Models using more indices are direct extensions of the two-index model.

## A.  Two-Index Model Development

Consider a two-index simplified portfolio analysis model with $N$ securities to be analyzed. Denote the first index $I_1$, and the second index $I_2$. These two indices might be GNP in dollars ($I_1$) and rates of return on the Standard and Poor's 500 Stocks Average ($I_2$) or anything else that has a significant correlation with the securities' returns. Assume the first $M$ securities, numbered $1, 2, \ldots, M$, where $M < N$, correlate most highly with index 1, $I_1$. Assume the remaining $(N - M)$ securities numbered $M + 1, M + 2, \ldots, N$ are correlated most highly with index 2, $I_2$. Then the return on the $i$th security can be written

$$r_i = a_{i1} + b_{i1}I_1 + e_{i1} \qquad \text{if } 0 < i \leq M, \qquad (7.19)$$

$$r_i = a_{i2} + b_{i2}I_2 + e_{i2} \qquad \text{if } M < i \leq N, \qquad (7.20)$$

where $a_{i1}$ and $b_{i1}$ are the regression parameters for the $i$th security which is correlated with $I_1$ and $e_{i1}$ is a random-error term (with the five assumptions pertaining to the error term listed earlier in this chapter still applicable). Equation (7.20) is the similar regression model for $I_2$ and securities $M + 1$, $M + 2, \ldots, N$. Both (7.19) and (7.20) are analogous to equation (4.4).

The variance of the $i$th security is defined below in equations (7.21) and (7.22).

$$\text{var}(r_i) = (b_{i1})^2 \, \text{var}(r_{I_1}) + \sigma^2_{(r_i \mid I_1)} \qquad \text{if } i \leq M, \qquad (7.21)$$

$$\text{var}(r_i) = (b_{i2})^2 \, \text{var}(r_{I_2}) + \sigma^2_{(r_i \mid I_2)} \qquad \text{if } i > M. \qquad (7.22)$$

The covariance terms are defined as:

$$\text{cov}(r_i, r_j) = (b_{i1})(b_{j1}) \, \text{var}(r_{I_1}) \qquad \text{if } i \text{ and } j \leq M \qquad (7.23)$$

$$\text{cov}(r_i, r_j) = (b_{i1})(b_{j2}) \, \text{cov}(I_1, I_2) \qquad \text{if } \begin{cases} i \leq M \text{ and } j > M \\ \text{or } j \leq M \text{ and } i > M, \end{cases} \qquad (7.24)$$

$$\text{cov}(r_i, r_j) = (b_{i2})(b_{j2}) \, \text{var}(r_{I_2}) \qquad \text{if } i \text{ and } j \geq M, \qquad (7.25)$$

where cov $(I_1, I_2)$ is the covariance of the rates of change in the two indices. In the simple case that the two indices are not correlated with each other, the following simplifications are possible:

$$x_{n+1} = \sum_{i=1}^{M} x_i b_{i1},$$ (7.26)

$$x_{n+2} = \sum_{i=M+1}^{N} x_i b_{i2}.$$ (7.27)

Using equations (7.26) and (7.27), the return and variance of the portfolio can be expressed as

$$E(r_p) = \sum_{i=1}^{N+2} a_i x_i,$$ (7.28)

$$\text{var } (r_p) = \sum_{i=1}^{N+2} x_i^2 \text{ var } (e_i),$$ (7.29)

where $E(r_{I_1}) = a_{n+1}$ and $a_{n+2} = E(r_{I_2})$ denote expected returns on the indices, and var $(r_{n+1})$ and var $(r_{n+2})$ measure the uncertainty surrounding the estimates of the indices.

The Lagrangian objective function to be maximized as shown in equations (7.30) and (7.31):

$$z = \phi E(r_p) - \text{var } (r_p) + \lambda_1 \left( \sum_{i=1}^{N} x_i - 1 \right)$$

$$+ \lambda_2 \left( \sum_{i=1}^{M} x_i b_i - x_{n+1} \right) + \lambda_3 \left( \sum_{i=m+1}^{N} x_i b_i - x_{n+2} \right),$$ (7.30)

$$= \phi \sum_{i=1}^{n+2} x_i a_i - \sum_{i=1}^{n+2} x_1 \text{ var } (e_i) + \lambda_1 \left( \sum_{i=1}^{N} x_i - 1 \right)$$

$$+ \lambda_2 \left( \sum_{i=1}^{M} x_i b_i - x_{n+1} \right) + \lambda_3 \left( \sum_{i=m+1}^{N} x_i b_i - x_{n+2} \right).$$ (7.31)

### B. Comparing the One- and Two-Index Models' Portfolios

Limited work has been done to determine whether the loss of computational efficiency resulting from introducing additional indices is offset by an increase in the efficiency of the portfolios generated. As mentioned above, Cohen and Pogue found that the single-index model outperformed a two-index model—a rather surprising conclusion. Wallingford, on the other hand, found that two-index models generated more efficient portfolios than single-index models.[16] Wallingford's sample was only 20 securities; he experimented with simulated data and actual historical data.

Figure 7.3 shows efficient frontiers Cohen and Pogue generated with Sharpe's single-index model, a multiindex model, and the Markowitz full-

---

[16]B. A. Wallingford, "A Survey and Comparison of Portfolio Selection Models," *Journal of Financial and Quantitative Analysis,* June 1967, pp. 85–106.

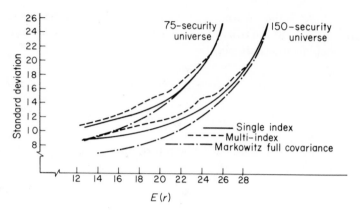

Figure 7.3. Different Efficient Frontiers Generated by Cohen and Pogue (their Fig. 2)

covariance model for two universes.[17] In one universe, 150 randomly selected common stocks were analyzed for possible inclusion in the efficient set. In the other universe, a randomly selected subset of 75 securities from the 150-security universe was used. Figure 7.3 shows clearly that the desirability of the efficient frontier generated varies directly with the size of the sample analyzed.

Cohen and Pogue, like Wallingford, find that the Markowitz full-covariance model generates the dominant efficient frontier. Unlike Wallingford, Cohen and Pogue point out that their sample is homogeneous (that is, only common stocks) enough that it is amenable to the single-index assumptions.[18]

Dr. G. Alexander has published empirical studies that clarify some ambiguities between the Cohen and Pogue results and the results reported by Wallingford. First, Alexander's evidence indicates that the single-index market model using the simplified diagonal covariance matrix, and also, the multiple-index model, are both able to generate efficient frontier portfolios that are highly similar to the efficient portfolios generated using the

---

[17]K. J. Cohen and G. A. Pogue, "An Empirical Evaluation of Alternative Selection Models," Fig. 2, pp. 178–181.

[18]More recently, B. K. Stone theorized a two-parameter model which explicitly deals with interest rates and market risk: "Systematic Interest-Rate Risk in a Two-Index Model of Returns," *Journal of Financial and Quantitative Analysis*, November 1974, pp. 709–721. Stone's model has been tested empirically with favorable results. However, the model has not yet been applied to the generation of an efficient frontier. J. D. Martin and A. J. Keown, "Interest Rate Sensitivity and Portfolio Risk," *Journal of Financial and Quantitative Analysis*, June 1977, pp. 181–195. W. P. Lloyd and R. A. Shick, "A Test of Stone's Two-Index Model of Returns," *Journal of Financial and Quantitative Analysis*, September 1977, pp. 363–376.

full-covariance Markowitz model. Second, Alexander found that the multiple-index model was able to generate efficient portfolios that dominated those obtained with the single-index model when heterogeneous assets (namely, common stocks, corporate bonds, and U.S. Treasury Bonds) were analyzed.[19] But, when a sample limited to common stocks is being analyzed, the single-index model used with a well-diversified stock market index generates more desirable efficient portfolios than does the multiple-index model.[20] These findings bode well for users of the simplified models.

### 7.4 Conclusions

In addition to the single-index and multiple-index models explained above, other simplified models to do portfolio analysis exist which are even simpler. By making different assumptions about the return generating process (namely, the characteristic regression line) it is possible to logically develop numerous simplified portfolio analysis models.

Sharpe developed a simplified model that ignored diversifiable risk completely. This portfolio analysis model was designed to be formulated as a linear programming problem.[21] And, for small problems involving few securities, the model could readily be solved graphically.

Jacob went on to specify and empirically test several other simplified portfolio analysis models. In particular, Jacob developed a linear programming model for small investors which delineates efficient portfolios composed of very few securities.[22] Some people find these highly simplified and special-purpose models useful if they (1) have small computer facilities, (2) have linear programming software but not QP software, or (3) have only limited access to input statistics for portfolio analysis.[23]

---

[19]G. J. Alexander, "Mixed Security Testing of Alternative Portfolio Selection Models," *Journal of Financial and Quantitative Analysis*, December 1977, pp. 817–832.

[20]G. J. Alexander, "A Re-Evaluation of Alternative Portfolio Selection Models Applied to Common Stocks," *Journal of Financial and Quantitative Analysis*, March 1978, pp. 71–78.

[21]W. F. Sharpe, "A Linear Programming Algorithm for Mutual Fund Portfolio Selection," *Management Science*, Vol. 13, 1967, pp. 499–510.

[22]N. L. Jacob, "A Limited-Diversification Portfolio Selection Model for the Small Investor," *Journal of Finance*, June 1974, pp. 847—856.

[23]See also E. J. Elton, M. J. Gruber, and M. W. Padberg, "Simple Rules for Optimal Portfolio Selection: The Multi-Group Case," *Journal of Financial and Quantitative Analysis*, September 1977, pp. 329–346; S. A. Buser, "Mean–Variance Portfolio Selection with Either a Singular or a Non-singular Variance–Covariance Matrix," *Journal of Financial and Quantitative Analysis*, September 1977, pp. 347–362; E. J. Elton, M. J. Gruber, and M. W. Padberg, "Optimal Portfolio Selection via Simple Decision Rules," *Journal of Finance*, December 1977.

**Selected References**

Cohen, K. J., and G. Pogue, "An Emprical Evaluation of Alternative Portfolio Models," *Journal of Business*, Vol. 40, No. 1, 1967, pp. 166–193. Reprinted in *Security Evaluation and Portfolio Analysis*, edited by E. J. Elton and M. J. Gruber. Englewood Cliffs, N.J.: Prentice-Hall, Inc., 1972.

The Cohen–Pogue article explains, analyzes, and tests empirically the single-index and a multiple-index model for simplified portfolio analysis. Algebra and statistics are employed.

Jacob, N. L., "A Limited Diversification Portfolio Selection Model for the Small Investor," *Journal of Finance*, June 1974, pp. 847–856.

This article proposes and tests empirically several simplified portfolio analysis models. The models require minimal input data and computational resources.

## Questions and Problems

1. List three sources where the general public can purchase monthly stock price data over the past five years for the 1000 largest stocks traded on the New York Stock Exchange. What would the data cost from each of these sources?

2. Markowitz's full-covariance model for portfolio analysis requires $n$ average returns, $n$ variances, and $(n^2 - n)/2$ covariances in order to analyze $n$ possible securities and delineate the efficient frontier. What input data are needed to analyze $n$ assets using the single-index model? Using a two-index model? Explain the differences.

3. It is possible to do simplified portfolio analysis without a computer when 20 securities are being considered as possible investments. How about 50 securities? How could the noncomputerized analysis be done? Would it yield accurate solutions? Explain.

4. Simplified portfolio analysis models have been developed for several reasons.

   (a) To minimize computer running time used in delineating efficient portfolios.
   (b) To enable portfolio analysis to be done on smaller computers.
   (c) To delineate efficient portfolios (which are only slightly dominated by efficient portfolios obtained with Markowitz's full-covariance model), but which require far fewer input statistics.

The original simplified portfolio analysis models were developed in the early 1960s when the second generation of computers (using transitors, small memories, and primitive input–output hardware) were just emerging. Empirical data were costly to obtain in the early 1960s, too. However, by the end of the 1970 decade, empirical data and QP programs were widely available. Also, huge third-generation computers which operated more than 100 times faster than the second-generation computers and had sophisticated peripheral equipment were also widely available to buy or rent. In light of these developments, do you think the cost savings associated with the simplified portfolio analysis algorithms are worth the small loss in efficiency which is associated with these portfolios? Do a benefit–cost study to answer this question.

# Section Three

# PORTFOLIO THEORY

THE chapters of Section Three move on to a higher level of abstraction than the portfolio analysis chapters in Section Two. The portfolio theories of Section Three presume (1) that the probabilistic risk concepts explained in Section One are generally valid, and (2) that all investors prefer Markowitz efficient portfolios and work to delineate and acquire shares in them. Given these two additional assumptions, Chapter VIII traces out the asset pricing implications of portfolio analysis—an equilibrium capital asset pricing model is developed. Chapter IX delves into various ideas about how a portfolio should be diversified. Chapter X explains several competing single-parameter portfolio performance evaluation tools which consider risk and return simultaneously—these performance measures yield individual index numbers for each portfolio which are suitable for performance rankings.

```
8888888888888888888888888888888888888888888888888888888888888888888888888888888888888888888888
8888888888888888888888888888888888888888888888888888888888888888888888888888888888888888888888
888888888888888888888888    8888888888888    888    888    888    8888888888888888888888888888
888888888888888888888888888    88888888888    8888    888    888    8888888888888888888888888888
88888888888888888888888888    888888888    88888    888    888    8888888888888888888888888888
88888888888888888888888888888    8888888    888888    888    888    8888888888888888888888888888
8888888888888888888888888888888    88888    8888888    888    888    8888888888888888888888888888
8888888888888888888888888888888888    888    88888888    888    888    8888888888888888888888888888
88888888888888888888888888888888888    '8    888888888    888    888    8888888888888888888888888888
888888888888888888888888888888888888888    8888888888    888    888    8888888888888888888888888888
8888888888888888888888888888888888888888    88888888888    888    888    8888888888888888888888888888
8888888888888888888888888888888888888888888888888888888888888888888888888888888888888888888888
8888888888888888888888888888888888888888888888888888888888888888888888888888888888888888888888
```

# Capital Market Theory

Aﬀﬃ Markowitz developed the two-parameter portfolio analysis model, analysts began to wonder what were the stock market implications if all investors were to use the two-parameter model.[1] As a result, what shall be referred to here as *capital market theory* was developed. The capital market theory set out here is not the only theory that could be called a "capital market theory." Such notions as the Dow theory and many others could be called capital market theories, too. Perhaps a more descriptive title for this chapter would have been "The Capital Market Theory of the Two-Parameter Model." However, for the sake of brevity, it will simply be called *capital market theory*.

---

[1]The reader who wishes to follow the original development of capital market theory is directed to the following items, especially the third (the list is not exhaustive): Harry M. Markowitz, *Portfolio Selection*, Cowles Foundation Monograph 16 (New York: John Wiley and Sons, Inc., 1959), pp. 98–101; W. F. Sharpe, "A Simplified Model for Portfolio Analysis," *Management Science*, Vol. 9, No. 2, 1963, pp. 277–293; see especially Part 4, on the diagonal model. Reprinted in many readings books; W. F. Sharpe, "Capital Asset Prices: A Theory of Market Equilibrium Under Conditions of Risk," *Journal of Finance*, September 1964, pp. 425–442; reprinted in S. H. Archer and C. A. D'Ambrosio, *The Theory of Business Finance* (New York: Macmillan Publishing Co., Inc., 1967), Reading 42; J. L. Treynor, "How to Rate Management of Investment Funds," *Harvard Business Review*, January–February 1965, pp. 63–75; John Lintner, "Security Prices, Risk, and the Maximal Gains from Diversification," *Journal of Finance*, December 1965, pp. 587–615; E. F. Fama, "Risk, Return and Equilibrium: Some Clarifying Comments," *Journal of Finance*, March 1968, pp. 29–40.

## 8.1 Assumptions Underlying the Theory

Capital market theory is based on the assumptions underlying portfolio analysis, since the theory is essentially a description of the logical (that is, mathematical and economic) implications of portfolio analysis. These assumptions are as follows:

1. The rate of return from an investment adequately summarizes the outcome from the investment, and investors see the various possible rates of return in a probabilistic fashion—that is, a probability distribution of rates of return.

2. Investors' risk estimates are proportional to the variability of return they visualize.

3. Investors are willing to base their decisions on only two parameters of the probability distribution of returns: the expected return and the variance (or its square root, the standard deviation) of returns. Symbolically, $U = f(E(r), \sigma)$, where $U$ denotes the investor's utility. For any risk class, investors prefer a higher to a lower rate of return. Symbolically, $\partial U/\partial E(r) > 0$. Or, conversely, among all securities with the same rate of return, investors prefer less, rather than more, risk. Symbolically, $\partial U/\partial \sigma < 0$.

This assumption is the logical implication of positive but diminishing marginal utility of wealth or returns combined with either (a) a quadratic utility function, or (b) rates of return that are distributed according to a two-parameter distribution such as the normal distribution.

4. The assets and liabilities are reviewed at the end of a one-period investment period with an eye toward maximizing the portfolio owner's utility over that one, or perhaps more, periods.

5. The assets and liabilities are perfectly liquid. That is, the assets and liabilities have infinite elasticity of supply, so that the portfolio's purchases and sales will not affect the market prices and expected returns.

The preceding assumptions are not new to economic model builders. But, the capital market theory is based on some new assumptions which are listed below.

An investor who conforms to the preceding assumptions will prefer Markowitz-efficient portfolios over other portfolios. Such investors will be referred to as *Markowitz-efficient investors*. With this background, it is possible to begin to discuss capital market theory. Following is a fairly exhaustive list of the assumptions necessary to generate the theory.

1. All investors are Markowitz-efficient diversifiers who delineate and seek to attain the efficient frontier.

2. Money may be borrowed or lent at the risk-free rate of interest denoted $R$. The return on short-term U.S. government bonds may be used as a proxy for $R$. Money may not be borrowed at any other rate.

3. "Idealized uncertainty" prevails. That is, all investors visualize identical probability distributions for future rates of return—or "homogeneous expectations."

4. All investors have the same one-period investment horizon.
5. All investments are infinitely divisible: fractional shares may be purchased in any portfolio or any individual asset.
6. No taxes and no transactions cost for buying and selling securities exist.
7. No inflation and no change in the level of interest rates exist—or all changes are fully anticipated.
8. The capital markets are in equilibrium.

The reader who is unaccustomed to economic analysis is probably confused and discouraged by a theory that begins with a list of unrealistic assumptions. Such should not be the case. These assumptions are only necessary to get started and will be relaxed later. The assumptions provide a concrete foundation upon which a theory can be derived by applying the forces of logic, intuition, and mathematics. Without these assumptions, the analysis would degenerate into a polemic discussion. Discussions of which historical facts, what folklore, and which institutions were significant, which were insignificant, what their relationships were, and what conclusions might be reached by a "reasonable man" are not very productive. Such thinking usually gets bogged down short of the objective.

Traditionally, economists have based their analysis on as few and as simple assumptions as possible. Then a theory is derived with conclusions and implications that are incontestable, given the assumptions. Then the assumptions are relaxed one at a time to determine what can be expected in more realistic circumstances.

### 8.2   The Capital Market Line

With little loss of realism, an opportunity set such as the one shown in Fig. 8.1 can be assumed.[2] This opportunity set is composed of the individual investments found in the capital markets plus the infinite number of port-

---

[2]In some of the financial literature the reader will find Fig. 8.1 as produced here in Fig. 8.1 (Alternate). Of course, the two figures represent identical situations, merely having their axes switched. Figure 8.1 reflects the custom of placing the independent variable on the horizontal axis and the dependent variable on the vertical axis.

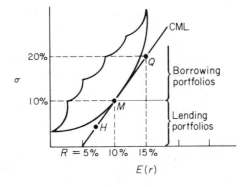

Figure 8.1. (Alternate)

folios that can be formed from these individual investments.[3] As was shown earlier (see Fig. 3.10), owing to the effects of diversification, the opportunity set will be composed of curves that are convex to the $E(r)$ axis. According to the assumption of idealized uncertainty (assumption 3), all investors will envision opportunity sets that are exactly identical. Thus, the following discussion can treat Fig. 8.1 as if it were clearly implanted in each investor's mind. This allows moot questions of investors' ignorance, different tax brackets, and so on to be postponed. The $E(r)$ is the cost of capital for the assets in the graph—it varies directly with the risk class of the asset in this model.

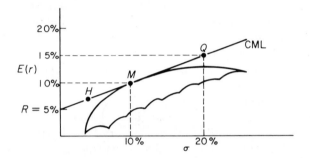

Figure 8.1. The Opportunity Set in Risk-Return Space

Assuming any amount of money may be borrowed and lent by anyone at rate $R$ (that is, assumption 2), the CML follows. The CML is generated by drawing a straight line out from the riskless rate $(R)$ into $(E(r), \sigma)$ space. This line is then swung down as far as possible until it is just tangent to the opportunity set as shown in Fig. 8.1. If $R$ or the opportunity set moves, the resulting CML would move, too. The point where the CML is tangent to the efficient frontier of the opportunity set is denoted point $M$.

Points between $R$ and $M$ on Fig. 8.1 represent *lending portfolios*. The portfolios are comprised of varying proportions of $R$ (for example, short-term U.S. government bonds held to maturity) and $M$. A point like $H$, located halfway between $R$ and $M$, represents a portfolio of half $R$ and half $M$.

Points on the CML that lie above $M$ represent *borrowing portfolios* (that is, leveraged portfolios), since their creation requires borrowing at rate $R$ to increase total investable capital. The total investable capital is then invested in $M$, and the return on equity and its variability (that is, risk) are increased. Consider a numerical example of how a leveraged portfolio's expected return and risk is determined to lie above $M$ on the CML.

---

[3]If the CML is thought of as representing the community's indifference line between risk and return, an interesting interpretation of $R$ is possible. The risk-free asset $R$ can be thought of as the *certainty equivalent* of the risky assets along the CML, such as $H$, $M$, and $Q$.

A.  Numerical Example of a Leveraged Portfolio

Suppose that one share of investment $M$ cost $1000 and offered a 50–50 chance of returning either $1000 or $1200. The expected return for the holding period is 10 percent:

$$E(r) = \sum_{i=1}^{2} p_i r_i = (0.5)\left(\frac{1000 - 1000}{1000}\right) + (0.5)\left(\frac{1200 - 1000}{1000}\right)$$

$$= (0.5)0 + (0.5)(20\%) = 0 + 10\% = 10 \text{ percent.}$$

The standard deviation of returns is 10 percent for $M$.

$$\sigma = \sqrt{\sum p_i [r_i - E(r)]^2} = \sqrt{(0.5)(0 - 0.1)^2 + (0.5)(0.2 - 0.1)^2}$$

$$= \sqrt{(0.5)(0.01) + (0.5)(0.01)} = \sqrt{0.01} = 0.1 = 10 \text{ percent.}$$

Now, if an investor borrows $1000 at $R = 5$ percent and buys a second share of $M$, he has a 50–50 chance of receiving $950 or $1350 on his $1000 of original equity, as follows:

| | Two Alternative Outcomes | |
| --- | --- | --- |
| | 1 | 2 |
| Original equity | $1000 | $1000 |
| Principal amount borrowed at 5% | 1000 | 1000 |
| Total amount invested in $M$ | $2000 | $2000 |
| Return on two shares of $M$ | $2000 | $2400 |
| Repayment of loan principal | ⟨1000⟩ | ⟨1000⟩ |
| Payment of interest at 5% | ⟨50⟩ | ⟨50⟩ |
| Net return on original equity | $950 | $1350 |
| Probability of outcome | 50% | 50% |

The expected return on $M$ leveraged is 15 percent. The calculations follow.

$$E(r) = \sum_{i=1}^{2} p_i r_i = (0.5)\left(\frac{950 - 1000}{1000}\right) + (0.5)\left(\frac{1350 - 1000}{1000}\right)$$

$$= (0.5)(-0.05\%) + (0.5)(35\%) = -2.5\% + 17.5\%$$

$$= 15 \text{ percent.}$$

The standard deviation of returns on the leveraged portfolio is 20 percent:

$$\sigma = \sqrt{\sum p_i [r_i - E(r_i)]^2} = \sqrt{(0.5)(-5\% - 15\%)^2 + (0.5)(35\% - 15\%)^2}$$

$$= \sqrt{(0.5)(-20\%)^2 + (0.5)(20\%)^2} = \sqrt{(0.5)(0.04) + (0.5)(0.04)}$$

$$= \sqrt{(0.02) + (0.02)} = \sqrt{0.04} = 0.2 = 20 \text{ percent.}$$

These results are shown graphically in Fig. 8.1 as point $Q$.

## B. The CML Is Linear

It is simple to prove the CML is linear in $(E(r), \sigma)$ space for all possible portfolios of $M$ and $R$. The expected return is a linear function:

$$E(r) = x_R R + (1 - x_R)E(r_M).$$

Since investment in $R$ has zero risk, $\sigma_R = 0$, the formula for the variance of a portfolio of $R$ and $M$ is a special case of equations (2.9) and (2.10).

$$\sigma = \sqrt{x_R^2 \sigma_R^2 + (1 - x_R)^2 \sigma_M^2 + 2x_R(1 - x_R)\sigma_{RM}},$$

which reduces to

$$\sigma = \sqrt{(1 - x_R)^2 \sigma_M^2} = (1 - x_R)\sigma_M \qquad \text{when } \sigma_R = 0.$$

Thus, the risk and expected return of any two-security portfolio containing one riskless asset $(R)$ is a linear function. So the CML must be linear in $(E(r), \sigma)$ space.[4]

## C. Unanimous Investment Decision

Since the CML dominates the opportunity set and the assumptions assure that all investors are rational and Markowitz-efficient, all investors will buy security $M$ in some combination (that is, they will seek to be on the CML). No other investment or combination of investments available are as efficient as $M$ or portfolios made of $M$. The decision to purchase $M$, the *investment decision,* will be unanimous among investors under the present assumptions.

After completing the investment decision, the investor will determine how to finance his purchase of $M$ based on his personal risk–return preferences. An aggressive investor, whose utility isoquants are graphed in the upper part of Fig. 8.2, will reach his highest level of utility $(U_3)$ by borrowing at $R$ to buy portfolio $B$. A conservative investor will prefer dividing his funds between $R$ and $M$ to form a lending portfolio: his highest indifference curve is just tangent to the CML at a point like $L$ in Fig. 8.2. The preceding observation is the basis for the separability theorem.

*Separability theorem, or, two-fund theorem*    The investment decision (to buy $M$) is independent of the financing decision (to buy some $R$ or leverage the portfolio).

---

[4]The slope of the CML is $dE(r)/d\sigma$. This slope is the constant

$$\frac{dE(r)}{d\sigma} = \frac{dE(r)}{dx_R} \cdot \frac{dx_R}{d\sigma}.$$

See Appendix 8A for completion of this proof that the CML is linear.

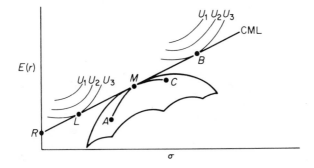

Figure 8.2. Risk-Return Indifference Curves Determine Financing

Given the situation and assumptions above, the theorem follows directly. The separability theorem implies that all investors, timid and aggressive, should hold the same mix of stocks in their portfolio. They should then use borrowing or lending to attain their preferred risk class. This conclusion is diametrically opposed to the popular "financial interior decorator" concept of portfolio management. The "financial interior decorator" school of portfolio management teaches that the portfolio manager should skillfully design a portfolio to match his client's personality. Thus, a timid investor's portfolio would contain a completely different set of securities than an aggressive investor's portfolio. This analysis shows that they should both own the same portfolio and differ only in financing it.

### 8.3 Market Portfolio[5]

Imagine a capital market such as the one graphed in Fig. 8.2, which is in equilibrium. By the definition of equilibrium in a market, excess demand is zero for all goods.[6] That is, all securities in the market must belong to some owner. Since all investors unanimously want $M$, it follows that in equilibrium $M$ must be a huge portfolio containing *all* marketable assets in the proportions $x_i$, where

$$x_i = \frac{\text{total value of the } i\text{th asset}}{\text{total value of all assets in the market}}$$

And, in equilibrium, $R$ must be the interest rate that equates the supply of, and demand for, loanable funds. Let $M$ be designated as the *market portfolio*. The market portfolio is the unanimously desirable portfolio containing all

[5]For a discussion of the market portfolio, see Fama, "Risk, Return and Equilibrium," pp. 32–33.

[6]Excess demand = demand less supply. Thus, when supply and demand are equal, excess demand is zero.

securities in exactly the proportions they are supplied in equilibrium.[7] The return on the market portfolio is the weighted average return of all securities in the market. The market portfolio is a risky portfolio—its risk is $\sigma_M$.

Of course, there is no observable market portfolio. However, it is a useful theoretical construct, since the return on $M$ is the return the Dow Jones Average, Standard and Poor's, the New York Stock Exchange Index, and other market indices are estimating.[8]

---

[7]Sharpe envisioned in his paper "Capital Asset Prices" a different equilibrium picture. Fama, "Risk, Return and Equilibrium," comments on this in his footnote 11 (p. 33).

Sharpe's equilibrium does not appear as the one graphed in Fig. 8.2. In Sharpe's case, $M$ (the point of tangency between the ray from the return on the riskless asset and the efficient frontier—Sharpe calls it $\phi$) is just one "optimal combination of risky assets" (Sharpe, "Capital Asset Prices," p. 433). In the "beginning," as Sharpe sees it, only portfolio $M$ will be in demand. Consequently, prices of assets in $M$ will rise and their expected returns will fall. Prices of assets not in $M$ will fall and their expected returns will rise.

Thus, a condition represented in the Fig. 8.3 emerges. Several portfolios lie along the CML—all those along the line segment $AMB$. Any of these combinations could be combined with borrowing or lending at $R$. Equilibrium is attained when all assets are included in combinations lying along $AMB$ and they are included in such proportions as they are supplied to the market.

Consider the implications of diversification theory for the equilibrium shown in Fig. 8.3. It was shown (in Fig. 3.10) that when two or more assets plot in a straight line in $(E(r), \sigma)$ space they must be perfectly, positively correlated. Thus, assets like $A$, $M$, $B$, and all other combinations along $AMB$ must be perfectly, positively correlated.

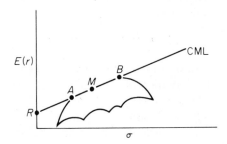

Figure 8.3. The CML with Multiple Tangencies

The risky combinations of assets along $AMB$ vary due to some common cause—variation in the overall economic, psychological, and market situation. The returns on combinations $A$, $M$, and $B$ will vary together systematically. All other variability of return (that is, risk) due to causes unrelated to movements in market conditions has been reduced by diversification. An equilibrium where many assets were tangent to the CML could be expected to emerge if most investors could not delineate the true efficient frontier or used naive diversification. Thus, Sharpe's multiple-tangency model is realistic, but it violates our first assumption for capital market theory.

[8]The divergence between the theoretical market portfolio and the empirically observed surrogates for it are considerable. In theory the market portfolio contains *all* market assets—that is, commodities, art objects, bonds, real estate, and other assets. Since the commonly used stock market indices are poor substitutes for the theoretical market portfolio, this means

## 8.4 Systematic and Unsystematic Risk

Sharpe has designated that portion of assets' variability of returns which is attributable to a common source as *systematic risk*.[9] Treynor has called this same common variability of return *undiversifiable risk*.[10] Systematic or undiversifiable risk is the minimum level of risk that may be achieved by means of diversification across a large group of randomly selected assets. The independent variations in the returns of the individual assets in such a portfolio average out to zero, and only systematic variability of return is left. This remaining common or systematic variability among all assets is due to changes in the economic, psychological, and political environment that affect all assets simultaneously.[11]

The independent or unsystematic variability of return in an asset has been called *unsystematic risk* by Sharpe, *residual variance* by Lintner,[12] and *diversifiable risk* by Treynor. This unsystematic risk is caused by events that are unique to the firm, such as strikes, inventions, management errors, and so on. Unsystematic risk and systematic risk sum to total risk as measured by the variance of returns of a security.

### A. Linear Relation with the Market

The nature of systematic and unsystematic risk is seen most graphically in terms of the following simple linear regression model, which Sharpe has called the *single-index model*.[13] Treynor called the same model the *characteristic line for the $i$th asset*.[14] Later writers have called equation (8.1) the *market model*. These names are synonymous.

$$r_{it} = a_i + b_i r_{Mt} + e_{it}, \tag{8.1}$$

---

that no valid empirical tests of the capital market theory have been published. See Richard Roll, "A Critique of the Asset Pricing Theory's Tests: Part I; On Past and Potential Testability of the Theory," *Journal of Financial Economics*, March 1977.

[9]Sharpe, "Capital Asset Prices."

[10]Treynor, "How to Rate the Management of Investment Funds."

[11]J. C. Francis, "Intertemporal Differences in Systematic Stock Price Movements," *Journal of Financial and Quantitative Analysis*, June 1975, pp. 205–219.

[12]Lintner, "Security Prices, Risk and Maximal Gains."

[13]Sharpe, "A Simplified Model for Portfolio Analysis"; see Part 4 on the diagonal model. The index which the $i$th security's returns are regressed onto should not be the same stock price index containing the $i$th security, or the model will be misspecified. For example, consider the following least-squares model $r_{it} = a + b r_{Mt} + e_{it}$. This model has cov $(e_t, r_M) \neq 0$ and cov $(r_M, r_i) \neq 0$ because $M$ contains the $i$th security (by definition of $M$). As a result the regression statistics are not minimum-variance, unbiased estimators of the parameters $a$ and $b$. To simply assume cov $(e_t, r_M) = 0$ and/or cov $(r_M, r_i) = 0$ would result in overspecification of the model. In this particular case, the caveat is to ensure correct application of mathematical regression theory and should not be interpreted to mean that the least-squares model above is worthless. Fama discusses this problem and its significance in "Risk, Return and Equilibrium: Some Clarifying Comments," pp. 37–39. Fama reaches the correct conclusion that the error introduced by the least-squares model above is infinitesimally small.

[14]Treynor, "How to Rate Management of Investment Funds."

where $r_{it}$ is the $t$th observation of the $i$th firm's rate of return; $r_{Mt}$ is the $t$th rate of return for the market portfolio; $e_{it}$ is the $t$th random-error term, which has an expected value of zero, constant finite variance, and is independent of other $e_{it}$'s; and $a_i$ and $b_i$ are least-squares regression coefficients.[15]

In equation (8.1) variation in $r_i$ is introduced from two sources: variation in $r_M$ and variation in $e_i$.

$$\text{var } (r_i) = \text{var } (a + b_i r_M + e_i)$$
$$= \text{var } (b_i r_M) + \text{var } (e_i),$$
$$\text{total risk} = \text{systematic risk} + \text{unsystematic risk}.$$

The partition of the variance above shows clearly the two sources of variability in $r_i$.

For prediction of $r_i$ the conditional expectation of equation (8.1), which is shown below, may be used.

$$r_i = E(r_i | r_M) = a_i + b_i r_M. \tag{8.2}$$

Two possible forms equation (8.2) may assume are shown in Figs. 8.4 and 8.5. Figure 8.4 is a graph of equation (8.2) fit to a firm that has returns that are positively correlated with the returns on some market index $(r_I)$. Figure 8.5 is the graph of equation (8.2) fit to a market asset that has returns that are negatively correlated with the market.

In terms of capital-market-theory language, the asset in Fig. 8.4 has more systematic risk than the firm in Fig. 8.5. The asset in Fig. 8.4 has a positive

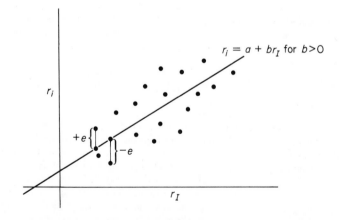

Figure 8.4. Regression Line for a Market Asset with Cyclical Returns

---

[15]According to the Gauss–Markov theorem, equation (8.2) is a minimum-variance, linear, unbiased estimator if the assumptions beneath (8.1) are met.

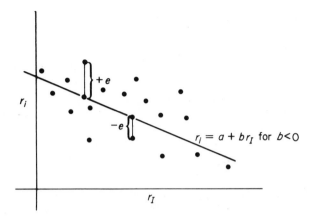

Figure 8.5. Regression Line for a Market Asset with Countercyclical Returns

slope coefficient [$b_i$ in equations (8.1) and (8.2)], positive covariance of returns with the returns on $M$, and positive correlation of returns with returns on $M$. The asset in Fig. 8.5, on the other hand, has returns that move countercyclically. The asset in Fig. 8.5 has a negative regression coefficient ($b_i$), negative covariance, and a negative correlation with $M$. Thus, adding the asset in Fig. 8.5 to a portfolio will decrease the risk of a portfolio that is correlated with $M$—as most portfolios are—more than adding the firm in Fig. 8.4 to the portfolio. Most simply, the firm in Fig. 8.5 is the better candidate for Markowitz diversification purposes. The $b_i$ coefficient is an index of systematic risk. It is sometimes called the *beta coefficient* or a measure of *volatility*.

Whenever equation (8.1) produces a correlation coefficient below 1, the observations will not all lie on the regression line—of course, this is the typical case graphed in Figs. 8.4 and 8.5. The vertical deviations of the observations from the regression line are called residual errors and are denoted $e$ in equation (8.1) and Figs. 8.4 and 8.5. Although the least-squares regression technique used to derive equation (8.2) minimizes the sum of the squared errors $\left( \text{that is, } \sum_{i=1}^{T} e_{it}^2 \right)$ over all $T$ observations, the sum is still a positive value. The term $\sigma^2(r_i | r_M)$ is called the "residual variance around the regression line" in statistical terms or "unsystematic risk" in capital-market-theory language.

$$\sigma^2(r_i | r_M) = \frac{\sum\limits^{T} e_i^2}{T} = \frac{\sum\limits^{T} [r_i - (a_i + b_i r_M)]^2}{T}. \tag{8.3}$$

The residual variance is the squared standard error in regression language; it is a measure of unsystematic variance and diversifiable risk.

### B.  Only Portfolios Efficient Enough for CML

Only *combinations* of risk assets (that is, portfolios) are efficient enough to lie on the CML in equilibrium. An individual security's risk will consist not only of the systematic risk of portfolios along the CML, but, in addition, an individual security's risk will contain unsystematic risk. Thus, all individual assets must be more risky than points on the CML. Empirical evidence bears this out. King concluded "that the typical stock has about half of its variance explained by an element of price change that affects the whole market."[16] That is, systematic risk comprises about half the risk in the typical stock by King's estimates.

Individual securities (as opposed to portfolios) will be located *within* the opportunity set instead of *on* the CML. In terms of Fig. 8.2 individual securities will be located at points such as *A* and *C*. Only through the benefits of successful diversification can *A* and *C* be held in efficient portfolios such as *M*.

### 8.5   Security Market Line

Thus far in this chapter, the analysis has determined that in the type of equilibrium situation assumed, the expected return of *portfolios* is a linear function of the portfolios' standard deviation of returns. This linear relation has been denoted the CML. Next, consider a model for the determination of the equilibrium rate of return of an *individual security* or a portfolio.

For an *n*-security portfolio the variance is

$$\operatorname{var}(r_p) = \sum_{i=1}^{n} x_i^2 \operatorname{var}(r_i) + \sum_{i=1}^{n} \sum_{j=1}^{n} x_i x_j \sigma_{ij} \qquad \text{for } i \neq j. \qquad (2.9)$$

Note that within the expression for the risk of a portfolio of any size are covariance terms between all possible pairs of securities in the portfolio. The essence of effective diversification is to combine securities with either low or negative covariances. Therefore, demand for securities that have low or negative covariance of returns with most other securities will be high. Those securities whose returns covary inversely or are independent of the returns from the market portfolio will have their prices bid up. Securities that have high covariance with *M*—that is, high systematic risk—will experience low demand. As a result, the prices of securities with high systematic risk will fall, and securities with low systematic risk will have their prices bid up. Since equilibrium rates of return move inversely with the price of the security, securities with high covariance with the market will

---

[16]B. F. King, "Market and Industry Factors in Stock Price Behavior," *Journal of Business*, January 1966, *Security Prices: A Supplement*, pp. 139–190.

have relatively low prices and high average or expected returns. Conversely, securities with low or negative covariances will have relatively high prices and, therefore, experience low expected rates of return in equilibrium. This relationship is depicted in Fig. 8.6 and equation (8.4). The $E(r_i)$ in the SML is the appropriate discount rate to use in valuing the $i$th asset's income—it is the cost of capital.

$$E(r_i) = R + \text{cov}(r_i, r_M) \left\{ \left[ E(r_M) - \frac{R}{\sigma_M^2} \right] \right\}. \tag{8.4}$$

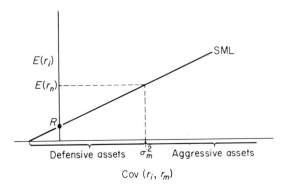

Figure 8.6. The Security Market Line (SML)

In words, Fig. 8.6 says that in equilibrium an *asset's expected return is a positive linear function of its covariance* of returns with the market. That is, the expected return from a security is an increasing function of its systematic risk as measured by its covariance with the market. Since systematic risk is the portion of a security's total risk that hinders rather than helps diversification, this relationship is intuitively appealing. The more risk a security has that cannot be eliminated by diversification, the more return investors will require to induce them to hold that security in their portfolios. The locus of equilibrium points in Fig. 8.6 will be called the *security market line* (SML)—a separate and distinct relation from the CML.[17]

In equilibrium, every individual common stock's expected return and risk observation will lie *on* the SML and *off* the CML. But, in equilibrium, only efficient portfolios' $E(r)$ and $\sigma$ will lie on the CML and also on the SML. Thus, even under idealistic assumptions and at static equilibrium, the CML will not include all points if portfolios and individual securities are plotted together on one graph. However, all assets should lie on the SML in equilibrium, because both portfolios' and individual securities' returns are determined by systematic risk.

---

[17]The name "security market line" can be attributed to Sharpe, "Capital Asset Prices." Some later writers call the SML the *capital asset pricing model* (CAPM).

## A. Defensive and Aggressive Securities

In Fig. 8.6 the portion of the horizontal axis representing low or negative covariances is marked as including *defensive securities*—defensive in the sense that they offer the opportunity to reduce portfolio risk by including them in a portfolio that is correlated with $M$, as nearly all portfolios will be. This definition is similar but not identical to the term "defensive security" as used by security salesmen, financial analysts, and others. Traditionally, when speaking of defensive securities, financial analysts gave examples of firms that are unlikely to experience decreases in earning power. Since these people tend to define risk ambiguously—if at all—their definitions of a defensive security are hard to pin down. In any event, the definition of defensive securities given here is similar to the more common definition.

The *aggressive securities* are securities that offer opportunities for speculation; their dividend and price reactions to changes in market conditions are more dramatic than the reactions of defensive securities.

## B. SML Restated in Terms of Sharpe's Beta Coefficient

In the discussion of systematic risk above, the regression coefficient $b_i$ from equations (8.1) and (8.2) was suggested as a possible measure of systematic risk. The covariance of returns with $M$ was also suggested as a measure of systematic risk. Two methods of defining the SML are possible. Figure. 8.7 defines the SML in terms of the regression coefficient $b_i$. In terms of $b_i$, defensive and aggressive securities can be delineated more easily. It is intuitively appealing to think of securities with $b_i < 1$ as being defensive and aggressive securities as having $b_i > 1$.

The SML defined in terms of cov $(r_i, r_M)$ is shown in Fig. 8.8. It is equivalent to Fig. 8.7. The only difference between Figs. 8.7 and 8.8 is that the

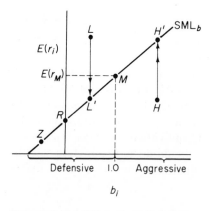

Figure 8.7. The SML in $[b, E(r)]$ Space]

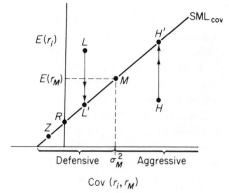

Figure 8.8. The SML in $[cov, E(r)]$ Space

horizontal scale of Fig. 8.7 is $(1/\sigma_M^2)$ times the length of the horizontal scale of Fig. 8.8. This is due to the definition of the regression slope coefficient— that is, Sharpe's beta coefficient—as shown in equation (8.5).

$$b_{(i|M)} = \frac{\text{cov } (r_i, r_M)}{\sigma_M^2} = \text{cov } (r_i, r_M) \cdot \left(\frac{1}{\sigma_M^2}\right) \tag{8.5}$$

$$= \frac{\rho_{iM}\sigma_i\sigma_M}{\sigma_M^2} \tag{8.5a}$$

$$= \frac{\rho_{iM}\sigma_i}{\sigma_M}, \tag{8.5b}$$

where $\rho_{iM}$ is the correlation coefficient of $r_i$ and $r_M$, and $\sigma_i$ and $\sigma_M$ are the standard deviations of returns for asset $i$ and the market portfolio, respectively. Since $\sigma_M^2$ is a constant for all assets in the market, $b_i$ is simply a linear transformation of cov $(r_i, r_M)$. Note that when $b_{(i|M)} = 1$, then cov $(r_i, r_M) = \sigma_M^2$. This relation reveals why the divisions between defensive and aggressive securities in Figs. 8.6, 8.7, and 8.8 are comparable. Equation (8.6) is thus a formula for the SML in Fig. 8.7 which is mathematically equivalent to the SML formula of equation (8.4), as shown in equation (8.5).

$$E(r_i) = R + b_i[E(r_M) - R]. \tag{8.6}$$

### C. Over- and Underpriced Securities

Figures 8.7 and 8.8 and the SML have security-price implications. Points between the SML and the $E(r)$ axis, such as point $L$ in Figs. 8.8 and 8.7, represent securities whose prices are lower than they would be in equilibrium. Since points such as $L$ represent securities with unusually high returns for the amount of systematic risk they bear, they will enjoy strong demand, which will bid their prices up until their equilibrium rate of return is driven back onto the SML at point $L'$.

Likewise, securities represented by points between the SML and the systematic risk axis represent securities whose prices are too high. Securities such as point $H$ in Figs. 8.7 and 8.8 do not offer sufficient return to induce rational investors to accept the amount of systematic risk they bear. As a result, their prices will fall, owing to lack of demand. Their prices will continue to fall until the denominator of the expected return formula

$$E(r) = \frac{E(\text{capital gains or losses} + \text{dividends})}{\text{purchase price}}$$

is low enough to allow the return to reach the SML at a point such as $H'$. Then the capital loss will cease and an equilibrium will emerge until a change in the firm's systematic risk, a change in $R$, or some other change causes another disequilibrium. After considering the effect the SML can have on the market price of an asset, it is easy to see why some writers call it the capital asset pricing model.

### D.  The Single-Index Market Model's Alpha Intercept

Although the single-index market model is essentially a time-series regression model for a single market asset which must be estimated across many rates of return and, in contrast, the SML is a cross-sectional (that is, across many assets) equilibrium relationship between the expected returns of many different market assets, the expected values of the two models may be equated to gain insight into the alpha intercept of the single-index market model. Equation (8.2a) shows the expectation of the single-index model (or characteristic line or market model).

$$E(r_M) = a_i + b_i E(r_m). \tag{8.2a}$$

Equating equations (8.2a) and (8.6) yields equation (8.7). Solving (8.7) for the alpha yields equation (8.7a).

$$\text{Eq. (8.2a)} = a_i + b_i E(r_M) = R + b_i[E(r_M) - R] = \text{Eq. (8.6)}, \tag{8.7}$$

$$a_i = R - b_i R = R(1 - b_i). \tag{8.7a}$$

Equation (8.7a) shows that the capital market theory models suggests that the alpha intercept in the single-index market model is a positive function of the $i$th asset's beta systematic risk index and the riskless interest rate.

### E.  Negative Correlation with M

Consider point $Z$ in Figs. 8.7 and 8.8. Point $Z$ represents a defensive security that has an equilibrium rate of return below the return on riskless assets $(R)$. Upon observing rates of return that were consistently below $R$, the traditional financial analyst would typically attribute the low return to a high price for the security, which was bid up in expectation of growth that failed to materialize. But, capital market theory provides a second rationalization of points such as $Z$; their prices are maintained at high levels owing to the Markowitz diversification benefits they offer.

### 8.6  Relaxing the Assumptions

As promised, the assumptions underlying the derivation of capital market theory will now be aligned more to conditions existing in the "real world." First, assumption 2 (that is, one interest rate—$R$) will be relaxed.

A. Multiple Interest Rates

In more realistic capital markets, the borrowing rate $(B)$ is higher than the lending rate $(L)$. In Fig. 8.9, this is represented by two lines emerging from points $L$ and $B$. The dashed portions of these two lines do not represent actual opportunities and are included merely to indicate the construction of the figure. The line formed by the solid sections of the two lines and a section of the opportunity locus is the relevant efficient frontier when the borrowing and lending rates differ. As a result, the CML has a curved section between $M_L$ and $M_B$ in Fig. 8.9. The curved section is the front of the opportunity locus.

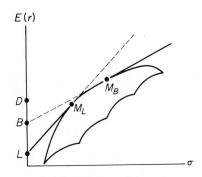

Figure 8.9. The CML When Borrowing and Lending Rates Differ

Of course, not all investors can borrow at rate $B$. Investors with poor credit ratings must pay a higher borrowing rate than investors with good credit ratings. Thus, the proverbial "deadbeat" might be able to borrow money only by paying rate $D$ in Fig. 8.9. Obviously, the more difference between the lending and the various borrowing rates, the more curved the CML will become. And, the CML will change for each individual as his credit rating changes. Likewise, the CML for the market in general will change with credit conditions. These complications would reduce the stability and the commonality of the CML. The reader may graph these complications as an exercise.[18]

In Fig. 8.9, points $M_L$ and $M_B$ are two separate tangency portfolios for lending and borrowing, respectively, if only one lending and one borrowing rate is recognized. The existence of two tangency portfolios creates problems.

[18]K. L. Hastie, "The Determination of Optimal Investment Policy," *Management Science*, August 1967, pp. B-757 through B-774.

The formulas[19] for the SML are as follows:

$$E(r_i) = R + (E(r_M) - R) \cdot \frac{\text{cov }(r_i, r_M)}{\sigma_M^2} \qquad (8.6a)$$

$$= R + [E(r_M) - R] \cdot \frac{\rho_{iM}\sigma_i}{\sigma_M} \qquad \text{substituting eq. (8.5)}$$

$$= R + [E(r_M) - R] \cdot b_i \qquad (8.6)$$

where $[E(r_M) - R]$ may be referred to as the "risk premium for the market portfolio."

If separate borrowing $(B)$ and lending $(L)$ rates are assumed to exist, two SML's emerge:

$$E(r_i) = B + (E(r_{MB}) - B) \cdot \frac{\text{cov }(r_i, r_{MB})}{\sigma_{MB}^2} \qquad (8.6B)$$

for $E(r_i) \geq E(r_{MB})$, and

$$E(r_i) = L + (E(r_{ML}) - L) \cdot \frac{\text{cov }(r_i, r_{ML})}{\sigma_{ML}^2} \qquad (8.6L)$$

for $E(r_i) \leq E(r_{ML})$.

These two SML's will not only have different horizontal axis intercepts; they will have different slopes, since $[E(r_M) - R]$ will be different. Also, since the covariances are with two different tangency portfolios (that is, $M_L$ and $M_B$), even the covariances differ. As a result, it is impossible to specify the relation between the two SML's without adding to, rather than reducing, the number of assumptions. In Fig. 8.10, one possible relationship between $SML_L$ and $SML_B$ is shown.[20]

As a result of divergent borrowing and lending rates, no equilibrium prices are possible for all individual securities. Since further relaxation of assumption two would clutter Figs. 8.9 and 8.10 without yielding any additional insights, this task is left to the reader's imagination.

## B. Limiting Short Sales and/or Leverage

The second capital market theory assumption was modified to acknowledge that the borrowing rate exceeded the lending rate. However, further modifications in the second assumption are needed to limit portfolios' bor-

---

[19]Equation (8.5) is derived formally in Appendix 8A, which deals explicitly with the mathematical foundations of capital market theory.

[20]This relationship was in the 1970 edition of this book. It was also analyzed by M. J. Brennan, "Capital Market Equilibrium with Divergent Borrowing and Lending Rates," *Journal of Financial and Quantitative Analysis*, Vol. 6, December 1971. For further discussion of this and related points, see E. Fama, *Foundations of Finance*, Basic Books, New York, 1976, Chapter 8.

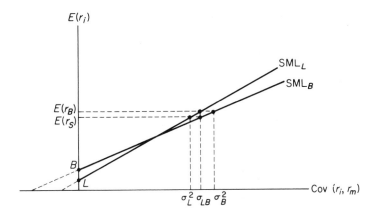

Figure 8.10. Two SML's When Borrowing and Lending Rates Differ

rowing activities to realistic levels. In particular, short selling and borrowing are activities that portfolios can use to raise funds, but only with constraints imposed by lenders. Before these constraints are explained, however, the nature of short selling and margin buying by portfolios is briefly reviewed.

Selling a security short is somewhat like printing and issuing a security as a liability to raise funds. With short selling a security that the portfolio does not own is sold and then the security is borrowed from a third party to deliver to the buyer. Thus, the portfolio has a liability to repay the borrowed shares. This is essentially the same position the portfolio would have been in if it had printed and sold a debt instrument with the same risk and negative rate of return (that is, interest on the borrowed amount) as the security that was sold short. Short selling and using financial leverage are similar in another respect—there are limits on lenders willingness to lend both securities and cash.

The U.S. Federal Reserve's margin requirements, the collateral requirements of lending institutions, and similar credit restrictions limit all borrowers' use of financial leverage. Likewise, those who loan securities to short sellers are not characterized by infinite amounts of charity in their lending. As a result, a realistic interpretation of the second capital market theory assumption would only allow "reasonable amounts" of borrowing. If *unlimited borrowing* (that is, the use of financial leverage, margin buying, and/or short sales) were allowed the investment opportunity set shown in Fig. 8.9 would extend infinitely far on the right-hand side, as shown in Fig. 8.11. And, the SML's in Fig. 8.10 would also extend upward to infinity.[21]

---

[21]The opportunity set has been analyzed by R. C. Merton, "An Analytic Derivation of the Efficient Portfolio Frontier," *Journal of Financial and Quantitative Analysis*, September 1972, pp. 1151–1172.

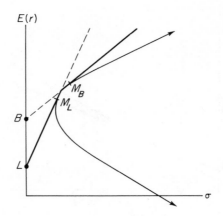

Figure 8.11. Unrestricted Short Sales and Leverage Leave Risk and Return
Unbounded on the Right-Hand Side in $[\sigma, E(r)]$ Space

Realistic extensions of lending are represented by the escalloped quarter-moon-shaped opportunity sets in $[\sigma, E(r)]$ space which have closed right-hand sides, and the limited SML's typically drawn in this chapter.

### C. Transaction Costs

If assumption 6 (that is, no transactions costs) were dropped, the CML and SML would have "bands" on their sides as shown in Figs. 8.12 and 8.13. Within these bands, it would not be profitable for investors to buy and sell securities and generate the price revisions necessary to attain equilibrium—transactions costs would consume the profit that induces such trading. As a result, the markets would never reach the theoretical equilibrium as described here, even if the other assumptions were retained.

In Chapter IX, empirical evidence will be examined, showing that investors need not diversify over many securities to obtain portfolios near the

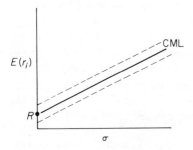

Figure 8.12. Transactions Costs Obscure
CML

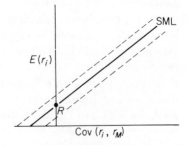

Figure 8.13. Transactions Costs
Obscure SML

CML. Thus, the effects of transactions costs need not be particularly detrimental to the equilibrium picture derived in theory.

## D. Indivisibilities

If all assets were not infinitely divisible—that is, if assumption 5 were discontinued—the SML would degenerate into a dashed line: each dash would represent an opportunity attainable with an integral number of shares. Little profit is to be gained from further examination of this trivial situation.

## E. General Uncertainty

To jettison assumption 3 (that is, idealized uncertainty) would require drawing an opportunity locus and CML composed of "fuzzy" curves and lines. The more investors' expectations differed, the "fuzzier" all lines and curves would become.[22] As a result of general uncertainty, the analysis becomes determinate only within limits. Only major disequilibriums will be corrected. Similarly, the picture of the SML becomes blurred. Statements cannot be made with certainty, and predictions must contain a margin for error.

## F. Different Tax Brackets

To recognize the existence of different tax rates on ordinary income and capital gains would blur the picture more. Equation (1.1a) for the after-tax rate of return $(r_{AT})$ is

$$r_{AT} = \frac{(\text{capital gains}) \cdot (1 - T_G) + (\text{dividends}) \cdot (1 - T_O)}{\text{price at beginning of the holding period}}, \quad (1.1a)$$

where $T_G$ is the capital gains tax rate and $T_O$ is the tax rate applicable to ordinary income. In terms of after-tax returns, every investor would see a slightly different CML and SML, depending on his particular tax situation. Thus, a static equilibrium could never emerge under existing tax laws, even if all the other assumptions were rigorously maintained.

---

[22]Cheng-Few Lee has shown econometrically how to estimate the length of the single period over which the single-period returns that compose the capital market theory are measured, "Investment Horizon and the Functional Form of the Capital Asset Pricing Model," *Review of Economics and Statistics*, Vol. 58, No. 3, 1976, pp. 356–363. Preliminary empirical work suggests that the SML may not be linear over all differencing intervals: Cheng-Few Lee, "On the Relationship Between the Systematic Risk and the Investment Horizon," *Journal of Financial and Quantitative Analysis*, December 1976, pp. 803–815.

### G.  Inflation and Varying Productivity of Capital

The interest rates observed in reality are *nominal* interest rates rather than *real* interest rates. Symbolically, the riskless nominal rate of interest may be decomposed,

$$R_Z = \text{mpk} + E\left(\frac{\Delta P}{P}\right) + f(\text{risk}) + \text{transactions costs}, \qquad (8.6)$$

where $R_Z$ is the *nominal* rate of interest per period (for example, the Treasury bill rate) seen in each day's newspapers, which varies unsystematically. The symbol mpk denotes the marginal productivity of capital or *real* rate of interest per period, and $E(\Delta P/P)$ is the expected percentage change in the general price level per period—that is, the expected rate of inflation or deflation.[23] This discussion will omit the impact of risk premiums, transactions costs, and the term structure of interest rates in determining $R_Z$. The marginal productivity of capital and the rate of inflation fluctuate with technology, the level of investment, monetary policy, fiscal policy, and consumers' tastes; it follows that $R_Z$ fluctuates, too.

Relaxing assumption seven means that even if $R_Z$ is the interest rate of U.S. short-term government bonds, it must, nevertheless, vary. Thus, there is no true riskless asset: even default-free securities will experience variability of return.[24] Graphically, this means that point $R$ in Fig. 8.14 ceases to exist as a lending possibility and is replaced by a point such as $R_Z$. The efficient frontier is now the curve from $S$ to $Q$ or from $S'$ to $Q$, assuming that all money is borrowed at rate $R_Z$. Portfolio $S$ or $S'$ is the minimum-risk portfolio—it may or may not contain default-free securities and it may or may not have zero risk as $S'$ does. A point such as $S'$ will emerge if returns on $R_Z$ and $M$ are perfectly negatively correlated. A point like $S$ will be the minimum-

---

[23]$\Delta$ is used to mean "change." Thus, technically speaking,

$$\frac{\Delta P}{P} = \frac{\text{change in price level per period}}{\text{price level at the beginning of the period}} = \text{rate of inflation or deflation.}$$

The mpk is the rate at which capital reproduces itself.

[24]K. L. Hastie, "The Determination of Optimal Investment Policy." Black has refined Hastie's original model of the market without a perfectly riskless rate (that is, a zero variance asset) in a theoretical article: F. Black, "Capital Market Equilibrium with Restricted Borrowing," *Journal of Business*, Vol. 45, July 1972, pp. 444–454. Black's model was tested empirically in an article by F. Black, M. Jensen, and M. Scholes entitled "The Capital Asset Pricing Model: Some Empirical Tests," which was published in a book of readings edited by M. Jensen entitled *Studies in the Theory of Capital Markets* (New York: Praeger Publishers, Inc., 1972). Black's model was mathematically correct, but the monthly returns estimated empirically by Black, Jensen, and Scholes contained significant positive correlation between the market portfolio and the zero-beta-positive-variance surrogate for the riskless asset. Thus, the zero-beta portfolio actually had a significantly positive beta index of systematic risk. Fama discusses Black's model and some alternative specifications in *Foundations of Finance* (New York: Basic Books, Inc, 1976), pp. 277–300.

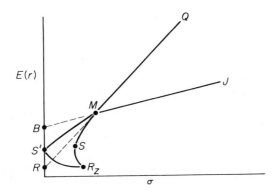

Figure 8.14. Lack of Riskless Rate Obscures CML

variance portfolio if returns on $R_Z$ and $M$ are uncorrelated but not perfectly negatively correlated.[25] If borrowing at rate $B$, rather than at rate $R$, is considered, the efficient frontier becomes $SMJ$ or $S'MJ$, depending on whether $S$ or $S'$ is the minimum-variance portfolio.

Lack of a riskless interest rate makes the lower section of the SML imprecise. Above $E(r_{M_B})$ the formula for the SML is given by equation (8.7):

$$E(r) = B + \left(\frac{E(r_{M_B}) - B}{\sigma^2_{M_B}}\right) \cdot (\text{cov}(r_i, r_{M_B})). \qquad (8.7)$$

Figure 8.15 shows the SML, assuming that $B$ does not vary. Below $E(r_{M_B})$ the locus of equilibrium returns lies in the neighborhood of the dashed segment of the SML. However, since a riskless rate and a market portfolio of maximum efficiency for lending are not defined when $\sigma_R > 0$, it is impossible to specify the SML below $E(r_{M_B})$ with any precision.

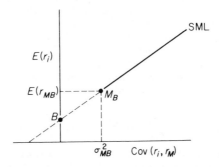

Figure 8.15   SML Obscured by Lack of Risk-Free Rate

---

[25]See Fig. 3.10 and the accompanying discussion of how the correlation coefficient determines the degree of convexity.

## H.  Mathematical Allowances for Varying Inflation

Chen and Boness analyzed the effects of inflation on security returns.[26] Then, Friend, Landskroner, and Losq[27] extended the work of Chen and Boness to allow for the effects of uncertain rates of inflation.

Equation (8.8) shows the SML adjusted for the effects of purchasing power risk resulting from stochastic rates of inflation. Friend, Landskroner, and Losq derived this model by assuming that all investors had similar risk-averse utility functions.[28]

$$E(r_i) = R + \sigma_{i\pi} + \frac{E(r_m) - R - \sigma_{m\pi}}{\sigma_m^2 - (\sigma_{m\pi}/x_i)}\left(\sigma_{im} - \frac{\sigma_{i\pi}}{x_i}\right), \qquad (8.8)$$

where $\sigma_{i\pi}$ measures the covariance of the inflation rate, denoted $\pi$, with the $i$th asset's nominal (as contrasted with real) rates of return; $\sigma_{m\pi} = \text{cov}(r_m, r_\pi)$; and $x_i$ denotes the weight (or proportion) of the $i$th risky asset in the market portfolio.[29] Comparing the inflation-adjusted SML shown in equation (8.8) with classic SML formula shown in equation (8.4) suggests that the market price of risk in the classic SML, denoted $\{[E(r_m) - R]/\sigma_m^2\}$ in equation (8.4), is misstated if the inflation rate is nonzero. If varying rates of inflation which are positively correlated with the market are expected (that is, the most realistic assumption), the traditional SML understates the market price of risk, as shown in inequality (8.9).

$$\frac{E(r_m) - R}{\sigma_m^2} < \frac{E(r_m) - R - \sigma_{m\pi}}{\sigma_m^2 - (\sigma_{m\pi}/x_i)}, \qquad (8.9)$$

$$\begin{pmatrix}\text{traditional market price of} \\ \text{risk from eq. (8.4)}\end{pmatrix} < \begin{pmatrix}\text{inflation adjusted market} \\ \text{price of risk}\end{pmatrix}, \quad (8.9a)$$

---

[26]A. H. Chen and J. A. Boness, "Effects of Uncertain Inflation on the Investment and Financing Decisions of the Firm," *Journal of Finance*, May 1975.

[27]Irwin Friend, Yoram Landskroner, and Etiene Losq, "The Demand for Risky Assets Under Uncertain Inflation," *Journal of Finance*, December 1976.

[28]Friend, Landskroner, and Losq assumed that all investors were characterized by constant proportional risk aversion in the Pratt–Arrow sense. This risk-aversion measure is defined and explained graphically in Chapter XI.

[29]Assuming further that all investors pay a proportion, $I$, of their income to the government as income taxes (where $0 < I < 1.0$) suggests modifying the inflation-adjusted SML of equation (8.8) to the inflation-and-income-tax-adjusted SML:

$$E(r_i) = R + \sigma_{i\pi} + \frac{E(r_m) - R - \sigma_{m\pi}}{\sigma_m^2 - \{\sigma_{m\pi}/[x_i(1 - I)]\}}\left[\sigma_{im} - \frac{\sigma_{i\pi}}{x_i(1 - I)}\right].$$

The income tax variable, $I$, may be viewed as a weighted average income tax rate averaged over all investors. It is comforting to note that when inflation and taxes are nonexistent (that is, $\sigma_{i\pi} = \sigma_{m\pi} = I = 0$), the model above simplifies to equation (8.4), the traditional SML. See Friend, Landskroner, and Losq, "The Demand for Risky Assets Under Uncertain Inflation," equation (12a) on p. 1291.

assuming $\sigma_{m\pi} > 0$. If inflation covaries inversely with the market returns, cov $(r_m, r_\pi) > 0$, inequality (8.9) should be reversed. Essentially, a positive (negative) correlation between the rate of inflation and the market returns implies that the market price of risk in the traditional SML understates (overstates) the true market price of risk.[30]

As a result of the inflation-adjusted SML characterized by equations (8.8) and (8.9), empirical observations of the SML measured in nominal rates of return will be flatter than the traditional SML of equation (8.4). Figures 8.16 and 8.17 illustrate the difference between the zero-inflation or traditional SML shown in Fig. 8.16 and the inflation-adjusted SML of equations (8.8) and (8.9) and Fig. 8.17.

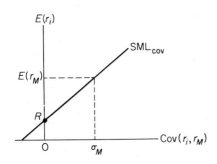

Figure 8.16. Traditional SML          Figure 8.17. Adjusted SML Is Flatter

Considering further the most realistic assumption of expected inflation rates, which rise and fall cyclically with the business cycle and stock market returns, $\sigma_{m\pi} > 0$, has implications for the CML, too. The risk of the $i$th asset is overstated because the rising returns associated with bullish market conditions embody decreased purchasing power per dollar of income because of the positively correlated inflation rates. This result may be seen graphically by comparing Fig. 8.18 of the traditional CML with the inflation-adjusted CML shown in Fig. 8.19.

Other realistic adjustments in the risk–return theory suggest that the empirically observed CML and SML will be flatter than the classic models. Chen, Kim, and Kon (CKK hereafter) have analyzed the effects on a portfolio of cash holdings.[31] For example, mutual funds typically hold 5 to

---

[30]Chen and Boness have suggested that Friend, Landskroner, and Losq have misinterpreted some of their original results which were not discussed here, "The Demand for Risky Assets Under Uncertain Inflation: A Clarifying Comment," an unpublished 1977 manuscript of six pages obtainable from Chen or Boness.

[31]A. H. Chen, E. H. Kim, and S. J. Kon, "Cash Demand, Liquidation Costs and Capital Market Equilibrium Under Uncertainty," *Journal of Financial Economics*, September 1975, pp. 293–308.

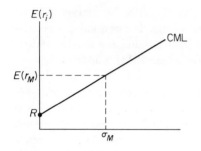

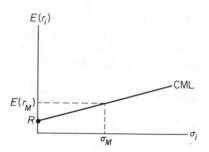

Figure 8.18. Traditional CML            Figure 8.19. Adjusted CML Is Flatter

10 percent of their total assets in cash to pay operating expenses and maintain the liquidity necessary to buy back any shares in the portfolio which are presented for redemption. Other portfolios face similar liquidity needs. Since cash is a nonearning asset, a portfolio's expected return is diminished by cash holdings.

CKK derive modified risk–return models which allow for the effects of portfolios holdings on nonearning cash. Essentially, CKK show that the CML is flatter after allowing for cash holdings—Figs. 8.18 and 8.19 depict the effects of this realistic modification. Allowing for portfolio liquidity also flattens the slope of the SML, this effect may be seen graphically by comparing Figs. 8.16 and 8.17.

## I.  Equilibrium

The assumption of equilibrium (assumption 8) is, of course, heroic. Information arrives to various investors at different times. Thus, investors' expectations do not change in unison. As a result, there is no reason to expect assets' prices to adjust so that all investors are satisfied with their holdings (that is, excess demand is zero for all assets) at any point in time. Instead, assets' prices are in a continuous, dynamic disequilibrium. Hopefully, most of the time this disequilibrium is minor.

## J.  Concluding Remarks on Capital Market Theory Assumptions

Thus far, all except the first assumption underlying capital market theory have been relaxed one at a time, and it was observed in each case that the previous analysis was somewhat obscured. If all were relaxed simultaneously, the result would be even less determinate. However, the fact that the analysis is not exactly determinate under realistic assumptions does not mean that it has no value. The analysis still rationalizes much observed behavior, explains such hitherto unexplained practices as diversification, and offers realistic suggestions about directions prices and returns should follow when they deviate significantly from equilibrium.

If the first assumption—that all investors were efficient Markowitz diversi-fiers—was partially relaxed, the SML would be obscured correspondingly. A market of naively diversified investors would most likely adjust asset prices until returns were proportional to the total risk in an asset. In such a market the CML would have multiple tangencies as shown in Fig. 8.3 and would explain more behavior than the SML.

### K. Ex Ante Versus Ex Post

The capital market theory implies that equilibrium *expected* returns are determined by *expected* risk. Or, as economists say, ex ante returns are a func-tion of expected risk. Historical, or ex post, returns are not what investors use as a basis for their decisions about the future, although their expectations can be affected by ex post behavior. Thus, it should be noted that a "jump" is made in going from the ex ante theory to the ex post data. If the probability distribution of historical returns has remained stationary over time, then the historical expected returns and variances can be used to estimate future returns. However, historical data play no role in the theory itself.

To test capital market theory, expectations must be observed—an impos-sible task if conducted on a meaningful scale. Of course, expectations may be formed from historical observations.[32] But, unless historical investors were clairvoyant, historical data will not be satisfactory to completely validate the theory.

### 8.7 Empirical Tests of Capital Market Theory

Capital market theory offers a number of clear-cut hypotheses in a mathe-matical form suitable for empirical testing. However, empirical data cannot be expected to verify every phase of capital market theory for the following reasons:

1. Since investors' expectations sometimes differ from the ex post results, empirical data cannot furnish an entirely satisfactory vehicle for tests. Un-fortunately, investors' expectations cannot be measured directly.[33]

2. As pointed out above, capital market theory is based on certain simplify-ing assumptions. To the extent that these assumptions oversimplify, the theory is simply inadequate.

---

[32]See Table 10.1, Fig. 10.1, and the related discussion for a test of the CML using historical data.

[33]This does not mean that a surrogate for expectations cannot be used to validate the theory. After numerous attempts by other economists, Meiselman found a surrogate for expectations of interest rates and made a step toward validating the expectations hypothesis concerning the term structure of interest rates. See D. Meiselman, *The Term Structure of Interest Rates* (Englewood Cliffs, N.J.: Prentice-Hall, Inc., 1962). Perhaps capital market theory will lend itself to such subtle analysis and testing someday.

3. Although some portions of the theory are supported with the empirical data, other portions of the theory may not be so well supported empirically. For example, if most investors operated under the naive definition of diversification instead of Markowitz diversification techniques, then the CML might be supported empirically while the SML might not be supported by the data.

4. Variability-of-return measures are only risk *surrogates*. Although the variability-of-return measures are used widely by academic researchers, it is not difficult to imagine that better risk surrogates may be developed in the future.

5. The regression coefficients and correlation coefficients found by the usual least-squares techniques are biased downward, owing to errors that enter into both the expected-return estimates and the expected-risk estimates. More sophisticated techniques than are commonly employed in regression and correlation work must be employed to test capital market theory adequately.[34] Other econometric problems that can hinder empirical work also exist.[35]

6. The important market portfolio which is central to much of the capital market theory has never been precisely defined—stock market indices are simply used as a surrogate for the market portfolio in most empirical work.

In spite of this awesome list of hinderances, meaningful econometric tests of the capital market theory can nevertheless be formulated. Consider some empirical estimates of the SML which were prepared.

Black, Jensen, and Scholes (BJS hereafter) estimated the SML by first estimating the beta coefficients and average rates of return from time-series regressions for each stock in their different sample of hundreds of NYSE

----

[34]To test the CML, suppose that the true relation is

$$E(R) = A + B(\Sigma). \tag{a}$$

Suppose that only $E(r)$ and $\sigma$ can be observed empirically, where

$$E(r) = E(R) + v, \tag{b}$$

$$\sigma = \Sigma + u, \tag{c}$$

and $u$ and $v$ are random errors. Substituting (b) and (c) into (a) gives (d).

$$E(r) = a + b(\sigma) + w, \tag{d}$$

where $w = v - Bu$. Model (d) violates the assumptions of the commonly employed least-squares techniques, since $\text{cov}(\sigma, w) = -B \text{ var}(u)$ even if $u$ and $v$ are independent. J. Johnston, *Econometric Methods* 2nd ed. (New York: McGraw-Hill Book Company, 1972) analyzes this common problem in Sec. 9.4.

[35]Random coefficients is a problem discussed in *Principles of Econometrics* by Henri Theil, (New York: John Wiley & Sons, Inc., 1971); see Sec. 12.4. Empirical tests suggest that the beta systematic risk coefficient is a random coefficient: F. J. Fabozzi and J. C. Francis, "Beta as a Random Coefficient," *Journal of Financial and Quantitative Analysis*, March 1978.

stocks—call this their *first-pass regressions*. Then, a separate second-pass cross-sectional regression was prepared to estimate the SML for each different sample period by regressing the average returns onto the betas from the first-pass regressions. However, some econometric problems made the process BJS actually followed more complicated, as explained below.

## A. First-Pass Regressions

First BJS estimated the single-index market model, equation (8.1), using 60 monthly rates of return for each stock which were taken from the CRSP tape.[36] Thirty-five different 5-year samples, composed of as few as 584 and as many as 1094 NYSE stocks, which were each one year ahead of the next sample, from 1926 through 1964, were used to estimate equation(8.1). But, then, BJS were reluctant to estimate the SML that characterized any of the 5-year sample periods by simply regressing the sampled stocks' average returns onto their betas. King had shown that the residual errors from equation (8.1) were correlated between many stocks.[37] This nonindependence between stocks could introduce bias and/or inefficiencies that could confound the second-pass cross-sectional regressions to be estimated later.

## B. Ten Portfolios Grouped on Betas

To reduce the econometric problems in estimating the SML caused by measurement errors, and to expedite their computations, BJS formed 10 portfolios of stocks grouped into risk deciles.[38] To eliminate selection bias in forming the 10 equal-sized portfolios to be used to estimate the SML, BJS grouped their stocks into risk deciles based on their calculated 5-year betas.[39] Then they calculated these 10 portfolios' rates of return in the following sixth year without measuring their betas again. Having avoided selection bias, BJS proceeded to generate large portfolios of stocks (always in excess of 58 stocks per risk decile portfolio) from 5 years of data and then to measure each of the 10 portfolios' returns in the sixth year. The 5-year average beta for each decile portfolio was calculated and paired with the sixth-year return averaged over all stocks in each decile portfolio. This procedure was replicated for each years' annual returns from 1931 to 1965.

---

[36]CRSP stands for the computer tape compiled at the Center for Research on Security Prices which contains monthly observations of all NYSE stocks.

[37]King, "Market and Industry Factors in Stock Price Behavior."

[38]Black, Jensen, and Scholes, "The Capital Asset Pricing Model"; see Figs. 6 and 7, especially.

[39]Jan Kmenta, *Elements of Econometrics* (New York: Macmillan Publishing Co., Inc., 1971); see Sec. 9-2; or J. Johnston, *Econometric Methods*, 2nd ed. (New York: McGraw-Hill Book Company, Inc., 1972); see Sec. 7.5.

## C. Second-Pass Regression Estimates of SML

After BJS calculated 35 years of betas and average annual returns for each of the 10 beta decile portfolios, they were able to undertake the cross-sectional second-pass regression estimates of the SML using equation (8.10):

$$\bar{r}_{it} = z_t + X_t b_{it} + y_{it} \qquad \text{for } i = 1, 2, \ldots, 10 \text{ decile portfolios.} \quad (8.10)$$

where $\bar{r}_{it}$ denotes the average rate of return (for the sixth year) from the $i$th risk decile portfolio in the $t$th sample period; $b_{it}$ represents the $i$th decile portfolio's average beta measured over the $t$th 5-year sample period; $X_t$ is regression equation (8.10)'s slope coefficient, which estimates the slope of the SML during sample period $t$, that is, $X_t = [E(r_{mt}) - R_t]$; $z_t$ is the regression's intercept estimate of the SML's riskless rate intercept; and $y_i$ is the residual return for the $i$th risk decile portfolio in sample period $t$, $E(y_{it}) = 0$.

The SML shown graphically in Fig. 8.20 was estimated with regression equation (8.10) over the 10 betas and returns averaged from each of the 10 risk decile portfolios from the total 35-year period analyzed by BJS.

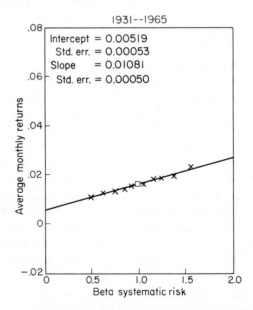

Figure 8.20. Average Monthly Returns Versus Systematic Risk for the 35-Year Period 1931–1965 for the 10 Portfolios and the Market Portfolio

Source: F. Black, M. Jensen, and M. Scholes, "The Capital Asset Pricing Model: Some Empirical Tests," reprinted in *Studies in the Theory of Capital Markets*, edited by M. C. Jensen, (New York: Praeger Publishers, Inc., 1972), Figure 7.

### D. Empirical Estimates of the SML

Each cross on Fig. 8.20 represents the average beta and average rate of return for one of the 10 portfolios grouped on beta deciles. The small square near the center of the 10 crosses represents the risk and return for the market's overall average. The straight line through the 10 crosses in Fig. 8.20 is an empirical estimate of the SML prepared with regression equation (8.10). This long-run average SML may be considered to be the best empirical estimate of the equilibrium SML developed by BJS, because it averages over bull and bear periods to measure the market's average tendencies.

When shorter sample periods are used for second-pass regression estimates of the SML, it sometimes assumes positions that surprise students who have not considered the implications of capital market theory for the dynamic disequilibria that characterize short-run buying and selling. Figure 8.21 shows estimates of the SML which BJS prepared from four different sample periods of 105 months each. The SML from the April 1957 to December 1965 sample slopes downward. This SML slopes downward because the sample period contained steep market declines in 1957, 1960, 1962, and 1965. During bearish periods the high-beta stocks experience the greatest negative rates of return, and this pulls their average return down below what was earned by less risky low-beta stocks. Conversely, in prevailing bullish samples, such as occurred from January 1931 to September 1939, following the Great Crash of 1929, the SML slopes steeply upward because the high-beta stocks experience the highest average rates of return. If one-month estimates of the SML were shown, their intercept and slope coefficients would vary even more dramatically than the $8\frac{3}{4}$-year SML's shown in Fig. 8.21.[40]

The preceding discussion of the empirical work by Black, Jensen, and Scholes contains two valuable insights. First, it provides good empirical estimates of the SML at different points in time.[41] Second, it demon-

---

[40]The $z_t$ intercept from regression equation (8.10) is the empirical estimate of the rate of return in sample period $t$ from the zero-beta-positive-variance portfolio developed by Black in order to specify the capital market theory without a riskless rate: Black, "Capital Market Equilibrium with Restricted Borrowing." Unpublished empirical work by the authors found the monthly values of $z_t$ to be significantly positively correlated with the returns from the market portfolio. Thus, the zero-beta portfolio appears to be misspecified econometrically—it contains significant systematic risk. Black's mathematical derivation of the zero-beta portfolio theory is sound, however.

[41]Other empirical estimates of the SML were published. See, for example, W. F. Sharpe and G. M. Cooper, "Risk–Return Classes of New York Stock Exchange Common Stocks, 1931–1967," *Financial Analysts Journal*, Vol. 28, No. 2, 1972, pp. 413–446. This Sharpe–Cooper article also suggests econometric problems related to what econometricians call the random-coefficient model.

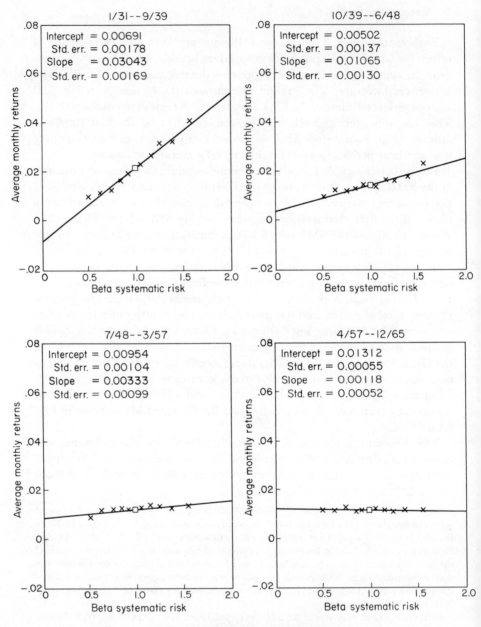

Figure 8.21. Empirical Estimates of SML

*Source:* F. Black, M. Jensen, and M. Scholes, "The Capital Asset Pricing Model: Some Empirical Tests," reprinted in *Studies in the Theory of Capital Markets*, edited by M. C. Jensen (New York: Praeger Publishers, Inc., 1972), Figures 8, 9, 10, and 11.

strates how applied econometricians deal with problems in their empirical work.[42]

## 8.8  Partial Versus General Equilibrium Analysis

One of the unresolved problems of capital market theory which causes theoretical as well as empirical problems revolves around defining which assets should be included in the market portfolio. This question is important because of the central role that portfolio $M$ plays in both the mathematical theory and the econometric empirical models.

If the market portfolio is narrowly construed to include only *equity shares*, then a stock market index can be used as a surrogate for portfolio $M$ in empirical tests. This is the approach typically used. As a result of this *narrow view* of the assets in the market portfolio, the capital market theory must be viewed as a *partial equilibrium* model for the stock market which has no further implications. It is a partial equilibrium model because it only explains diversification among common stocks and has asset pricing implications for common stocks. Bonds, options (that is, puts and calls), commodities, cash, savings, real estate, and other possible investments are all exogenous to this narrowly defined capital market theory—that is, it only rationalizes a partial or single-market (namely, a stock market) equilibrium.

Some economists have chosen to give a broader interpretation to the market portfolio. These analysts wish to include stocks, bonds, options, savings, cash, real estate, art objects, human capital, and all other types of investment opportunities in the market portfolio. No empirical surrogate or market index exists for this broadly defined market portfolio; so no empirical work has been done with this more ambitious interpretation of the capital market theory. But mathematical theoreticians are working to reformulate the capital market theory as a *general equilibrium theory* by extending it to include all investments. The solution to such a general equilibrium model would have implications for equilibrium conditions in *different markets*. And, of course, as more different investment opportunities are included in the analysis, it becomes possible to derive more dominant efficient frontiers in $[\sigma, E(r)]$ space.

Advocates of the general equilibrium approach have criticized the partial

---

[42]Since Black, Jensen, and Scholes published their study other significant econometric problems relevant to estimating the SML have come to light. The beta coefficient estimated in the first-pass regressions appears to be a random coefficient, as explained in Sec. 12.4 of Theil's *Principles of Econometrics*. Empirical research into the single-index-market model by one of the authors indicates that the beta is a random coefficient: Fabozzi and Francis, "Beta as a Random Coefficient." In a different vein it has been shown that the stock market averages used as a surrogate for the market portfolio also impart problems to empirical work: see Roll, "A Critique of the Asset Pricing Theory's Tests."

equilibrium research that has been done as being myopic and incomplete.[43] Although such criticisms are true, it does not mean that the partial equilibrium analysis has no value. The equity market studies published in the past two decades have yielded substantial advancements in knowledge, and further stock market research ls needed. Thus, the capital market theory is useful for partial equilibrium analysis and is also useful for work of a more general nature.

### 8.9  Capital Market Theory Conclusions

The capital market theory explained in this chapter is the first economic theory about security market equilibrium which has ever gained general acceptance in the academic community at large. Practically all business finance professors and economic theory professors in the world generally subscribe to and support the theory.

Since securities markets fascinate many people, the capital market theory is widely discussed and debated. Sometimes the debate becomes shrill and it may appear as if disagreement exists; this is not the case, however. Actually, practically all the intellectual polemics about capital market theory are about small esoteric aspects of the overall theory and/or how to apply it. The capital market theory model is generally well received.

Capital market theory is also receiving increasing acceptance among business managers.[44] Most security analysts and portfolio managers are still naive about it. But most of them are embarassed to admit their naivety and are attempting to learn and implement the theory—it is increasingly the "in" thing to do in the Wall Street community. Thus, it behooves today's business finance students to study capital market theory if they expect a career in investment management.

### Appendix 8A
### The Mathematical Foundations of Capital Market Theory*

At the beginning of Chapter 8 the assumptions underlying capital market theory were listed. These assumptions ensure that the capital markets will maintain an equilibrium as graphed in Fig. 8.1.[1] As long as these assumptions

---

[43]Roll, "A Critique of the Asset Pricing Theory's Tests: Part I, On Past and Potential Testability of the Theory, *Journal of Financial Economics*, March 1977, Vol. 4, No. 2, pp. 129–176.

[44]See C. Welles, "The Beta Revolution: Learning to Live with Risk," *Institutional Investor*, 1971, for a Wall Street news reporter's view of the impact of capital market theory.

*This appendix takes up mathematics that is not necessary for a basic understanding.

[1]Actually, the assumptions may also represent an equilibrium where more portfolios than just $M$ are tangent to the CML, as shown in Fig. 8A.1 (alternate). The propositions developed in this chapter are not altered by using this approach.

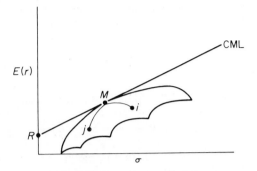

Figure 8A.1. Opportunities in Risk-Return Space

are not violated, several important propositions about capital market theory may be proven mathematically. Throughout this appendix reference will be made to Fig. 8A.1 as some propositions are proved.

### 8A.1 Capital Market Line

*Proposition I*     *The capital market line (CML) is linear in $(E(r), \sigma)$ space.*

*Proof*     Every point on the CML is some combination of $R$ and $M$. Thus, the measure of risk for points on the CML is given by the formula for $\sigma_h$, where $h$ stands for the "hypothetical portfolio" containing two assets, $R$ and $M$.

$$\sigma_h = \sqrt{x_R^2 \sigma_R^2 + (1 - x_R)^2 \sigma_M^2 + 2x_R(1 - x_R)\rho_{RM}\sigma_R\sigma_M}. \qquad (8A.1)$$

By definition, $R$ is the riskless asset and must have $\sigma_R = 0$. Thus, equation (8A.1) may be rewritten as (8A.1a) by substituting zero for $\sigma_R$.

$$\begin{aligned}\sigma_h &= \sqrt{0 + (1 - x_R)^2 \sigma_M^2 + 0} \\ &= (1 - x_R)\sigma_M = \sigma_M - \sigma_M x_R.\end{aligned} \qquad (8A.1a)$$

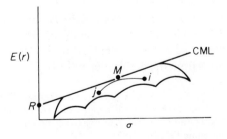

Figure 8A.1 (Alternate)

The change in $\sigma_h$ as $x_R$ is varied (that is, moving up and down the CML) is given by the derivative of (8A.1a) with respect to $x_R$.

$$\frac{d\sigma_h}{dx_R} = -\sigma_M. \tag{8A.2}$$

The return of portfolios on the CML is given by equation (8A.3):

$$E(r_h) = x_R R + (1 - x_R) \cdot E(r_M). \tag{8A.3}$$

The change in $E(r_h)$ as $x_R$ is varied (that is, moving up and down the CML) is given by the derivative of (8A.3) with respect to $x_R$.

$$\frac{dE(r_h)}{dx_R} = R - E(r_M). \tag{8A.4}$$

The slope of the CML is represented by the differential equation $dE(r_h)/d\sigma_h$. This differential may be evaluated by applying the chain rule to equations (8A.4) and (8A.2) as shown in equation (8A.5).

$$\frac{dE(r_h)}{d\sigma_h} = \frac{dE(r_h)}{dx_R} \cdot \frac{dx_R}{d\sigma_h} = \frac{E(r_M) - R}{\sigma_M}. \tag{8A.5}$$

Since (8A.5) is a constant and it is the formula for the slope of the CML, the CML is linear in $(E(r), \sigma)$ space.     Q.E.D.

### 8A.2  Beta Coefficient and SML

In a 1964 article, Sharpe hypothesized the CML and therefrom derived the SML.[2] He derived the SML using the regression coefficient from equation (8.2) as a measure of systematic risk.

$$E(r_i|r_I) = a + b_i r_I. \tag{8.2}$$

As discussed in Chapter VIII, the $b_i$ is a measure of systematic risk. The $b_i$ is sometimes called *Sharpe's beta coefficient*.

Sharpe's mathematical derivation of the SML is to be found in footnote 22 of his original 1964 article. The derivation of the SML in terms of Sharpe's beta coefficient presented below is identical to Sharpe's original derivation. Proposition II follows from the derivation of the SML in terms of $b_i$.

---

[2]W. F. Sharpe, "Capital Asset Prices: A Theory of Market Equilibrium Under Conditions of Risk," *Journal of Finance*, September 1964, pp. 425–442. Reprinted on pp. 653–670 of S. H. Archer and C. A. D'Ambrosio, *The Theory of Business Finance: A Book of Readings* (New York: Macmillan Publishing Co., Inc., 1967).

*Proposition II*    The expected return from the ith asset is a positive linear function
of the beta coefficient for that security.

*Proof*    Recall that point $M$ in Fig. 8A.1 is the market portfolio. Also recall
that every point on the CML is some combination of $M$ and the risk-free
security represented by point $R$. Let $\alpha$ be the weight of security $i$ in any
hypothetical portfolio composed of $i$ (or $j$) and $M$. The hypothetical portfolio
will move along the curve $iM$ in Fig. 8A.1 as $\alpha$ varies. And, let $(1 - \alpha)$ be
the weight of $M$ in the hypothetical portfolio. In equilibrium, the price of
any security such as $i$ must adjust so excess demand for it is zero. When excess
demand for securities such as $i$ is zero, the market portfolio will contain all
securities in the proportions they exist. Also, the curve $iM$ must be tangent
to the CML, reflecting the equality of the rate of exchange available in the
market (that is, the slope of CML) and investor's marginal rate of transformation of risk for return (that is, the slope of $iM$ at $\alpha = 0$). These tangency
conditions imply (1) the appropriate risk measure for individual securities,
and (2) equilibrium security prices.

The risk of the hypothetical $(h)$ portfolio is given were as $\sigma_h$:

$$\sigma_h = \sqrt{\alpha^2 \sigma_i^2 + (1 - \alpha)^2 \sigma_M^2 + 2\rho_{iM}\alpha(1 - \alpha)\sigma_i\sigma_M}, \tag{8A.6}$$

where $i$ is the portfolio represented by point $i$ in Fig. 8A.1. Of course, equation (8A.6) is the square root of equation (2.9) for the two-security case.

Moving from $i$ to $M$ along the curve in Fig. 8A.1, $\alpha$ approaches zero at
$M$, where the curve is tangent to the CML. The concomitant change in $\sigma_h$
with respect to the change in $\alpha$ is shown by differentiating equation (8A.6)
with respect to $\alpha$.

$$\frac{d\sigma_h}{d\alpha} = \frac{2\alpha\sigma_i^2 - 2\sigma_M^2 + 2\alpha\sigma_M^2 + 2\rho_{iM}\sigma_i\sigma_M(1 - 2\alpha)}{2\sigma_h}, \tag{8A.7}$$

which simplifies to (8A.7a) at $\alpha = 0$:

$$\left.\frac{d\sigma_h}{d\alpha}\right|_{\alpha=0} = \frac{-1}{\sigma_h}(\sigma_M^2 - \rho_{iM}\sigma_i\sigma_M). \tag{8A.7a}$$

But at $\alpha = 0$, the hypothetical portfolio is identical to the market portfolio,
so $\sigma_h = \sigma_M$ at $\alpha = 0$. This equality means that equation (8A.7a) simplifies
to (8A.8) by substituting $\sigma_M$ for $\sigma_h$.

$$\left.\frac{d\sigma_h}{d\alpha}\right|_{\alpha=0} = -(\sigma_M - \rho_{iM}\sigma_i). \tag{8A.8}$$

The expected return of the hypothetical portfolio is given by equation (8A.9):

$$E(r_h) = \alpha E(r_i) + (1 - \alpha)E(r_M).\qquad(8A.9)$$

The change in $E(r_h)$ with respect to a change in $\alpha$ is

$$\frac{dE(r_h)}{d\alpha} = -[E(r_M) - E(r_i)].\qquad(8A.10)$$

Applying the chain rule to equations (8A.10) and (8A.7) yields the slope of the curve from $i$ to $M$.

$$\frac{dE(r_h)}{d\sigma_h}\bigg|_{\alpha=0} = \frac{dE(r_h)}{d\alpha} \cdot \frac{d\alpha}{d\sigma_h}\bigg|_{\alpha=0} = \frac{-[E(r_M) - E(r_i)]}{-(\sigma_M - \rho_{iM}\sigma_i)}.\qquad(8A.11)$$

Since equation (8A.11) is tangent to the CML where $\alpha = 0$, the slopes of the curve from $i$ to $M$ (that is, the marginal rate of substitution available to investors) is equal to the slope of the CML (that is, the rate of substitution available in the market). This condition of market equilibrium means that equations (8A.11) and (8A.5) must be equal at $\alpha = 0$. Specifically,

$$\frac{dE(r_h)}{d\sigma_h}\bigg|_{\alpha=0} = \frac{E(r_M) - E(r_i)}{\sigma_M - \rho_{iM}\sigma_i} = \frac{E(r_M) - R}{\sigma_M},\qquad(8A.12)$$

where the right side of (8A.12) is (8A.5). It is well known that the $b_i$, slope parameter, in (8.2) is variously defined as follows:

$$b_i = \frac{\text{cov }(r_i, r_M)}{\sigma_M^2} = \frac{\rho_{iM}\sigma_i\sigma_M}{\sigma_M^2} = \frac{\rho_{iM}\sigma_i}{\sigma_M}.\qquad(8A.13)$$

Equation (8A.12) may be solved in terms of $b_i = (\rho_{iM}\sigma_i/\sigma_M)$ to find $E(r_i)$ as follows:

$$\frac{E(r_M) - E(r_i)}{\sigma_M^2 - \rho_{iM}\sigma_i\sigma_M} = \frac{E(r_M) - R}{\sigma_M^2} = \frac{1}{\sigma_M} \text{ multiplied by (8A.12),}$$

$$(\sigma_M^2 - \rho_{iM}\sigma_i\sigma_M)[E(r_M) - R] = (\sigma_M^2)[E(r_M) - E(r_i)],$$

$$E(r_M)\sigma_M^2 - E(r_M)\rho_{iM}\sigma_i\sigma_M - R\sigma_M^2 + R\rho_{iM}\sigma_i\sigma_M$$
$$= E(r_M)(\sigma_M^2) - E(r_i)(\sigma_M^2),$$

$$[R - E(r_M)] \cdot \rho_{iM}\sigma_i\sigma_M = [-E(r_i) - E(r_M)]\sigma_M^2 + [E(r_M) + R]\sigma_M^2;$$

$$\frac{\rho_{iM}\sigma_i}{\sigma_M} = \frac{[-E(r_i) - E(r_M)]\sigma_M^2 + [E(r_M) + R]\sigma_M^2}{[R - E(r_M)]\sigma_M^2},$$

$$= \frac{-E(r_i) - E(r_M) + E(r_M) + R}{R - E(r_M)};$$

$$-E(r_i) + R = \frac{\rho_{iM}\sigma_i}{\sigma_M}[R - E(r_M)],$$

$$E(r_i) = R + \frac{\rho_{iM}\sigma_i}{\sigma_M}[E(r_M) - R],$$

$$= R + (b_i)[E(r_M) - R]. \tag{8A.14}$$

In words, equation (8A.14) says that the expected return on the *i*th security is equal to the riskless rate of return ($R$) plus the product of $b_i$ times the risk premium on the market portfolio. Equation (8A.14) is graphed in Fig. 8A.2. Q.E.D.

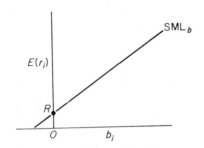

Figure 8A.2. Security Market Line

## 8A.3  Fama's Derivation of the SML in Terms of cov (*i*, *M*)

Fama showed a different approach to deriving the SML.[3] Fama formulates the SML in terms of the covariance of the *i*th security's returns with the returns of the market portfolio—cov ($r_i$, $r_M$), referred to below as simply cov ($iM$). Fama's derivation proves proposition III.

*Proposition III      The expected return from the ith security is a positive linear function of the covariance of that security's returns with the market.*

*Proof*      Again using Fig. 8A.1 as a graphical reference, Fama's derivation is presented below. Like Sharpe, Fama differentiates the curve from *i* to *M* with respect to a change in $\alpha$—the proportion of the hypothetical portfolio invested in *i*. He then sets $\alpha = 0$ and solves the equation for the slopes of the CML and the curve *iM* at their tangency point, *M*, for the SML formula.

Taking the change in $E(r_h) = \alpha E(r_i) + (1 - \alpha)E(r_M)$ with respect to a change in $\alpha$, Fama finds that

$$\frac{dE(r_h)}{d\alpha} = -[E(r_M) - E(r_i)], \tag{8A.15}$$

[3]E. F. Fama, "Risk, Return and Equilibrium: Some Clarifying Comments," *Journal of Finance*, March 1968, pp. 29–39.

which is identical to equation (8A.10). Then, differentiating

$$\sigma_h = \sqrt{\alpha^2\sigma_i^2 + (1-\alpha)^2\sigma_M^2 + 2\alpha(1-\alpha)\,\text{cov}\,(iM)}$$

with respect to the change in $\alpha$, Fama finds equation (8A.16):

$$\frac{d\sigma_h}{d\alpha} = \frac{-2\sigma_M^2 + 2\alpha\sigma_M^2 + 2\alpha\sigma_i^2 + 2\,\text{cov}\,(iM) - 4\alpha\,\text{cov}\,(iM)}{2\sigma_h}. \quad (8A.16)$$

Where $\alpha = 0$ and the curve $iM$ is tangent to the CML, equation (8A.16) simplifies to equation (8A.16a) below at $\alpha = 0$.

$$\left.\frac{d\sigma_h}{d\alpha}\right|_{\alpha=0} = \frac{1}{2\sigma_h}[-2\sigma_M^2 + 2\,\text{cov}\,(iM)] = \frac{\text{cov}\,(iM) - \sigma_M^2}{\sigma_h}. \quad (8A.16a)$$

Applying the chain rule to equations (8A.15) and (8A.16a) yields

$$\left.\frac{dE(r_h)}{d\sigma_h}\right|_{\alpha=0} = \frac{dE(r_h)}{d\alpha} \cdot \left.\frac{d\alpha}{d\sigma_h}\right|_{\alpha=0} = \frac{E(r_i) - E(r_M)}{[\text{cov}\,(i,M) - \sigma_M^2]/\sigma_h}. \quad (8A.17)$$

Setting the slope of the CML [equation (8A.5)] equal to the slope of the curve $iM$ at point $M$ [equation (8A.17)] yields the following equality.

$$\underbrace{\frac{E(r_M) - R}{\sigma_M}}_{\text{Eq. (8A.5)}} = \underbrace{\frac{E(r_i) - E(r_M)}{[\text{cov}\,(i,M) - \sigma_M^2]/\sigma_h}}_{\text{Eq. (8A.17)}} = \left.\frac{dE(r_h)}{d\sigma_h}\right|_{\alpha=0}. \quad (8A.18)$$

At the tangency point $M$, where $\alpha = 0$, the fact that $\sigma_M = \sigma_h$ facilitates algebraic manipulation. Solving equation (8A.18) for $E(r_i)$ yields the SML. The algebra is as follows:

$$\frac{E(r_M) - R}{\sigma_M} = \frac{E(r_i) - E(r_M)}{[\text{cov}\,(iM) - \sigma_M^2]/\sigma_h}, \quad (8A.18)$$

$$\sigma_M^2[E(r_i) - E(r_M)] = [E(r_M) - R]\cdot[\text{cov}\,(iM) - \sigma_M^2],$$

$$\sigma_M^2[E(r_i) + E(r_M) - R - E(r_M)] = [E(r_M) - R]\,\text{cov}\,(iM),$$

$$E(r_i) = R + \frac{E(r_M) - R}{\sigma_M^2}\,\text{cov}\,(iM). \quad (8A.19)$$

In words, equation (8A.19) says the expected return on the $i$th security equals the riskless return ($R$) plus the product of the slope coefficient

$$\frac{E(r_M) - R}{\sigma_M^2}$$

times the covariance of returns for security $i$ with the market. More simply, expected return on the $i$th security is a linear function of its systematic risk as measured by cov $(iM)$.   Q.E.D.

Equation (8A.19) is graphed in Fig. 8A.3. Fama's equation for the SML [that is, (8A.19)] is identical to a scale factor to Sharpe's equation [that is,

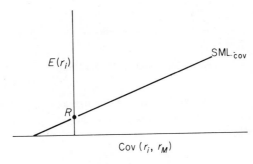

Figure 8A.3. Security Market Line

(8A.14)] for the SML. The scale factor is $(1/\sigma_M^2)$. More specifically,

$$b_i = \frac{\text{cov } (iM)}{\sigma_M^2}. \qquad (8A.13)$$

Equation (8A.13) shows that Figs. 8A.2 and 8A.3 are identical except that 8A.2 has a scaled-down horizontal axis.

The preceding paragraph proves Proposition IV.

*Proposition IV*    *Figures 8A.2 and 8A.3 are equivalent*. That is, Sharpe's and Fama's derivations of the SML are equivalent.

## 8A.4  Third Form of the SML

It is possible to restate equation (8A.19) [using the relation shown in equation (2.6)] as equation (8A.20).

$$E(r_i) = R + \frac{E(r_M) - R}{\sigma_M^2} \text{ cov } (r_i, r_M)$$

$$= R + \frac{E(r_M) - R}{\sigma_M^2} (\rho_{iM})(\sigma_i)(\sigma_M) \qquad (8A.19)$$

$$= R + \frac{E(r_M) - R}{\sigma_M} (\rho_{iM})(\sigma_i). \qquad (8A.20)$$

Equation (8A.20) is graphed as Fig. 8A.4. This third statement of the SML highlights the facts that (1) the individual security's total variability as

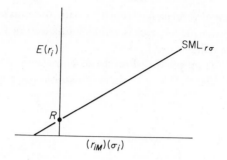

Figure 8A.4 Security Market Line

measured by $\sigma_i$, and (2) its correlation with the market $(\rho_{iM})$, are the essential determinants of the security's systematic risk. Figure 8A.4 is equivalent to Figs. 8A.2 and 8A.3.

## 8A.5 Lintner's Derivation Leads to the SML

Taking a different approach Lintner sought to determine the conditions for a stock market equilibrium by studying the relationships within the market portfolio $(M)$.[4] To find the asset most desired by Markowitz efficient investors (that is, $M$), Lintner used standard calculus techniques to maximize $\theta$. The term $\theta$ is the slope of a line from $R$ to an asset in risk–return space as measured from the horizontal dashed line out of $R$. As shown in Fig. 8A.5, point 2 is more desirable than point 1, since $\theta_1 < \theta_2$.[5]

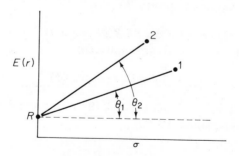

Figure 8A.5. Lintner's $\theta$

---

[4]Lintner did not use the terminology "market portfolio"—however, that is what he was studying. Lintner's article attempted to find a more general equilibrium than that of Sharpe's 1964 article, "Capital Asset Prices." See John Lintner, "Security Prices, Risk and Maximal Gains from Diversification," *Journal of Finance*, December 1965, pp. 587–615. Fama clarified the issue and removed the seeming disparity between Lintner and Sharpe: Fama, "Risk, Return and Equilibrium," especially pp. 35–36.

[5]Equations (8A.21) and (8A.21a) are Lintner's equation (7) on p. 595.

$$\theta = \frac{E(r_p) - R}{\sigma_{r_p}} = \frac{\text{risk premium of the portfolio}}{\text{risk of the portfolio}} \qquad (8A.21)$$

$$= \frac{\sum x_i E(r_i) - R}{\sqrt{\sum_i \sum_j x_i x_j \sigma_{ij}}} = \frac{\text{Eq. (2.8) less } R}{\text{Eq. (2.9)}}. \qquad (8A.21a)$$

For an $n$-security case, the securities weights in the maximum-$\theta$ portfolio are found by simultaneously solving the first partial derivatives for the weight vector:[6]

$$\frac{\partial \theta}{\partial x_1} = \frac{[E(r_1) - R] - [E(r_p) - R](1/\sigma_p^2)(\sum_i x_i \sigma_{i1})}{\sigma_p} = 0,$$

$$\frac{\partial \theta}{\partial x_2} = \frac{[E(r_2) - R] - [E(r_p) - R](1/\sigma_p^2)(\sum_i x_i \sigma_{i2})}{\sigma_p} = 0,$$

$$\vdots \qquad (8A.22)$$

$$\frac{\partial \theta}{\partial x_n} = \frac{[E(r_n) - R] - [E(r_p) - R](1/\sigma_p^2)(\sum_i x_i \sigma_{in})}{\sigma_p} = 0.$$

The partial derivative of the $i$th security from the system of equations (8A.22) may be restated as follows.

$$\frac{\partial \theta}{\partial x_i} = \frac{[E(r_i) - R] - [E(r_p) - R](1/\sigma_p^2)(\sum_j x_j \sigma_{ji})}{\sigma_p} = 0, \quad (8A.22a)$$

$$E(r_i) - R = \frac{E(r_p) - R}{\sigma_p^2} \left(\sum_i x_i \sigma_{ij}\right)$$

$$= \lambda \, \text{cov} \, (r_i, r_M), \qquad (8A.19)$$

where $\lambda = [E(r_p) - R]/\sigma_p^2$ and $\sum_i x_i \sigma_{ij} = \text{cov} \, (r_i, r_M)$ if the portfolio in (8A.21) contains all assets in the market. Note that (8A.22a) has been reduced to (8A.19), the SML in terms of cov $(r_i, r_M)$. Thus, Lintner's approach also yields the SML, just as Sharpe's and Fama's methods did.

### 8A.6  Black's Zero-Beta Portfolio

In order to restate the capital market theory with fewer simplifying assumptions, Black[7] refined and extended Hastie's[8] concept of a zero-beta-positive-variance portfolio shown above in Fig. 8.14. The one-period returns

---

[6]This system comprises Lintner's equations (11) on p. 596.

[7]F. Black, "Capital Market Equilibrium with Restricted Borrowing," *Journal of Business*, Vol. 45, July 1972, pp. 444–454.

[8]K. L. Hastie, "The Determination of Optimal Investment Policy," *Management Science*, August 1967, pp. B-771 through B-772.

on this zero-beta portfolio vary unsystematically so that it has zero covariance (or beta) with the market portfolio's returns, cov $(r_z, r_m) = 0$. However, the zero-beta portfolio's unsystematic risk is positive, var $(r_z) > 0$, so that it has diversifiable risk. Black formed a portfolio of the zero-beta portfolio, denoted $Z$, and the market portfolio, denoted $M$, and by using short sales and/or leverage was able to approximate the SML without a riskless rate of interest. Consider the portfolios that may be formed from two risky assets such as $Z$ and $M$ in more detail before proceeding to Black's model.

Figure 8A.6 illustrates various portfolios that can be derived from the two risky assets denoted $Z$ and $M$, $\sigma_M > \sigma_Z > 0$. The expected rate of return from these portfolios is denoted $E(r_p)$ and is defined by equation (8A.23).

$$E(r_p) = x_Z E(r_Z) + (1 - x_Z)E(r_M), \tag{8A.23}$$

where $x_M = 1 - x_Z$. The portfolios' risk is measured with equation (8A.24).

$$\text{var}(r_p) = x_Z^2 \sigma_Z^2 + (1 - x_Z)^2 \sigma_M^2 + 2x_Z(1 - x_Z)\sigma_{ZM} \tag{8A.24}$$
$$= x_Z^2 \sigma_Z^2 + (1 - x_Z)^2 \sigma_M^2 + 2x_Z(1 - x_Z)\sigma_M\sigma_Z\rho_{MZ}. \tag{8A.24a}$$

The opportunity loci in Fig. 8A.6 represent three different correlations between the returns from risky assets $Z$ and $M$—perfect positive correlation, $\rho_{ZM} = 1.0$, zero correlation, $\rho_{ZM} = 0$, and perfect negative correla-

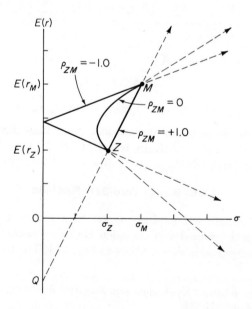

Figure 8A.6. Portfolios That May Be Generated from Two Risky Assets Denoted $Z$ and $M$ with Leverage and/or Short Sales

tion, $\rho_{ZM} = -1.0$. The opportunity loci, which are illustrated with solid lines, represent portfolios without short sales (or equivalently, leverage or margin trading). But the dashed lines represent opportunities that can only be attained by selling short (or issuing) one of the assets to raise additional capital to buy the other asset. The dashed lines extend infinitely far toward the direction of increasing risk to represent the use of infinite quantities of short sales or financial leverage. Since the zero-beta portfolio (by definition) has zero correlation with the market, the zero correlation curve in Fig. 8A.6 represents the hyperbolic opportunity set available without a riskless asset but with short sales (or issuing) of the two risky assets $Z$ and $M$.

Sharpe[9] and later Black have shown that in an equilibrium, with short sales and/or leverage allowed, investment opportunities in $[b, E(r)]$ space will be linear. Black[10] has shown that this linear locus of portfolios and individual assets is defined by equation (8A.25).

$$E(r_s) = E(r_z)(1 - b_s) + E(r_M)b_s, \qquad (8A.25)$$

where $b_s$ is the beta systematic risk of asset $s$.[11] The term $E(r_z)$ denotes the expected rate of return from the zero-beta-positive-variance portfolio, and it can be shown that $R < E(r_z) < E(r_m)$.

If lending at the riskless rate, $R$, is allowed, but funds can only be obtained be selling short or issuing a risky asset like $Z$, the capital market line (CML) is replaced by the capital market curve through the points $RTMC$ in Fig. 8A.7. And the security market line (SML) is replaced by equation (8A.25), which passes through points $E(r_z)TMC$ in Fig. 8A.8. Point $T$ in Figs. 8A.7 and 8A.8 is a tangency portfolio derived from portfolios $Z$ and $M$. In Fig. 8A.8 the efficient portfolios will not lie on the line $E(r_z)TMC$, representing equation (8A.25); instead, they lie along the two straight lines from $R$ to $T$ and then through $TMC$. The efficient lending portfolios along the two rays $RT$ in Figs. 8A.6 and 8A.7 have a one-to-one correspondence. The beta coefficient of these efficient portfolios is $x_T b_T$ for $0 < x_T < 1.0$. Below point $T$ efficient portfolios expected returns are equal to the quantity $[x_T E(r_T) + (1 - x_T)R]$.

Individual risky assets and imperfectly diversified portfolios are on the curve $ZTMC$ in Fig. 8A.7; these assets lie along the line in Fig. 8A.8 that represents equation (8A.25) and passes through points $E(r_z)TMC$. The individual assets and naively diversified portfolios on the ray from $E(r_z)$ to $T$ dominate the efficient portfolios on the ray from $R$ to $T$ in Fig. 8A.8. This

---

[9]Sharpe, "Capital Asset Prices."

[10]Black, "Capital Market Equilibrium with Restricted Borrowing."

[11]Equation (8A.25) is the linear relation Black, Jensen, and Scholes estimated empirically to obtain estimates of the rates of return from the zero-beta portfolio in "The Capital Asset Pricing Model: Some Empirical Tests," in *Studies in the Theory of Capital Markets.*

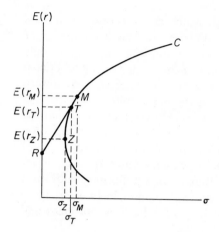

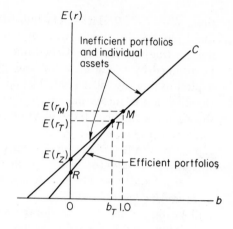

Figure 8A.7 Efficient Frontier Is RTMC When Riskless Lending, But Not Riskless Borrowing, Is Possible

Figure 8A.8. Relationship Between Beta and Expected Return When Riskless Lending, But Not Riskless Borrowing, Is Possible

is not true in $[\sigma, E(r)]$ space, however. The same efficient portfolios that appeared to be dominated by individual assets below point $T$ in Fig. 8A.8 lie on the dominant ray $RT$ in Fig. 8A.7.[12]

One of the realistic aspects of the models shown in Figs. 8A.7 and 8A.8 is that lending at the riskless rate is fairly realistic. Also, the slope of equation (8A.25) is less than the slope of the SML, $[E(r_m) - E(r_z)] < [E(r_m) - R]$, as the empirical data suggest.[13]

---

[12]For an extended discussion of Figures 8A.7 and 8A.8 see M. C. Jensen, "Capital Markets," *Bell Journal of Economics and Management Science*, Autumn 1972, Vol. 3, No. 2, pp. 357–398; see Figures 4 and 5 and their related discussion.

[13]Other empirical estimates of the SML were published by W. F. Sharpe and G. M. Cooper, "Risk–Return Classes of NYSE Common Stocks, 1931–1967," *Financial Analysts Journal*, March–April 1972.

## Selected References

Sharpe, W. F., "Capital Asset Prices: A Theory of Market Equilibrium Under Conditions of Risk," *Journal of Finance*, September 1964, pp. 425–442.
This classic investments paper was the first complete statement of the capital market theory. Algebra and statistics are used. A crucial derivation employing elementary differential calculus is relegated to a footnote and may be omitted with no loss in continuity.

Tobin, James, "Liquidity Preference as Behavior Towards Risk," *Review of Economic Studies*, Vol. 26, No. 1, 1958, pp. 68–86.
This classic paper on monetary economics develops much of the machinery and concepts that underlie the capital market theory. Algebra and statistics are used.

Both articles above are reprinted in *The Theory of Business Finance* by S. H. Archer and C. A. D'Ambrosio, published by Macmillan Publishing Co., Inc., New York, 1967.

## Questions and Problems

1. "As the market changes from bullish in one year and bearish in another year, the security market line (SML) will change from a positive slope to a negative slope if it is estimated separately with the one-year returns from the bullish and bearish years." True, false, or uncertain? Explain.

2. Define and discuss (a) systematic risk, and (b) unsystematic risk. Give verbal definitions, use formulas with all symbols labeled, and, use graphs with all parts labeled.

3. Assume that you have three investment opportunities:
(a) you can lend at the riskless rate, denoted $R$.
(b) you can borrow at the riskless rate.
(c) you can invest in the risky market portfolio, denoted $M$.
Given these opportunities, draw a graph in risk–return space with all parts labeled of the best investment opportunities you could generate. Show math derivations for the model you drew in the graph.

4. Define and discuss systematic risk verbally, mathematically, and graphically. How are assets' prices affected by systematic risk? By unsystematic risk?

5. "The capital market theory suggests that the price of an individual asset (for example, a share of stock or a bond) should adjust in such a manner that its expected rate of return was on a linear function, called the capital market line (CML), of the asset's total risk (as measured by its standard deviation of returns)." Is this sentence true, false, or uncertain? Explain. (*Hint:* It is false.)

6. Suppose that you owned a highly cyclical steel mill and its common stock had a beta coefficient of 1.5. If you had an opportunity to merge your steel mill with a countercyclical company of equal size and total market value, would you do it? The countercyclical merger candidate manufactures red ink (which sells well in recessions) and its stock has a negative beta of $-0.5$. How would you evaluate this merger opportunity in light of the capital market theory?

7. Consider the following three assets:

| Asset | Characteristic Line | $\rho$ | $E(r)$ (%) | var $(r)$ |
|-------|---------------------|--------|-----------|-----------|
| 1 | $r_{1t} = 0.05 + 1.1r_{mt} + e_t$ | 0.9 | 9 | 0.3 |
| 2 | $r_{2t} = 0.04 + 1.0r_{mt} + e_t$ | 0.7 | 10 | 0.2 |
| 3 | $r_{3t} = 0.03 - 0.2r_{mt} + e_t$ | 0.1 | 4 | 0.4 |

Assume that you are managing a portfolio comprised mainly of common stocks. The Wharton econometric forecast, to which your portfolio subscribes, shows a recession starting four quarters in the future. As a result,

194

you are worried about a bear stock market. Which of the three assets above should you add to your portfolio in a situation like this? Why? What factors did you consider?

8. Define Markowitz diversification verbally. Use formulas to show how the benefits of using Markowitz diversification vary inversely with the correlation coefficients between the assets. Use a small portfolio of two risky assets, and graphically show how Markowitz diversification works.

```
999999999999999999999999999999999999999999999999999999999999999999999999999999999
999999999999999999999999999999999999999999999999999999999999999999999999999999999
99999999999999999999999999999999  999   99999   99999999999999999999999999999999
999999999999999999999999999999999  9999   999   9999999999999999999999999999999999
99999999999999999999999999999999  99999    9   9999999999999999999999999999999999
99999999999999999999999999999999  999999       99999999999999999999999999999999
99999999999999999999999999999999  9999999   9999999999999999999999999999999999999
99999999999999999999999999999999  999999       99999999999999999999999999999999
99999999999999999999999999999999  99999    9   99999999999999999999999999999999
999999999999999999999999999999999  9999   999   9999999999999999999999999999999999
99999999999999999999999999999999  999   99999   99999999999999999999999999999999
999999999999999999999999999999999999999999999999999999999999999999999999999999999
999999999999999999999999999999999999999999999999999999999999999999999999999999999
```

# The Limits of Diversification

**N**AIVE *diversification* was defined as "not putting all your eggs in one basket." Naive diversification suggests owning many different securities—presumably, the more the better. Naive diversification ignores the covariance between securities and leads to superfluous diversification. Portfolios containing many securities selected by chartists or fundamental analysts would be examples of naively diversified portfolios, since they typically ignore covariances.

*Markowitz diverisfication* was defined as combining securities that are less than perfectly positively correlated in an effort to reduce risk in the portfolio without reducing the portfolio's expected return. To the extent that securities' returns are all positively correlated, the risk-reduction benefits to be gained from Markowitz diversification are limited.

It is an unfortunate fact that nearly all securities' returns are positively correlated with each other and with the market.[1] The portion of a security's variability of return that is correlated with the rest of the market was designated *systematic risk*; it cannot be eliminated from a portfolio containing many assets with any kind of diversification.

Using a sample of 63 firms from the New York Stock Exchange, B. F. King estimated what portion of the average security's risk is systematic. He used monthly price changes from 1927 to 1960 for 63 firms from six industries for his study. King concluded that "the typical stock has about half of its vari-

---

[1]B. F. King, "Market and Industry Factors in Stock Price Behavior," *Journal of Business*, Vol. 39, January 1966 Supplement, pp. 149–150.

ance explained by an element of price change that affects the whole market."[2] This finding can be summarized as follows:

| | |
|---|---|
| Systematic risk, which is undiversifiable | 50% |
| Plus: unsystematic risk, which is diversifiable | 50% |
| Total risk | 100% |

Of course, the risk statistics above are only averages and will vary from industry to industry as well as from company to company.

### 9.1  Naive Diversification Analyzed

Nearly every security has a high proportion of undiversifiable systematic risk which results from changes in the basic economic forces (for example, booms and recessions) that affect the value of all securities. As a result, precious few securities covary negatively with the market or with each other. This means that risk cannot be reduced to zero in portfolios of any size.[3] However, studies have shown that portfolios of randomly selected securities (that is, naively diversified portfolios) have risk that asymptotically decreases to a minimum level equal to the systematic risk in the market as the portfolio's size is increased. Figure 9.1 depicts the exact nature of this relationship.

Figure 9.1 represents the main conclusions of the Evans–Archer work.[4] The data for the figure came from 470 firms from the New York Stock Exchange. First, a data bank of semiannual rates of return for the decade from 1958 to 1967 for 470 firms was stored in the memory of a computer. Then, a random-number generator was used to select individual securities from the data bank and form them into equally weighted portfolios. Sixty portfolios—each containing two randomly selected securities—were formed. The standard deviation of returns was calculated on the 60 portfolios containing two securities each. Then the averages of the 60 portfolios' standard deviations were calculated and found to be 0.161. This process of generating 60 portfolios was done for portfolios of size 3, 4, 5, . . . , 38, 39, and 40 securities, respectively. Thus, a total of 60 random portfolios were formed of each size from 1 to 40 securities inclusive. The average standard deviation of returns for the 60 portfolios at each of the 40 different sizes was calculated. Figure 9.1 is a graph with the average standard deviation of returns plotted for each of the 40 different sizes of naively diversified portfolios. Figure 9.1 is a graph of naive diversification at work.

---

[2]Ibid., p. 151.

[3]J. L. Evans and S. H. Archer, "Diversification and the Reduction of Dispersion: An Empirical Analysis," *Journal of Finance*, December 1968, pp. 761–769. For interesting extensions, see: W. H. Wagner and S. Lau, "The Effect of Diversification on Risk," *Financial Analyst's Journal*, Vol. 26, November–December 1971, pp. 2–7.

[4]Ibid.

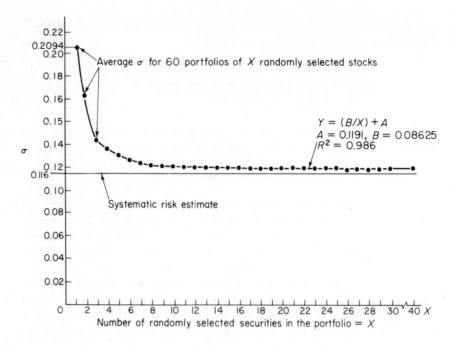

Figure 9.1. Naive Diversification Reduces Risk to the Systematic Level

Naive diversification reduces risk to the systematic level by allowing the independent random errors (that is, unsystematic variability of return) from the combined securities to average out to zero, leaving only the systematic risk. Lintner says:[5]

> Apart from negatively correlated stocks, all the gains from diversification come from "averaging over" the independent components of the returns and risks of individual stocks. Among positively correlated stocks, there would be no gains from diversification if independent variations (i.e., unsystematic risk) were absent.

Since naive diversification ignores covariances, it does not generally reduce risk below the systematic level.

### 9.2 Diversification Across Industries

Salesmen who need easy answers to tell their clients (for example, stockbrokers who are "churning" their customers to maximize their own commission income) are probably the primary advocates of naive diversification.

---

[5]John Lintner, "Security Prices, Risk, and Maximal Gains from Diversification," *Journal of Finance*, December 1965, p. 1965, p. 589 (words in parentheses added).

More sophisticated investors, such as investment advisers who are selling their services, advocate diversification across industries. Diversification across different industries is a time-honored axiom; it is presumably based on the idea that different industries are statistically independent of each other. However, whether or not this is true seems to go unquestioned by many investors.[6] In fact, Fig. 9.2 shows that the different stock price indices tend to rise and fall together in a systematic fashion, even the indices from different industries. Therefore, it seems as if diversification across industries may be a venerable tradition that needs closer scrutinizing.

L. Fisher and J. Lorie published an enlightening study of the risk-reduction benefits of diversifying across industries.[7] Their research methodology involved forming portfolios of 8, 16, 32, and 128 N.Y. Stock Exchange stocks. These portfolios were formed using two different approaches to diversification. The first approach was based on *naive diversification* and selected the stocks for each portfolio randomly, which essentially is how stock price chartists, "hot-tip" chasers, or security analysts who operate without a portfolio management plan handle the diversification problem. The second approach utilized industry classification for every stock and stressed *diversifying across different industries*. This second approach categorized all the NYSE stocks into 34 different industry classifications, and the portfolios were formed so that no portfolios of fewer than 34 stocks had two stocks in the same industry. Monthly rates of return were used and 20 sucessive one-year portfolios were drawn from each year from 1946 to 1965 inclusive. The risk and return statistics in Table 9.1 summarize the results.

The standard deviations of the various portfolios rates of return are shown in the far right-hand column in Table 9.1. These total risk statistics are each the average of 20 successive one-year portfolios' standard deviations. They show that total portfolio risk declined, on average, slightly when more than eight securities were included in the portfolios. This finding confirms the Evans–Archer result shown in Fig. 9.1.

Additional insight may be gained from Table 9.1 by comparing the risks of the randomly selected portfolios with the risk of the portfolios which are diversified across industries. There is no difference in the portfolios' total risk statistics, which results from the two different approaches to diversification. Furthermore, the two different diversification procedures also did not limit

---

[6]Published data shows that most industries are high positively correlated. Thus, diversification across different industries seems naive. See B. F. King, "Market and Industry Factors in Price Behavior," pp. 139–190; K. V. Smith, "A Portfolio Analysis of Conglomerate Diversification," *Journal of Finance*, June 1969, p. 422; L. Fisher and J. Lorie, "Some Studies of Variability of Returns on Investments in Common Stocks," *Journal of Business*, April 1970, pp. 99–134.

[7]Fisher and Lorie, "Some Studies of Variability of Returns on Investments in Common Stocks."

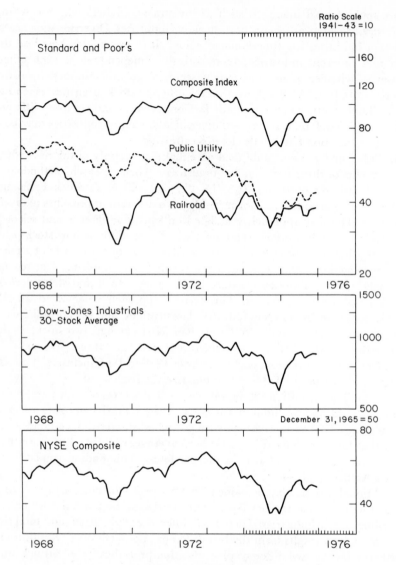

Figure 9.2. Stock Price Indexes

*Source: Monthly Chart Book*, Federal Reserve System, March 1976, p. 70.

the portfolios *downside risk* (that is, capital losses) significantly. For the two different eight-stock portfolios, for example, the worst rate of return was $-0.47 = -47.0$ percent for both diversification techniques. These and the other statistics in Table 9.1 suggest that diversifying across industries is merely another form of naive diversification.

TABLE 9.1   Statistics Obtained by Use of Different Diversification Techniques*

| Stocks in Portfolio | Technique Used to Diversify | 20th and 80th Percentiles (the middle 60%) | Min. Rate of Return | Max. Rate of Return | Mean Rate of Return | Average Std. Dev. of Returns |
|---|---|---|---|---|---|---|
| 8 | Random across industries | −0.06 to 2.9 −0.06 to 2.9 | −0.47 −0.47 | 1.64 1.58 | 0.13 0.13 | 0.22 0.22 |
| 16 | Random across industries | −0.06 to 0.28 −0.06 to 0.28 | −0.37 −0.35 | 1.21 1.21 | 0.13 0.13 | 0.21 0.21 |
| 32 | Random across industries | −0.05 to 0.27 −0.05 to 0.27 | −0.31 −0.29 | 0.98 0.93 | 0.13 0.13 | 0.20 0.20 |
| 128 | Random | −0.04 to 0.27 | −0.29 | 0.76 | 0.13 | 0.19 |

*Fisher and Lorie used wealth relatives $p_t/p_{t-1} = 1 + r_t$, so unity was deducted to obtain the one-period rates of return reported in the table. The standard deviation was not changed, since var $(1 + r) = $ var $(r)$.

Source: L. Fisher and J. Lorie, "Some Studies of Variability of Returns on Investments in Common Stocks," Journal of Business, April 1970, p. 112, Table 5.

Naive diversification across up to eight randomly selected NYSE stocks was shown in Fig. 9.1 to effectively cut a portfolio's total risk roughly in half. This is a substantial reduction in a portfolo's variability of return and is valuable to the portfolio's owners. Two discouraging aspects of the diversification research findings are still hard to ignore, however. First, naive diversification can be achieved by selecting assets with an unaimed dart. Second, traditional diversification techniques suggest no way to manage a portfolio that is better than using a dart or other randomizing technique.

## 9.3   Superfluous Diversification

This analysis highlights the folly of the time-honored axioms about diversification currently used by most investment fund managers and legislators. The traditional investment fund manager naively defines diversification as "not putting all your eggs in one basket." Such thinking seems to imply that a 20-security portfolio is twice as well diversified as a 10-security portfolio. This type of thinking was apparently the basis for the Investment Company Act of 1940, Subchapter M of the Internal Revenue Code, and various state laws. These laws require that an open-ended investment company (that is, mutual fund) hold no more than 5 percent of its total assets in any given security if it is to obtain favorable tax treatment.

Most large mutual fund managers and their staffs of fundamental analysis and chartists have carried the dubious logic of naive diversification too far by spreading their assets over dozens of different securities. In fact, it is quite common for large mutual funds to hold well over 100 different securities in their portfolios. Of course, such superfluous diversification will probably reduce risk to the systematic level. But the average return of such superfluously diversified portfolios is doomed to remain below the highest return available in that risk class for the following reasons:

1. Excessive management costs of maintaining up-to-date information on the excessive number of securities held in the portfolio.
2. Acceptance of securities with poor returns resulting from a policy of owning numerous securities rather than a few efficient ones.

### 9.4  Correlation and Diversification

The nihilistic nature of preceding research into traditional forms of diversification does not imply that good diversification techniques do not exist. The results in Sections 9.1 through 9.3 merely imply that the *traditional* approaches to diversification are no better than selecting securities with an unaimed dart. But better techniques, which focus on the correlation coefficient (or covariance) between securities, do exist.

Consider two hypothetical securities named Alpha (A) and Omega ($\Omega$). Table 9.2 shows several successive time periods' rates of return from the two assets, as well as the returns from a portfolio named Pi ($\pi$), which is composed half and half of Alpha and Omega. That is, the single-period returns from portfolio Pi are calculated as follows for the $t$th period:

$$r_{\pi t} = x_A r_{At} + (1 - x_A)r_{\Omega t} \qquad \text{where } x_A = 0.5.$$

A glance at Table 9.2 reveals that Alpha and Omega experience considerable variability of return. Portfolio Pi, however, experiences zero variance of returns even though it is completely invested in the risky assets, Alpha and Omega. The key to understanding this seeming paradox is the correlation between the two assets' returns.

Alpha and Omega have *perfectly negatively correlated* returns ($\rho_{A\Omega} = -1.0$), so their *prices move inversely.* That is, the gains on Alpha exactly offset the

TABLE 9.2  A Riskless Portfolio Constructed from Two Risky Securities

| Time Period | $t = 1$ | $t = 2$ | $t = 3$ | $t = 4$ | var $(r)^*$ |
|---|---|---|---|---|---|
| Alpha's performance | $r_{A1} = 10\%$ | $r_{A2} = 5\%$ | $r_{A3} = 15\%$ | $r_{A4} = 5\%$ | $\sigma_A^2 = 0.0015$ |
| Omega's performance | $r_{\Omega1} = 20\%$ | $r_{\Omega2} = 25\%$ | $r_{\Omega3} = 15\%$ | $r_{\Omega4} = 25\%$ | $\sigma_\Omega^2 = 0.0021$ |
| Pi's performance | $r_{\pi1} = 15\%$ | $r_{\pi2} = 15\%$ | $r_{\pi3} = 15\%$ | $r_{\pi4} = 15\%$ | $\sigma_\pi^2 = 0$ |

$*\text{var } (r_A) = \frac{1}{4} \sum\limits^{4} (r_{At=1} - 0.088)^2 = 0.00612/4 = 0.00153$

$\text{var } (r_\Omega) = \frac{1}{4} \sum\limits^{4} (r_{\Omega t=1} - 0.2125)^2 = 0.0085/4 = 0.00212$

$\text{var } (r_\pi) = \frac{1}{4} \sum\limits^{4} (r_{\pi t=1} - 0.15)^2 = 0.$

losses on Omega, and vice versa, so that the portfolio Pi experiences zero variability of returns. In short, a riskless portfolio was constructed from two risky assets whose prices covary inversely. This is familiar stuff, of course; it is merely a numerical example of what was shown graphically in Fig. 3.10. But, this focus on the way assets covary is the key to understanding Markowitz diversification.

### 9.5 Markowitz Diversification

Markowitz diversification, as explained earlier, is defined as combining assets that are less than perfectly positively correlated in order to reduce total risk without sacrificing any expected return. At the optimum, two perfectly negatively correlated assets (such as Alpha and Omega in Table 9.2) can be combined in the proper proportion to reduce risk to zero. As a practical matter, however, negatively correlated assets are rare. In recent decades the average correlation between NYSE stocks was about 0.5, for example. Figure 3.10 on page 45 graphically depicts the modest risk-reduction opportunities available with such levels of correlation. Nevertheless, Markowitz diversification still outperforms naive diversification.

Johnson and Shannon published a study that compares the risk and return from Markowitz portfolio analysis with the results that can be obtained from naive diversification.[8] Johnson and Shannon used 30 quarterly price change plus cash dividend returns measured over a sample period from 1965 through 1972 for 50 NYSE stocks. They formed portfolios using two different procedures. First, they used naive diversification—like Evans and Archer—to form portfolios of 3, 5, 7, 9, 11, 13, 15, and 17 randomly selected stocks which were weighted equally (for example, in the 17-security naive portfolio, each stock had a participation level of $\frac{1}{17} = 0.0588 = x_i$ for $i = 1$, $2, \ldots, 17$ stocks). The second set of portfolios were formed with Markowitz portfolio analysis using a quadratic program and a full covariance matrix to select the proportions of each security. Table 9.3 shows the summary statistics from the traditional naive technique as well as the scientific Markowitz technique.

Johnson and Shannon used the first 10 of their 30 quarterly returns to calculate risk and return statistics for each of their 50 stocks. Then they tested their portfolios over each of the remaining 20 quarterly returns. By moving forward in time one quarter for each test, Johnson and Shannon were able to generate new risk and return statistics and test their portfolios over successively more recent one-year test periods as they deleted the oldest quarter and added a more recent quarter for each test data. Thus, 20 tests

---

[8]K. H. Johnson and D. S. Shannon, "A Note on Diversification and the Reduction of Dispersion," *Journal of Financial Economics*, Vol. 1, No. 4, 1974, pp. 365–372.

TABLE 9.3 Average Quarterly Returns and Variability Measures
for Two Allocation Strategies and Alternative Portfolio Sizes

| | Equal Allocation | | Quadratic Programming Variable Proportions Allocation | | |
|---|---|---|---|---|---|
| Available Portfolio Size $K*$ | Average Quarterly Returns | Variability Measure, $VAP_p$ | Average Number of Securities in Portfolio† | Average Quarterly Returns | Variability Measure, $VAR_p$ |
| 3 | 1.99 | 0.0240 | n.a. | n.a. | n.a. |
| 5 | 1.82 | 0.0160 | n.a. | n.a. | n.a. |
| 7 | 2.21 | 0.0146 | 2.58 | 4.10 | 0.0150 |
| 9 | 1.89 | 0.0134 | 3.06 | 3.72 | 0.0133 |
| 11 | 1.99 | 0.0128 | 3.40 | 3.78 | 0.0115 |
| 13 | 1.95 | 0.0130 | 3.57 | 3.68 | 0.0137 |
| 15 | 2.32 | 0.0125 | 4.19 | 4.31 | 0.0117 |
| 17 | 2.04 | 0.0127 | 4.43 | 4.40 | 0.0125 |

*For the equal allocation strategy, $K$ represents the number of securities in the portfolio; for the quadratic programming allocations, $K$ represents the number of securities from which the portfolios were selected (i.e., many of the securities will have zero weights).

†The average number of securities in solution with nonzero weights.

were performed for each portfolio size. The summary risk and return statistics shown in Table 9.3 and Fig. 9.3 are the averages of these 20 test replication statistics.

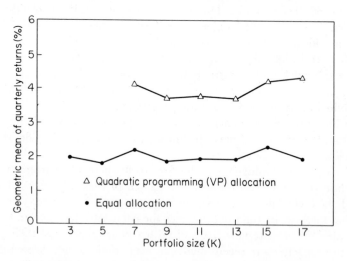

Figure 9.3. Average Ex-Post Portfolio Returns for Alternative Portfolio Sizes and Allocation Strategies

*Source:* K. H. Johnson and D. S. Shannon, "A Note on Diversification and the Reduction of Dispersion," *Journal of Financial Economics*, Vol. 1, No. 4, 1974, Table 1, Figs. 1 and 2.

The main conclusions can be seen in Table 9.3 and Fig. 9.3. First, from a given small universe of securities (namely, 3, 5, 7, 9, 11, 13, 15, or 17 securities) from which to select, the Markowitz full-covariance model did not reduce the portfolios total risk below the levels that could be achieved through naively selecting securities with an unaimed dart to form equally weighted portfolios. The second finding, which may be seen in Table 9.3, is that the Markowitz model was able to form portfolios with risk equal to the naively diversified portfolios with far *fewer* stocks. By varying the proportions the stocks in each portfolio optimally, the Markowitz model set most stocks' weights to zero (that is, $x_i = 0$), so the Markowitz portfolios all contained less than half as many securities as the naively diversified portfolios. By purchasing larger quantities of fewer securities, the Markowitz model will save commission costs, even if it will not reduce risk lower than naive diversification. However, the Markowitz model has another benefit to suggest itself over the traditional naive diversification technique.

Table 9.3 and Fig. 9.3 show that the Markowitz portfolios had returns that averaged approximately twice as high as the returns from the naively diversified protfolios. This means that the Markowitz model can generate portfolios which dominate in risk–return space the portfolios formed by traditional techniques. And, if the commission cost savings obtained by using the Markowitz procedure were considered, its margin of superiority would be even better.[9]

### 9.6  Conclusions About Diversification

The traditional technique of diversifying across industries and the scientific Markowitz technique were both unable to reduce the risk of their average portfolios much below the risk levels attainable by throwing an unaimed dart to select about 10 random securities for a naively diversified portfolio. Although easy to obtain, this amount of risk reduction was, nevertheless, substantial. Figure 9.1 shows that investment *risk can be cut in half* by randomly diversifying across less than a dozen NYSE stocks. This raises the question of why practically all mutual funds and other "professional money managers" hold over 100 different securities in their common stock portfolios.

The empirical evidence reviewed in the chapter suggests that no kind of diversification will ever be able to develop portfolios of any size which have zero risk (unless short sales, options, and other securities that have not yet been considered in the published empirical portfolio research are used).

---

[9]The Johnson and Shannon study also investigated the advisability of revising the portfolios periodically versus maintaining fixed proportions which were optimal only at an initial date. Johnson and Shannon found that periodic revision was beneficial. However, the discussion of portfolio revision is postponed until Chapter XII.

However, of the alternatives that have been tested, Markowitz portfolio analysis appears to be superior. The Markowitz model was able to delineate portfolios which had risk levels that averaged as low as could be obtained by diversifying across industries. But the Markowitz portfolios had rates of return that averaged *twice as high* as the average stock's return, and the *commission savings* available by buying Markowitz portfolios containing only a few securities would make them even more desirable (since it costs about 1 percent of the value of the securities to buy in large quantities, and another 1 percent commission to sell).

The superiority of the Markowitz model stems from the power of mathematics to analyze the returns, risks, and covariances of numerous different assets simultaneously and select the best simultaneous balance of risk and return. Since the human mind is unable to consider more than a few things at once, portfolio management is a job that requires the assistance of scientific portfolio management models which can simultaneously evaluate a large number of alternative investments.[10]

### Appendix 9A
### Diversification Can Increase the Geometric Mean Return

In this chapter it was shown that Markowitz diversification was at least as effective at reducing risk as naive diversification. It was pointed out that the Markowitz diversification could also increase portfolio's expected return. In fact, diversification of any kind can be expected to *increase* a portfolio's geometric mean rate of return over time. A simple numerical example will be used to illustrate this point.

TABLE 9A.1   Hypothetical Data for Three Assets

| Asset | $1 + r_1$ | $1 + r_2$ | $[(2 + r_1 + r_2)/2] = \overline{VR}$ |
|-------|-----------|-----------|----------------------------------------|
| A | 1.4 | 1.0 | 1.2   portfolio N |
| B | 1.4 | 1.0 | 1.2   portfolio N |
| C | 1.0 | 1.4 | 1.2   portfolio M |

All three assets in Table 9A.1 have an *arithmetic average* value relative (that is, $VR = 1 + r$) of 1.2 over the two periods. If assets $A$ and $B$ are combined half and half into a portfolio, call it $N$, the variance of the portfolio's *value relatives* is calculated as follows:

$$\text{var}(VR_N) = \sum_{i=1}^{2} p_i (VR_i - \overline{VR})^2 = \tfrac{1}{2}(1.4 - 1.2)^2 + \tfrac{1}{2}(1.0 - 1.2)^2$$

$$= \tfrac{1}{2}(0.04) + \tfrac{1}{2}(0.04) = 0.04.$$

---

[10]Paul Slovic, "Psychological Study of Human Judgment: Implications for Investment Decision-Making," *Journal of Finance*, September 1972, pp. 779–799.

If assets $B$ and $C$ are combined half and half into a portfolio, the portfolio's average value relative is also 1.2. However, this portfolio of inversely correlated assets has a variance of zero. This Markowitz diversified portfolio, denote it $M$, has a variance of zero because the portfolio's value relative equals 1.2 in both periods.

The geometric mean of the value relatives for portfolios $M$ and $N$ are calculated as follows:

$$gr_N = \sqrt[2]{(1.4)(1.0)} = \sqrt{1.40} = 1.18,$$
$$gr_M = \sqrt[2]{(1.2)(1.2)} = \sqrt{1.44} = 1.2.$$

Portfolio $M$ grew to 144 percent of its beginning value while portfolio $N$ only grew to 140 percent of its beginning value. Portfolio $M$ had a higher geometric mean value relative than portfolio $N$, although both had an arithmetic mean value relative of 1.2, because portfolio $M$ had less variance. Better diversification reduced portfolio $M$'s variance to zero. Thus, portfolio $M$ grew at a constant factor of 1.2 and outperformed its poorly diversified counterpart, which grew erratically.

In general, the product of $n$ value relatives with a given arithmetic average $[(1/n) \sum_{i=1}^{n} VR_i = \overline{VR}]$, will be larger the less the variance of those $n$ value relatives. In terms of the geometric mean returns $(gr)$ and arithmetic mean returns $(ar)$, this relationship may be restated as equation (9A.1.).[1]

$$gr \cong (ar^2 - \sigma^2)^{1/2}. \qquad (9A.1)$$

Clearly, $gr$ increases as the variance of the period-by-period rates of return decreases.

| Period | Asset | $M$ | $Q$ | $N$ |
|---|---|---|---|---|
| 1 | $VR_1 = 1 + r_1$ | 1.2 | 1.3 | 1.4 |
| 2 | $VR_2 = 1 + r_2$ | 1.2 | 1.1 | 1.0 |
| | Arithmetic average return | 20% | 20% | 20% |
| | Geometric mean return | $\sqrt[2]{(1.2)(1.2)}$ $gr_M = \sqrt{1.44}$ > | $\sqrt[2]{(1.3)(1.1)}$ $gr_Q = \sqrt{1.43}$ > | $\sqrt[2]{(1.4)(1.0)}$ $gr_N = \sqrt{1.40}$ |

[1]W. E. Young, "Common Stock Ex Post Holding Period Returns and Portfolio Selection," Ph.D. thesis, University of North Carolina, 1968, Chapel Hill, N.C.; W. E. Young and R. H. Trent, "Geometric Mean Approximations of Individual Security and Portfolio Performance," *Journal of Financial and Quantitative Analysis*, Vol. 4, June 1969; E. F. Renshaw, "Portfolio Balance Models in Perspective: Some Generalizations That Can Be Derived from the Two Asset Case," *Journal of Financial and Quantitative Analysis*, Vol. 2, June 1967, pp. 123–149; Harry M. Markowitz, *Portfolio Selection* (New York: John Wiley & Sons, Inc., 1959), p. 122.

The data above summarize the teaching point of this appendix. Three portfolios—say, *M*, *Q*, and *N*—all having an arithmetic average rate of return of 20 percent per period, are shown. But all three portfolios have different geometric mean returns over the two periods they are in existence. The portfolio with the least variability of return (that is, *M*) has the highest geometric mean return over the two periods.

## Selected References

Latane, H., and W. Young, "Test of Portfolio Building Rules," *Journal of Finance*, September 1969, pp. 595–612.

An empirical study of diversification by means of various portfolio building plans. The results are presented in terms of the geometric mean (or long-run compounded) rate of return from various approaches to diversification.

Wagner, W. H., and S. C. Lau, "The Effect of Diversification on Risk," *Financial Analysts Journal*, Vol. 27, No. 6, 1971, pp. 48–53.

This easy-to-read numerical analysis of empirical data shows various effects of diversification. No mathematics is used.

## Questions and Problems

1. The *central limit theorem* (CLT) is one of the most powerful theorems in all of mathematical statistics. Stated very simply, the CLT essentially says: If some random variable denoted $r$ possesses a finite probability distribution with a mean value of $u_r$ and a standard deviation of $\sigma_r$, then the sample mean, $\bar{r}$, based on a sample of size $n$, will tend to be distributed according to a normal probability distribution with a mean of $u_r$ and a standard deviation of $(\sigma_r/\sqrt{n})$. As $n$ increases, the approximation improves: (1) $\bar{r}$ tends to converge on $u_r$, (2) the sample mean's standard deviation tends to converge on $(\sigma_r/\sqrt{n})$, and, (3) the sample mean tends to be normally distributed. What does the CLT suggest about naive or random diversification to reduce portfolio risk (assuming that the single-period returns have finite variances)?

2. Can diversification across a large number of stocks or bonds which all have the same high quality rating (for example, AAA) decrease the portfolio's risk? Explain.

3. Suppose that you were the manager of some wealthy young heir's $50 million portfolio. Your instructions are to maximize the portfolio's terminal wealth at the end of 30 years so that the young heir can then found a prestigious university which is to be named after his family and thus perpetuate his family's good name in a favorable context (for example, Stanford University, Carnegie-Mellon University, Vanderbilt University). Should you plan to reinvest in a series of high-risk speculations of only one or a few assets (that is, take big risks to earn big returns) every year for the next 30 years? Or, should you diversify to reduce risk in each of the 30 years? Which approach should maximize the portfolio's terminal wealth? (*Hint*: See Appendix 9A.)

4. Is there any kind of trade-off between (a) the gains to be had from diversification, and (b) the correlation between the assets in the portfolio that is to be diversified?

5. Assume that the average stock costs $30 per share and that only 100-share round-lot purchases should be made, to obtain lower brokerage commissions. What are the implications of this situation for the small private investor who has only $10,000 to invest? Explain.

6. Can an individual security have a positive variance (that is, total risk) and yet make a negative contribution to the total risk of a portfolio? Explain.

1010101010101010101010101010101010101010101010101010101010101010101010101010
1010101010101010101010101010101010101010101010101010101010101010101010101010
101010101010101010101010101010101010101    10101    101010101010101010101010101010101010
101010101010101010101010101010101010    010    0101010101010101010101010101010101010
1010101010101010101010101010101010101    1    101010101010101010101010101010101010
1010101010101010101010101010101010101010    0101010101010101010101010101010101010
1010101010101010101010101010101010101010101    10101010101010101010101010101010101010
101010101010101010101010101010101010    0101010101010101010101010101010101010
1010101010101010101010101010101010101    1    101010101010101010101010101010101010
101010101010101010101010101010101010    010    0101010101010101010101010101010101010
1010101010101010101010101010101010101    10101    1010101010101010101010101010101010
1010101010101010101010101010101010101010101010101010101010101010101010101010
1010101010101010101010101010101010101010101010101010101010101010101010101010

# Portfolio Performance Evaluation

MUTUAL funds and other large public portfolios are widely advertised and the subject of much conversation. But few analytical studies or studies grounded in portfolio analysis have been made of their performance.[1] There is institutional and descriptive material out on various portfolios explaining their corporate charters, their management structure, the value and composition of their holdings, and so on. But, not enough work has been done to discredit or support widely held beliefs within the industry concerning the use of charting, traditional views on diversification, the fundamental analyst's approach to searching out undervalued securities, the interrelation of security price movements, and other vital subjects. Hopefully, more research will be done in these areas in the future and will reach the hands of investment fund managers and the investing public.

An abundance of erroneous but widely accepted folklore is used in the investments industry. Only when erroneous beliefs are discredited and the

---

[1] J. L. Treynor, "How to Rate Management of Investment Funds," *Harvard Business Review*, January–February 1965, pp. 63–75; W. F. Sharpe, "Mutual Fund Performance," *Journal of Business*, January 1966, pp. 119–138; M. C. Jensen, "The Performance of Mutual Funds in the Period 1945–1964," *Journal of Finance*, May 1968, pp. 389–416; D. E. Farrar, *The Investment Decision Under Uncertainty* (Englewood Cliffs, N.J.: Prentice-Hall, Inc., 1962); M. C. Jensen, "Risk, The Pricing of Capital Assets, and the Evaluation of Investment Portfolios," *Journal of Business*, April 1969; *Institutional Investor Study Report of the S.E.C.*, (Washington, D.C.: Government Printing Office), Chap. Four.

folklore replaced with an awareness of ignorance will the foundation be laid for acceptance of analytical techniques such as portfolio analysis. In the meantime, loanable funds will be misallocated and resources squandered to pay for the services of charlatans.

To evaluate the performance of portfolios in a realistic setting empirical data from well-known public portfolios is analyzed in this chapter. In particular, mutual funds' performances are evaluated because (1) mutual fund advertisements promising investors the benefit of "professional money management" raise questions as to whether this "professional management" is worth having, and (2) mutual funds' data are made public by law. The first step in evaluating the performance of these open-ended investment companies is to calculate their one-period rates of return over some sample period. Mutual fund share owners can receive three types of income from their shares: (1) disbursements of interest and cash dividends on securities the fund owns, denoted $cd_t$ for time period $t$; (2) disbursements of capital gains realized when securities the portfolio owned are sold to realize a capital gain, denoted $cg_t$ for period $t$; and (3) unrealized gains or losses on securities held in the portfolio; this is called a change in the fund's net asset value (*nav*) and is denoted $\Delta nav_t$ for period $t$. Since mutual fund shares must be purchased at their net asset values, their one-period rates of return, denoted $r_t$, are calculated as follows:

$$r_t = \frac{cd_t + cg_t + \Delta nav_t}{nav_t}.$$

These single-period returns are analogous to common stock returns shown in equation (1.1).

### 10.1   Testing the Capital Market Line

In Chapters 3 and 8 the rationale was developed for the Capital Market Line (CML). The theory hypothesized that the expected return of an efficient portfolio should be a positive linear function of the portfolio's risk as measured by its standard deviation of returns. Perhaps a good place to begin examining funds is to compare empirical evidence about their performance with what the theory predicts. Although the theory is cast in terms of expectations, it is not unreasonable to expect historical data to conform to the hypothesis in at least some rough sense.

To test the CML, data previously tabulated and reported by W. F. Sharpe will be used.[2] Table 10.1 shows the historical average annual rates of return ($\bar{r}$) in column 1 and standard deviation of these annual returns ($\sigma$) in column

---

[2]See W. F. Sharpe, "Risk Aversion in the Stock Market: Some Empirical Evidence." *Journal of Finance*, September 1965, pp. 416–422.

TABLE 10.1  Performance of 34 Mutual Funds, 1954–1963

| Mutual Fund | Average Annual Return (%) | Std. Dev. of Annual Return (%) | Risk Premium to Standard Deviation Ratio* |
|---|---|---|---|
| Affiliated Fund | 14.6 | 15.3 | 0.75896 |
| American Business Shares | 10.0 | 9.2 | 0.75876 |
| Axe-Houghton, Fund A | 10.5 | 13.5 | 0.55551 |
| Axe-Houghton, Fund B | 12.0 | 16.3 | 0.55183 |
| Axe-Houghton, Stock Fund | 11.9 | 15.6 | 0.56991 |
| Boston Fund | 12.4 | 12.1 | 0.77842 |
| Broad Street Investing | 14.8 | 16.8 | 0.70329 |
| Bullock Fund | 15.7 | 19.3 | 0.65845 |
| Commonwealth Investment Company | 10.9 | 13.7 | 0.57841 |
| Delaware Fund | 14.4 | 21.4 | 0.53253 |
| Dividend Shares | 14.4 | 15.9 | 0.71807 |
| Eaton and Howard, Balanced Fund | 11.0 | 11.9 | 0.67399 |
| Eaton and Howard, Stock Fund | 15.2 | 19.2 | 0.63486 |
| Equity Fund | 14.6 | 18.7 | 0.61902 |
| Fidelity Fund | 16.4 | 23.5 | 0.57020 |
| Financial Industrial Fund | 14.5 | 23.0 | 0.49971 |
| Fundamental Investors | 16.0 | 21.7 | 0.59894 |
| Group Securities, Common Stock Fund | 15.1 | 19.1 | 0.63316 |
| Group Securities, Fully Administered Fund | 11.4 | 14.1 | 0.59490 |
| Incorporated Investors | 14.0 | 25.5 | 0.43116 |
| Investment Company of America | 17.4 | 21.8 | 0.66169 |
| Investors Mutual | 11.3 | 12.5 | 0.66451 |
| Loomis-Sales Mutual Fund | 10.0 | 10.4 | 0.67358 |
| Massachusetts Investors Trust | 16.2 | 20.8 | 0.63398 |
| Massachusetts Investors—Growth Stock | 18.6 | 22.7 | 0.68687 |
| National Investors Corporation | 18.3 | 19.9 | 0.76798 |
| National Securities—Income Series | 12.4 | 17.8 | 0.52950 |
| New England Fund | 10.4 | 10.2 | 0.72703 |
| Putnam Fund of Boston | 13.1 | 16.0 | 0.63222 |
| Scudder, Stevens & Clark Balanced Fund | 10.7 | 13.3 | 0.57893 |
| Selected American Shares | 14.4 | 19.4 | 0.58788 |
| United Funds—Income Fund | 16.1 | 20.9 | 0.62698 |
| Wellington Fund | 11.3 | 12.0 | 0.69057 |
| Wisconsin Fund | 13.8 | 16.9 | 0.64091 |

*Ratio = (average return −3.0 percent)/variability. The ratios shown were computed from original data and thus differ slightly from the ratios obtained from the rounded data shown in the table. These ratios may be thought of as being a sort of index of desirability that considers risk and return simultaneously.

2 over the decade from 1954 to 1963 for 34 mutual funds. These 34 funds were selected by Sharpe from the Weisenberger data because they had annual returns published for 10 consecutive years. This criteria may bias the sample because new, small funds were not included.

Using the standard least-squares technique, a simple linear regression line of the form $\bar{r}_i = a + b\sigma_i + e_i$ was fitted to the 34 pairs of observations, where $a$ and $b$ are the intercept and slope regression statistics. The regression line over the range that the data cover is shown in Fig. 10.1 as the solid line. This regression line represents the average performance that could be achieved using naive diversification. The regression slope coefficient ($b = 0.475$) is significantly different than zero at the 0.01 level of significance.[3] The correlation coefficient is 0.835. The percentage of variation explained by the regression line (that is, the coefficient of determination) is 69.8 percent. The historical data conform to the CML hypothesis.[4]

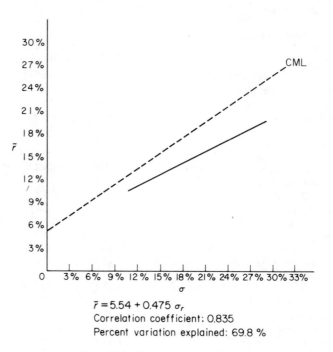

$$\bar{r} = 5.54 + 0.475\ \sigma_r$$
Correlation coefficient: 0.835
Percent variation explained: 69.8 %

Figure 10.1. Estimates of the CML

---

[3]The standard error of $b$ is 0.055, so $t = (b - B)/\sigma_b = (0.475 - 0)/0.055 = 8.6$ for the null hypothesis $b = 0$.

[4]Sharpe, "Risk Aversion in the Stock Market: Some Empirical Evidence." For a critique of Sharpe's study, see R. R. West, "Mutual Fund Performance and the Theory of Capital Asset Pricing: Some Comments," *Journal of Business*, April 1968, pp. 230–234.

Sharpe's regression slope parameter is probably biased. Both variables in the regression model represent observations that are subject to various errors. It has been shown that this "errors-in-variables" problem results in inconsistent, inefficient, and biased regression slope coefficients: J. Johnston, *Econometric Methods*, 2nd ed. (New York: McGraw-Hill Book Company, 1972), Sec. 9-4.

## A. Funds Not Efficient

In Fig. 10.1 a dashed line labeled the CML has been graphed to show a subjective estimate of where the true efficient frontier would lie. Although the regression line conforms to the relationship hypothesized in the capital market theory, it is dominated by the true CML, owing to several poor management practices followed by mutual funds. These inefficiencies are discussed next.

*Superfluous diversification*    In Chapter IX it was shown that portfolio risk could typically be reduced to near the minimum level imposed by systematic variation with as few as eight *randomly* selected securities—see Fig. 9.1 for a graphical summary of the analysis leading to this conclusion. It was also pointed out that by using portfolio analysis fewer securities could achieve even more reduction in risk.

Various legal guidelines require open-ended mutual funds to spread their assets across a minimum of 20 different portfolios in order to obtain certain income tax exemptions. This requirement does not seem to frustrate the mutual funds, pension funds, and so forth. In fact, most funds have well over 100 securities in their portfolios by choice. As a glance at Fig. 9.1 reveals, such excessive diversification tends to reduce portfolio risk to the minimum level imposed by systematic variation. But this is no impressive accomplishment, since the number of securities owned is excessive and leads to at least three types of portfolio inefficiency.

First, experience with the portfolio analysis techniques discussed in this book shows that unleveraged Markowitz-efficient portfolios without any constraints on the number of securities held are frequently composed of less than 20 securities. Furthermore, the lowest-risk portfolios in the efficient set typically contain *less than the systematic level of risk*. These minimum-risk portfolios are composed of only a few uncorrelated securities.[5] As additional securities are forced into a Markowitz-efficient portfolio, it becomes more risky, and its risk asymptotically approaches the level of risk in the market portfolio—that is, the level of systematic risk. Superfluous diversification can *increase* risk rather than reduce it. Thus, the larger portfolios are more prone to fluctuate with the market than the lowest-risk Markowitz-efficient port-folios. Even if they used portfolio analysis, most investment funds are simply too large to be well diversified—they are forced by their size to pursue superfluous diversification.

---

[5]Homestake Mining, Pan-Am, General Portland Cement, and Pepsi-Cola were found to have negatively correlated returns with the market over a recent 10-year period. Such securities allow portfolio risk to be reduced below the systematic level if this countercyclical behavior can be expected to continue.

Second, a portfolio that has 120 securities has at least 100 more securities than it needs to be efficient or to satisfy the law. The *administrative cost* of keeping current information on these 100 excess securities and the recurring management cost of reviewing them periodically runs up unduly high management fees for the mutual fund. This reduces the net return to owners. In fact, Sharpe's data indicate that mutual funds with a *low* ratio of management expense to net assets do *better* than funds that spend a larger proportion on management.[6] Such evidence speaks poorly for mutual fund managements.

Third, mutual funds that purchase many different securities will be forced to accept securities offering lower and lower returns. In highly efficient markets such as the New York Stock Exchange, very few significantly undervalued investments (that is, disequilibrium returns) will exist at any moment. Thus, a portfolio containing over 100 securities must surely contain a majority of lackluster performers.

The three effects of superfluous or naive diversification discussed above explain why the CML in Fig. 10.1 must surely dominate the regression-line fit to the actual data. In defense of the charge they diversify superfluously, investment fund managers frequently reply that their fund is too large to own only a few securities. That is, if a large fund invested all its assets in less than 20 securities, its activities would affect the price of these issues. Of course, these contentions are correct. Thus, the law would do better to limit the total dollar size of funds than to require superfluous diversification.

*Searching for underpriced securities*     Most mutual funds devote resources to searching for underpriced securities in hopes of earning substantial capital gains. This search is typically performed either by fundamental security analysts or technical analysts (that is, chartists). It is unlikely that such activity will ever earn a return above a naive buy-and-hold strategy.[7]

Charting-reading is based on the assumption that the successive price changes of securities are not random. But impressive evidence has been gathered showing that these price changes are actually random.[8] Meanwhile, the chartists have offered little in the way of economic rationale or proof that their activity has any merit.[9]

---

[6]Sharpe, "Mutual Fund Performance," p. 132.

[7]The phrase "naive buy-and-hold strategy" refers to the process of randomly selecting securities (for example, with a dart or a roulette wheel), buying them, and holding them as long-run investments. See L. Fisher and J. Lorie, "Rates of Return on Investments in Common Stock," *Journal of Business*, July 1968.

[8]E. F. Fama, "Efficient Capital Markets: A Review of Theory and Empirical Work," *Journal of Finance*, May 1970, pp. 383–417.

[9]Levy has articulated a case for technical analysis better than most. R. A. Levy, "Random Walks: Reality or Myth," and M. C. Jensen, "Random Walks: Reality or Myth—Com-

Fundamental analysis, on the other hand, is a more defensible process. It involves collecting facts and then reaching a rather subjective estimate of the intrinsic value of a security based on these facts.

In spite of its rationale, fundamental analysis offers a negligible opportunity to earn a return above what could be achieved with a naive buy-and-hold strategy. There are thousands of full-time professional fundamental analysts constantly pouring over new information as it becomes available and constantly rechecking market values against their own estimates of intrinsic value. Thus, market prices in efficient markets such as the New York Stock Exchange at any moment are excellent, unbiased, up-to-the-moment estimates of the securities' true intrinsic value. The efforts of an "army" of fundamental analysts cause market prices to be so accurate that fundamental analysis offers virtually no possibility of consistently finding a significantly undervalued security—or an overvalued one for that matter. This should not be interpreted to mean that no fundamental analyst (or chartist or dart-thrower) will not "pick a winner" and know it from time to time. Rather, the point is, after deducting the losses from the "losers" and the costs of fundamental analysis (or charting), the net returns from fundamental analysis (or charting) will not exceed what could have been earned with random selection.

Lorie and Fisher found that about a 10 percent before-tax annual return compounded annually could be earned over recent decades by selecting many securities randomly (for example, with a dart) and holding them.[10] Over a period of years, the studies published seem to indicate that no large open-ended mutual fund has been able to consistently outperform these naive buy-and-hold strategies.

Charting and fundamental analysis have not only failed to earn average returns exceeding those attainable by randomly selecting securities, but the costs of this fruitless search seem to have lowered mutual funds' *net returns to below* what could be attained by using a dart.[11]

---

ment," both in November–December 1967, *Financial Analysts Journal*, pp. 69–85. "Random Walks: Reality or Myth—Reply," *Financial Analysts Journal*, January–February 1968, pp. 129–132. Also see Ben Branch, "The Predictive Power of Stock Market Indicators, *Journal of Financial and Quantitative Analysis*, June 1976, pp. 269–285.

[10]J. Lorie and L. Fisher, "Rates of Return on Investments in Common Stock," *Journal of Business*, Vol. 40, No. 3, 1968, pp. 1–26. Or, for a scientific study of the results of naively buying and holding common stocks, corporate bonds, and U.S. Treasury Bonds, see R. G. Ibbotson and R. A. Sinquefield, "Stocks, Bonds, Bills, and Inflation: The Year-By-Year Historical Returns (1926–1974)," *Journal of Business*, Volume 49, No. 1, January 1976, pp. 11–47.

[11]See Fama's comments, "Behavior of Stock Prices," *Journal of Business*, January 1965, pp. 90–92. Also see T. Kim, "An Assessment of the Performance of Mutual Fund Management: 1969–1975," *Journal of Financial and Quantitative Analysis*, Vol. XIII, No. 3, September 1978, pp. 385–406.

Perhaps if the capital market theory of Chapter 8 were used to highlight securities whose prices were in disequilibrium[12] and then fundamental analysis performed on these, the search for undervalued securities could be made fruitful. At this time, however, the authors know of no investment fund that uses such analytical techniques. Instead, they more or less aimlessly conduct an expensive and evidently fruitless search for undervalued securities.

### B.  No Consistently Superior Funds

In an effort to determine if any open-ended mutual funds were consistently superior, Fama ranked 39 common stock funds that were in existence throughout the decade from 1951 to 1960. Calculating annual rates of return with dividends reinvested and compounded, Fama ranked all 39 funds based on their annual returns in each of the 10 years. These data are shown in Table 10.2.

As Fama points out, the most striking feature of Table 10.2 is the inconsistency of the rankings. Although some funds did significantly better than average in some years, no fund consistently ranked high. Of the 39 funds, no single fund consistently had returns high enough to place it among the top 20 funds in each of the 10 years.

In column 1 of Table 10.2 the funds' compound rate of return over the decade is shown. The average return of all 39 funds is 14.1 percent for the decade. This is the return on the shareholder's actual investment after load charges (salesman's commissions). This return on net investment flatters the funds. Their return on gross investment (that is, on the actual investment, plus the salesman's commission) would be lower, of course. The Lorie and Fisher data showed that the market average return over this same period was 14.7 percent. This means that the average investor who used a dart to select securities for the decade from 1951 to 1960 would have earned a higher return than the average mutual fund share owner.

### C.  Near Efficiency

Probably the most complimentary remarks about mutual fund performance in an analytical study were made by Farrar.[13] Using monthly observations from 1946 to 1956 on 23 mutual funds, the risk–return of each portfolio and the efficient frontier were determined. These results are shown in Fig. 10.2.[14]

---

[12]See the discussion accompanying Figs. 8.8 and 8.7. For an insightful analysis of how security analysis and portfolio analysis should interact, see J. Treynor and F. Black, "How to Use Security Analysis to Improve Portfolio Selection," *Journal of Business*, January 1973.

[13]D. E. Farrar, *The Investment Decision Under Uncertainty* (Englewood Cliffs, N.J.: Prentice-Hall, Inc., 1962).

[14]Ibid., p. 73.

# TABLE 10.2  Year-by-Year Ranking of Individual Fund Returns*

| Fund | Return on Net (1) | 1951 (2) | 52 (3) | 53 (4) | 54 (5) | 55 (6) | 56 (7) | 57 (8) | 58 (9) | 59 (10) | 1960 (11) |
|---|---|---|---|---|---|---|---|---|---|---|---|
| Keystone Lower Price | 18.7 | 29 | 1 | 38 | 5 | 3 | 8 | 35 | 1 | 1 | 36 |
| T. Rowe Price Growth | 18.7 | 1 | 33 | 2 | 8 | 14 | 15 | 2 | 25 | 7 | 4 |
| Dreyfuss | 18.4 | 37 | 37 | 14 | 3 | 7 | 11 | 3 | 2 | 3 | 7 |
| Television Electronic | 18.4 | 21 | 4 | 9 | 2 | 33 | 20 | 16 | 2 | 4 | 20 |
| National Investors Corp. | 18.0 | 3 | 35 | 4 | 19 | 27 | 4 | 5 | 5 | 8 | 1 |
| De Vegh Mutual Fund | 17.7 | 32 | 4 | 1 | 8 | 14 | 4 | 8 | 15 | 23 | 36 |
| Growth Industries | 17.0 | 7 | 34 | 14 | 17 | 9 | 9 | 20 | 5 | 6 | 11 |
| Massachusetts Investors Growth | 16.9 | 5 | 36 | 31 | 11 | 9 | 1 | 23 | 4 | 9 | 4 |
| Franklin Custodian | 16.5 | 26 | 2 | 4 | 13 | 33 | 20 | 16 | 5 | 9 | 4 |
| Investment Co. of America | 16.0 | 21 | 15 | 14 | 11 | 17 | 15 | 23 | 15 | 15 | 15 |
| Chemical Fund, Inc. | 15.6 | 1 | 39 | 14 | 27 | 3 | 33 | 1 | 27 | 4 | 23 |
| Founders Mutual | 15.6 | 21 | 13 | 25 | 8 | 2 | 20 | 16 | 11 | 13 | 28 |
| Investment Trust of Boston | 15.6 | 6 | 3 | 25 | 3 | 14 | 26 | 31 | 20 | 29 | 20 |
| American Mutual | 15.5 | 14 | 13 | 4 | 22 | 14 | 13 | 16 | 25 | 25 | 4 |
| Keystone Growth | 15.3 | 29 | 15 | 25 | 1 | 1 | 1 | 39 | 11 | 13 | 38 |
| Keystone High | 15.2 | 10 | 7 | 3 | 27 | 23 | 36 | 5 | 27 | 25 | 11 |
| Aberdeen Fund | 15.1 | 32 | 23 | 9 | 25 | 9 | 7 | 10 | 27 | 7 | 30 |
| Massachusetts Investors Trust | 14.8 | 8 | 9 | 14 | 16 | 9 | 15 | 20 | 18 | 32 | 28 |
| Texas Fund Inc. | 14.6 | 3 | 15 | 9 | 32 | 23 | 26 | 5 | 27 | 37 | 7 |
| Eaton & Howard Stock | 14.4 | 14 | 9 | 4 | 17 | 20 | 15 | 13 | 37 | 29 | 17 |
| Guardian Mutual | 14.4 | 21 | 26 | 25 | 34 | 31 | 29 | 13 | 20 | 15 | 2 |
| Scudder, Stevens, Clark | 14.3 | 14 | 23 | 14 | 19 | 27 | 15 | 29 | 9 | 15 | 30 |
| Investors Stock Fund | 14.2 | 8 | 28 | 21 | 22 | 27 | 20 | 23 | 5 | 29 | 23 |
| Fidelity Fund, Inc. | 14.1 | 21 | 26 | 25 | 34 | 31 | 29 | 13 | 20 | 15 | 23 |
| Fundamental Inv. | 13.8 | 14 | 15 | 31 | 15 | 9 | 11 | 31 | 18 | 25 | 30 |
| Century Shares | 13.5 | 14 | 28 | 35 | 25 | 3 | 20 | 23 | 31 | 34 | 2 |
| Bullock Fund Ltd. | 13.5 | 29 | 9 | 21 | 19 | 14 | 9 | 20 | 34 | 34 | 20 |
| Financial Industries | 13.0 | 26 | 15 | 31 | 13 | 19 | 29 | 34 | 20 | 9 | 35 |
| Group Common Stock | 13.0 | 38 | 8 | 25 | 27 | 27 | 33 | 8 | 20 | 34 | 17 |
| Incorporated Investors | 12.9 | 14 | 13 | 37 | 6 | 3 | 13 | 37 | 11 | 18 | 39 |
| Equity Fund | 12.9 | 14 | 27 | 21 | 32 | 31 | 33 | 13 | 31 | 18 | 23 |
| Selected American Shares | 12.8 | 21 | 15 | 21 | 31 | 23 | 20 | 23 | 15 | 32 | 30 |
| Dividend Shares | 12.7 | 32 | 7 | 14 | 34 | 20 | 32 | 4 | 37 | 37 | 11 |
| General Capital Corp. | 12.4 | 10 | 28 | 9 | 38 | 35 | 39 | 23 | 34 | 13 | 23 |
| Wisconsin Fund | 12.3 | 32 | 26 | 4 | 37 | 35 | 38 | 10 | 34 | 18 | 7 |
| International Resources | 12.3 | 10 | 37 | 39 | 22 | 35 | 1 | 37 | 39 | 1 | 11 |
| Delaware Fund | 12.1 | 36 | 23 | 25 | 27 | 39 | 26 | 29 | 9 | 23 | 30 |
| Hamilton Fund | 11.9 | 38 | 28 | 9 | 34 | 35 | 36 | 10 | 31 | 18 | 17 |
| Colonial Energy | 10.9 | 10 | 15 | 35 | 39 | 20 | 4 | 36 | 20 | 39 | 10 |

*E. F. Fama, "Behavior of Stock Prices," *Journal Business*, January 1965, Table 18, p. 93.

The figure shows that the funds are near the Markowitz-efficient frontier. Farrar says:[15]

---

[15]Ibid., p. 74.

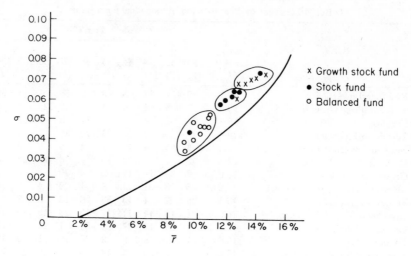

Figure 10.2. Data on 23 Mutual Funds

The plots do seem to follow closely along the frontier of optimal portfolios. Even more encouraging, however, is the tendency of the funds to cluster along the boundary in almost perfect groups of balanced funds, stock funds, and growth funds, respectively.

## 10.2 One-Parameter Portfolio Performance Measures

In an effort to measure the performance of investment portfolios, various devices have been proposed.[16] The more sophisticated of these techniques sought to take both the risk and return of a portfolio into consideration. Treynor and Sharpe have developed models for portfolio performance measurement that consider both risk and return and allow the portfolios to be ranked. These models develop one ordinal number to measure the performance of each portfolio. This number is a function of the portfolio's risk and return.

All the portfolio performance measures discussed in the remainder of this chapter are outgrowths of capital market theory. As such, they are based upon the simplifying assumptions listed and discussed in Chapter VIII.

### A. Sharpe's Ranking Technique

Sharpe analyzed 34 mutual funds' performance over the decade from 1954 to 1963 inclusive. His data are shown in Table 10.1. He subtracted from each fund's gross average return ($\bar{r}$) his estimate of the riskless return over

---

[16]Treynor, "How to Rate the Management of Mutual Funds"; Sharpe, "Mutual Fund Performance"; Jensen, "The Performance of Mutual Funds in the Period 1945–1964"; Jensen, "Risk, Capital Assets, and the Evaluation of Investment Portfolios."

the decade—that is, 3 percent. The difference is a *risk premium* for investing in assets with more than zero risk. He then divided each security's risk premium by its standard deviation of annual returns ($\sigma$), a measure of the portfolio's total risk. The resulting number is the ratio of risk premium per unit of risk borne. Let this ratio of risk premium per unit of risk borne be denoted $S_p$ for the $p$th mutual fund.

$$S_p = \frac{\bar{r} - 0.03}{\sigma_p} = \frac{\text{risk premium}}{\text{total risk}}. \tag{10.1}$$

$S$ is Sharpe's index of desirability. $S$ is developed for comparing assets in different risk classes. Consider Fig. 10.3, which graphically represents $S_p$ for assets 1, 2, and 3. Asset 1 is the most desirable, since $S_1 > S_2 > S_3$. These $S_p$'s or reward-to-variability ratios for the 34 mutual funds are shown in column 3 of Table 10.1. Sharpe then calculated the same ratio for the Dow Jones Industrial Averages (DJIA) and prepared Fig. 10.4.[17]

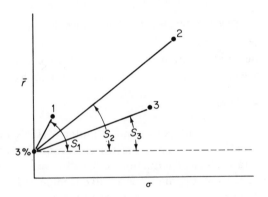

Figure 10.3. Sharpe's Ranking Technique

The average ratio for the 34 funds was 0.633, which is considerably below the 0.667 for the DJIA. Of the 34 funds, only 11 did better than the DJIA in Sharpe's ranking. Had Sharpe netted out sales commissions (which are typically 8 percent of the original investment), the mutual funds would have done even worse in comparison with the DJIA.

If a superior open-ended mutual fund existed, Sharpe's study did not detect it. In general, most funds seems to earn a gross return a little below that which would be achieved using a naive buy-and-hold strategy. The net return they pay to shareholders is significantly below what the investor could have averaged with a naive buy-and-hold strategy. None of the mutual

---

[17]Sharpe, "Mutual Fund Performance," Fig. 9, p. 136.

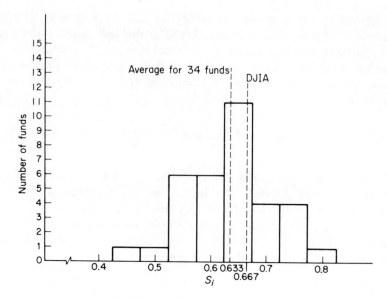

Figure 10.4. Frequency Distribution of Risk Premium-to-Variability Ratios

funds discussed here were Markowitz-efficient:[18] A discussion of other models for evaluating investment funds is provided in the remainder of this chapter.

### B. Treynor's Ranking Device

In Chapter IV [equations (4.4)] and Chapter VIII [equations (8.1)], individual securities' returns were regressed on the market index to determine Sharpe's beta coefficient [equation (8.5)]. Sharpe's beta coefficient is an index of a security's systematic or undiversifiable risk. Similarly, the returns on portfolio $p$, denoted $r_p$, may be regressed on the returns of a market index, denoted $r_I$.

$$r_{pt} = a_p + b_p(r_{It}) + e_{pt}, \tag{10.2}$$

where the $e_p$'s are random errors and it is assumed that

1. $E(e_p) = 0$.
2. Var $(e_p)$ = some finite constant.
3. Cov $(e_p, r_I) = 0$.
4. Cov $(e_{p,t}, e_{p,t+k}) = 0$.

---

[18]These conclusions agree with those of Ira Horowitz, "The Varying Quality of Investment Trust Management," *Journal of the American Statistical Association*, December 1963, pp. 1011–1032; Jensen, "The Performance of Mutual Funds in the Period 1945–1964," especially p. 406; and Jensen, "Risk, The Pricing of Capital Assets, and the Evaluation of Investment Portfolios."

These assumptions assure that the regression parameters $a_p$ and $b_p$ are minimum-variance, unbiased estimates of the true values of $a_p$ and $b_p$ for the $p$th portfolio.[19]

The expected value of equation (10.2) is the conditional expectation (that is, regression line) shown in equation (10.3):

$$E(r_p | r_I) = a + b(r_I). \tag{10.3}$$

This regression line will be called the "characteristic line of the portfolio." Two possible forms the characteristic line might assume are graphed in Fig. 10.5.

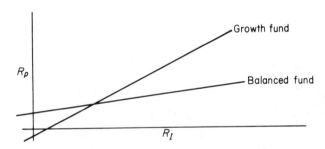

Figure 10.5. Characteristic Lines

The regression slope coefficient ($b$) in equations (10.2) and (10.3) will be referred to as the *portfolio's beta*—it is a measure of the systematic risk of the portfolio. A portfolio's beta coefficient is a measure of the volatility or responsiveness of the portfolio to changes in the market index.[20] Portfolios classified as "balanced funds" would have lower $b_p$'s than "growth funds." The portfolio beta is the weighted average of the Sharpe's beta coefficients of the securities in the portfolio. Symbolically,

$$b_p = \frac{\text{cov}(r_p, r_I)}{\sigma_I^2} \quad \text{by definition}$$

$$= \frac{\text{cov}\left(\sum_i^{i \in p} x_i r_i, r_I\right)}{\sigma_m^2} \quad \text{substituting } \sum_i^{i \in p} x_i r_i = r_p$$

$$= \sum_i^{i \in p} x_i \frac{\text{cov}(r_i, r_I)}{\sigma_I^2}$$

$$= \sum_i^{i \in p} x_i b_i \quad \text{since } b_i = \text{cov}(r_i, r_I)/\sigma_I^2 \tag{10.4}$$

---

[19]By the Gauss–Markov theorem.

[20]Treynor, "How to Rate Management of Investment Funds." Treynor calls equation (10.2) the *characteristic line* of a portfolio and the slope coefficient ($b$) a measure of its *volatility*.

Treynor's portfolio-ranking device utilizes the portfolio beta to measure risk. Treynor's index of portfolio desirability, denoted $T_p$ for the $p$th portfolio, is defined in equation (10.5):

$$T_p = \frac{E(r_p) - R}{b_p} = \frac{\text{risk premium}}{\text{systematic risk index}}. \tag{10.5}$$

Graphically, Treynor's ranking device is represented in Fig. 10.6. Portfolio 1 is more desirable than portfolio 2 because $T_1 > T_2$. The $T_p$ measures the slope of a straight line from $R$ to the $p$th asset. Assuming that portfolio 2 in Fig. 10.6 is on the security market line (SML) implies that portfolio 1 is undervalued. High values of $T_p$ indicate that the $i$th portfolio is a "good buy."

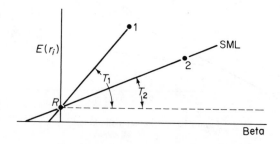

Figure 10.6. Treynor's Ranking Device

In an effort to determine if some mutual funds managers were able to outguess the ups and downs of bull- and bear-market periods, Treynor and Mazuy[21] reformulated the characteristic line as shown in equation (10.6).

$$r_{pt} = a_p + b_{1p} r_{It} + b_{2p} r_{It}^2 + e_{pt}. \tag{10.6}$$

The $a_p$ is the regression intercept, and $b_{1p}$ and $b_{2p}$ are regression coefficients on the market index returns and the markets returns squared, respectively. Equation (10.6) is like the characteristic line in equation (10.2) except that it has a second-order explanatory variable, $r_{It}^2$, added to allow for a curvilinear relation between portfolio $p$ and the market.

If the managers of portfolio $p$ can foresee a bull market ahead, they will shift into high-beta stocks to maximize their portfolio's capital gains. If a bear market is foreseen, the portfolio's managers would liquidate equity securities and hold cash (or sell stocks short, or write calls, or invest in bonds, etc.) to earn positive returns while the stock market falls (that is, $r_{It} = \, < 0$).

---

[21]J. L. Treynor and K. K. Mazuy, "Can Mutual Funds Outguess the Market?," *Harvard Business Review*, July–August 1966, pp. 131–166.

As a result of such adept trading, portfolio $p$ would have the upward-curved, $d^2 r_{pt}/dr_{It}^2 > 0$, characteristic line shown in Fig. 10.7.

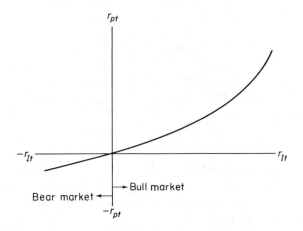

Figure 10.7. Curvilinear Characteristic Line for a Portfolio That Outguesses the Market

Treynor and Mazuy estimated equation (10.6) using 10 annual returns for 57 mutual funds—25 growth funds and 32 balanced funds. They found that $b_{2p}$ was not significantly different from zero for any of the 57 mutual funds except one. One fund's $b_2$ was marginally above zero, so its characteristic line displayed slightly discernible curvature upward. But, since the value of $b_{2p}$ that fits the returns best was zero for the other 56 mutual funds, curvilinear equation (10.6) reduced to linear equation (10.2). This absence of $b_{2p}$'s which were larger than zero is statistical evidence showing that essentially none of the 57 portfolios examined by Treynor and Mazuy were managed by people who could forecast the stock market's turns. Thus, the linear characteristic line is more descriptive of their performance than the curvilinear model.

## C. Jensen's Measure

Jensen developed a one-parameter portfolio performance measure that differs from Sharpe's or Treynor's measures. Like Treynor's measure, Jensen's measure is based upon the asset-pricing implications of the SML.[22] In Chapter VIII (see the proof of Proposition 2 in Appendix 8A) the formula for the SML was shown to be equation (8.5).

$$E(r_i) = R + b_i[E(r_I) - R]. \tag{8.5}$$

---

[22]Jensen, "The Performance of Mutual Funds in the Period 1945–1964," and Jensen, "Risk, the Pricing of Capital Assets, and the Evaluation of Investment Portfolios."

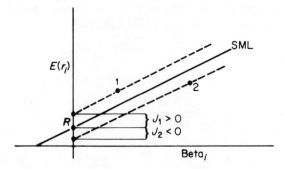

Figure 10.8. Jensen's Measure

The SML is shown graphically in Fig. 10.8. Two hypothetical portfolios are represented by points 1 and 2 in Fig. 10.8. Portfolio 1 is underpriced and offers a high expected return relative to the equilibrium prices and returns represented by the SML.

Jensen measures the desirability of portfolios with the coefficient $J_p$ in equation (10.7).

$$E(r_p) = R + J_p + B_p[E(r_I) - R]. \qquad (10.7)$$

$J_p$ measures the vertical distance which portfolio $p$'s return lies above or below the SML shown in Fig. 10.8. High values of $J_p$ represent underpriced portfolios with unusually high returns, such as $J_1$ in Fig. 10.8. $J_2 < 0$ implies that portfolio 2 is overpriced and offers a poor return for the amount of systematic risk associated with that portfolio. Since $J_p$ only measures vertical deviations from the SML (but ignores the risk dimension), it cannot be used for one-parameter portfolio rankings as well as the $S_p$ and $T_p$ measures.

Jensen suggests measuring $J_p$ by fitting regression equation (10.8) for $t = 1, 2, \ldots, T$ time periods (for example, $T = 60$ months).

$$r_{pt} - R_t = J_p + B_p(r_{It} - R_t) + e_{pt}. \qquad (10.8)$$

Over $T$ periods the $e_{pt}$'s will average zero and $J_p$ will be the regression intercept coefficient. Jensen suggests using a different value for the risk-free rate ($R_t$) in each period to hold the variation in the level of interest rates constant while $J_p$ is estimated. Equation (10.7) is the mathematical expectation of equation (10.8).[23] The slope coefficient, $B_p$, is called Jensen's beta coefficient.

---

[23]Although the SML in Figure 10.8 is similar *conceptually* to the SML models used elsewhere in this monograph (namely, in Chapter 8), the SML in Figure 10.8 is *slightly different* from the other SML models *numerically*. This slight difference arises because the beta systematic risk

### D. Conclusions About One-Parameter Portfolio Performance Measures

Sharpe's technique measures risk premium per unit of total risk and is satisfactory for portfolio selection but not for ranking the desirability of individual assets. The individual assets' total risk contains diversifiable unsystematic risk which is not relevant to the asset-pricing implications of the SML. Treynor's measure considers systematic risk and is suitable for individual assets or portfolios. Jensen's measure is useful for portfolios and individual assets, too, but unfortunately is not as useful for ranking investments.

All three of the portfolio performance measures discussed above have one serious flaw that exerts a bias against selection of high-risk portfolios. As discussed in Chapter VIII, the borrowing and lending rates differ. This causes the CML and SML to become nonlinear (for example, Figs. 8.10 and 8.9). The nature of these nonlinearities implies lower equilibrium expected returns for the high-risk portfolios than indicated by the CML and SML. Since none of the three portfolio-evaluation models discussed above makes adjustments for this, they all tend to be slightly biased against high-risk portfolios.[24]

The question of similarity between the Sharpe, Treynor, and Jensen portfolio performance measures should also be considered. It will be shown algebraically below that all three are positive linear transformations of each other. Equation (8.5) represents portfolio $p$, which is located on the SML. If all assets are correctly priced, all $(b_p, E(r_p))$ pairs fit equation (8.5). To recognize explicitly that not all assets are in equilibrium, equation (10.7) may be rewritten as equation (10.7a).

$$E(r_p) - R = J_p + B_p[E(r_I) - R], \qquad (10.7a)$$

where $J_p$ is a measure of disequilibrium for asset $p$. If $J_p = 0$, then portfolio $p$ is correctly priced—this is Jensen's measure.

---

coefficient estimated with equation 10.8 and used in equation 10.7 and Figure 10.8 is defined as shown below:

$$\text{Jensen's beta} = B_p = \frac{\text{Cov}\,[(r_{pt} - R_t),\,(r_{It} - R_t)]}{\text{Var}\,(r_{It} - R_t)}$$

If, and only if, the riskless rate is constant (for example, as it is in the static equilibrium theory), so that Var $(R_t) = 0$, will Jensen's beta then be equal to the classic beta coefficient defined in the capital market theory (in particular, the classic beta defined in equation 8.5). In empirical work, Var $(R_t) > 0$, and, as a result, Jensen's beta differs numerically a little bit from the classic beta, $B_p \neq b_p$. See Chapter 4, Appendix B for a more thorough discussion of this difference. Conceptually, however, Jensen's beta and the classic beta are identical.

[24]I. Friend and M. Blume, "Measurement of Portfolio Performance Under Uncertainty," *American Economic Review*, September 1970. Also, R. C. Klemkosky, "The Bias in Composite Performance Measures," *Journal of Financial and Quantitative Analysis*, June 1973, pp. 505–514.

Treynor's one-parameter portfolio performance measure, denoted $T_i$, is obtained by dividing both sides of (10.7a) by the beta coefficient to obtain equation (10.8). This assumes var $(R) = 0$, so the $B_p = b_p$.

$$T_p = \frac{E(r_p) - R}{B_p} = \frac{J_p}{B_p} + [E(r_I) - R]. \tag{10.8}$$

Equation (10.8) shows that Treynor's measure is a linear transformation of Jensen's measure, $J_p$, since $[E(r_I) - R]$ is a constant. Sharpe's portfolio performance index $(S_p)$ may be derived from (10.7a) by noting that $B_p = [(\rho_{pI})(\sigma_p)(\sigma_I)]/\sigma_I^2$, as shown in equation (10.9).

$$E(r_p) - R = J_p + \frac{(\rho_{pI})(\sigma_p)(\sigma_I)}{\sigma_I^2} \cdot [E(r_I) - R]. \tag{10.9}$$

For *efficient* portfolios, $\rho_{pI} = +1.0$. Dropping the unitary correlation coefficient and dividing (10.9) by $\sigma_p$ yields Sharpe's portfolio measure, $S_p$, as shown in equation (10.10).

$$\frac{E(r_p) - R}{\sigma_p} = \frac{J_p}{\sigma_p} + \frac{E(r_I) - R}{\sigma_I} = S_p. \tag{10.10}$$

Since $[E(r_I) - R]/\sigma_I$ is a constant, $S_p$ is seen to be a transformation of Jensen's $J_p$. That is, $S_p = (J_p/\sigma_p) + $ (constant).

The models above are formulated in terms of ex ante quantities. Equation (10.8) may be used in place of (10.7a) if these quantities are to be estimated with ex post data.

$$r_{pt} - R_t = J_p + B_p(r_{It} - R_t) + e_{pt}, \tag{10.8}$$

where $R_t$ is the riskless interest rate at time period $t$, $B_p$ the portfolio $p$'s beta systematic risk coefficient, and $e_{pt}$ the residual error for portfolio $p$ in period $t$. The intercept coefficient, $J_p$, is Jensen's portfolio performance measure.

### E.   More Recent Data

McDonald estimated the Sharpe, Treynor, and Jensen portfolio performance measures for 123 mutual funds using monthly data from a more recent decade, 1960 to 1969 inclusive.[25] He estimated equation (10.8) over $t = 1, 2, \ldots, 120$ months of data using high-grade 30-day commercial paper yields as market estimates of $R_t$. McDonald divided the 123 mutual funds stated investment objectives into the five different categories shown

[25]J. G. McDonald, "Objectives and Performance of Mutual Funds," *Journal of Financial and Quantitative Analysis*, June 1974, pp. 311–333.

below, based on each fund's written statement (which is required by law) of intent to undertake risk to attain higher returns.

1. Maximize capital gains—18 funds.
2. Growth (that is, high capital gains)—33 funds.
3. Growth and income (that is, capital gains and dividend income, with the priority going to capital gains)—36 funds.
4. Income and growth (that is, cash dividends and capital gains with the priority on the dividends)—12 funds.
5. Balanced (that is, conservation of principal while seeking fair returns)—12 funds.
6. Income (that is, cash dividends and interest income)—12 funds.

Table 10.3 shows graphically how the 123 mutual funds stated objectives compared with their actual performance, as measured by their beta systematic risk coefficients and standard deviations of returns.

TABLE 10.3  Comparison of Stated Investment Goals and Empirical Risk Statistics

10.3a.  Objective and Systematic Risk

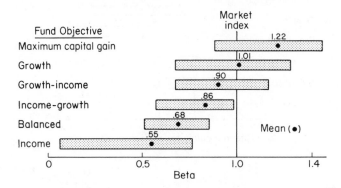

10.3b.  Objective and Total Variability (Standard Deviation of Return)

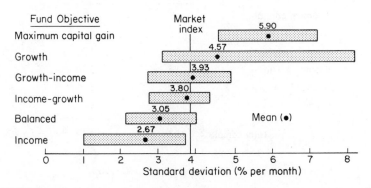

*Source:* J. G. McDonald, "Objectives and Performance of Mutual Funds," *Journal of Financial and Quantitative Analysis,* June 1974, p. 316, Fig. I.

Table 10.3 shows that, on *average*, the mutual funds' stated willingness to assume risk aligned with their actual assumption of both systematic and total risk. But there are some notable individual exceptions. For example, some mutual funds with a stated objective of high capital gains (that is, growth) assumed less risk than the average balanced fund (which usually holds large proportions of bonds), and some assumed more risk than the most aggressive funds seeking to maximize capital gains. These findings indicate that potential mutual fund investors might do better to look at the fund's quantitative risk measures than to read its written objective statement.

Table 10.4 shows how the mutual funds excess returns, $(r_{pt} - \bar{R}_t)$, averaged over the decade measured up. All the funds averaged returns above

TABLE 10.4   Mutual Funds' Actual Returns and Stated Objectives

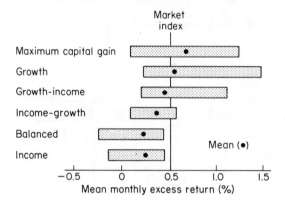

|                       | Number of funds | Mean monthly excess return (%) |
|-----------------------|:---------------:|:------------------------------:|
| Maximum capital gain  | 18              | .693                           |
| Growth                | 33              | .565                           |
| Growth-income         | 36              | .476                           |
| Income-growth         | 12              | .398                           |
| Balanced              | 12              | .214                           |
| Income                | 12              | .252                           |
|                       | ———             | ———                            |
| Total sample          | 123             | .477                           |
| NYSE index            |                 | .510                           |

Measurement period: Monthly returns, 1960-1969

*Source:* J. G. McDonald, "Objectives and Performance of Mutual Funds," *Journal of Financial and Quantitative Analysis,* June 1974, p. 317, Fig. II.

the riskless rate, that is, $r_{pt} > \bar{R}_t$ for all $p$. But the majority of the funds did not perform as well as the NYSE Index—a weighted average of all NYSE stocks. This finding suggests that mutual fund investors might be better off picking stocks within whatever risk class they prefer with an unaimed dart. The "professional money management" skills provided are of dubious value.

The average performance statistics for each of the five groupings based on stated objectives are shown in Table 10.5. One of the general conclusions suggested by the data is that the funds with extreme objectives—that is, both the maximum risk and the maximum safety funds—tended to have the most disappointing risk-adjusted return performances. After eliminating the groups with the extreme objectives, a performance pattern appears for the middle three groupings, which is evident for the Sharpe, Treynor, and Jensen performance measures. The more aggressive funds tend to earn more return per unit of risk assumed than the less aggressive managers. However, the final generality discernible from Table 10.5 is less positive; that is, on

TABLE 10.5 Performance Statistic Means by Stated Objective

| | Risk | | | Performance Measures | | |
|---|---|---|---|---|---|---|
| Objective of Fund | System- atic Risk (Beta) | Total Vari- ability (Std. Dev.) | Mean Monthly Excess Return (%) | Sharpe* Measure | Treynor† Measure | Jensen‡ Measure |
| Maximum capital gain | 1.22 | 5.90 | 0.693 | 0.117 | 0.568 | 0.122 |
| Growth | 1.01 | 4.57 | 0.565 | 0.124 | 0.560 | 0.099 |
| Growth–income | 0.90 | 3.93 | 0.476 | 0.121 | 0.529 | 0.058 |
| Income–growth | 0.86 | 3.80 | 0.398 | 0.105 | 0.463 | 0.004 |
| Balanced | 0.68 | 3.05 | 0.214 | 0.070 | 0.314 | −0.099 |
| Income | 0.55 | 2.67 | 0.252 | 0.094 | 0.458 | −0.002 |
| Sample means | 0.92 | 4.17 | 0.477 | 0.112 | 0.518 | 0.051 |
| Market-based portfolios | — | — | — | 0.133 | 0.510 | 0 |
| Stock Market Index | 1.00 | 3.83 | 0.510 | 0.133 | 0.510 | 0 |
| Bond Market Index§ | 0.18 | 1.42 | 0.093 | 0.065 | 0.516 | N.A. |

*Reward-to-variability ratio: mean excess return divided by the standard deviation of fund return.

†Reward-to-volatility ratio: mean excess return divided by beta.

‡Alpha = estimated constant from least-squares regression of fund excess returns on market excess returns.

§Proxy measure based on arithmetic means of results for Keystone B-1 and B-4 funds, with returns adjusted for 0.042 percent per month average management fee.

Source: J. G. McDonald, "Objectives and Performance of Mutual Funds," Journal of the Financial and Quantitative Analysis, June 1974, Table 1, p. 319.

average, the mutual funds do not appear to have outperformed the market averages in terms of earning high returns or in terms of reducing risk. These conclusions are generalities, however. Other tools to dissect the performance are explained in the final section of this chapter.

## 10.3 Evaluating Various Aspects of Portfolio Performance

It is possible that a rational Markowitz-efficient investor may desire to own shares in several Markowitz-*inefficient* portfolios. If the shares in these inefficient portfolios are assembled into an overall portfolio that is Markowitz-efficient, the investor has ultimately made an efficient investment. Thus, it is not clear that a portfolio manager's objective should necessarily be to maintain a Markowitz-efficient portfolio. In fact, at least two portfolio objectives suggest themselves: (1) selection of undervalued securities in an effort to earn returns above those appropriate for the securities' risk class, or (2) maintaining a Markowitz-efficient portfolio (that is, risk reduction).

Since either or both of these two portfolio objectives may be appropriate, it seems that multiple criteria may be required for evaluating the performance of portfolios. Some new theoretical apparatus will be required to carry out this evaluation.

### A. Naive Market Portfolio—The Index

Consider the Dow Jones Average or some other index $(I)$ that is used as a surrogate for the market portfolio $(M)$. These real-life analogs to $M$ are like a naively formed market portfolio. They differ from $M$ in two respects: (1) the indices are not Markowitz-efficient portfolios. The indices did not have their risk minimized. (2) The indices are not perfectly positively correlated with $M$. Since the indices only enjoyed the benefits of naive diversification (see Fig. 9.1), their risk is equal to or above the systematic level—the indices most likely contain unsystematic risk.

As was mentioned above, the stock market indices used in the financial world are surrogates for $M$. The indices are not Markowitz-efficient portfolios. If the average return and standard deviation of returns for some index are plotted in $(E(r), \sigma)$ space, a point such as $I$ in Fig. 10.9 would result.

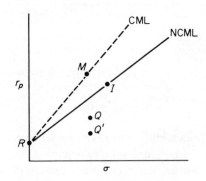

Figure 10.9. Naive Capital Market Line

232

Then, if the riskless rate $(R)$ is estimated and plotted, a *naive capital market line* (NCML) may be constructed. The NCML is the line passing through $R$ and $I$. The NCML should correspond to a regression line for naively diversified portfolios' expected returns and standard deviations (such as the solid line in Fig. 10.1). Of course, the NCML will be dominated by the CML because $M$ is Markowitz-efficient and $I$ is not. The CML (developed in Chapter VIII) is drawn in Fig. 10.9 as a dashed line. The solid line in Fig. 10.1 is analogous to the NCML.

Both the NCML or CML may be used to evaluate the performance of portfolios such as mutual funds, trust funds, and pension funds. Portfolios on the CML are Markowitz-efficient and perfectly positively correlated. Portfolios between the NCML and the CML in Fig. 10.9 are more efficient than the average portfolio—but they are not Markowitz-efficient. Portfolios lying below the NCML in Fig. 10.9 are not only inefficient, they are more inefficient than a naively selected portfolio.

A portfolio may not be Markowitz-efficient because (1) its securities have poor returns, or (2) the portfolio's risk is not being properly reduced, or (3) a combination. In the remainder of this chapter a portfolio-evaluation model is outlined that will enable analysts to determine which of these weaknesses is the cause of any given inefficient portfolio. This model may also be used to determine if a portfolio is efficient owing to its ability to find securities that earn abnormally high returns although it is poorly diversified. That is, portfolios that are able to "pick winners" may be detected.

### B. Portfolio Betas and the SML

Earlier in this chapter it was shown that the returns on portfolio $p$, denoted $r_p$, may be regressed on the returns of a market index—denoted $r_I$

$$r_p = a + b(r_I) + e_p, \qquad (10.2)$$

where the $e_p$'s are random errors and conform to the assumptions of regression analysis. This was called the portfolio's characteristic line.

Since portfolios' expected returns and beta coefficients are merely linear combinations of the expected returns and betas of the securities in the portfolio, portfolios' returns and beta coefficients should also be on the SML in equilibrium. The SML is graphed in Fig. 10.10. The SML represents the linear relationship between a portfolio's or individual security's systematic risk and its expected return in equilibrium.

If a portfolio is doing an average job of finding undervalued securities, its $E(r_p)$ and $b_p$ should plot *on* the SML. But, if a portfolio's $E(r_p)$ and $b_p$ plot between the SML and the $E(r)$ axis, the portfolio is better than average at "picking winners." Conversely, a portfolio located below the SML is picking overvalued securities (that is, "losers").

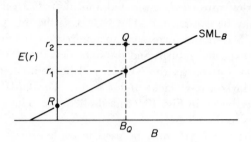

Figure 10.10. Security Market Line

If a portfolio such as $Q$ in Fig. 10.10 is investigated further, it may turn out to be efficient or inefficient. As shown in Fig. 10.9, portfolio $Q$ is less efficient than average. In fact, portfolio $Q$ would be at a point like $Q'$ in Fig. 10.9 if it were not so adept at picking winners that it raised its average return to point $Q$. It can be concluded that portfolio $Q$ is good at picking capital gains and poor at diversification. Portfolio $Q$ is less efficient than average and far from being Markowitz-efficient.

### C. The Index of Total Portfolio Risk and $b_p$

The relationship between a portfolio's systematic risk (as measured by $b_p$) and its total risk (as measured by $\sigma_p$) may be more clearly seen in terms of Fig. 10.11. Figure 10.11 is like Fig. 10.10 except that an additional variable has been graphed on the horizontal axis. The additional variable is the *index of total portfolio risk*,[26] as measured by the ratio $\sigma_p/\sigma_I$.

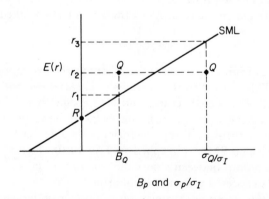

$B_p$ and $\sigma_p/\sigma_I$

Figure 10.11. Tools for Evaluating Portfolio Performance

---

[26] The index of total portfolio risk is

$$\frac{\sigma_p}{\sigma_I} = \frac{\text{standard deviation of returns on the portfolio}}{\text{standard deviation of returns on the index}}.$$

234

Relationships between $b_p$ and $\sigma_p/\sigma_I$ may be developed from equations (10.2) and (10.3). The returns on the $p$th security can be represented as a linear function of the index's returns $(r_I)$. The $p$th security's variance of returns can be partitioned into two sources, as shown in equation (10.11a).

$$\text{var } (r_p) = \text{var } (a + b_p r_I + e_p) \tag{10.11}$$

$$= \text{var } (b_p r_I) + \text{var } (e_p) = b_p^2 \text{ var } (r_I) + \text{var } (e_p) \tag{10.11a}$$

$$= \text{systematic variance} + \text{unsystematic variance} = \text{total risk.}$$

If the $p$th security is efficient, its unsystematic variance must be zero by the definition of efficiency—namely, var $(e_p) = 0$. Thus, equation (10.11a) can be rewritten as follows for an efficient asset.

$$\text{var } (r_p) = b_p^2 \text{ var } (r_I) + 0. \tag{10.11b}$$

The relation between $b_p$ and the index of total portfolio risk for *efficient* portfolios is derived from equation (10.12b):

$$\text{var } (r_p) = b_p^2 \text{ var } (r_I) + 0 \qquad \text{since var } (e_p) = 0, \tag{10.11b}$$

$$\frac{\text{var } (r_p)}{\text{var } (r_I)} = \frac{\sigma_p^2}{\sigma_I^2} = b_p^2 \qquad \text{by dividing by var } (r_I)$$

$$\frac{\sigma_p}{\sigma_I} = b_p. \tag{10.12}$$

The same relationship can be derived by examining the definition of the beta coefficient.

$$b_p = \frac{\text{cov } (r_p, r_I)}{\sigma_I^2} = \frac{(\rho_{pI})(\sigma_p)(\sigma_I)}{\sigma_I^2} = \frac{\sigma_p}{\sigma_I},$$

since $\rho_{pI} = 1$ for all *efficient* portfolios. Thus, $b_p$ is identical to the index of total portfolio risk for an efficient portfolio; they are in the same units. For an *inefficient portfolio,*

$$\sqrt{\frac{\text{var } (r_p)}{\text{var } (r_I)}} = \sqrt{\frac{\text{var } (b_p r_I) + \text{var } (e_p)}{\text{var } (r_I)}} > b_p \qquad \text{since var } (e_p) > 0.$$

It was shown in Fig. 9.1 that naive diversification can reduce portfolio risk to the systematic level. At that point $\sigma_p = \sigma_I$ and the index of total portfolio risk equals unity, $b_p = 1$ when $\sigma_p = \sigma_I$. When risk is above the systematic level, $b_p > 1$ and $\sigma_p > \sigma_I$. Likewise, when $b_p < 1$, then $\sigma_p < \sigma_I$ for an efficient portfolio. The ratio $\sigma_p/\sigma_I$ is in the same units as $b_p$, and $\sigma_p/\sigma_I$ will equal $b_p$ when the portfolio is efficient.

Referring to portfolio Q again, Fig. 10.11 shows that portfolio Q earned a higher return $(r_2)$ than normal $(r_1)$ for its level of systematic risk $(b_Q)$.

This is just what Fig. 10.10 showed. But Fig. 10.11 *also* shows that for its level of total portfolio risk $(\sigma_q/\sigma_I)$ portfolio $Q$ had a return $(r_2)$ below normal $(r_3)$—this is what Fig. 10.9 showed. The apparent paradox between the evidence about portfolio $Q$ shown in Figs. 10.9 and 10.10 is resolved in Fig. 10.11. The multiaspect portfolio performance evaluation tool shown in Fig. 10.11 resolved the seeming paradox by showing that portfolio $Q$ "picked winners" but that it did not diversify well.[27]

It was pointed out at the beginning of this section that a portfolio manager's objective need not necessarily be to operate an efficient portfolio. Thus, Markowitz-efficient investors may want to buy shares in portfolio $Q$ in an effort to reap the abnormally high return. But they must combine shares of $Q$ with shares of other assets if they are going to minimize risk. To the extent that such multiple criteria are applicable, the more discriminating tools shown here are necessary for portfolio evaluation.

### 10.4  Conclusions About Performance Evaluation

Although the rate of return is the single most important outcome from an investment, the rate of return is insufficient information on which to adequately evaluate a portfolio's performance. This chapter has shown the importance of considering both risk and return simultaneously in evaluating portfolios' performance. In addition, there are other aspects of an investment's performance that may be worth considering. The broker's sales commission (or load fee),[28] the skewness[29] of returns, possible nonlinearities[30] in

---

[27]The model for simultaneously evaluating different aspects of a portfolio's performance is discussed more fully by E. F. Fama in "Risk and Evaluation of Pension Fund Portfolio Performance," *Measuring the Investment Performance of Pension Funds*, Bank Administration Institute, Park Ridge, Ill., 1968; and also "Components of Investment Performance," *Journal of Finance*, June 1972, pp. 551–567. Both these articles are reprinted as readings 27 and 28 in *Modern Developments in Investment Management*, edited by J. Lorie and A. Brealey (New York: Praeger Press, Inc., 1972).

[28]F. Modigliani and G. Pogue, "Alternative Investment Fee Arrangements and Implications for the SEC Regulatory Policy," *The Bell Journal of Economics*, Spring 1975, pp. 127–159.

[29]F. D. Arditti suggested a three-parameter portfolio performance system which considers the first three moments, "Another Look at Mutual Fund Performance," *Journal of Financial and Quantitative Analysis*, June 1971. Francis argued that although skewness was theoretically relevant, it could not be measured empirically with sufficient reliability to justify considering it: "Skewness and Investors' Decisions," *Journal of Financial and Quantitative Analysis*, March 1975. C. G. Martin published an independent study that supported Francis's findings in *Review of Business and Economic Research* entitled, "Ridge Regression Estimates of Ex Post Risk-Return Trade-off on Common Stock," Spring 1978, pp. 1–15.

[30]Cheng-Few Lee has analyzed the nonlinearity problem from several points of view in the following three articles: "Investment Horizon and the Functional Form of the Capital Asset Pricing Model," *Review of Economics and Statistics*, Vol. 48, August 1976; "On the Relationship Between Systematic Risk and the Investment Horizon," *Journal of Financial and Quantita-*

the risk–return relationship, the portfolio's cash holdings,[31] the quality of the portfolio's security analysis,[32] the timing[33] of the portfolio's purchases and sales of security holdings, shifting risk statistics,[34] and the length of the time interval over which the investment period is measured[35] are all factors that can also affect an investor's well-being.[36] As a result of the multiplicity of relevant considerations, portfolio performance evaluation is a complicated task.

---

*tive Analysis*, December 1976, pp. 803–815; "Functional Form, Skewness Effect, and the Risk–Return Relationship," *Journal of Financial and Quantitative Analysis*, March 1977, pp. 55–72. See also J. C. Francis and C. F. Lee, "Investment Horizon, Risk Surrogates and Mutual Fund Performance," unpublished manuscript, October 1978.

[31]A. H. Chen and J. C. Francis, "Investment Performance Evaluation Including Explicit Liquidity Evaluation," unpublished manuscript, September 1977. A. H. Chen, E. H. Kim, and S. J. Kon, "Cash Demand, Liquidation Costs and Capital Market Equilibrium Under Uncertainty," *Journal of Business*, April 1967.

[32]J. L. Treynor and F. Black, "How to Use Security Analysis to Improve Portfolio Selection," *Journal of Business*, January 1973. Amir Barnea and D. E. Logue, "Evaluating the Forecasts of a Security Analyst," *Financial Management*, Summer 1973.

[33]It has been suggested that the difference between a portfolio's geometric mean (or time-weighted) rate of return and its dollar weighted (or internal) rate of return is the result of good or bad timing. See H. D. Mills, "On The Measurement of Fund Performance," *Journal of Finance*, No. 25, December 1970, pp. 1125–1132; also K. B. Gray and R. B. K. Dewar, "Axiomatic Characterization of Time Weighted Rate of Return," *Management Science*, Vol. 18, No. 2, 1971, pp. B32–B35.

[34]F. J. Fabozzi and J. C. Francis, "Beta as a Random Coefficient," *Journal of Financial and Quantitative Analysis*, March 1978, also, J. C. Francis and F. J. Fabozzi, "Macro-Economic Changes and the Stability of the Alpha and Beta Coefficients, *Journal of Financial and Quantitative Analysis*, forthcoming 1979.

[35]Evidence that security risk and return statistics change over any given sample, depending upon whether daily, monthly, quarterly, or annual differencing intervals are used to calculate the rates of return, has been published. See the following references: Gerald A. Pogue and Bruno H. Solnik, "The Market Model Applied to European Common Stocks: Some Empirical Results," *Journal of Financial and Quantitative Analysis*, December 1974, pp. 917–944; E. I. Altman, B. Jacquillant, and M. Levasseur, "Comparative Analysis of Risk Measures: France and the U. S.," *Journal of Finance*, December 1974, pp. 1495–1511; J. C. Francis, "Skewness and Investors Decisions," *Journal of Financial and Quantitative Analysis*, March 1975, pp. 163–172; H. E. Phillips and J. P. Seagle, "Data: A Mixed Blessing in Portfolio Selection," *Financial Management*, Autumn, 1975, pp. 50–53; R. A. Schwartz and David K. Whitcomb, "The Time-Variance Relationship: Evidence on Autocorrelation in Common Stock Returns," *Journal of Finance*, March 1977; K. V. Smith, "The Effects of Intervaling on Estimation Parameters of the Capital Asset Pricing Model," *Journal of Financial and Quantitative Analysis*, June 1978; H. Levy, "Portfolio Performance and the Investment Horizon," *Management Science*, Vol. 18, 1972, pp. 867–887; and D. Levhari and H. Levy, "The Capital Asset Pricing Model and the Investment Horizon," *The Review of Economics and Statistics*, Vol. 49, 1977, pp. 92–104.

[36]Institutional Investor Study Report of the Securities and Exchange Commission. 92nd Congress, 1st Session, House Document No. 92–64, March 10, 1974. In particular, Volume 4 of the eight-volume report, which was written by Professor Gerald Pogue, deals with portfolio performance evaluation.

As multiple millions of dollars flow into U.S. federal-law-controlled pension funds each year, portfolio performance evaluation can be expected to become more important for financial executives in the future. Corporations will seek to control their pension costs by evaluating their pension portfolio managers' performances in detail. Thus, portfolio performance evaluation may be an important determinant of the success of more financial managers.

## Selected References

Jensen, M. C., "Risk, the Pricing of Capital Assets, and the Evaluation of Investment Portfolios," *Journal of Business*, Vol. 42, April 1969, pp. 167–247.

Jensen analyzes his portfolio performance measure in a risk–return context and contrasts it with other performance measures. Mutual fund management practices are also discussed. Algebra and statistics are used.

McDonald, J. G., "Objectives and Performance of Mutual Funds," *Journal of Financial and Quantitative Analysis*, June 1974, pp. 311–333.

This statistical study compares the Sharpe, Treynor, and Jensen portfolio performance measures using a decade of sample data.

Sharpe, W. F., "Mutual Fund Performance," *Journal of Business*, January 1966, pp. 119–138.

This classic article explicates the Sharpe and Treynor portfolio performance measures and compares them empirically. Algebra and statistics are used.

## Questions and Problems

1. Suppose that you are vice-president of finance and that managing the corporation's pension funds is one of your responsibilities. Assume further that you have the annual rates of return for the most recent 10 years from 100 different mutual funds, banks' trust departments, investment advisory services, and life insurance companies that want to manage your pension funds (for fees that are all identical). How should you select three portfolio managers from these 100 candidates to each manage one-third on your firm's pension funds? Should you select the three that had the highest return in the most recent year, or the three with the highest average return over several years, or the portfolio managers whose portfolios had the least risk, or what?

2. Some statistics describing the performance of three mutual funds over a recent decade are listed below. During this decade the riskless rate was $R = 5.0$ percent $= 0.05$.

| Mutual Fund | Average Return, $\bar{r}$ | Standard Deviation, $\sigma$ | Beta Coefficient, B | Correlation with Market, $\rho$ |
|---|---|---|---|---|
| A | 15% = 0.15 | 5% = 0.05 | 0.8 | 0.98 |
| B | 20% = 0.2 | 10% = 0.1 | 1.0 | 0.95 |
| C | 10% = 0.1 | 10% = 0.1 | 1.1 | 0.85 |

Use the Sharpe and the Treynor single-parameter portfolio performance measures to rank the performance of these three. Use graphs to illustrate your analysis. Which portfolio performed the best? The worst? (*Warning:* This case contains some sophistry to make you think.)

3. The beta-based portfolio performance measures developed by Treynor and Jensen both require returns from some market index when using these models for performance evaluation work. In contrast, Shape's portfolio efficiency measure requires fewer data than the Treynor and Jensen measures. In view of this difference in the data requirements, which of these three evaluation tools would you use if you had to compare the performance of mutual funds, closed-ended funds, commodity futures trading portfolios, international portfolios which are totally invested in foreign securities, portfolios of money market instruments (for example, large-denomination certificates of deposit), and portfolios that invest only in bonds? What market index or indexes would you use if you wanted to employ one of the beta-based measures?

4. When using Sharpe's portfolio efficiency measure, does it make any difference whether the total risk measure used in the denominator is the standard deviation or the variance? Prepare graphs of the results using both the standard deviation and the variance to illustrate the difference. Is the difference in the curvature good, bad, or irrelevant? Explain.

5. If you had to compare the risk-adjusted rate of return performance of several different New York Stock Exchange stocks, would you use the Sharpe, Treynor, or Jensen measure? Explain. (*Hint:* One of the three measures is entirely inappropriate.)

6. Do you think that the correlation coefficient for the characteristic line (or single index market model) is higher, the same, or lower for mutual funds than for individual stocks? Why?

7. Suppose that some mutual fund manager adeptly shifted into high-beta assets during bullish market times and into low-beta assets during bearish periods in an effort to improve the portfolio's risk-adjusted return. How would this affect the Sharpe, Treynor, and Jensen performance measures?

8. From a recent four-year period, gather 48 monthly observations on the following:

(a) Monthly price change plus cash dividend rates of return from some stock market index (for example, Standard and Poor's 500);

(b) Two money-market interest rates (for example, U.S. Treasury bill yields and commercial paper rates).

(c) Monthly price change plus cash disbursement returns from two different mutual funds.

With these data, calculate the Sharpe, Treynor, and Jensen performance measures for the two mutual funds. Do all three performance measures assign the best performance to the same fund? Will the ranking always be consistent when different performance measures are used? Calculate the Jensen measure twice for each mutual fund—one time using each of the different money market interest rates. Are the Jensen results sensitive to which interest rate is used? Since interest rates and stock market indices have different elasticities with respect to the inflation rate, do you think that varying rates of inflation might distort the Jensen measure? Explain.

# Section Four

# UTILITY ANALYSIS

CHAPTERS XI and XII analyze the logic of selecting Markowitz-efficient portfolios. Investment decisions involving risk are rationalized in terms of the expected utility model. Chapter XI delves into single-period investment decisions, and differences between different utility functions are analyzed in terms of the Pratt–Arrow risk-aversion measures. Chapter XII studies multiperiod investment decisions from two different perspectives. Considered first is maximizing the utility of terminal wealth (or equivalently, of the geometric mean rate of return) if no intermediate investment withdrawals are made. Second, a multiperiod utility function is maximized when the investor is presumed to have the opportunity to withdraw investment funds for consumption in every period. An examination of portfolio revision concludes Chapter XII.

# Single-Period Utility Analysis

WHEN economists discuss a person's derived happiness, they call it utility. That is, *utility* measures the magnitude of satisfaction someone derives from something. Utility is a subjective index of preference. If a person is faced with a decision, the alternative with the highest utility (that is, the most utiles) is the preferred choice. Thus, if the utility of candy is less than the utility of ice cream, the ice cream is preferred to the candy. Symbolically, this preference may be written: $U(\text{candy}) < U(\text{ice cream})$.

Utility is derived from numerous things. For example, people derive utility from portfolios. Thus, choices among portfolios may be rationalized with utility analysis. The task of this chapter is to analyze single-period portfolio decisions. The length of time covered by the "single period" discussed in this chapter may be as short as a day or as long as a decade. Essentially, an investor's period of reference is the length of the person's investment planning horizon. Multiperiod utility analysis is the topic of the following chapter.

## 11.1 Basic Axioms of Utility Analysis

Utility analysis is based on the following six assumptions[1]:

1. People have complete and consistent preferences. Thus, given a choice between $A$ and $B$, a person can tell whether he prefers $A$ to $B$, $U(A) > U(B)$;

---

[1]For the classic discussion of the basic assumptions see John von Neumann and Oskar Morgenstern, *Theory of Games and Economic Behavior*, 3rd ed. (Princeton, N.J.: Princeton

is indifferent between $A$ and $B$, $U(A) = U(B)$; or prefers $B$ to $A$, $U(B) > U(A)$.

2. A person's choices are transitive. Thus, if a man preferred $A$ to $B$ and preferred $B$ to $C$, it follows directly that $A$ is preferred to $C$.

3. Objects with equal utility are equally desirable. Symbolically, if $U(A) = U(D)$ and $U(A) > U(B)$, then $U(D) > U(B)$ follows directly, since $A$ and $D$ are desired equally.

4. If $U(A) > U(B)$ and $U(B) > U(C)$, there is some risky lottery involving $A$ and $C$ that is as satisfying as $B$. Symbolically,

$$P(A) \cdot U(A) + P(C) \cdot U(C) = U(B)$$

for some values of $P(A)$ and $P(C)$, where $P(A)$ and $P(C)$ are probabilities of $A$ and $C$.

5. If someone has ranked objects of choice, then adding some irrelevant additional object to each of the already ranked alternative objects of choice does not change their ranking. Symbolically, if $U(A) > U(B)$, then $[U(A) + U(E)] > [U(B) + U(E)]$, where $E$ does not affect $A$ or $B$.

6. The expected-utility maxim: The utility of a risky object is equal to the *expected* utility of the possible outcomes. Symbolically, if an object has $n$ possible outcomes, its expected utility is

$$E(U) = \sum_{i=1}^{n} P(O_i) \cdot U(O_i),$$

where $O_i$ is the $i$th outcome and $P(O_i)$ is the probability of $O_i$ occurring. All utility analysis is based on these six assumptions.

One of the reasons economists perform utility analysis is to mathematically analyze the implications of their models to see if they are realistic. For example, positive but diminishing marginal utility is one of the things economists expect to find in a realistic economic model. *Diminishing positive marginal utility* simply means that as you get more and more units of a good, you enjoy each additional unit less. All people experience diminishing marginal utility when they eat several ice cream cones, for example, as shown below symbolically.

$$U(\text{1st cone}) > U(\text{2nd cone}) > U(\text{3rd cone}) > \cdots.$$

University Press, 1953), Chap. 3. For a less rigorous discussion, see W. J. Baumol's *Economic Theory and Operations Analysis*, 2nd ed. (Englewood Cliffs, N. J.: Prentice-Hall, Inc., 1965), Chap. 22. Much of the other important utility literature is in the following books: S. H. Archer and C. A. D'Ambrosio, *The Theory of Business Finance: A Book of Readings* (New York: Macmillan Publishing Co., Inc., 1967), readings 2, 3, 4, 39, and 42; Harry M. Markowitz, *Portfolio Selection*, Cowles Foundation Monograph 16 (New York: John Wiley & Sons, Inc., 1959), Chaps. 10–13; and J. L. Bicksler and P. A. Samuelson, *Investment Portfolio Decision-Making* (Lexington, Mass.: Lexington Books, 1974), readings 1–8 and 14–18.

If you have *positive* marginal utility of ice cream (or dollars, or returns, or new suits of clothes, etc.) that just means that you like ice cream (or whatever). *Diminishing* positive marginal utility means that even though you like something, as you receive more of the good you start to become satisfied and your desire for additional units of the same good decreases. The realism of this is obvious—who would want the tenth ice cream cone as badly as the first one?

## 11.2  The Utility of Wealth Function

Economists do not usually analyze the utility from particular commodities (such as ice cream cones, new clothes, perfume, etc.) because everyone has different tastes and preferences for particular items. Instead, economists analyze the utility of purchasing power because real purchasing power allows the purchase of, say, hair styling to be compared with the purchase of medical care. That is, economists focus on the utility of wealth, denoted $U(w)$, to facilitate the analysis of different purchasing decisions which all either have dollar costs or to which dollar costs can be imputed (for example, an hour of leisure time has a cost equal to the hourly wage lost by loafing).

A utility of wealth function is a formula or a graph of a formula that shows how much utility (or how many utiles, or how much happiness) a person derives from different levels of wealth. Figure 11.1 shows a graph of a utility-of-wealth function. The notion of marginal utility is a little more complex; it involves segments of the utility-of-wealth function. In words, "marginal utility" of wealth may be defined as the additional utility a person gets from a change in his or her wealth. Mathematically, marginal utility is the first derivative of the utility function—that is, $dU/dw$, or $U'(w)$. To determine whether marginal utility is rising or falling, the slope of the utility function or the sign of the second derivative of the utility function must be observed. Decreasing marginal utility is present when the utility function

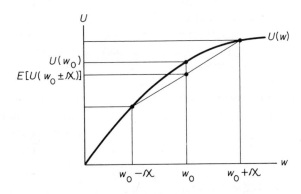

Figure 11.1. Diminishing Marginal Utility of Wealth

rises at a less steep rate or when the second derivative of the utility function is negative, $d^2U/dw^2 < 0$ or $U''(w) < 0$.

Utility analysis is useful for analyzing the logic, or lack of it, in decisions involving risk. The expected-utility maxim given in assumption 6 is the heart of utility analysis. The expected-utility maxim implies that people act so as to maximize their *expected utility* rather than so as to maximize the *utility of the expected outcome*.

Maximizing expected utility is different from simply maximizing utility if the possible outcomes are risky. To understand the difference, consider the definition of expected utility. The expected utility from a decision to undertake some risky course of action is the weighted average of the utiles from the possible outcomes that are calculated, using the probability of each outcome as the weights. For example, if you decide to enter into a coin-tossing gamble, you have made a decision to undertake a risky course of action. There are two possible outcomes—heads or tails. The probability of getting heads is denoted $P(\text{head})$, and the probability of a tail is written as $P(\text{tail})$. The utility from the gamble which results if heads turns up is represented by $U(\text{head})$ and the utility of getting the tail is $U(\text{tail})$. Thus, the expected utility of the gamble is written symbolically as

$$E[U(\text{coin toss})] = P(\text{head}) \times U(\text{head}) + P(\text{tail}) \times U(\text{tail}).$$

To understand this more clearly, consider some examples.

### 11.3  Diminishing Marginal Utility and Risk Aversion

Risk-averse behavior will result if the investor has diminishing marginal utility of wealth. A diminishing marginal utility-of-wealth function is graphed in Fig. 11.1, it is concave to the horizontal axis.[2]

Diminishing marginal utility of wealth leads to risk-avoiding behavior, since, from any point on the utility-of-wealth or utility-of-returns curve, a risky investment has a lower expected utility than a safe investment with the same expected outcome. That is, if an investment offers a 50–50 chance of increasing or decreasing a given level of starting wealth by $X$ dollars, the loss of utility from the bad outcome is larger than the gain in utility from the favorable outcome. Symbolically, $(0.5)U(w_0 - x) + (0.5)U(w_0 + x) \leq U(w_0)$. Thus, the person with diminishing utility of wealth would prefer to keep $w_0$ rather than make a risky investment or bet to attain $(w_0 + x)$ or $(w_0 - x)$ with equal probability. Figure 11.1 represents this situation graphically. Since the utility of the certain starting wealth, $U(w_0)$, is larger than the expected utility of an equal amount of uncertain wealth, $E[U(w_0)]$, the risk

---

[2] By definition, a function $U$ is concave if and only if $U(x) \geq \alpha U(x - y) + (1 - \alpha)U(x + y)$ for $1 \geq \alpha \geq 0$. A concave (to the horizontal axis) utility function results in risk aversion.

averter prefers not to assume the risk, $U(w_0) > E[U(w_0)]$. The risk averter prefers simply to hold $w_0$ cash rather than assume risks in an effort to increase this wealth. If the chance for gains from the risky investment were large enough, however, the risk-averse investor would find it sufficient compensation to assume the risk. Thus, risk averters may gladly accept risky investments if they feel the odds are in their favor.

### 11.4 Equality of Wealth and Return Utility Functions

Utility preference orderings are invariant under a positive linear transformation of the utility function. Graphically speaking, this means that any utility curve (such as the one in Fig. 11.1) can be raised or lowered (that is, can have a constant added or subtracted), can be scaled down without having its shape changed (that is, can be divided by a positive constant), or can be expanded without changing its curvature (that is, can be multiplied by a positive constant) without changing the way the utility curve would rank the desirability of a set of investment opportunities. These transformations would change the number of utils assigned to any given outcome, but the preference *rankings* would be invariant under a positive linear transformation. The one-period rate of return is another kind of positive linear transformation. A given investor's return is simply a linear transformation of his or her wealth. Thus, the investor's utility curves shown in Figs. 11.1 and 11.2 are merely linear transformations of identical preferences for single-period

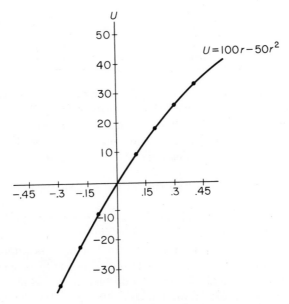

Figure 11.2. Risk-Averter's Quadratic Utility of Returns Function

changes in wealth or equivalent one-period rates of return. The positive
linear transformation between one-period changes in wealth and the rate of
return is as follows:

$$w_1 = w_0(1 + r) \tag{11.1}$$

$$= w_0 + w_0 r$$

$$w_1 - w_0 = w_0 r$$

$$\frac{w_1 - w_0}{w_0} = r, \tag{11.1a}$$

where $w_0$ denotes the beginning of period wealth (a positive constant), $w_1$ the
end-of-period wealth (a random variable), and $r_t$ the one-period rate of
return (also a random variable).

In discussing investments, financial economists often prefer to analyze the
speed or rate at which the investor gets wealthy rather than the wealth itself.
The one-period measures the rate at which beginning wealth of $w_0$ increases
to end-of-period wealth of $w_1$. Of course, if the rate of return is negative, the
investor is getting poorer, not wealthier. It is easier to analyze the utility of
returns, denoted $U(r)$, than it is to analyze the utility of wealth, because the
analysis is not distorted by differences in the dollar amount of the investment
(economists call this *scaling differences*). Thus, a $15 per share security named
$A$ can yield as much utility as security $B$, which costs $150 per share, if they
both grow at a rate of 33.3 percent:

| Security | Purchase Price Per Share | End-of-Period Sale Price | One-Period Rate of Return |
|----------|--------------------------|--------------------------|---------------------------|
| $A$ | $15 | $20 | $r_A = 33.3\%$ |
| $B$ | $150 | $200 | $r_B = 33.3\%$ |

An investor who was naive would prefer investment $B$ because it yielded
more dollars of capital gain ($50) than security $A$ (only $5). But a rational
investor would realize that 10 shares of security $A$ would provide the identical gain as one share of security $B$ and thus evaluate the two investments
equally, $U(r_A) = U(r_B) = U$ (33.3 percent), in terms of their returns.

## 11.5 Expected Utility of Returns Analysis

Investors' utility of returns are analyzed in the remainder of this chapter.
In the real world, investments involve risk. Therefore, before the analysis of
risky alternatives can be performed, the analyst must be supplied with a
probability distribution of returns and a utility function to assign utiles to the
returns. In selecting among alternative portfolios, a probability distribution
of returns is needed for each portfolio. Only after the utility function and the
probability distributions are known may utility analysis proceed.

TABLE 11.1 Probability Distributions for Three Portfolios' Returns

| Portfolio | | Portfolios' Outcomes and Their Probabilities | | | | | Portfolio Characteristics | |
|---|---|---|---|---|---|---|---|---|
| | Outcomes: | −3% | 0 | 3% | 6% | 9% | $E(r)$ | $\sigma_p$ |
| A | | 0.5 | | + | | 0.5 = 1.0 | $E(r_A) = 3\%$ | $\sigma_A = 6.0\%$ |
| B | Probabilities: | | 0.5 | + | 0.5 | = 1.0 | $E(r_B) = 3\%$ | $\sigma_B = 3.0\%$ |
| C | | | | 1.0 | | | $E(r_C) = 3\%$ | $\sigma_C = 0$ |

Consider three objects of choice—portfolios named, say, $A$, $B$, and $C$. Table 11.1 defines the probability distribution of returns for portfolios $A$, $B$, and $C$. The three portfolios' characteristics are calculated using equations (2.1a) and (2.3a) as shown below.

$$E(r_A) = \sum_{i=1}^{2} p_i r_i = \tfrac{1}{2}(-0.03) + \tfrac{1}{2}(0.09) = 0.03 = 3 \text{ percent,}$$

$$E(r_B) = \tfrac{1}{2}(0) + \tfrac{1}{2}(0.06) = 3 \text{ percent,}$$

$$E(r_C) = (1.0)(0.03) = 3 \text{ percent,}$$

$$\sigma_A = \sqrt{\sum p_i [r_i - E(r)]^2}$$
$$= \sqrt{\tfrac{1}{2}(-0.03 - 0.03)^2 + \tfrac{1}{2}(0.09 - 0.03)^2} = \sqrt{0.0036}$$
$$= 6 \text{ percent,}$$

$$\sigma_B = \sqrt{\tfrac{1}{2}(0 - 0.03)^2 + \tfrac{1}{2}(0.06 - 0.03)^2}$$
$$= \sqrt{\tfrac{1}{2}(0.0009) + \tfrac{1}{2}(0.0009)} = 3 \text{ percent,}$$

$$\sigma_C = \sqrt{(1)(0.03 - 0.03)^2} = 0.$$

Figures 11.2, 11.3, and 11.4 represent the utility functions for a risk-averting, risk-indifferent, and risk-seeking investor, respectively. Since investments $A$, $B$, and $C$ all offer the same expected return of 3 percent, it is clear that the three investors will rank these three investments differently *purely* because of their differences in risk.

The risk-averter's expected utility from $A$, $B$, and $C$ is calculated as follows:

$$E[U(A)] = \sum_{i=1}^{2} p_i U(r_i)$$
$$= \tfrac{1}{2}[U(-0.03)] + \tfrac{1}{2}[U(0.09)]$$
$$= \tfrac{1}{2}(-3.045) + \tfrac{1}{2}(8.595)$$
$$= 2.785 \text{ utiles,}$$

$$E[U(B)] = \tfrac{1}{2}[U(0)] + \tfrac{1}{2}[U(0.06)]$$
$$= 0 + \tfrac{1}{2}(5.82)$$
$$= 2.91 \text{ utiles,}$$

$$E[U(C)] = 1[U(0.03)]$$
$$= 1(2.955)$$
$$= 2.955 \text{ utiles.}$$

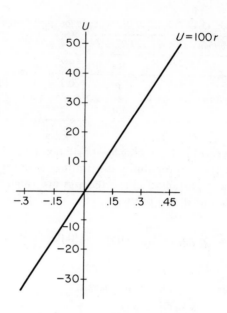

Figure 11.3. Risk-Indifferent Investor's Linear Utility of Returns Function

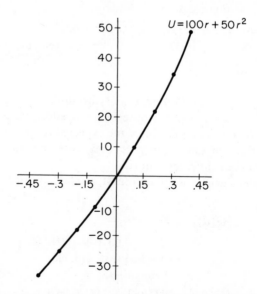

Figure 11.4. Risk-Lover's Quadratic Utility of Returns Function

The risk averter derives the most satisfaction from investment $C$, which has the least variability of return.

The risk-indifferent investor's expected utiles from the three investments are calculated as follows:

$$E[U(A)] = \tfrac{1}{2}[U(-0.03)] + \tfrac{1}{2}[U(0.09)]$$
$$= \tfrac{1}{2}(-3) + \tfrac{1}{2}(9)$$
$$= 3 \text{ utiles,}$$
$$E[U(B)] = \tfrac{1}{2}[U(0)] + \tfrac{1}{2}[U(0.06)]$$
$$= 0 + \tfrac{1}{2}(6)$$
$$= 3 \text{ utiles,}$$
$$E[U(C)] = 1[U(0.03)]$$
$$= 1(3)$$
$$= 3 \text{ utiles.}$$

Since investments $A$, $B$, and $C$ differ only with respect to their risk, the risk-indifferent investor assigns the same utility to all three. Symbolically, $E[U(A)] = E[U(B)] = E[U(C)]$ for the risk-indifferent investor.

The risk-lover's utility calculations follow.

$$E[U(A)] = \tfrac{1}{2}[U(-0.03)] + \tfrac{1}{2}[U(0.09)]$$
$$= \tfrac{1}{2}(-2.055) + \tfrac{1}{2}(9.405)$$
$$= 3.225 \text{ utiles,}$$
$$E[U(B)] = \tfrac{1}{2}[U(0)] + \tfrac{1}{2}[U(0.06)]$$
$$= 0 + \tfrac{1}{2}(6.18)$$
$$= 3.09 \text{ utiles,}$$
$$E[U(C)] = 1[U(0.03)]$$
$$= 1(3.045)$$
$$= 3.045 \text{ utiles.}$$

The risk-lover prefers the large variability of return exhibited by investment A. The three investors' expected utilities are summarized in Table 11.2.

TABLE 11-2. Different Investment Preferences for Risky Investments

| Investor | Asset A—Most Risky $E(r_A) = 3\%, \sigma_A = 6\%$ | Asset B $E(r_B) = 3\%, \sigma_B = 3\%$ | Asset C—Least Risky $E(r_C) = 3\%, \sigma_C = 0$ |
|---|---|---|---|
| Risk-averter | $EU(A) = 2.785$ | $EU(B) = 2.91$ | $EU(B) = 2.955$ |
| Risk-indifferent | $EU(A) = 3$ | $EU(B) = 3$ | $EU(B) = 3$ |
| Risk-lover | $EU(A) = 3.225$ | $EU(B) = 3.09$ | $EU(B) = 3.045$ |

Investments $A$, $B$, and $C$ all have identical expected returns of 3 percent, $E(r) = 3$ percent; only their variability of returns differs. The lower expected utilities assigned to $A$ and $B$ by the risk-averse investor are due to their larger variability of returns, which seems distasteful. And the larger expected utility the risk lover associates with investments $A$ and $B$ reflects this investor's preference for risk. Thus, the two parameters—mean and variance of returns —are both reflected in expected utility. In all cases, expected utility reflects the effects of the investment's $E(r)$ and also its risk. Symbolically, $EU(r)$ $= f[E(r), \sigma]$, where $f_1 > 0, f_2 < 0$.

The mathematical convention

$$f[E(r), \sigma] = E[U(r)]$$

is what economists call an *indifference curve* or *utility isoquant* in $[\sigma, E(r)]$ space. Figures 11.6, 11.7, and 11.8 illustrates three different sets of indifference curves for three different investors. Figure 11.6 is a risk-averter's indifference map in $[\sigma, E(r)]$ space which corresponds to the utility of returns function of Fig. 11.2. That is, the utility isoquants in Fig. 11.6 can be mathematically derived from a utility of returns function like the one in Fig. 11.2. Likewise, Fig. 11.7 is a set of utility isoquants for a risk-indifferent investor. Figure 11.7 can be mathematically derived from a linear utility-of-returns function such as the one in Fig. 11.3. The risk-lover's indifference map shown in Fig. 11.8 follows directly from a risk-lover's utility-of-returns function such as the one in Fig. 11.4. Note, however, that all of these indifference maps are in the two-dimensional space of (1) standard deviation and (2) expected return. The next section explains why expected utility is a function of the first two statistical moments of the probability distribution of returns.

### 11.6  Portfolio Analysis Is Based on Only the First Two Moments

One of the basic assumptions underlying portfolio analysis is that investors can base their decisions on only the first two statistical moments of the probability distribution of returns. Symbolically, $U = f(E(r), \sigma)$. Figure 11.6 is a graph of a utility map for a risk-averter's utility function of the form $U = f(E(r), \sigma)$. Every point on any given indifference curve is equally satisfying to the person represented by the indifference map. Indifference curves are *utility isoquants*. Where the utility isoquants intersect the $E(r)$ axis $\sigma = 0$ and the expected return is known with certainty. Thus, on indifference curve $U_2$ in Fig. 11.6, it can be seen that riskless asset $R$ is the *certainty equivalent* of risky asset $RS$.[3] The assumption that utility is a function of only variability of return and expected return begs several important questions.

First, students of the *expected-utility maxim* often wonder how it can satisfactorily rationalize risky portfolio decisions based on the mean and variance of

---

[3] D. E. Farrar, *The Investment Decision Under Uncertainty* (Englewood Cliffs, N.J.: Prentice-Hall, Inc., 1962), see Sec. 1.4.

returns when it does not even consider the variance of utility—only expected utility. The numerical example given earlier should suffice to explain this confusing point. Portfolios $A$, $B$, and $C$ all had 3 percent $E(r)$, and only their variances of returns differed. The lower expected utilities assigned to $A$ and $B$ by the risk-averse investor are due to their larger variability of returns. The larger expected utility the risk lover associated with portfolio $A$ reflects this investor's preference for risk. Thus, the two parameters—mean and variance of returns—are both reflected in expected utility. Risk is incorporated into utility analysis without resort to the variance of utility. Of course, if the utility function in Fig. 11.2 had been drawn convex to the $r_i$ axis (for a risk lover), the preference ordering for the three portfolios would have been reversed. In either case, expected utility measures the effects of both $E(r)$ and $\sigma$.

A second question typically raised by students of the utility implications of portfolio analysis concerns the third and fourth moments of the probability distribution of returns. For example, imagine two portfolios with identical expected returns and variances but which have different third and fourth moments. In this situation the distribution most skewed to the left will have a larger probability of a large downward variation—perhaps even enough to bankrupt the portfolio. Or, if one of the distributions is platykurtic, the range of possible returns is wider than a normal distribution. In this situation the student may ask if portfolio analysis will find both securities equally desirable. The answer is yes.

Portfolio analysis techniques presented here ignore third and fourth moments. However, these are not flaws in the model for two reasons: (1) Statistical evidence shows that, historically, distributions of returns are approximately symmetrical.[4] Thus, consideration of skewness is not necessary. (2) Unless investors' utility functions are of degree 4, or higher, the fourth moment does not affect utility. Furthermore, there is some question about what the fourth moment actually measures.[5]

The assumption that utility is only a function of the first two moments begs a third question. How does the investor's level of wealth affect his utility of returns? That is, what consideration is given to the investor's wealth if utility is only a function of risk and return? The answer is that the investor's initial wealth affects the curvature of his utility-of-returns function.[6] Later in this chapter it is shown that the utility function for returns does imply certain things about the investor's utility of wealth.

---

[4]E. F. Fama, *Foundations of Finance* (New York: Basic Books, Inc., 1976). Chapters 1 and 2 argue in favor of using the normal distribution.

[5]I. Kaplansky, "A Common Error Concerning Kurtosis," *Journal of the American Statistical Association*, June 1945.

[6]Jan Mossin, "Optimal Multiperiod Portfolio Policies," *Econometrica*, October 1966, pp. 215–218.

## 11.7 Quadratic Utility Functions

A quadratic utility function implies certain things about the investor's utility. Consider the following quadratic utility function:

$$U = a + br - cr^2, \tag{11.2}$$

where $a$, $b$, and $c$ are positive constants.

Finding the expectation of the quadratic utility function yields an insight.

$$
\begin{aligned}
E(U) &= E(a + br - cr^2) \\
&= a + bE(r) - cE(r^2) \\
&= a + bE(r) - c[E(r)]^2 - c(\sigma^2), 
\end{aligned}
\tag{11.3}
$$

since $E(r^2) = [E(r)]^2 + \sigma^2$. Equation (11.3) shows that the expected utility of a quadratic utility function is determined by the first two moments. Symbolically, $E[U(r)] = f[E(r), \sigma]$. In equation (11.3) expected utility varies directly with $E(r)$ and inversely with risk, as shown below for the values to which $b$, $c$, and $r$ are constrained (namely, $r < b/2c$).

$$\frac{\partial E(U)}{\partial E(r)} = b - 2cE(r) > 0$$

$$\frac{\partial E(U)}{\partial \sigma^2} = c > 0.$$

Thus, investors with diminishing quadratic utility of wealth or returns desire both higher $E(r)$ and less risk. Solving equation (11.3) for $\sigma^2$ yields (11.4):

$$
\begin{aligned}
\sigma^2 &= \frac{a - E(U)}{c} + \frac{b}{c}E(r) - E(r)^2 \\
&= (\text{constant}) + \frac{b}{c}E(r) - E(r)^2.
\end{aligned}
\tag{11.4}
$$

Equation (11.4) is quadratic in $[E(r), \sigma]$ space. Varying the constant generates an indifference map in $[E(r), \sigma]$ space. For an investor with diminishing utility (that is, a risk averter), this indifference map must be composed of quadratic functions that are concave to the $E(r)$ axis as shown in Figs. 3.6, 3.7, 3.8 and Fig. 11.6. These figures show graphically that investors with diminishing quadratic utility functions will maximize their expected utility by selecting portfolios with the minimum risk for any given rate of return (that is, efficient portfolios). Thus, portfolio analysis can maximize expected utility for investors with quadratic utility functions. In fact, an investor with a utility of wealth (or returns) function of many forms may maximize expected utility using portfolio analysis if the probability distribution of returns is a two-parameter distribution (for example, a normal distribution) and marginal utility is diminishing but positive.[7]

### A. Problem with Quadratic Utility Functions

The marginal utility of returns of equation (11.2) is the change in utility with respect to a change in return:

$$\text{marginal utility of returns} = \frac{dU}{dr} = b - 2cr. \tag{11.5}$$

The marginal utility of additional returns is positive for $r < b/2c$. At $r = b/2c$, marginal utility is zero—this is where the utility curve in Fig. 11.5 reaches a peak. And for returns above $b/2c$, the investor receives *negative marginal utility*—that is, returns above $b/2c$ are distasteful! To avoid that unlikely portion of the indifference map where returns have negative marginal utility (that is, the dashed portion of Fig. 11.5), the analysis must be restricted to returns below $b/2c$. To assume that a quadratic utility-of-returns function has an upper bound is not so unrealistic. After all, people are not observed paying large prices for a small chance at an infinitely large return.

The preceding mathematical analysis showed how both $E(r)$ and $\sigma$ affect an investor's expected utility. Next, this same analysis will be replicated

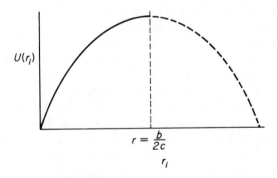

Figure 11.5. Quadratic Utility of Returns Function

---

[7]James Tobin, "Liquidity Preference as Behavior Towards Risk," *Review of Economic Studies*, February 1968, pp. 65–86, especially Sec. 3. Also see M. K. Richter, "Cardinal Utility, Portfolio Selection, and Taxation," *Review of Economic Studies*, June 1960, pp. 152–166, especially 153–154. Briefly, the proof goes as follows:

$$E[u(r)] = \int f(r \mid m_1, m_2) u(r) \, dr$$
$$= E[u(r) \mid m_1 m_2],$$

where $f(r \mid m_1, m_2)$ is a two-parameter probability distribution of rates of return. Clearly, expected utility is a function of $m_1$ and $m_2$ as long as the distribution is completely described by two parameters.

graphically to show how a rational, risk-averse, wealth-seeking investor will select investments that minimize risk at any given level of expected return and thus maximize expected utility in a world of uncertainty.

### B. Selecting Investments in Terms of Quadratic Risk and Return

Given the investor's utility function, we have seen how an individual will be able to select investment assets (either consciously or subconsciously) in terms of the investments' expected return and risk. Figure 11.6 shows graphically how an investor will select between investments by examining only their expected returns and risk. The exhibit is a graph in risk–return space of the six hypothetical securities listed below:

| Name of Security | Expected Return, $E(r)$ (%) | Risk, $\sigma$ (%) |
|---|---|---|
| American Telephone Works (ATW) | 7 | 3 |
| General Auto Corporation (GAC) | 7 | 4 |
| Big Tractor Company (BTC) | 15 | 15 |
| Fairyear Tire & Rubber (FTR) | 3 | 3 |
| Hotstone Tire Corporation (HTC) | 7 | 12 |
| Rears and Sawbuck Co. (RS) | 9 | 13 |
| Riskless Rate (R) | 2 | 0 |

Figure 11.6 also shows a utility map in risk–return space representing the preference of some risk-averse investor like the one whose utility of return function was shown in Fig. 11.2 and equation (11.4). In this indifference map the investor's utility is equal all along each curve. These curves are called *utility isoquants* or *indifference curves*. The graph is called an *indifference map in risk–return space*. Since investments $RS$, $R$, and $FTR$ are all on the same indifference curve (that is, $U_2$), the investor obtains equal expected utility from them, although their expected returns and risk differ considerably.

An infinite number of indifference curves could be drawn for the risk averter depicted in Fig. 11.6, but they would all be similar in shape and would all possess the following characteristics:

1. Higher indifference curves represent more investor satisfaction. Symbolically, $U_5 > U_4 > U_3 > U_2 > U_1$, because the investor likes higher expected return and dislikes higher risk.

2. All indifference curves slope upward. This is because the investor requires higher expected returns as an inducement to assume larger risks. Consider, for example, the investor's indifference between $FTR$, $R$, and $RS$. It is due to the fact that $RS$'s expected return is just enough above the expected return of $FTR$ to compensate the risk-averse investor for assuming the additional risk incurred in going from $FTR$ to $RS$. Riskless investment $R$ has just enough reduction in risk below the risk of $FTR$ to compensate the

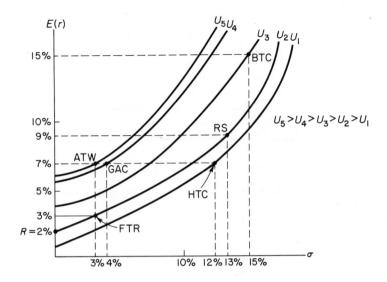

Figure 11.6. Opportunities and Preferences in Risk-Return Space

investor for accepting $R$'s lower rate of return and still be as happy as with *FTR* or *RS*. Investment $R$ is called the *certainty equivalent* of investments *FTR* and *RS* because it involves no risk.

3. The indifference curves grow steeper at higher levels of risk. This reflects the investor's diminishing willingness to assume risk as returns become higher. This is a characteristic that is unique to quadratic utility functions (and its logic is dubious).

Given the investment opportunities and the investor preferences shown in Fig. 11.6, we see that the investor prefers *ATW* over any of the other investments since *ATW* lies on a higher indifference curve than any other investment. In fact, Fig. 11.6 shows that

$$U(ATW) > U(GAC) > U(FTC) > U(R)$$
$$= U(RS) = U(FTR) > U(HTC).$$

### 11.8 Pathological Risk Attitudes

The indifference map graphed in Fig. 11.6 represents rational, normal, risk-averse preferences. Figure 11.6 is implied by a utility-of-returns function like the one in Fig. 11.2. Figures 11.7 and 11.8 represent radically different investment preferences, the preferences of a risk-indifferent investor and of a risk-loving investor, respectively.

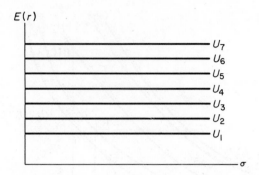

Figure 11.7. Risk-Indifferent Wealth Maximizer's Preferences in Risk–Return Space

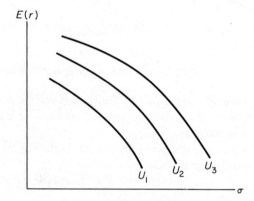

Figure 11.8. Risk Lover's Preferences in Risk–Return Space

Figure 11.7 is simply another way of representing the utility-of-returns function graphed in Fig. 11.3. Figure 11.8 results from a utility function such as the one in Fig. 11.4. These two pathological cases of investment preferences are presented merely as intellectual curiosities. They do not represent rational behavior.

### 11.9 Fractional Power Utility Functions

The preceding analysis of the quadratic utility function should not be construed to imply that quadratic utility is the only function which suggests selecting Markowitz-efficient investments to maximize expected utility. Other forms of utility functions also imply positive but diminishing utility of wealth and have their expected utility maximized by selecting Markowitz-efficient portfolios. The fractional power utility function is one such function.

In order to facilitate analysis of a specific power utility function, assume that the fractional exponent is one-half, as shown in equation (11.6).[8]

$$U = \sqrt{r} = r^{0.5}, \tag{11.6}$$

where $U$ is the number of utiles and $r$ is the rate of return. Figure 11.9 represents equation (11.6) graphically.

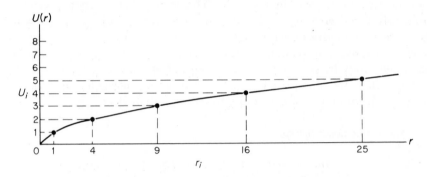

Figure 11.9. Square Root Utility of Returns Function

Unless wealth becomes undesirable at some point, marginal utility should be a positive function of returns. That is, if $r_2 > r_1$, then $U(r_2) > U(r_1)$ for all $r$ if more wealth is always desirable. Mathematically, this means the first derivative of the utility function, which measures marginal utility, should be positive. Specifically,

$$\frac{dU}{dr} = \frac{1}{2}(r)^{-1/2} > 0 \qquad \text{for all } r > 0.$$

Risk aversion requires diminishing marginal utility. Mathematically, whether marginal utility is increasing or decreasing is measured by the

---

[8]The only power utility functions which are sufficiently realistic to be of economic interest have positive fractions as exponents and are of the general form

$$U(w) = w^{1-x} \qquad \text{if } 0 < x < 1.$$

For the square-root function $x = 0.5$. Arguments favoring the square-root utility function may be found: Daniel Bernoulli, "Exposition of a New Theory on the Measurement of Risk," *Econometrica*, January 1954, pp. 23–36. Reprinted in *The Theory of Business Finance*, (New York: Macmillan Publishing Co., Inc., 1967), edited by S. H. Archer and C. A. D'Ambrosio. This classic paper was originally published 200 years ago and since translated and republished. The square-root utility offers insights into solving the Petersburg paradox.

second derivative, it should be negative for the diminishing marginal utility, which causes risk aversion.

$$\frac{d^2U}{dr^2} = \frac{-1}{4(\sqrt{r^3})} = \left(\frac{-1}{4}\right)r^{-3/2} < 0 \qquad \text{for all } r > 0.$$

Clearly, utility function (11.6) is for an investor who prefers more wealth to less wealth but is nevertheless a risk averter, since he experiences diminishing marginal utility (that is, the second derivative is negative). These same conclusions can be seen in Fig. 11.9. The square-root function rises continuously at a decreasing rate; that is, it is concave toward the returns axis. To show that an investor with a square-root (or any other positive fractional power, negative exponential, or logarithmic) utility function maximizes his expected utility by selecting Markowitz-efficient portfolios, it is necessary to assume that the one-period rates of return are normally distributed, $f[E(r), \sigma]$, with mean of $E(r)$ and standard deviation of $\sigma$.

### A. Efficient Portfolios Selected

The expected utility of returns for a square root (or any positive fractional power, negative exponential, or logarithmic) utility function, denoted simply $U(r)$ for generality, is defined in equation (11.7).

$$E[U(r)] = \int_{-\infty}^{\infty} U(r)f(r\,|\,E(r), \sigma)\,dr, \qquad (11.7)$$

where $f[r\,|\,E(r), \sigma]$ represents a normal distribution of returns. The well-known unit-normal variable is defined in equation (11.8).

$$z = \frac{r - E(r)}{\sigma}. \qquad (11.8)$$

Rewriting equation (11.7) in terms of the unit-normal variable produces the equivalent equation, (11.9).

$$E[U(r)] = E[E(r), \sigma] = \int_{-\infty}^{\infty} U[E(r) + \sigma z]f(z\,|\,0, 1)\,dz. \qquad (11.9)$$

The slope of an indifference curve in risk–return space which is defined by equation (11.9) may be determined by differentiating it with respect to $\sigma$, setting the derivative equal to zero, and solving as shown in equation (11.10).

$$0 = \int_{-\infty}^{\infty} U'[E(r) + \sigma z]\left[\frac{dE(r)}{d\sigma} + z\right]f(z\,|\,0, 1)\,dz. \qquad (11.10)$$

Equation (11.10) may be rearranged to obtain equation (11.11) for the slope of a utility isoquant in $[\sigma, E(r)]$ space.

$$\frac{dE(r)}{d\sigma} = -\frac{\int_{-\infty}^{\infty} z U'(r) f(z \mid 0, 1) \, dz}{\int_{-\infty}^{\infty} U'(r) f(z \mid 0, 1) \, dz}. \tag{11.11}$$

The marginal utility of returns, $U'(r)$, in equation (11.11) is assumed to be positive but diminishing—a realistic assumption. It follows from the algebra of the signs that the utility isoquant is positively sloped, $dE(r)/d\sigma > 0$, which in turn implies risk-averting behavior. It is further shown below that the shape of the investor's indifference map in $[\sigma, E(r)]$ space is related to the shape of the utility function.

Suppose that the two points $[E(r), \sigma]$ and $[E(r)', \sigma']$ lie on the same utility isoquant, so that $g[E(r), \sigma] = g[E(r)', \sigma']$. Now consider whether or not the point

$$g(\{[E(r) + E(r)']/2\}, \{(\sigma + \sigma')/2\})$$

is on the same, or a higher, or a lower utility isoquant. In the case of declining marginal utility we know that for every $z$ the following inequality holds[9]:

$$0.5U[E(r) + \sigma z] + 0.5U[E(r)' + \sigma' z]$$
$$< U[\{(E(r) + E(r)')/2\} + \{(\sigma + \sigma')/2\}z]. \tag{11.12}$$

Inequality (11.12) implies that $g(\{[E(r) + E(r)']/2\}, \{[\sigma + \sigma']/2\})$ is greater than $g[E(r), \sigma]$ or $g[E(r)', \sigma']$, and the point $g(\{[E(r) + E(r)']/2\}, \{(\sigma + \sigma')/2\})$, which lies between $g[E(r), \sigma]$ and $g[E(r)', \sigma']$, is on a higher utility isoquant than those points. Thus, it is shown that a risk-averter's utility isoquant in $[\sigma, E(r)]$ space is concave toward the $E(r)$ axis. As a result, the investor will diversify and obtain the maximum expected utility from Markowitz-efficient portfolios. Graphing the utility isoquants in $[\sigma, E(r)]$ space for an investor with a square root (or any fractional power, or negative exponential, or logarithmic) utility function will thus yield something similar to Fig. 11.6.[10]

---

[9]The derivation of equations (11.9) through (11.12) is from James Tobin, "Liquidity Preference as Behavior Towards Risk"; see equation (3.7). This classic article is widely reprinted; for example, in *The Theory of Business Finance*, edited by S. H. Archer and C. A. D'Ambrosio (New York: Macmillan Publishing Co., Inc., 1967).

[10]For an analysis of the power, negative exponential, and logarithmic utility functions' implications for the investment decisions, see M. J. Brennan and A. Kraus, "The Geometry of Separation and Myopia," *Journal of Financial and Quantitative Analysis*, June 1976, pp. 171–193. This article is also relevant to the analysis of multiple-period portfolio problems discussed in Chapter XII.

The paragraphs above were general and probably leave many readers unconvinced. Therefore, the same analysis will be replicated below, specifically in terms of the square-root utility function. Rewriting expected utility equation (11.9) in terms of the square-root function obtains equation (11.9a).

$$E[U(r)] = E[E(r), \sigma] = \int_{-\infty}^{\infty} [E(r) + \sigma z]^{0.5} f(z \,|\, 0, 1)\, dz \quad (11.9a)$$

The partial derivative of $E[U(r)]$ with respect to $\sigma$ from equation (11.9a) is shown in equation (11.10a).

$$0 = \int_{-\infty}^{\infty} 0.5[E(r) + \sigma z]^{-0.5} \left[ \frac{\partial E(r)}{\partial \sigma} + z \right] f(z \,|\, 0, 1)\, dz. \quad (11.10a)$$

Equation (11.10a) is rearranged to obtain (11.11a), which represents the slope of a utility isoquant in $[\sigma, E(r)]$ space.

$$\frac{\partial E(r)}{\partial \sigma} = \frac{-\int_{-\infty}^{\infty} z \cdot 0.5 r^{-0.5} f(z \,|\, 0, 1)\, dz}{\int_{-\infty}^{\infty} 0.5 r^{-0.5} f(z \,|\, 0, 1)\, dz}. \quad (11.11a)$$

The sign of the denominator in differential equation (11.11a) is positive because (1) the marginal utility, $U'(r) = 0.5 r^{-0.5} > 0$, is positive, and (2) the area under the unit normal curve integrates (that is, sums up) to positive unity. Thus, the numerator of equation (11.11a) must determine the sign of $dE(r)/\partial \sigma$. To analyze the numerator's sign it is rewritten in equation (11.13) for integration by parts.

$$-\left[ \int_{-\infty}^{\infty} z \cdot 0.5 r^{-0.5} f(z \,|\, 0, 1)\, dz \right] = \text{numerator of equation (11.11a)}$$

$$= -\left[ \int_{-\infty}^{0} z \cdot 0.5 r^{-0.5} f(z \,|\, 0, 1)\, dz + \int_{0}^{\infty} z \cdot 0.5 r^{-0.5} f(z \,|\, 0, 1)\, dz \right].$$

$$(11.13)$$

For a risk-averse investor with a square-root utility function, the negative values of $z$ in the range from negative infinity up to zero are weighted by the larger marginal utilities which risk averters obtain from small returns. The positive values of $z$ from zero up to positive infinity are multiplied by smaller marginal utilities and thus the quantity in the large square brackets in equation (11.13) is negative. Taking the negative of this negative quantity means that the numerator of equation (11.11a) is positive for a risk averter with a square root (or logarithmic) utility-of-returns function. This proves that the slope of the indifference curves are positive in $[\sigma, E(r)]$ space, $\partial E(r)/\partial \sigma > 0$.

The next subsections compares fractional power functions such as the square-root function to the quadratic utility function to obtain some informative contrasts.

### B. Comparing Power and Quadratic Functions

In comparing the quadratic and power utility functions, several advantages to using the power function become evident. First, the power function exhibits positive marginal utility that remains positive over all ranges. In contrast, the quadratic function's marginal utility becomes negative for large wealth or large returns (as shown graphically in Fig. 11.5)—an unrealistic and perplexing problem that must be dealt with by appending bounds to the function.

Another advantage of the power function relative to the quadratic is that the investor's wealth and returns are separable with the power function, but not with the quadratic. For example, suppose that an investor has the power utility of terminal wealth function shown in equation (11.14).

$$U = w_T^p, \tag{11.14}$$

where $p = \frac{1}{2}$ for the square-root function (or $p$ equals any other positive value) and $w_T$ denotes the end-of-period terminal wealth. Equation (11.14) may be rewritten equivalently as (11.14a) by using equation (11.1).

$$U = w_T^p \tag{11.14}$$
$$= [w_0(1 + r)]^p$$
$$= [(w_0)^p(1 + r)^p]. \tag{11.14a}$$

The first term on the right-hand side of equation (11.14a), $(w_0)^p$, is a positive constant that can be ignored since utility function's preference orderings are invariant under positive monotonic transformations. Thus, the utility analysis can focus on the term involving the returns, $(1 + r)^p$, without being distorted by changes in the investor's wealth (unless $p$ changes with $w$). The quadratic function does not allow separation of the investor's wealth level from his returns. A quadratic wealth function implies a quadratic returns function, but the coefficients of the returns function are dependent upon the level of wealth.

Another realistic and convenient utility function is the logarithmic.

### 11.10  Logarithmic Utility Function

Consider an investor whose utility function (or, if you prefer, happiness function) is logarithmic in wealth, or equivalently, logarithmic in returns. The investor's beginning wealth, $w_0$, is separable from the rate of return, $r$, as shown in equation (11.15a).

$$U(w_T) = \ln (w_T) \tag{11.15}$$

$$= \ln [w_0(1 + r)]$$

$$= \ln (w_0) + [\ln (1 + r)]. \tag{11.15a}$$

Naperian (or natural) logarithms are usually used (instead of common or base 10 logs).[11] Figure 11.10 graphically depicts the log utility function in wealth.

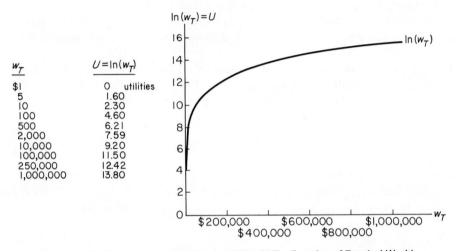

Figure 11.10. The Natural or Naperian Logarithm Utility Function of Terminal Wealth

The log utility functions in wealth and in returns both have continuously positive and continuously diminishing marginal utility. These desirable economic characteristics are evidenced by the unrestricted positive first derivatives shown below.

$$\frac{\partial U}{\partial w_T} = \frac{1}{w_T} > 0 \tag{11.16}$$

$$\frac{\partial U}{\partial r} = \frac{1}{1 + r} > 0. \tag{11.16a}$$

The negative second derivatives represent continuously diminishing marginal utility.

---

[11]Natural logs are preferred for two main reasons: (1) the calculus is simpler, and (2) the natural log of a price relative equals the continuously compounded rate of return, $r_t = \ln (p_t/p_{t-1})$, where ln denotes natural logarithm. The latter point is discussed in detail in Chapter XIV.

$$\frac{\partial^2 U}{\partial w_T^2} = \frac{-1}{w_T^2} < 0 \tag{11.17}$$

$$\frac{\partial^2 U}{\partial r^2} = \frac{-1}{(1 + r^2)} < 0. \tag{11.17a}$$

It can also be shown that if the rates of return are normally distributed, the logarithmic expected utility will be maximized by selecting Markowitz-efficient portfolios. The proof is omitted here because it is identical to the proof for the fractional power function. If $U(r)$ in equation (11.7) denoted a logarithmic utility function instead of a power function, then the analysis is identical. That is, equations (11.9), (11.11), and (11.13) and their implications apply equally to the log and power utility functions.

The logarithmic utility function also possesses several other qualities. However, additional tools must be introduced in the remainder of this chapter and in the next chapter to appreciate deeper dimensions of utility analysis.

### 11.11  Arrow–Pratt Risk-Aversion Measures

Kenneth Arrow and John Pratt[12] suggested measuring an investor's absolute risk aversion, denoted $AR(w)$, and relative risk aversion, denoted $RR(w)$, as shown in equations (11.18) and (11.19), respectively.

$$AR(w) = -\frac{U''(w)}{U'(w)} \tag{11.18}$$

$$RR(w) = -\frac{U''(w)w}{U'(w)}. \tag{11.19}$$

As explained previously, it is known that rational risk-averse people have positive but diminishing marginal utility; this means that $U'(w) > 0$ and $U''(w) < 0$. The negative signs on the right-hand sides of equations (11.18) and (11.19) converts these ratios to positive values. Thus, the larger the values of $AR(w)$ and $RR(w)$, the more risk aversion the utility-of-wealth function represents.

The values of $AR(w)$ and $RR(w)$ for any given utility function change as the level of wealth, $w$, is varied unless the risk aversion is constant. However, the $AR(w)$ and $RR(w)$ measures are both invariant under positive linear transformations of the utility function. The meanings of the risk-aversion measures are interpreted graphically and verbally below.

---

[12]J. E. Pratt, "Risk Aversion in the Small and in the Large," *Econometrica*, January–April, 1964, pp. 122–136; K. Arrow, "Comment on Duesenberry's "The Portfolio Approach to the Demand for Money and Other Assets," *Review of Economics and Statistics*, supplement, February 1963.

## A. Interpreting the Risk-Aversion Measures

Figures 11.11 and 11.12 each represent three different families of indifference maps for three different investor attitudes toward risk. In both figures the family of *dashed* utility isoquants that grow *steeper* represents values of $AR(w)$ and $RR(w)$ that increase with the investor's level of wealth—this is called *increasing* absolute and relative risk aversion, respectively. The sets of *solid* curves which are *parallel* represent *constant* absolute and relative risk aversion in Fig. 11.11 and 11.12, respectively, and represent constant values for $AR(w)$ and $RR(w)$ as $w$ increases. The set of curves formed from *dashes and dots* which are *flatter* in Figs. 11.11 and 11.12 represent absolute and relative risk aversion which *diminishes*, respectively, and is measured by values of $AR(w)$ and $RR(w)$ which are also positive but decrease with the investor's wealth.

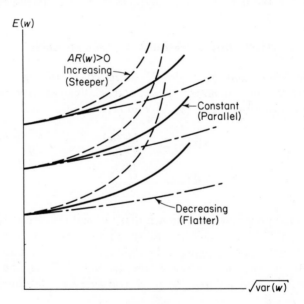

Figure 11.11. Three Families of Indifference Curves for Different Absolute Risk Aversion

A risk-indifferent investor who had linear utility of wealth and returns functions like those in Figs. 11.3 and 11.7 would have zero values for $AR(w)$ and $RR(w)$. The risk lover represented by Figs. 11.4 and 11.8 would have negative values for $AR(w)$ and $RR(w)$.

The $RR(w)$ measure yields to more intuitive interpretations than $AR(w)$. The $RR(w)$ measure is analagous to the elasticity of marginal utility with

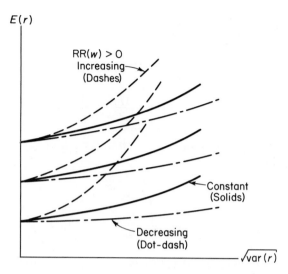

Figure 11.12. Three Families of Indifference Curves for Different Relative Risk Aversion

respect to the investor's wealth. Arrow has interpreted the value of $RR(w)$ as follows:

> Thus, broadly speaking, the relative risk aversion must hover around 1, being, if anything, somewhat less for low wealths and somewhat higher for high wealths. Two conclusions emerge: (1) it is broadly permissible to assume that relative risk aversion increases with wealth, though theory does not exclude some fluctuations; (2) if, for simplicity, we wish to assume a constant relative risk aversion, then the appropriate value is 1. As can easily be seen, this implies that the utility of wealth equals its logarithm, a relation already suggested by Bernoulli. To be sure, the logarithm is not bounded at either end, but it may still be regarded as an approximation to a bounded utility function, for if the relative risk aversion were ever so slightly greater than 1 at the high end of the wealth scale and ever so slightly less at the lower end, the utility function would be bounded at both ends and yet essentially logarithmic throughout the greater part of the range.[13]

### B. Risk Aversion of Different Utility Functions

One of the uses of the Arrow–Pratt measures is in comparing and contrasting risk aversion in different utility functions. The risk aversion of the logarithmic, power, and quadratic functions are compared below.

---

[13]K. Arrow, *Essays in the Theory of Risk-Bearing* (Chicago: Markham Publishing Company, 1971), p. 98.

The logarithmic utility equation (11.15) has decreasing absolute risk aversion, as shown by equality (11.20).

$$\text{AR}(w) = -\frac{U''(w)}{U'(w)} \tag{11.18}$$

$$= -\frac{-1/w^2}{1/w} = \frac{1}{w}. \tag{11.20}$$

The log function has constant relative risk aversion of unity, as shown in equation (11.21).

$$\text{RR}(w) = \frac{-U''(w)w}{U'(w)} \tag{11.19}$$

$$= \frac{-(-1/w^2)w}{1/w} = 1.0. \tag{11.21}$$

Table 11.3 summarizes the risk-aversion measures for the three types of utility functions discussed in this chapter.

TABLE 11.3   Risk-Aversion Measures for Three Different Utility Functions

| Utility Function | Absolute Risk Aversion | Relative Risk Aversion |
|---|---|---|
| Quadratic equation (11.2) | Increasing $\text{AR}(w) = 2c/(b - 2cw)$ | Increasing $\text{RR}(w) = 2cw/(b - 2cw)$ |
| Square-root equation (11.6) | Decreasing $\text{AR}(w) = 0.5/w$ | Constant $\text{RR}(w) = 0.5$ |
| Logarithmic equation (11.15) | Decreasing $\text{AR}(w) = 1/w$ | Constant $\text{RR}(w) = 1.0$ |

The decreasing absolute risk aversion of the square-root and logarithmic utility functions are realistic and logical because rational, risk-averse people may be expected to assume more risk as they grow wealthier. But the increasing absolute risk aversion of the quadratic utility function is perplexing. Increasing absolute risk aversion means that if a rich man and his poor twin brother were both offered the same bet, the rich twin brother would be more afraid of the bet than his poorer brother, although the two men were identical except for their wealth. Such unlikely implications cast doubts of the quadratic utility function's ability to adequately describe reality.

Although economists generally agree that reasonable utility of wealth functions should exhibit (1) positive but diminishing marginal utility, and (2) decreasing absolute risk aversion, there is no concensus about whether realistic relative risk-aversion measures should increase, remain constant, or decrease. The square-root and logarithmic functions' constant risk aversion, however, is highly reasonable because it implies that if a person's wealth and the size of a bet both increase proportionally, that person's willingness to undertake the bet will remain constant. It will be shown in the next chapter that the logarithmic and square-root functions also imply other pleasing and reasonable forms of investment behavior.

### 11.12  Conclusions

A. D. Roy is widely quoted for saying that, "A man who seeks advice about his actions will not be grateful for the suggestion that he maximize his expected utility."[14] While true, such light remarks do not depreciate the rigor or the usefulness of utility analysis. The logic of advising investor's to select Markowitz-efficient portfolios was mathematically proven to be the logical implication of rational, wealth-seeking, risk-averse behavior in this chapter.

Rationally seeking to increase one's wealth in a risk-averse fashion was, early in this chapter, shown to imply positive but diminishing marginal utility of wealth or returns. Utility functions with positive but dimishing marginal utility are those with positive first derivatives and negative second derivatives. Graphically speaking, such functions are positive monotone functions which are concave toward the wealth or returns axis (see Figs. 11.1 or 11.2). Next, the expected utility axiom was used to analyze how investors made choices involving risk that would maximize their happiness (that is, expected utility).

The quadratic, the positive fractional power (in particular, the case when the exponent is $\frac{1}{2}$), and the logarithmic utility functions were examined. All three functions were found to have positive but diminishing marginal utility, to yield indifference maps in risk–return space for selecting between investments such as the one shown in Fig. 11.6, and to have their expected utility maximized by selecting Markowitz-efficient portfolios. Of these three functions the quadratic was shown to be a troublesome function to work with because of some unrealistic implications it possesses (namely, possible negative marginal utility, and increasing absolute risk aversion). But by assuming that the rates of return are normally distributed, it is possible to employ other, more logical utility functions, such as the positive fractional power and the logarithmic, to prove that Markowitz diversification maximizes expected utility [see equations (11.9), (11.11), and (11.13)].[15]

Chapter XII delves into questions that arise in managing a portfolio over a long period of time—more specifically, two or more planning periods. The utility analysis tools developed in this chapter are used to analyze the implications of employing Markowitz's single-period portfolio analysis model in a multiple-period portfolio management contest.[16]

---

[14]A. D. Roy, "Safety First and the Holding of Assets," *Econometrica*, July 1952, p. 433.

[15]The negative exponential utility is of the form $U(w) = -w^{1-x}$ if $x > 1$. It is also an economically logical utility function.

[16]Two references that provide excellent discussions of the relevant single-period utility considerations are: M. Friedman and L. Savage, "The Utility Analysis of Choices Involving Risk," *Journal of Political Economy*, August 1948, pp. 279–304, and Harry M. Markowitz, *Portfolio Selection* (New York: John Wiley & Sons, Inc., 1959), Part IV.

## Selected References

Friedman, M., and L. J. Savage, "The Expected Utility Hypothesis and the Measurability of Utility," *Journal of Political Economy*, December 1952.

This article uses graphs and simple algebra to teach basic utility theory.

Pratt, J. E., "Risk Aversion in the Small and in the Large," *Econometrica*, January–April 1964.

This article uses calculus to analyze some investment implications of various utility functions.

## Questions and Problems

1. What does it mean to say that an investor's preferences are invariant under any positive monotone alteration in the investor's utility function?

2. Show algebraic proof supplemented with graphs that a risk-averse investor will not willingly enter into a fair gamble.

3. How do the first two moments of an investor's probability distribution of returns affect the investor's utility of wealth function?

4. Why does the expected utility theory of decision making ignore the variance of utility when the variance of wealth and the variance of returns are both used to rationalize decision making in uncertainty under this theory?

5. Consider the following two finite probability distributions of returns for risky investments $A$ and $B$:

| Investment A | | Investment B | |
|---|---|---|---|
| Probability | Return | Probability | Return |
| $\frac{1}{2}$ | 4% | $\frac{1}{2}$ | 2% |
| $\frac{1}{2}$ | 8% | $\frac{1}{2}$ | 16% |
| 1.0 | | 1.0 | |

(a) What is the expected utility from investments $A$ and $B$ for an investor who has the logarithmic utility function: $U(r) = [\ln (r)/2.0] - 10$. Will this investor select $A$ or $B$? Explain.

(b) What is the expected utility from investments $A$ and $B$ for the following log utility function?

$$U(r) = \ln (r).$$

Which investment will this second investor select? Are the log functions in (a) and (b) similar? Do they imply similar decisions? Explain.

(c) What is the expected utility from investments $A$ and $B$ for an investor who had the following quadratic utility function?

$$U(r) = 1.0 + 2r - 10r^2.$$

Will the quadratic utility function prefer investment $A$ or $B$? Is there anything irrational about the quadratic utility function? Explain.

6. What utility functions exhibit constant relative risk aversion? To what does "isoelastic utility" refer?

```
12121212121212121212121212121212121212121212121212121212121212121212121212
121212121212121212121212121212121}2121212121212121212121212121212121212121212
1212121212121212121212121212121    12121    121    121    1212121212121212121212
1212121212121212121212121212121212    212    2121    121    1212121212121212121212
121212121212121212121212121212121    1    12121    121    1212121212121212121212
1212121212121212121212121212121212        212121    121    1212121212121212121212
121212121212121212121212121212121212121    1212121    121    1212121212121212121212
1212121212121212121212121212121212        212121    121    1212121212121212121212
1212121212121212121212121212121212121    1    12121    121    1212121212121212121212
1212121212121212121212121212121212    212    2121    121    1212121212121212121212
121212121212121212121212121212121    12121    121    121    1212121212121212121212
12121212121212121212121212121212121212121212121212121212121212121212121212121212
12121212121212121212121212121212121212121212121212121212121212121212121212121212
```

# Multiperiod Portfolio Analysis*

Markowitz portfolio analysis is a single-period model. The risk and return statistics for the assets being considered are estimated for one period, and, then the Markowitz-efficient portfolios which are designed to span that period are delineated. The length of this single period is the portfolio manager's *investment horizon*—it may be as short as a day or as long as a decade. As a practical matter, the length of the investment horizon for most portfolios is probably only a year or two, because it is difficult to forecast risk and return statistics with any accuracy further into the future. In any event, it is doubtful that the length of the most heroically long investment horizon should realistically exceed a decade. Therefore, those portfolios that must be managed for over a decade clearly involve *multiperiod*, as contrasted with single-period, portfolio analysis.

Billions of dollars of portfolio assets are in portfolios with multiperiod lives. Life insurance companies portfolios, money held in lifetime fiduciary trust agreements, endowment funds of universities and charities, pension funds, and other portfolios are often intended to be continually invested for multiple periods. Thus, the question naturally arises: Is Markowitz's single-period portfolio theory relevant to the manager of a multiperiod portfolio? The answer is: yes. It will be shown that revising and selecting a series of single-

---

*Chapter XII presumes a mastery of the topics in Chapter XI.

period Markowitz-efficient portfolios can maximize the portfolio owner's multiperiod welfare (namely, expected utility).

### 12.1 Maximizing Expected Utility of Terminal Wealth

The manager of a multiperiod investment from which *no withdrawls* will be made should maximize the owner's utility from the investment's *terminal wealth*, denoted $w_T$, as shown in equation (12.1).

$$\max U(w_T). \tag{12.1}$$

The terminal wealth results from an initial investment of $w_0$ dollars and $T$ different intermediate states of wealth, denoted $w_t$, which were the stepping stones between $w_0$ and $w_T$. Equation (12.1a) decomposes equation (12.1) to reveal the multiperiod nature of this problem.

$$\max U(w_T) = U\left[w_0\left(\frac{w_1}{w_0}\right)\left(\frac{w_2}{w_1}\right)\cdots\left(\frac{w_{T-1}}{w_{T-2}}\right)\left(\frac{w_T}{w_{T-1}}\right)\right]. \tag{12.1a}$$

The wealth relatives may be rewritten as link relatives, denoted $(1 + r_t)$ $= (w_t/w_{t-1})$, to restate equation (12.1a) equivalently as (12.1b) and distinguish between beginning wealth and the $T$ different one-period portfolio returns.

$$\max U(w_T) = U[(w_0)(1 + r_1)(1 + r_2)\cdots(1 + r_{T-1})(1 + r_T)]. \tag{12.1b}$$

It is assumed that the $T$ different one-period returns are independent and identically distributed random variables—this is the well-known *random walk model*. Since such returns involve risk, the portfolio owner's expected utility should be maximized, as shown in equation (12.1c) by using the $E$ operator.

$$\max E\{U(w_T)\} = E\{U[(w_0)(1 + r_1)(1 + r_2)\cdots(1 + r_{T-1})(1 + r_T)]. \tag{12.1c}$$

Equation (12.c) explicitly depicts the stochastic and the multiperiod aspects of the portfolio management problems being considered in Section 12.1. Consider a dynamic programming formulation of this problem.

### A. Dynamic Programming (DP)

Bellman's fundamental principle of dynamic programming (DP hereafter) may be stated as follows: The optimum path between any two states (such as the wealth states $w_t$ and $w_{t+1}$) is neither a function (namely, the function denoted $F$ in this chapter) of how one gets to the first state (in a forward DP) nor of where one goes after the second state (as in a backward DP).[1] This principle is useful because backward induction is used to formulate and solve the multiperiod portfolio problem as a DP. *Backward induction* involves optimizing the $t$th period's decision based on the presumption that all subsequent periods' decisions will also be optimally determined.

Equation (12.2) shows the portfolio manager's decision variables which link the liquidating value of a portfolio at time period $t$ to its value at period $(t + 1)$.

$$w_{t+1} = \sum_{i=1}^{n} (1 + r_{it})x_{it}w_t, \tag{12.2}$$

where $r_{it}$ = one-period return in period $t$ for the $i$th asset from equation (1.1), for example

$x_{it}$ = proportion of total investable wealth, $w_t$, in the $i$th asset during period $t$; if $x_{it} = 0$, this merely means that the $i$th asset was not included in the portfolio in period $t$; of course, $\sum_{i=1}^{n} x_{it} = 1.0$

$n$ = total number of assets considered as potential investments during period $t$; one of these $n$ assets can be the riskless asset, so that $r_{it} = R_t$ for some asset, if desired.

A recursive relationship suitable for DP can be derived from equation (12.2).

Let $F_t(w_t)$ denote the expected utility of following an optimum portfolio management policy from period $t$ to the horizon $T$, given that $w_t$ dollars were invested at the start of period $t$. For the terminal period, $t = T$, this implies identity (12.3).

$$F_T(w_T) \equiv E[U(w_T)]. \tag{12.3}$$

For the next-to-the-last period, $t = T - 1$, equation (12.3) implies (12.3a).

$$F_{T-1}(w_{T-1}) = \max_{x_{i,(T-1)}} E[F_T(w_T)]. \tag{12.3a}$$

Equation (12.3a) is a DP recursive relationship between period $(T - 1)$ and the terminal period which states that the decision variables, $x_{it}$ for $i = 1, 2, \ldots, n$ assets should be varied at the start of period $(T - 1)$ in such a way

---

[1]For background on dynamic programming, see Richard Bellman, *Dynamic Programming* (Princeton, N.J.: Princeton University Press, 1957). For various financial applications of DP, see E. J. Elton and M. J. Gruber, *Finance as a Dynamic Process* (Englewood Cliffs, N.J.: Prentice-Hall Inc., 1975), especially Chap. V. Some specific portfolio problems are analyzed by Samuelson and Merton: P. A. Samuelson, "Lifetime Portfolio Selection by Dynamic Stochastic Programming," *Review of Economics and Statistics*, August 1969, pp. 239–246, and R. C. Merton, "Lifetime Portfolio Selection Under Uncertainty: The Continuous Time Case," *Review of Economics and Statistics*, August 1969, pp. 247–257. The papers by Merton and Samuelson are companion pieces.

as to derive the portfolio which maximizes the expected utility of terminal wealth. Restating equation (12.2) in terms of the last two periods, as shown in (12.2a), depicts the relevant random variables ($r_{it}$ for $i = 1, 2, \ldots, n$), invested wealth ($w_{T-1}$), and their relationship in maximizing equation (12.3a).

$$w_T = \sum_{i=1}^{n} (1 + r_{it})x_{it}w_{T-1}. \tag{12.2a}$$

After moving from equations (12.2) and (12.3) to equations (12.2a) and (12.3a), the equation (12.4) is a straightforward generalization for any time period $t$. Equation (12.4) is a general recursive relationship that may be analyzed as a DP.

$$F_t(w_t) = \max_{x_{it}} E[f_{t+1}(w_{t+1})], \tag{12.4}$$

where $w_{t+1}$ is defined in equation (12.2).

The term $f_{t+1}(\ )$ in recursive equation (12.4) is derived from $F_T(\ )$ in equation (12.3). The function $f_{t+1}(\ )$ is derived from $F_t(\ )$ through the intermediation of $F_{t+2}(\ ), F_{t+3}(\ ), \ldots, F_{T-1}(\ )$ and assumes sequential optimization of all the intermediate functions. The form of the derived utility function need not be identical to the form of the utility of terminal wealth function. But the optimal behavior of maximizing the utility of one-period wealth is identical with both functions, $F_T(\ )$ and $f_t(\ )$.

Although the derived utility function $f_t(\ )$ may differ in form from other derived utility functions, $f_{t+1}(\ )$, for example, for the same investor's portfolio, and these may differ from the terminal wealth utility function, $F_T(\ )$, it is still possible to make statements about the forms of these various utility functions. Consider a utility of terminal wealth function which has positive but diminishing marginal utility (for example, the logarithmic or square-root functions), because these were shown in Chapter XI to imply rational investing in Markowitz-efficient portfolios. In this case, the derived utility function would *also* have positive but diminishing marginal utility. The derived utility function would have *positive* marginal utility because income from intermediate investment periods contributes to terminal wealth and is thus desirable, too. The marginal utility of the derived functions would be *diminishing* because the expected utility of terminal wealth function is merely the sum of the derived functions, and utility orderings are invariant under a linear-transformation-like addition. To complete the outlines of this proof, it only remains to be shown that if $F_T(w_T)$ is concave, then $f_t(w_t)$ is also concave. This proof is simple and its outline is as follows. When the multi-period case is reduced to the single-period investment shown in equation (12.3a), then both $F_{T+1}(w_{T+1})$ and $F_T(w_T)$ must be concave. This concavity is generalized to the $t$th period case to complete the proof. The concept is just that simple—however, the mathematical notation can be quite cumbersome.

The DP formulation of the multiperiod portfolio problem has produced an important insight: it is possible to derive a single-period utility function such that *maximization of single-period expected utility is consistent with maximizing the expected utility of terminal wealth.* Furthermore, if the utility of terminal wealth function is concave, then so are the derived utility functions. These findings show similarity between the single-period portfolio problem and the multiperiod problem. However, the DP must be solved at every level of wealth to delineate the portfolio that maximizes each single-period derived utility function. This computationally cumbersome procedure can be simplified by using certain isoelastic utility functions that were discussed in Chapter XI.

### B. Isoelastic Utility Functions

The Arrow–Pratt relative risk-aversion measure may be interpreted as a measure of the elasticity of utility with respect to wealth. Therefore, those classes of utility functions that have constant relative risk aversion may be called *isoelastic* utility functions. Isoelastic utility functions allow wealth and returns to be separated so that the investor's utility can be maximized by analyzing investment returns without reference to the investor's level of wealth—that is, the optimum portfolio is invariant to changes in the investor's wealth. This *separability property* greatly simplifies the analysis of investors' utility in a multiperiod context where the investor likely begins every period with a different amount of investable wealth. Investors with isoelastic utility functions can maximize the same utility of returns function in every period regardless of how their wealth varies—this myopic behavior is both simple and optimal.

Among those classes of utility of wealth function that possess positive but diminishing marginal utility, Mossin has shown that three classes of utility functions are isoelastic.[2]

1. $U(w) = \ln(w)$—logarithmic.
2. $U(w) = w^{1-p}$ for $0 < p < 1$—postive fractional power.
3. $U(w) = -w^{1-p}$ for $p > 1$—negative exponential.

The logarithmic and a positive fractional power (namely, the square root) single-period utility functions were analyzed in Chapter XI. They were shown to have constant relative risk aversion (see Table 11.3). Wealth and returns were shown to be separable for the logarithmic and positive fractional power utility functions. These conditions allow use of the Markowitz single-period portfolio model in multiperiod applications.

---

[2]Jan Mossin, "Optimal Multi-period Portfolio Policies," *Journal of Business*, April 1968, pp. 215–229.

### C. Myopic Markowitz Analysis Is Optimal

An investor who disregards past and future periods in making investment decisions for the current period is said to behave *myopically*. Since Markowitz portfolio analysis is a single-period analysis, it may thus be described as a mode of myopic economic behavior. Happily, however, simply delineating and selecting a Markowitz-efficient portfolio is optimal behavior, which may be called myopic, but will nevertheless maximize multiperiod expected utility under certain realistic conditions. These necessary conditions are listed below.

1. The investor has positive but diminishing utility of terminal wealth, $U'(w_T) > 0$, $U''(w_T) < 0$.
2. The investor's utility is some form (namely, any positive linear transformation) of one of the classes of isoelastic utility functions.
3. The single-period rates of return are distributed according to the two-parameter normal distribution.

These three conditions simplify the mathematics sufficiently to prove that Markowitz analysis can maximize expected utility in the multiperiod case as well as the single-period case. The implications of each of the three conditions and how they relate is summarized below.

In Chapter XI the logarithmic and the positive fractional power (in particular, the square root) single-period utility functions were shown to represent investors with positive but diminishing marginal utility—see the discussion below square-root equation (11.6) and equations (11.14) and (11.15) for the other functions. These two functions were also shown to have constant relative risk aversion and thus be isoelastic—see Table 11.3. The resulting separability of wealth and returns was shown explicitly in equations (11.14a) and (11.15a) for the positive fractional power and log functions, respectively. As a result of this separability, an investor's single-period utility of returns function does not change with the amount of wealth invested each period. More specifically, the derived single-period utility functions, $f_t(w_t)$, are identical to the utility of terminal wealth function, $F_T(w_T)$, in the DP formulation when the utility functions are isoelastic. It follows that if an investor's utility of terminal wealth were a logarithmic or any other positive but diminishing marginal utility, the single-period utility would be the same. Finally, assuming that the single-period returns are normally distributed allows them to be analyzed in terms of their mean and variance. Equations (11.7) through (11.11) showed proof that Markowitz-efficient portfolios maximized the expected utility from the logarithmic and positive fractional power functions if returns were normally distributed. These preceding facts all considered in unison imply directly that myopically selecting efficient portfolios leads to optimal multiperiod expected utility; it can also maximize the terminal value of wealth invested over the long run of multiple periods.

### D. Terminal Dollar Value Maximized

Markowitz has shown that selecting portfolios that maximize the expected utility of single-period returns is a portfolio management procedure which (in addition to maximizing the multiperiod expected utility) will also maximize the terminal liquidating value of the portfolio.[3] To see this, equation (12.1c) is rewritten as equations (12.1d) and (12.1e) with *log utility*.

$$\max E\{U(w_T)\} = E\{\ln\left[(w_0)(1+r_1)(1+r_2)\cdots(1+r_{T-1})(1+r_T)\right]\} \quad (12.1\text{d})$$
$$= \ln(w_0) + E\{\ln(1+r_1)\} + E\{\ln(1+r_2)\} + \cdots$$
$$+ E\{\ln(1+r_{T-1})\} + E\{\ln(1+r_T)\}. \quad (12.1\text{e})$$

Perusal of the last $(T-1)$ terms inside the square brackets on the right-hand side of equation (12.1d) reveals that this quantity is the geometric mean (or compound) rate of return, denoted $g$, as shown in equation (12.5).

$$(1+r_1)(1+r_2)\cdots(1+r_{T-1})(1+r_T) = (1+g)^T = \frac{w_T}{w_0}. \quad (12.5)$$

Equation (12.5) shows that maximizing the product of the $T$ different one-period link relative in equation (12.1d) is equivalent to both maximizing (1) the geometric mean rate of return, $(1+g)$, and (2) the terminal wealth, $w_T$ (since initial wealth, $w_0$, is a fixed constant). Equation (12.1e) goes on to show that the single-period expected utilities, $E[\ln(1+r_t)]$ for $t = 1, 2, \ldots, T$, must also be maximized independently to maximize equation (12.5).[4]

---

[3]Harry M. Markowitz, *Portfolio Selection* (New York: John Wiley & Sons, Inc., 1959), Chap. 6, and also, Markowitz, "Investment for the Long Run: New Evidence for an Old Rule," *Journal of Finance*, December 1976. Markowitz argues against the Mossin and Samuelson papers: Jan Mossin, "Optimal Multi-period Portfolio Policies," and P. A. Samuelson, "Lifetime Portfolio Selection by Dynamic Stochastic Programming." Essentially, Markowitz argues against the assumptions by the Mossin and Samuelson papers that (1) the utility of wealth is *unbounded*, and (2) the utility of wealth is constant.

[4]The investment objective of maximizing terminal wealth is a venerable topic supported by several writers. H. A. Latane, "Criteria for Choice Among Risky Ventures," *Journal of Political Economy*, April 1959; J. L. Kelly, Jr., "A New Interpretation of Information Rate," *Bell System Technical Journal*, pp. 917–956; L. Breiman, "Investment Policies for Expanding Businesses Optimal in a Long-Run Sense," *Naval Research Logistics Quarterly*, 1960, pp. 647–651; H. Latane, D. L. Tuttle, and C. P. Jones, *Security Analysis and Portfolio Management*, 2nd ed. (New York: The Ronald Press Co. 1975); E. J. Elton and M. J. Gruber, "On the Maximization of the Geometric Mean with Lognormal Returns Distribution," *Management Science*, December 1974; E. J. Elton and M. J. Gruber, "Portfolio Theory When Investment Relatives Are Lognormally Distributed," *Journal of Finance*, June 1974.

An additional point that may be observed in equations (12.1d) and (12.5) involves how much risk to assume in managing the one-period returns that ultimately determine terminal wealth. Suppose that a very greedy investor short-sightedly invests all his wealth in an "all-or-nothing" risky asset in the $t$th period. Further suppose that the worst possible outcome occurs and this hypothetical investor's speculative asset becomes completely worthless; that is, $1 + r_t = 0$ because $r_t = -100$ percent $= -1.0$. This could easily happen if the greedy investor was too hasty to take the time to diversify.

As a result of any one link relative becoming equal to zero, the investor loses *all* the wealth he had accumulated up to period $t$; that is, he goes bankrupt and his utility, namely, equation (12.1d), becomes as low as it can possible be. This shows that some risk aversion (that is, the fear of bankruptcy) is essential to maximize expected utility of terminal wealth over multiperiod reinvesting. Merely buying high-risk assets or "taking long shots" at the race track will not automatically yield riches. Quite to the contrary, the assumption of high risks period after period means that $r_t = -100$ percent $= -1.0$ may occur in one period and cause the geometric mean return and terminal wealth to become zero.

### 12.2 Maximize Utility of Multiperiod Consumption

The preceding analysis in this chapter focused on managing a multiperiod portfolio from which no withdrawls were made until the terminal period—this case is a comfortable situation that is beyond the means of many investors. Most individuals and businesses view their investment portfolio as an emergency reserve of funds that may be increased only by deposits during "good periods": that is, investment and consumption are competing uses for funds. During "bad periods" part of the investment capital may be consumed. Adopting such a consumption and investment formulation of the portfolio management problem allows the economic analyst to focus on maximizing the utility of multiperiod *consumption*, as represented by equation (12.6).

$$\max U(c_1, c_2, \ldots, c_{T-1}, c_T \mid \phi_T). \tag{12.6}$$

The symbol $c_t$ represents consumption (measured in dollars) in period $t$; $T$ is the terminal single period, so that, for example, $c_T$ may represent a bequest to heirs at death or the last payment into a retirement fund; and $\phi_T$ represents the set of information available up to the $T$th period. The available historical information, denoted $\phi_1, \phi_2, \ldots, \phi_{T-2}$ and $\phi_{T-1}$, is included in $\phi_T$ along with the most recent information about time period $T$.[5]

---

[5]Section 12.2 draws on an article by E. F. Fama, "Multi-period Consumption–Investment Decisions," *American Economic Review*, Vol. 60, March 1970, pp. 163–174. Fama's analysis is more extensive and interested readers should consult it for additional detail.

Transactions costs and other sources of income are ignored here to simplify the analysis. For the $t$th period, the investor invests a total amount of after-consumption wealth of $(w_t - c_t)$ dollars and earns a weighted average rate of return of $\sum_{i=1}^{n} x_{it} r_{it}$ on it from an $n$-asset portfolio. This consumption investment decision for period $t$ provides a portfolio worth of $w_{t+1}$, which may all be consumed, or all reinvested, or part consumed and part reinvested in period $(t + 1)$. This single-period investment consumption relationship is summarized in equation (12.7).

$$w_{t+1} = \sum_{i=1}^{n} x_{it}(1 + r_{it} | \phi_t)(w_t - c_t), \qquad (12.7)$$

where $\sum_{i=1}^{n} x_{it} = 1.0$, the usual balance sheet identity, is observed. The one-period rates of return, denoted $r_{it}$ for $i = 1, 2, \ldots, n$ different assets, represent $n$ independent and identically distributed random variables, which are defined by the information set given at period $t$, denoted $\phi_t$. Such returns conform to the random walk investment model. Equation (12.7) explicitly depicts the single-period portfolio decision of selecting proportions ($x_{it}$ for $i = 1, 2, \ldots, n$ assets) for a total investable wealth of $(w_t - c_t)$ dollars that will yield $w_{T+1}$ dollars for the next period. This equation facilitates representation of the multiperiod nature of the portfolio problem as a dynamic program (DP).

## A. Dynamic Programming (DP)

If an investor's situation is represented by $(c_1, c_2, \ldots, c_{T-1}, w_T | \phi_T)$ in period $T$, the multiperiod utility of consumption from this is $F_T(c_1, c_2, \ldots, c_{T-1}, w_T | \phi_T)$. Using this convention allows the terminal period recursive relationship to be written as shown in equation (12.8).

$$
\begin{aligned}
F_{T-1}&(c_1, c_2, \ldots, c_{T-2}, w_{T-1} | \phi_{T-1}) \\
&= \max_{x_i, T-1, c_{T-1}} E[F_T(c_1, c_2, \ldots, c_{T-1}, w_T | \phi_T). \qquad (12.8)
\end{aligned}
$$

The expected utility in equation (12.8) is maximized over the probability distribution of all the possible outcomes implied by $\phi_T$ by varying the investment proportions, $x_{i,T-1}$ for $i = 1, 2, \ldots, n$ assets, and consumption, $c_{T-1}$.

Equation (12.8) may be generalized for all periods and rewritten as equation (12.9) to obtain the recursive relalationship for any $t$th period.

$$
\begin{aligned}
F_t&(c_1, c_2, \ldots, c_{t-1}, w_t | \phi_t) \\
&= \max_{x_{it}, c_t} E[F_{t+1}(c_1, c_2, \ldots, c_t, w_{t+1} | \phi_{t+1})], \qquad (12.9)
\end{aligned}
$$

where $w_{t+1}$ is defined in equation (12.7). Equation (12.9) is solved iteratively at each period by selecting the optimum investment portfolio (that is, the investment weights) for whatever funds are left after the investor's consumption decision is made. The solution gives consideration to the given constants of past consumption, all historical information, and the available wealth of $w_t$. Then, over all possible states of nature in every period, the DP evaluates every combination of consumption–investment decisions to find the one that maximizes the expected multiperiod utility of consumption. Unfortunately, this may be a computationally infeasible problem. Suppose, for example, that there are $P$ periods remaining until the terminal period. If there are $C$ different consumption possibilities and $S$ different states of nature defined by the relevant information set, $\phi$, then $C^P S^P$ portfolio problems must be solved for period $(T-1)$, $C^{p-1}S^{p-1}$ problems for period $(T-2)$, and so on. It is clear that for realistic values of $C$, $S$ and $P$, the solution becomes overwhelming. Luckily, however, this DP problem can be simplified to a manageable single-period problem.

At the start of the $t$th period, the past consumption decisions have all been made so that $c_1, c_2, \ldots$ and $c_{t-1}$ are all known quantities in the information set $\phi_t$. This means that all the variables on the right-hand side of equation (12.9) are known quantities except $c_t$ and $w_{t+1}$. This allows equation (12.9) to be rewritten more simply, but equivalently, as equation (12.10).

$$F_t(c_1, c_2, \ldots, c_{t-1}, w_t \,|\, \phi_t)$$

$$= \max_{x_{it}, c_t} E[F_{t+1}(c_1, c_2, \ldots, c_t, w_{t+1} \,|\, \phi_{t+1}) \qquad (12.9)$$

$$= \max_{x_{it}, c_t} E[f_{t+1}(c_t, w_{t+1} \,|\, \phi_{t+1}), \qquad (12.10)$$

where $\phi_t$ contains $c_1, c_2, \ldots, c_{t-1}$ as given constants, and $f_{t+1}(\ )$ is constant and unchanging from period to period if the first three of the following six conditions prevail.[6]

1. The consumer's tastes are independent of the state of the world represented by $\phi$.

2. The investor–consumer acts as if the consumption opportunities and their prices are known in advance (that is, at the beginning of any previous period).

3. The distribution of one-period rates of return conforms to an independent and identically distributed normal distribution (that is, a random walk market is presumed).

4. The utility of consumption in one period is independent and separable from the utility of consumption in other periods.

---

[6] E. F. Fama, "Multi-period Consumption Investment Decisions."

5. The utility function, $F_t$, has positive but diminishing marginal utility, which, in turn, implies the same about $f_{t+1}$.

6. The utility function, $F_t(\ )$, is isoelastic (that is, logarithmic, positive fractional power, or negative exponential), so the single-period utility function, $f_t(\ )$, is a function of the one-period rates of return which is independent from the investor's wealth level.

The assumption that returns are normally distributed in condition 3, combined with the three further conditions 4, 5, and 6, imply that the investor's expected utility can be maximized by selecting Markowitz-efficient portfolios (as explained in Section 12.1C). Combined with the stability condition for the derived single-period utility functions implied by conditions 1, 2, and 3, the six conditions together imply that myopic period-by-period selection of Markowitz-efficient portfolios is optimal behavior that will maximize the expected utility from multiperiod consumption.

This analysis of maximizing the utility from multiperiod consumption reaches conclusions similar to the preceding analysis (in Section 12.1) of maximizing the utility of terminal wealth in spite of the greater generality of this consumption–investment analysis. But the analysis of consumption–investment behavior required additional simplifying assumptions (namely, conditions 1, 2, and 3) about the period-by-period independence and stability of the derived single-period utility functions. Furthermore, the consumption–investment analysis leaves some important questions un-answered. First, the analysis gives no clue as to how the investor–consumer will divide each period's wealth between consumption and reinvestment unless future period's information is assumed known in advance. Second, the assumption that each period's utility of consumption is independent and separable from other period's utility of consumption (that is, condition 4) may be an oversimplification.[7] After all, the utility from a home or an auto in any one period is inextricably intertwined with the expenditure to

---

[7]The separability of different period's utility of consumption has been employed either implicitly or explicitly by different analysts working on the multiperiod portfolio problem. Nils Hakansson, "Optimal Investment and Consumption Under Risk, An Uncertain Lifetime and Insurance," *International Economic Review*, Vol. 10, No. 3, 1969, pp. 443–466; "Risk Disposition and the Separation Property in Portfolio Selection," *Journal of Financial and Quantitative Analysis*, Vol. 4, No. 4, Dec. 1969, pp. 401–416; "An Induced Theory of the Firm Under Risk: The Pure Mutual Fund," *Journal of Financial and Quantitative Analysis*, Vol. 3, No. 2, 1970, pp. 155–178; "Optimal Investment and Consumption Strategies Under Risk for a Class of Utility Functions," *Econometrica*, Vol. 38, September 1970, pp. 587–607. Robert Merton, "Lifetime Portfolio Selection Under Uncertainty: The Continuous Time Case," *Review of Economics and Statistics*, Vol. 50, August 1969, pp. 247–257; "Optimal Consumption and Portfolio Rules in a Continuous Time Model," *Journal of Economic Theory*, Vol. 3, No. 4, 1971, pp. 373–413. Edmund Phelps, "The Accumulation of Risky Capital: A Sequential Utility Analysis," *Econometrica*, Vol. 30, October 1962, pp. 729–743. P. A. Samuelson, "Lifetime Portfolio Selection by Dynamic Stochastic Programming."

purchase the home or auto in an earlier period, as well as later expenditures for heating the home and fueling the auto and periodic maintenance outlays. These problems do not render the analysis of consumption–investment decisions void of intuitively appealing logic, however. The simple numerical example in the next subsection shows a simplified but realistic application of this analysis.

### B.  DP Numerical Example

Consider a consumer–investor facing a three-period consumption–investment problem. Assume that this economic unit has a square-root single-period utility of consumption function which is separable in each period and additive, as shown in equation (12.11).

$$U(c_1, c_2, c_3) = \sum_{t=1}^{3} U(c_t) \tag{12.11}$$

$$= \sqrt{c_1} + \sqrt{c_2} + \sqrt{c_3}. \tag{12.11a}$$

This is a very simple example of the type of problem analyzed in the preceding subsection and in the literature.

It is assumed that the economic unit leaves all wealth at the end of the terminal period to heirs and derives the same utility from this bequest as from consuming it personally. This bequest attitude is summarized in equation (12.12).

$$\sqrt{w_3} = \sqrt{c_3} = F_3(w_3). \tag{12.12}$$

The investor starts the $t$th period with $w_{t-1}$ dollars, consumes $c_t$ of it, and invests the other $w_{t-1} = z_t + c_t$ dollars to earn a one-period rate of return of either zero or 100 percent in the $t$th period. The suggested probability distribution of investment returns is shown in Table 12.1.

TABLE 12.1   Probability Distribution Investment Relatives for One Period

| Outcome | Probability | One-Period Return, $r_t$ | $1 + r_t = w_t/z_t$ |
|---|---|---|---|
| 1 | $P(1) = \frac{1}{2}$ | Zero | $1.0 = 100\%$ |
| 2 | $P(2) = \frac{1}{2}$ | 100% | $2.0 = 200\%$ |

Equation (12.13) summarizes the outcome of the investment in period $t$.

$$w_{t+1} = z_t(1 + r_t). \tag{12.13}$$

The following budget equation forces the $t$th period's beginning wealth to be either invested or consumed.

$$w_t = z_t + c_t. \tag{12.14}$$

Solving equation (12.14) for $z_t$ and substituting it into (12.13) yields (12.13a).

$$w_{t+1} = z_t(1 + r_t) = (w_t - c_t)(1 + r_t). \qquad (12.13a)$$

The only income the consumer has is assumed to come from his investments. The consumer–investor's multiperiod expected utility can be maximized by myopically maximizing the utility of consumption. Recursive equation (12.15) represents the DP formulation of the optimal strategy for period $t$.

$$F_t(w_t) = \max \left[ \sqrt{c_t} + E[F_{t+1}(w_{t+1})] \right] \qquad \text{for } t = 1, 2, \qquad (12.15)$$

where $F_t(w_t)$ is the utility from following an optimum consumption pattern from period $(t + 1)$ to the terminal period and $w_{t+1}$ is defined in equation (12.13a).

Assuming that the economic unit begins this multiperiod consumption investment example with $(w_0 = z_1 =)$ \$2 suggests the outcomes enumerated in Table 12.2. Equations (12.13a), (12.14), and (12.15) are used to solve this investor's portfolio management problem. The maximum consumption opportunity occurs in period 3 if the original \$2 is reinvested and doubles twice to yield $\sqrt{w_3} = \sqrt{c_3} = F_2(w_3) = \sqrt{\$8}$ utiles. In contrast, if the investor consumes all his wealth before period 3, then $\sqrt{w_3} = \sqrt{c_3} = \sqrt{0}$ utiles.

For periods 1 and 2, equations (12.13a) and (12.15) are used to determine the values and select the best strategy. For example, in period 1 the initial wealth of $z_0 = w_0 = \$2$ can all be consumed, $c_1 = \$2$, all be invested, $z_1 = \$2$, or half consumed, and half invested, $z_1 = c_1 = \$1$.

To obtain a more intuitive understanding of the backward induction nature of DP problem solving, the solution is illustrated below. To keep things simple, the problem limits the dollar outcomes to only integer amounts. At the beginning of the problem (that is, at $t = 0$), the problem is to decide how much to consume and how much to invest next period (that is, in period $t = 1$). Before the period one problem can be solved, however, the optimal solution for period 2 (that is, $t = 2$) must be delineated in order to use backward induction. Starting with \$2 at a time $t = 0$, there are four possible wealth levels available to begin period $t = 2$; they are $w_2$ equal to zero, one, two, or four dollars. The zero-dollar outcome (that is, $w_2 = 0$) is obviously not an optimum outcome, so only the other three values of $w_2$ (namely $w_2 = \$1$, \$2, or \$4) need be considered. Table 12.2 enumerates all the relevant outcomes for the backward optimization from period $t = 2$ for a period $t = 1$ decision.

Table 12.2 shows that first the time $t = 2$ optimal decisions for $w_2 = \$1$, \$2, and \$4 are determined. Then, the best of these three (namely, consume \$2 and invest \$2) is presumed to be what will happen in the future. Then and only then the decision currently needed for period $t = 1$ to enable the $t = 2$ decision of $z_2 = \$2$ and $c_2 = \$2$ can be determined. That is, only after the $t = 2$ optimal decision is derived can the analysis work backward to the optimal $t = 1$ decision of consuming \$1 and investing \$1 to obtain on expected multiperiod utility of 2.71 utils.

TABLE 12.2   Backward Optimization DP Enumeration for Period $t$ = 1 Decision

| Period 2 decisions: | | | | |
|---|---|---|---|---|
| | $c_2$ | $z_2$ | $\tilde{w}_3$ | $E[U(c_2, \tilde{w}_3)]$ |
| If $w_2 = 4$ | 0 | 4 | 8 / 4 | 2.41 |
| | 1 | 3 | 6 / 3 | 3.09 |
| | 2 | 2 | 4 / 2 | 3.12 (optimum) |
| | 3 | 1 | 2 / 1 | 2.94 |
| | 4 | 0 | 0 | 2.00 |
| If $w_2 = 2$ | 0 | 2 | 4 / 2 | 1.71 |
| | 1 | 1 | 2 / 1 | 2.21 (optimum) |
| | 2 | 0 | 0 | 1.41 |
| If $w_2 = 1$ | 0 | 1 | 2 / 1 | 1.21 (optimum) |
| | 1 | 0 ——— 0 | | 1.00 |
| Period 1 decisions (assuming optimality in period 2): | | | | |
| | $c_1$ | $z_1$ | $\tilde{w}_2$ | $E[U(c_1, \tilde{c}_2, \tilde{w}_3)]$ |
| $w_1 = 2$ | 0 | 2 | 4 / 1 | 2.67 |
| | 1 | 1 | 2 / 1 | 2.71 (optimum) |
| | 2 | 0 ——— 0 | | 1.41 |

Table 12.3 is also provided to enumerate all possible values without regard to the backward nature of the relevant DP solution.

TABLE 12.3 Three-Period DP Example Enumerated

| $t = 0$ | | $t = 1$ | | | | | $t = 2$ | | | $t = 3$ |
|---|---|---|---|---|---|---|---|---|---|---|
| $w_0 = z_0$ | $c_1$ | $z_1 = w_0 - c_1$ | $w_1$ | $F_1(w_1)$ | $c_2$ | $z_2 = w_1 - c_2$ | $w_2$ | $F_2(w_2)$ | | $F_3(w_3)$ |
| | | | | | 1 | 0 | 0 | $1 + 0 = 1$ | | $\sqrt{1} = 1.0$ |
| | | | | | 0 | 1 | 1,2 | $0 + \tfrac{1}{2}(1 + 1.41)$ $= 1.20*$ | | |
| 2 | 2 | 0 | 0 | $1.41 + 0 = 1.41$ | 2 | 0 | 0 | $1.41 + 0 = 1.41$ | | $\sqrt{2} = 1.41$ |
| | 1 | 1 | 1,2 | $1 + \tfrac{1}{2}(1.20 + 2.20)$ $= 2.70$ | 1 | 1 | 1,2 | $1 + \tfrac{1}{2}(1 + 1.41)$ $= 2.20*$ | | |
| | 0 | 2 | 2,4 | $0 + \tfrac{1}{2}(2.20 + 3.2)$ $= 2.66$ | 0 | 2 | 2,4 | $0 + \tfrac{1}{2}(1.41 + 2)$ $= 1.70$ | | |
| | | | | | 4 | 0 | 0 | $2 + 0 = 2$ | | $\sqrt{4} = 2.00$ |
| | | | | | 3 | 1 | 1,2 | $1.73 + \tfrac{1}{2}(1 + 1.41)$ $= 2.93$ | | |
| | | | | | 2 | 2 | 2,4 | $1.41 + \tfrac{1}{2}(1.41 + 2)$ $= 3.12*$ | | |
| | | | | | 1 | 3 | 3,6 | $1 + \tfrac{1}{2}(1.73 + 2.45)$ $= 3.09$ | | |
| | | | | | 0 | 4 | 4,8 | $0 + \tfrac{1}{2}(2 + 2.83)$ $= 2.42$ | | |
| | | | | | | | | | | $\sqrt{3} = 1.73$ |
| | | | | | | | | | | $\sqrt{6} = 2.45$ |
| | | | | | | | | | | $\sqrt{8} = 2.83$ |

*Indicates optimal strategy for period given $z_t$ wealth.

The preceding example was trival for the sake of expedition—it never considered which assets might enter the optimum portfolios or other important matters. Hopefully, however, the example was clarifying and, also, focused attention on the period-by-period problems of the investment changes caused by $z_t \neq z_{t+1}$. Dealing with such portfolio changes includes several related problems, all grouped under the heading "portfolio revision." These problems are examined in the next section. Practical questions will be considered: Why is portfolio revision needed? How often should it be done? What does it cost?

## 12.3 Portfolio Revision

After an optimal portfolio is selected and the funds are invested, the need for portfolio revision arises almost immediately. The investment proportions that define an optimum portfolio, $x_{it}$ for $i = 1, 2, \ldots, n$ assets, become suboptimal even if the investor's investment needs and wishes are identical every period because (1) cash dividends and interest income increase the cash holding, (2) some assets' actual weights decline from the optimal value because of capital losses, (3) some assets experience capital gains which inflate their weight in the portfolio above the optimal amount, (4) the risk classes of some assets change, (5) some expected returns change, and so on. Most of these changes cause the set of investment opportunities (for example, the efficient frontier) to shift minute by minute. Thus, an optimal portfolio needs revising almost as soon as it is purchased. This revision is necessary even if the portfolio owner's utility function is isoelastic (so that it does not change with the owner's wealth) and the owner experiences no change in preferences (so that the indifference map in risk–return space is stable). This situation is represented graphically in Fig. 12.1.

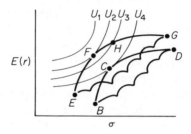

Figure 12.1. Known Utility Map and Changing Investment Opportunities

## A. The Problems and Costs of Portfolio Revision

In Fig. 12.1 an initial portfolio at $C$ was selected from the opportunity set bounded by $BCD$ based on the utility map in risk–return space. Then a better opportunity set, denoted $EFHG$, became available. Using the unchanged utility map, the portfolio manager could maximize the portfolio owner's expected utility by revising portfolio $C$ to become portfolio $F$. Such changes can be made if and only if the owner's utility map is explicitly known. This approach can be suggested as a practical policy only if the *individual* who owns the portfolio can consistently articulate sufficiently detailed investment objectives to allow the indifference map to be constructed. If the portfolio is owned by a group of people (for example, a mutual fund) or managed by a committee, it will be nearly impossible to delineate the preferences of the relevant group—that is, community or social welfare functions cannot be derived.[8]

---

[8]For a discussion of the problems associated with the construction of group preference orderings, the interested reader is directed to Henderson and Quandt's *Microeconomic Theory*, 2nd ed. (New York: McGraw-Hill Book Company, 1971). Those authors present a discussion of utility and group utility in Chapters 2 and 7. References are given. See Sections 7.5 and 7.6 about social welfare functions.

Different people do not desire the same portfolios; each person has a unique set of indifference curves. For example, a timid investor might prefer point $B$ in Fig. 12.1. An aggressive investor might simultaneously prefer portfolio $D$ on the curve $BCD$. Investors select the point where their highest-valued utility isoquant is just tangent to the then-current efficient frontier in order to maximize their utility. Clearly, not all points on the efficient frontier yield the same utility to an investor. Therefore, a portfolio with multiple owners, such as a mutual fund, should not be content to be just efficient. If a mutual fund was originally at point $C$ in Fig. 12.1, but changed to point $F$, for example, some shareholders of that fund might sell shares in the fund and buy shares in a different fund that would place them closer to point $C$ in order to maximize their utility. Or point $H$, which is in the same risk class as $C$, could be even more desirable.

Shareholders do not desire a fund that changes risk classes, because a mutual fund shareholder would maximize utility if he bought an efficient fund that stayed in some desired risk class. Thus, the *objective* of portfolio management of a portfolio with multiple owners becomes one of simply maximizing return in a "preferred risk habitat." In the initial formation of such a portfolio, management should select and publicize the risk class in which they plan to maintain the portfolio so that only investors whose preferences concur will be attracted to ownership. Of course, this is what is occurring (as a first approximation) when some mutual funds promote themselves as "growth funds" while other funds, for example, stress dividend income and limited risk exposure.

Although the manager of a portfolio that has multiple owners can usually maximize the owners' expected utility by seeking to maximize the portfolio's return in some preferred risk habitat, other problems related to portfolio revision arise. The portfolio revision process is further complicated by certain costs, which economists call *market imperfections*, because they keep supply and demand from functioning smoothly. Some market imperfections that cause the real world to differ from an economically idealistic model include the following transcactions costs:

1. Commissions for buying securities.
2. Commissions for selling securities.
3. Transfer taxes for buying and/or selling securities.
4. Capital gains taxes must be paid when capital gains are realized.
5. Revision costs, which include:
   (a) Data-gathering expenses, that is, security analysis.
   (b) Portfolio analysis costs, such as computer expenses.
   (c) Professional and clerical salaries for the portfolio manager's staff.

As a result of these unavoidable cash outlays, portfolio revision should not be done too frequently. Instead, portfolio revision should be undertaken on a limited basis using some objective benefit–cost criterion to determine when it is worthwhile to revise.

## B. Controlled Revision

K. V. Smith has suggested a policy he calls "controlled revision" to manage a multiperiod portfolio.[9] Smith's controlled revision procedure is less costly than a procedure of completely revising the portfolio as it becomes suboptimal. The policy of *complete revision* entails recomputation of the efficient set each time the security analyst's latest expectations indicate that the portfolio is "significantly" suboptimal. This will likely entail completely liquidating the portfolio and reinvesting the proceeds frequently. Such a policy will result in large revision costs. The amount of revision costs incurred by a policy of complete revision will depend on how significant a departure from the efficient frontier will be tolerated, how often a determination is made to detect suboptimality, and how revision costs are weighed in the decision to revise.

In contrast to complete revision, Smith's suggested policy of controlled revision is a heuristic policy that will tolerate suboptimal portfolios on a continuing basis. Unlike complete-revision policy, the controlled-revision policy will result in minor portfolio revisions. This *controlled revision process* would proceed as follows. First, securities are forced into the solution by varying their participation levels ($x_i$'s). The effects of the change in the weights on $E(r_p)$, $\sigma_{r_p}$, and the concurrent revision costs are noted. If the marginal return from bringing the asset or assets under consideration into the portfolio exceeds the revision costs, and the portfolio will not be removed from its preferred risk habitat by the change, the change is made. Then, the investigation reexamines all remaining nonparticipating assets to determine if other securities may profitably be brought into the portfolio.

Figure 12.2 shows three suboptimum portfolios—$A$, $B$, and $C$. Assuming that $\sigma_0$ is the desired risk class, portfolio $D$ is the optimum revision. The impact of inserting new securities into the suboptimum portfolios $A$, $B$, and $C$ is determined by calculating the resulting portfolios' returns and risk as various new securities are introduced. Any portfolio revision that does not increase the portfolio's return within the desired risk class ($\sigma_0$) is discarded. Of those portfolio revisions that do increase the portfolio's return within the desired risk class, the revision that offers the largest expected marginal net increment in portfolio returns should be selected. Equation (12.16) defines the marginal net increment of gain to the portfolio's owners. This gain equals the increase in the portfolio's rate of return resulting from the

[9]See K. V. Smith, "Alternative Procedures for Revising Investment Portfolio," *Journal of Finance and Quantitative Analysis,* December 1968. See also, E. J. Elton, M. G. Gruber, and M. W. Padberg, "Simple Criteria for Optimal Portfolio Selection," *Journal of Finance,* December 1976, Vol. 31, No. 5, pages 1341-1357.

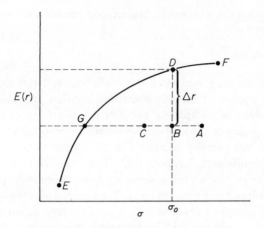

Figure 12 2. Portfolio Revision Possibilities

revision, denoted $\Delta r$, less the revision's cost as a percentage of the portfolio's assets.

$$(\Delta r) \text{ less ($ revision cost/total $ assets)}$$
$$= \text{net marginal return.} \quad (12.16)$$

The controlled-revision policy is based on iteratively performing marginal analysis. The objective of this revision policy is to capture the majority of the expected return that could be achieved with a complete revision but at a fraction of the revision cost.

If the portfolio's risk class is allowed to vary, such marginal analysis techniques are of dubious value. By allowing the portfolio's risk class to change, the relevant search area becomes the area within the triangular figure bounded by $GBD$ in Fig. 12.2. Searching within this area requires that consideration be given to both risk and return. If selection is to be made in $(E(r), \sigma)$ space, some weighting scheme must be devised to evaluate both risk and return simultaneously. Any such weighting scheme will not be satisfactory to all investors since risk–return preferences differ. Thus, portfolio revision should seek dominant portfolios in the preferred risk habitat if the portfolio has multiple owners.

### 12.4 The Attainable Efficient Frontier

As a result of portfolio revision costs, it is not possible for a revised portfolio to attain the true efficient frontier along the curve $EBCF$ in Fig. 12.3. Instead, the attainable efficient along the curve $E'C'F'$ represents the optimum attainable investments. The vertical difference between the unconstrained efficient frontier curve $EBCF$ and the attainable "efficient frontier" $E'C'F'$ is

292

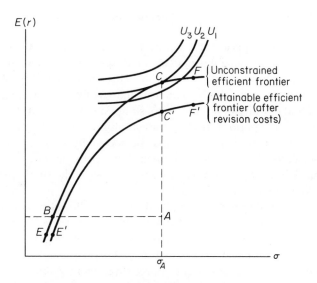

Figure 12.3. Portfolio Revision Possibilities

the revision costs as a percentage of the portfolio's total assets.[10] As shown in Fig. 12.3, the attainable efficient frontier is closer to the true efficient frontier for low-risk, low-return portfolios than for portfolios with higher returns. This is because the low-risk, low-return portfolios presumably contain many bonds and the sales commissions for buying and selling bonds are much lower than for stock; therefore, revision costs are less.

In situations such as the one depicted in Fig. 12.3, portfolio $A$ should be revised to attain point $C'$. Revisions of this nature should occur as often as they are possible according to the controlled revision policy—this may be a month, a quarter, or perhaps even longer after portfolio $A$ was originally purchased. There is no single optimum time schedule for portfolio revision. Owing to revision costs, it is impossible to attain the most efficient portfolio, $C$, in the desired risk class, $\sigma_A$. But there is no reason why portfolio $C'$ should not be obtained directly and immediately.[11] To maintain the portfolio in the risk class its investors chose when they bought shares in it, portfolios that are in significantly different risk classes should not be selected, even though they may dominate the portfolio under revision.

[10]A. H. Y. Chen, F. C. Jen, and S. Zionts, "The Optimal Portfolio Revision Policy," *Journal of Business*, Vol. 44, No. 1, 1971, pp. 51–61.

[11]K. H. Johnson and D. S. Shannon, "A Note on Diversification and the Reduction of Dispersion," *Journal of Financial Economics*, Vol. 1, No. 4, 1974, pp. 365–372. This study presents empirical evidence that revising a Markowitz full-covariance portfolio quarterly results in significantly better performance than initially determining the optimal participation levels and then maintaining these proportions unfixed period after period.

## 12.5 Conclusions

Markowitz's single-period efficient portfolio model was shown to be applicable to multiperiod portfolio management applications. Two multiperiod objectives were considered: (1) maximize the expected utility of terminal value of a portfolio from which no intermediate withdrawals were made; and (2) maximize the utility of a series of consumption–investment decisions that occur over multiple periods. Both of these multiperiod portfolio problems, as well as the single-period problem, can be solved by selecting Markowitz-efficient portfolios if it is merely assumed that (a) the investor has positive, but diminishing, marginal utility of wealth; and (b) the single-period rates of return are normally distributed.

To maximize *multiperiod* expected utility, the following assumptions (in excess of the two assumptions needed to justify the single-period analysis) are necessary: (c) The investor's utility is isoelastic (namely, logarithmic, positive fractional lower, or negative exponential). Furthermore, the multiperiod consumption–investment solution requires three more assumptions: (d) the consumer–investor's tastes and preferences are not effected by the changing states of the world; (e) the consumer–investor *acts as if future* information is known; and (f) the utility of consumption in every period is separable and independent of the utility from consumption in other periods. The dubious nature of these last three assumptions undermines somewhat the more general conclusions which can be drawn from the consumption–investment analysis. However, the realism of assumptions *a*, *b*, and *c* suggests that Markowitz analysis is a useful procedure for single-period and multiperiod portfolio management problems.

Transactions costs were admitted into consideration and, combined with the necessity of revising optimal portfolios to maintain optimality, these market imperfections were shown to preclude attainment of the Markowitz-efficient frontier. However, a policy of controlled revision to maximize a portfolio's expected return in some preferred risk class was suggested as a practical procedure that can maintain near-optimality over multiple periods.

## Selected References

Elton, E. J., and M. J. Gruber, "On the Optimality of Some Multiperiod Portfolio Selection Criteria," *Journal of Business*, April 1974.
This article uses utility theory and algebra to analyze several important conclusions about different multiperiod investment goals.

Fama, E. F., "Multi-period Consumption–Investment Decisions," *American Economic Review*, Vol. 60, March 1970, pp. 163–174.
This paper uses utility theory to rationalize myopic single-period selection of Markowitz-efficient portfolios as a solution to a lifetime's consumption and investment decisions.

Merton, R. C., "Lifetime Portfolio Selection Under Uncertainty: The Continuous Time Case," *Review of Economics and Statistics*, Vol. 50, August 1969, pp. 247–257.
This paper uses utility theory, mathematical statistics, calculus, and dynamic programming to derive optimal investment–consumption decisions in a continuous-time model.

Schreiner, John, "Portfolio Revision — A Turnover Constrained Approach", *Financial Management,* forthcoming 1979. This article (which was published after this book's first printing went on sale) formulates the portfolio revision problem mathematically and shows insightful empirical insights.

## Questions and Problems

1. The investment objective of maximizing the utility of terminal wealth is easier to solve mathematically than the multiperiod investment–consumption decision. However, when unchanging and separable utility functions are assumed (to expedite analysis of the investment–consumption problem over multiperiods), do the results differ from the results that maximize the utility of terminal wealth? Explain.

2. Do transactions costs affect the optimal solution to the utility of terminal wealth problem? Do they affect the optimal multiperiod investment–consumption decision?

3. Why do some utility functions make myopic decisions, period after period, an optimal policy? What trait characterizes these optimal myopic utility functions? Explain.

4. If a multiperiod investor faces a series of unknown and changing investment opportunities in the future periods, will this investor be able to maximize a multiperiod utility function? Explain.

5. How might the analysis of multiperiod utility functions in Chapter XII help an executive who had to formulate policies by which a large portfolio was to be managed?

# Section Five

# ASSET AND LIABILITY MANAGEMENT BY MEANS OF PORTFOLIO ANALYSIS

IN preceding chapters, Markowitz portfolio analysis and its various implications for *asset* management have been discussed. For simplicity, liabilities were purposely ignored in the earlier chapters. The discussion tended to focus on mutual funds because these portfolios have no liabilities—by law.

In Chapters XIII, the analysis is extended to include liabilities. This chapter shows how Markowitz portfolio analysis is used to select the optimum asset holdings and also the optimum liabilities to finance them.

# Portfolio Analysis of Assets and Liabilities Simultaneously

$\mathbf{M}$ARKOWITZ portfolio analysis can be used to delineate the optimal balance sheet proportions. The analysis evaluates the risk and return of every asset simultaneously with the risk and cost of capital of every liability. The solution is obtained by means of quadratic programming and tells which assets should be on the balance sheet, and in what proportions, as well as which liabilities should be used to raise the necessary capital. The analysis encompasses the capital allocation and financial leverage decisions. The firm is the portfolio and the efficient frontier obtained is a set of balance sheets for the firm which have the maximum rate of return on equity at each level of equity risk or, conversely, the minimum risk at each rate of return.

Since mutual funds have only equity as a source of funds, it is necessary to extend the analysis to more flexible forms of business organization which also include liabilities as a source of funds. The extended portfolio analysis model presented in this chapter is capable of analyzing proprietorships, partnerships, or corporations in any field.[1] However, it is easiest to analyze

---

[1]J. C. Francis first developed this portfolio analysis of a balance sheet working independently in 1971. George Oldfield offered valuable suggestions in 1972. John Wood read the paper in 1972 and commented that an analogous model had already been published by M. Parkin, "Discount House Portfolio and Debt Selection," *Review of Economic Studies*, October 1970, pp. 469–497. Unlike Parkin's model, however, this model abstracts from dollar

corporations that have liquid assets and liquid liabilities, because it is easiest to measure each period's cost for actively traded assets and liabilities. A commercial banking firm was selected as a vehicle for the example shown below.[2] However, with additional work, the analysis could be used on any firm.

### 13.1 Formulating the Balance Sheet Analysis

Markowitz portfolio analysis of a bank balance sheet is expedited because bank balance sheets essentially contain only five homogeneous asset categories and three homogenous liabilities, as shown in Table 13.1. Furthermore, average annual rate of return data are available for these eight balance sheet items from the Federal Reserve. Finally, banks are especially amenable to this analysis, because all eight of their balance sheet items are liquid.[3]

$$K_t r_{et} = (C_t r_{ct} + G_t r_{gt} + H_t r_{ht} + L_t r_{lt} + B_t r_{bt})$$
$$+ (-D_t r_{dt} - S_t r_{st} - F_t r_{ft}) - O_t. \qquad (13.1)$$

The capital letters $K_t, C_t, G_t, H_t, L_t, B_t, D_t, S_t, F_t$, and $O_t$ represent the dollar amounts of the bank's equity capital, cash, government bonds,[4] home mortgages, installment loans, business loans, demand deposits, savings deposits, certificates of deposit (CD's), and fixed overhead expense, respec-

---

quantities to facilitate comparing firms of different size and to enable solutions to be graphed in risk-return space. This model also deals with more assets and liabilities than Parkin's model, recognizes constraints, and differs in other respects. This model extends D. H. Pyle's model, "On The Theory of Financial Intermediation," *Journal of Finance*, June 1971, pp. 737–747. This model is essentially what F. Black suggested in "Bank Funds Management in an Efficient Market," *Journal of Financial Economics*, December 1975.

[2]This analysis draws heavily on an article by J. C. Francis, "Portfolio Analysis of Asset and Liability Management in Small-, Medium-, and Large-Sized Banks," *Journal of Monetary Economics*, August 1978, Vol. 4, No. 3, pp. 460–480.

[3]Even home mortgages which have an average life in excess of a decade are liquid in the secondary markets for insured mortgages maintained by Fannie Mae (FNMA), Ginnie Mae (GNMA), Freddie Mac (FHLMC), and Maggie Mae (MGIC). The three U.S. government agencies and Maggie Mae (which is sometimes also called Magic) are explained by J. C. Francis, "Helping Americans Get Mortgages," *Business Review*, Philadelphia Federal Reserve Bank, January 1974, pp. 14–21.

[4]Two significant asset categories which are not homogeneous were combined. Specifically, tax-exempt municipal bonds were added to U.S. government bonds to form one large item called, simply, government bonds. Although municipal bonds' returns differ significantly from the U.S. government bonds' returns because of their tax-exempt status, they are similar on an after-tax basis. Therefore, tax adjustments were used and both types of government bonds were combined as explained on page 10 of the 1971 *Functional Cost Analysis*. It is not clear why the Federal Reserve follows this procedure in its accounting for government securities. However, the available data are carefully prepared to aid in bank evaluations and review, according to the Federal Reserve officials. Since other data were not available, the tax-adjusted data on municipal bonds were used.

tively, on the books in period $t$. The lowercase $r_t$'s refer to the net rates of return (interest) of the bank's assets (liabilities) in period $t$. Thus, $Kr_{et}$ is the bank's taxable net income and equation (13.1) is a bank's income statement for period $t$. Abstracting from fixed overhead costs and dividing equation (13.1) through by $K_t$ yields equation (13.2), which defines the bank's rate of return on equity as a function of direct costs.[5]

$$r_{et} = (x_{ct}r_{ct} + x_{gt}r_{gt} + x_{ht}r_{ht} + x_{lt}r_{lt} + x_{bt}r_{bt})$$
$$+ (x_{dt}r_{dt} + x_{st}r_{st} + x_{ft}r_{ft}) \tag{13.2}$$

where $x_{it}$ is the weight of the $i$th asset or liability on the bank's balance sheet in period $t$ stated as a percentage of equity capital ($x_{ct} = C_t/K_t$, for example). The weights are the decision variables in this analysis.

The weights of assets are nonnegative, as shown in inequality (13.3), since they are not sold short or issued like liabilities.

$$x_{ct}, x_{gt}, x_{ht}, x_{lt}, x_{bt} \geq 0 \qquad \text{for all } t. \tag{13.3}$$

The weights of liabilities are nonpositive, as indicated in equation (13.4), since they represent debt.

$$x_{dt}, x_{st}, x_{ft} \leq 0 \qquad \text{for all } t. \tag{13.4}$$

Liabilities are essentially negative assets.[6]

Table 13.1 shows a balance sheet model for a typical large bank that is a member of the Federal Reserve System.[7] The balance sheet weights in the exhibit were obtained by averaging over 79 banks' balance sheets. The weight of total assets (that is, 1050 percent, or 10.5 times equity) exceeds total liabili-

---

[5]Economies of scale in check processing and other factors affecting a bank's cost function may be included in the analysis by adjusting the bank's overhead costs and/or reformulating equation (13.2) as a step function with costs that change as the size of the bank changes. This is an extension of the analysis which was not undertaken in this paper. About bank cost studies, see D. L. Daniel, W. A. Longbrake, and N. B. Murphy, "The Effects of Technology in Bank Economies of Scale for Demand Deposits," *Journal of Finance*, March 1973, pp. 131–146, and the included references.

[6]The conditions delineated in inequalities (13.3) and (13.4) must be imposed as constraints or the bank model will raise funds by collecting free cash (that is, $x_{ct} < 0$) rather than taking in demand deposits, which have a slight cost to the bank. Such solutions (that is, $x_{ct} < 0$, for example) are mathematically feasible but financially unrealistic.

[7]The income statement and balance sheet models, in equation (13.2) and Figure 13.1, respectively, were obtained by averaging over the balance sheets of 79 Federal Reserve banks for the year 1971. Any asset or liability that was not larger than the bank's total equity (including preferred stock and debentures) was omitted from the model. No significant asset or liability categories were thus omitted from the analysis, however, because banks' equity and other long-term capital always totaled less than 9.0 percent of total assets. Furthermore, the tiny "other asset" and "other liability" categories that were omitted contained a heterogeneous variety of items, many of which were probably held for reasons to which only vague estimated revenues and costs could be attributed.

TABLE 13.1   Simplified Bank Sheet, Common-Sized Percentages*

| Assets (Symbol) | Weight | Liabilities (Symbol) | Weight |
|---|---|---|---|
| Cash and uncollected funds (c) | 180% | Demand deposits (d) | −470% |
| Government bonds (g)† | 290% | Savings deposits (s) | −230% |
| Home and other mortgages (h) | 150% | Certificates of deposit (f) | −250% |
| Business loans (b) | 330% | Equity (e) | −100% |
| Installment loans (l) | 100% | | |
| Total assets | 1,050% | Total liabilities and net worth | 1,050% |

*See footnote 7 of the text.
†See footnote 4 of the text.
Source: *Functional Cost Analysis: 1971 Average Banks*, Board of Governors of the Federal Reserve System, Washington, D.C.

ties (of 950 percent, or 9.5 times equity) by the amount of equity, which is defined as a base number of 100 percent, or unity. All balance sheet items are stated as percentages of equity in Markowitz portfolio analysis to facilitate calculation of risk and return on equity. As a result the sum of all assets and liabilities weights must equal 1 as shown in the balance sheet identity, equation (13.5).

$$1.0 = \sum_{j=1}^{8} (x_j | j = c, g, h, l, b, d, s, f). \tag{13.5}$$

Equating equity with unity does not restrict its dollar value. Equity may be any positive amount and may vary from period to period.

The view of a bank as a portfolio in which balance sheet proportions are the relevant decision variables in no way implies that the rates of return on assets and liabilities are constant. Banks' rates of return (interest rates) on assets (liabilities) are random variables that effect the owners' income risk, as explained in section 13.2.

### 13.2   Minimizing Variability of Return on Equity

The banking model presumes that bank managers minimize the owners' variability of returns on equity at some rate of return which is sufficient to induce the owners to provide capital. The quadratic variance–covariance formula is used to measure risk and is the basis for risk management.

Minimizing a bank's risk involves minimizing quadratic equation (13.6). The symbol $\sigma_{ij}$ in equation (13.6) denotes the covariance of rates of return between items $i$ and $j$ on the bank's balance sheet when $i \neq j$ and the variance when $i = j$.

$$\sum_{i=1}^{8} \sum_{j=1}^{8} x_i x_j \sigma_{ij} = \text{var}(r_e), \tag{13.6}$$

where summation is over the eight balance sheet items. The $8 \times 8$ covariance matrix of equation (13.6) is shown below in matrix form.

$$
\begin{bmatrix}
\sigma_{cc} & \sigma_{cg} & \sigma_{ch} & \sigma_{cl} & \sigma_{cb} & \sigma_{cd} & \sigma_{cs} & \sigma_{cf} \\
\sigma_{gc} & \sigma_{gg} & \sigma_{gh} & \sigma_{gl} & \sigma_{gb} & \sigma_{gd} & \sigma_{gs} & \sigma_{gf} \\
\sigma_{hc} & \sigma_{hg} & \sigma_{hh} & \sigma_{hl} & \sigma_{hb} & \sigma_{hd} & \sigma_{hs} & \sigma_{hf} \\
\sigma_{lc} & \sigma_{lg} & \sigma_{lh} & \sigma_{ll} & \sigma_{lb} & \sigma_{ld} & \sigma_{ls} & \sigma_{lf} \\
\sigma_{bc} & \sigma_{bg} & \sigma_{bh} & \sigma_{bl} & \sigma_{bb} & \sigma_{bd} & \sigma_{bs} & \sigma_{bf} \\
\sigma_{dc} & \sigma_{dg} & \sigma_{dh} & \sigma_{dl} & \sigma_{db} & \sigma_{dd} & \sigma_{ds} & \sigma_{df} \\
\sigma_{sc} & \sigma_{sg} & \sigma_{sh} & \sigma_{sl} & \sigma_{sb} & \sigma_{sd} & \sigma_{ss} & \sigma_{sf} \\
\sigma_{fc} & \sigma_{fg} & \sigma_{fh} & \sigma_{fl} & \sigma_{fb} & \sigma_{fd} & \sigma_{fs} & \sigma_{ff}
\end{bmatrix} .
$$

The values of the variances and covariances used in equation (13.6) are shown in Table 13.2.[8] Credit risk statistics were added to the risk statistics in Table 13.2.[9] Figure 13.1 illustrates the five assets and three liabilities in $[\sigma, E(r)]$ space.

TABLE 13.2   Risk and Return Statistics for the Average Large Bank

| | $c$ | $g$ | $h$ | $l$ | $b$ | $d$ | $s$ | $f$ |
|---|---|---|---|---|---|---|---|---|
| Mean annual rate of return (or cost) (%) | 0 | 6.21* | 5.89 | 6.16 | 6.15† | 1.71 | 4.78 | 5.35 |
| Variance–covariance matrix | | | | | | | | |
| Cash and reserves ($c$) | 0 | 0 | 0 | 0 | 0 | 0 | 0 | 0 |
| Government bonds ($g$) | 0 | 0.77 | 0.38 | 0.32 | 0.69 | 0 | 0.28 | 0.46 |
| Mortgages on homes, etc. ($h$) | 0 | 0.38 | 0.34 | 0.19 | 0.22 | 0 | 0.18 | 0.19 |
| Installment loans ($l$) | 0 | 0.32 | 0.19 | 0.51 | 0.25 | 0 | 0.12 | 0.18 |
| Business loans ($b$) | 0 | 0.69 | 0.22 | 0.25 | 1.05 | 0 | 0.20 | 0.45 |
| Demand deposits ($d$) | 0 | 0 | 0 | 0 | 0 | 0 | 0 | 0 |
| Savings deposits ($s$) | 0 | 0.28 | 0.18 | 0.12 | 0.20 | 0 | 0.16 | 0.14 |
| Certificates of deposit ($f$) | 0 | 0.46 | 0.19 | 0.18 | 0.45 | 0 | 0.14 | 0.30 |

*See footnote 4 of the text about combining tax-exempt municipal bonds with taxable Treasury bonds.

†This statistic was adjusted upward for compensating balances.

[8]Six annual average returns were used to calculate the variance and covariances shown in Table 13.2. Six elements is a small sample. However, the law of large numbers suggests that mean returns drawn from a sampling distribution with over 68 observations underlying each of the means should yield nearly error-free estimates of banks' mean rate of return parameter in each of the year sampled. *Source: Functional Cost Analysis*, for 1966, 1967, 1968, 1969, 1970, and 1971, Federal Reserve System, Washington, D.C.

[9]The asymmetry of loan-loss rates will be summed in with the other rates of return and cost, and the central limit theorem suggests that the resulting rates of return on equity will tend to be normally distributed. Thus, the two-parameter analysis is appropriate for analyzing rates of return on equity. One objection to invoking the central limit theorem to justify assuming that returns on equity are normally distributed (thus making Markowitz's two-parameter analysis appropriate) is that the returns are not independent. Table 13.2 shows nonzero covariances between various rates. However, since the rates on assets and liabilities differ in sign, the returns on equity are differences that may be well approximated by the two-parameter distribution. Furthermore, the central limit theorem is robust.

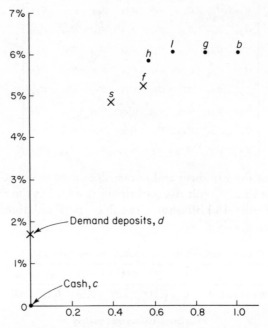

Figure 13.1. Five Assets and Three Liabilities in $[\sigma, E(r)]$ Space

## 13.3 Efficient Combinations of Banking Assets and Liabilities

The set of bank balance sheets which have the minimum total risk at each level of expected rate of return on equity are delineated by selecting the sets of balance sheet weights that minimize risk at each level of equity return or, conversely, maximize return on equity at each prespecified level of total variance. Wolfe's quadratic programming algorithm was used for the computations. The resulting efficient banking frontiers are discussed below.[10]

---

[10]The computations were performed at the University of Pennsylvania's computer center, Uni-Coll. Wolfe's quadratic programming algorithm was performed by a Uni-Coll library program named WOLFEQP. The bank model is outlined by equations (13.1) through (13.6). For the calculus-oriented reader, the model is summarized by the Lagrangian objective function:

$$\text{minimize } z = \text{var}(r_e) + \lambda_1[E(r_e) - E^*] + \lambda_2[\sum_{i=1}^{8} x_i - 1.0].$$

This equation is not as difficult to comprehend as it may seem. In equation (13.7), $z$ is the variable to be minimized; $z$ has no financial interpretation. The bank owners' total risk, var $(r_e)$, as defined in equation (13.6), is minimized subject to two Lagrangian constraints. The first constraint requires the bank to earn some expected rate of return on equity, $E(r_e)$, the expectation of equation (13.2), equal to $E^*$. The variables $\lambda_1$ and $\lambda_2$ are two Lagrangian multipliers. The second constraint requires that the balance sheet identity, equation (13.5), is not violated.

A. Unconstrained Efficient Frontier

Three different efficient banking frontiers are graphed in Fig. 13.2; the associated statistics are shown in Table 13.3. The risk and return of the average bank (shown in Table 13.3) is represented by point $A$ in Fig. 13.2. The dominant or unconstrained efficient frontier was delineated by minimizing quadratic equation (13.6) at each level of return on equity, equation (13.2), using the three definitions set out in equations (13.3), (13.4), and (13.5). The dominated or constrained efficient frontiers in Fig. 13.2 and Table 13.3 were generated by appending additional constraints which will be discussed in the following sections.

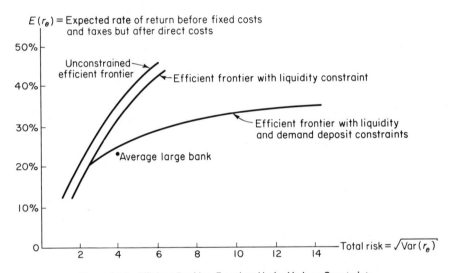

Figure 13.2. Efficient Banking Frontiers Under Various Constraints

As might be anticipated, the unconstrained efficient portfolios raised funds almost totally by accepting demand deposits $(x_d < 0)$, the lowest-cost source of funds available. The unconstrained efficient frontier has some interesting implications for normative economics. Most noteworthy perhaps is the fact that an efficient, unconstrained bank naturally *intermediates* and *diversifies*. Over all relevant ranges of risk and return, the unconstrained banking portfolios raised funds by issuing two liabilities (namely, certificates of deposit and demand deposit liability positions are indicated by $x_f < 0$ and $x_d < 0$, respectively, in Table 13.3). The proceeds from these deposits are invested in three assets (that is, holdings of home mortgages, installment loans, and business loans are indicated by positive values of $x_h$, $x_l$, and $x_b$ in Table 13.3).

TABLE 13.3 Efficient Portfolios of Banking Assets and Liabilities Under Different Constraints

| Net Return (%) Before Fixed Costs, Eq. (13-2) | Total Variance $var(r_e)$, Eq. (13-6) | Total Risk, $\sqrt{var(r_e)}$ | Weights of Items in Efficient Balance Sheets | | | | | | | | |
|---|---|---|---|---|---|---|---|---|---|---|---|
| | | | Assets | | | | | Liabilities | | | $\sum_{j=1}^{8} x_j$ |
| | | | $x_c$ | $x_g$ | $x_h$ | $x_l$ | $x_b$ | $x_d$ | $x_s$ | $x_f$ | |
| Unconstrained Efficient Frontier | | | | | | | | | | | |
| 15 | 1.98 | 1.40 | 0 | 0 | 1.76 | 0.63 | 0.40 | −1.53 | 0 | −0.27 | 1.0 |
| 20 | 3.84 | 1.96 | 0 | 0 | 2.42 | 0.87 | 0.55 | −2.48 | 0 | −0.37 | 1.0 |
| 25 | 6.51 | 2.55 | 0 | 0 | 3.09 | 1.11 | 0.71 | −3.43 | 0 | −0.47 | 1.0 |
| 30 | 10.23 | 3.20 | 0 | 0 | 3.75 | 1.35 | 0.86 | −4.39 | 0 | −0.57 | 1.0 |
| 35 | 15.44 | 3.92 | 0 | 0 | 4.42 | 1.59 | 1.01 | −5.35 | 0 | −0.68 | 1.0 |
| 45 | 33.80 | 5.81 | 0 | 0 | 5.74 | 2.07 | 1.32 | −7.25 | 0 | −0.88 | 1.0 |
| Efficient Frontier with Liquidity Constraint | | | | | | | | | | | |
| 15 | 2.85 | 1.68 | 1.5 | 0 | 2.10 | 0.76 | 0.48 | −3.52 | 0 | −0.32 | 1.0 |
| 20 | 5.03 | 2.24 | 1.5 | 0 | 2.76 | 0.99 | 0.63 | −4.47 | 0 | −0.43 | 1.0 |
| 25 | 8.26 | 2.87 | 1.5 | 0 | 3.43 | 1.23 | 0.79 | −5.42 | 0 | −0.53 | 1.0 |
| 30 | 12.67 | 3.55 | 1.5 | 0 | 4.09 | 1.47 | 0.94 | −6.38 | 0 | −0.63 | 1.0 |
| 35 | 18.92 | 4.35 | 1.5 | 0 | 4.75 | 1.71 | 1.10 | −7.33 | 0 | −0.73 | 1.0 |
| 45 | 41.58 | 6.45 | 1.5 | 0 | 6.08 | 2.19 | 1.40 | −9.24 | 0 | −0.93 | 1.0 |
| Efficient Frontier with Liquidity and Demand Deposit Constraints | | | | | | | | | | | |
| 15 | 2.84 | 1.68 | 1.5 | 0 | 2.10 | 0.76 | 0.48 | −3.52 | 0 | −0.32 | 1.0 |
| 20 | 5.09 | 2.58 | 1.5 | 0 | 2.76 | 0.99 | 0.63 | −4.47 | 0 | −0.43 | 1.0 |
| 25 | 10.25 | 3.20 | 1.5 | 0 | 4.05 | 1.29 | 1.67 | −4.7 | −0.02 | −2.8 | 1.0 |
| 30 | 38.96 | 6.24 | 1.5 | 0 | 5.94 | 1.61 | 2.53 | −4.7 | −1.56 | −4.33 | 1.0 |
| 35 | 177.82 | 13.33 | 1.5 | 0 | 7.82 | 1.93 | 3.39 | −4.7 | −3.09 | −5.86 | 1.0 |
| 45 | 3598.15 | 59.98 | 1.5 | 0 | 11.59 | 2.58 | 5.11 | −4.7 | −6.16 | −8.92 | 1.0 |
| Average Over 79 Banks for 1971 | | | | | | | | | | | |
| 26.2 | 19.65 | 4.43 | 1.8 | 2.9 | 1.5 | 1.0 | 3.3 | −4.7 | −2.3 | −2.5 | 1.0 |

Markowitz and others have demonstrated the risk-reducing benefits of diversification analytically and empirically.[11] Pyle has analyzed intermediation.[12] The results in Table 13.3 show the extent to which wealth-seeking, risk-averse bankers can be expected to intermediate. This evidence is insightful since it was obtained with the one-period portfolio analysis model. Subjective influences such as bank regulations or the "customer relationship" are not needed to rationalize intermediation and diversification.

Constrained solutions are more complicated than unconstrained solutions. Turning from normative to positive economics, two realistic constraints will be imposed on the solution to align the efficient portfolios of banking assets and liabilities more closely with those actually held by banks.

### B. Minimizing Liquidity Risk

Bank regulatory authorities are concerned with the stability of the economy and want to minimize the risk that banks become insolvent and create a "money panic." To ensure that banks will be able to meet large unexpected deposit withdrawals, the regulators require that a minimum amount of nonearning liquid assets be held. Statistics for the average bank indicate that cash and uncollected funds equal to 1.8 times equity are held.[13] Equation (13.7) is imposed as a realistic *liquidity constraint* to force the bank model to hold nonearning assets equal to 1.5 times equity.

$$x_{ct} \geq 1.5 \qquad \text{for all } t. \tag{13.7}$$

The efficient frontiers graphed in Fig. 13.2 and the statistics in Table 13.3 highlight the difference between the unconstrained efficient frontier and the efficient frontier attainable under the liquidity constraint; this difference may be viewed as the opportunity cost of solvency insurance. That is, holding nonearning assets actually decreases the bank's expected rate of return on equity.

### C. A Competitive Constraint on Demand Deposits

As a practical matter, most banks have difficulty drawing in more demand deposits. The average bank has demand deposits of 4.7 times its equity. Because of competition, the model bank is assumed to be powerless to

---

[11]Harry M. Markowitz, *Portfolio Selection* (New York: John Wiley and Sons, Inc., 1969).

[12]Pyle, "On the Theory of Financial Intermediation."

[13]As a practical matter, reserve requirements are stated as a fraction, denoted $R$, of deposits. This implies that a bank's reserves are $Rd$ dollars, where $d$ is the dollar amount of deposits. In the formulation employed here, deposits are stated as some proportion, $P$, of equity, $e$. Thus, deposits are $Pe = d$ and the banks reserves are $RPe = Rd$, where $RP \geq 1.5$ in equation (13.7). This shows that stating reserves relative to equity and stating reserves relative to deposits, as is customary, are equivalent procedures.

increase its demand deposits beyond 470 percent of equity. This assumption facilitates comparisons with the average bank; it is summarized in inequality (13.8).

$$x_{dt} \geq -4.7 \quad \text{for all } t. \tag{13.8}$$

The realistic *demand deposit constraint* begins binding just above $E(r_e) = 20$ percent, and the bank model reacts by selling certificates of deposit and taking in savings deposits to raise funds when no more low-cost demand deposits can be obtained, as shown in Table 13.3.

As shown graphically in Fig. 13.2, the demand deposit constraint forces the efficient bank to assume large increases in risk to increase its return on equity (before fixed costs and taxes) above 20 percent, $E(r_e) = 20$ percent. When the demand deposit constraint begins to bind, asset expansion must be financed with a decreasing proportion, $x_d/(x_d + x_s + x_f)$, of low-cost demand deposits. This causes the weighted average cost of liability capital (WACLC), equation (13.9), to increase above its lowest possible value, $E(r_d) = -1.71$ percent, asymptotically toward the cost of the highest-cost liability, $E(r_f) = -5.4$ percent, even though the costs of the individual liabilities are invariant.

$$\frac{x_d E(r_d) + x_s E(r_s) + x_f E(r_f)}{x_d + x_s + x_f} = \text{WACLC}. \tag{13.9}$$

Thus, as a bank increases its asset holdings by increasing debt financing, its WACLC increases while assets' returns do not change—this reduces the marginal profit and the incentive to expand. Also, the increasingly poor risk–return trade-off, $d^2 E(r_e)/d\sigma^2 < 0$, available above 20 percent return on equity, limits banks' willingness to increase their debt-to-equity ratio.

### D. Capital Adequacy Constraint

In addition to the liquidity constraint resulting from the requirement to hold liquid reserves and the demand deposit constraint imposed by competitive conditions, banks face a *capital adequacy constraint* imposed by Federal Reserve bank examiners. These examiners analyze the banks over which they have responsibility and conduct certain tests to ensure that the banks do not use too much financial leverage. Ratios are used to analyze banks' leverage and liquidity. A bank is allowed to borrow more heavily as it increases its liquidity and equity capitalization. The various ratios used by bank examiners were used to formulate a realistic capital adequacy constraint. However, the capital adequacy constraint was not binding; all the efficient portfolios shown in Table 13.3 obtained under the liquidity and demand deposit constraints were unchanged when the third realistic constraint was included. The capital adequacy constraint tends to coincide with the necessary and sufficient conditions for a minimum-risk portfolio at each level of return.

### 13.4 The Asset and Liability Structure of the Portfolios

Table 13.3 shows that the holdings of efficient banks with two realistic constraints are similar to the holdings of actual banks in many respects. Since it is impossible to tell which of the efficient portfolios is most desirable without knowing a bank owner's utility function (or at least the risk–return trade-off preferences), the efficient bank earning about the same rate of return on equity as the average bank, that is, $E(r_e) = 25$ percent, is compared and contrasted to the average bank below.

#### A. Savings Deposits

The constrained efficient bank demonstrates a preference to raise funds by selling certificates of deposit rather than from increased savings deposits. This departure from the average banking behavior may be the result of attempts by efficient banks to hedge against variability of return on equity. By financing asset expansion with CD's so that the bank's interest expense on CD's will fall and offset the lower rates of return available on some assets when market rates fall, the bank can hedge its income. This does not mean that savings deposits are not desirable; it means that because they are not highly correlated with asset returns, an efficient bank may prefer to obtain other types of deposits. Other differences between average banks and efficient banks occur on the asset side of the balance sheet.

#### B. Government Bonds

The efficient bank with two realistic constraints that earns 25 percent expected return on equity has holdings of most assets that are similar to the average bank. However, government bonds do not enter into solution. The large holdings of federal and municipal bonds which the average bank has did not enter the efficient portfolios, even after including the capital adequacy constraint imposed by bank examiners (as explained in Section 13.3D, the capital adequacy constraint was not binding). The municipal bonds were properly adjusted for taxes. (The returns on the tax-exempt bonds were raised to be comparable to taxable rates, as explained in the *Functional Cost Analysis* booklets before the analysis was undertaken. See footnote 4.) Therefore, only subjective hypotheses can be offered to explain why actual banks hold more government bonds than the efficient bank.

Casual expiricism suggests that the federal and municipal bonds which banks carry may result from five factors not included in the bank model: (1) indirect pressure from bank examiners to hold primary reserves in government bonds; (2) banks that have a Tax and Loan Account from the U.S. Treasury can use these deposits to pay for purchases of Treasury bonds but not other issuer's bonds; (3) some bank's willingness to buy municipal bonds to help the local community; (4) the bank may obtain the municipality's demand deposits if it buys the municipality's bonds; and (5) municipal bonds may be counted as reserves at some state-chartered banks. No adjustments were made for these considerations for the sake of brevity. The bank model with only two binding realistic constraints, equations (13.7) and (13.8), which earns a 25 percent return on equity furnishes a good approximation of the average bank's holdings.

## C. Bank Simulation

The fact that efficient banks make a smaller quantity of business loans than average banks may be the result of the failure of the model to allow explicitly for those considerations sometimes discussed under the rubric of "customer relationships." Customers who borrow from a bank tend to keep their deposits at that bank. Since banks benefit from interest-free demand deposits the bank should not ignore this source of profit in formulating its business loan policies. The average Federal Reserve bank has business loans equal to about half of its demand deposits, as shown in equation (13.10).[14] Essentially, equation (13.10) is a formalized *customer relationship constraint* for business loans.

$$x_{bt} = (-0.5)(x_{dt}). \qquad (13.10)$$

In order to take explicit cognizance of the value of the bank's relationship with its customers, equation (13.10) could be imposed as a realistic constraint. Likewise, the customer relationship could be used to increase savings account deposits; many people do save where they have their checking account, for convenience. Equation (13.11) represents the realistic relationship between checking and savings deposits observed, on average.

$$x_{st} = (0.5)(x_{dt}). \qquad (13.11)$$

Constraint equations (13.10) and (13.11) will bring business loans and savings in efficient banking portfolios yielding 25 percent return on equity up to levels observed in the average bank. However, the constraints would be imposed solely to emulate the average bank's proportions more closely rather than to obtain an optimum allocation. And, tying less desirable assets and/or

---

[14]Substituting the sign of deposits imposed by inequality (13.4) explains why the negative sign on the coefficient is necessary in equation (13.10). Equation (13.10), coupled with inequality (13.8), essentially constrains business loans, $x_b \geq 2.35$.

liabilities to demand deposits will reduce the quantity of demand deposits held by the efficient bank. To demonstrate the positive economic power of the bank portfolio model explained above, the number of realistic constraints employed is held to only two. However, the bank model can be made to emulate a wide range of rational and irrational practices simply by adding constraints to the bank model and adjusting the returns and costs to reflect relevant characteristics of the bank being simulated.[15]

## 13.5 Summary and Conclusions

Markowitz portfolio analysis was applied to a portfolio of banking assets and liabilities. Intermediation and diversification to maximize bank owner's expected return in some preferred risk habitat was rationalized by means of the analysis. Adding a liquidity constraint and a constraint to reflect banks' inability to increase their demand deposits indefinitely generates balance sheet proportions fairly similar to those of actual banks. Other constraints could be added to simulate different banking situations.[16] Thus, the model has both normative and positive economic applications.

The form of balance sheet analysis suggested above has advantages over other models. First, the approach is *comprehensive*. Legal constraints, costs, revenues, risks, competitive constraints, asset management, and liability management are all factors dealt with by the model. The second main advantage is the *simultaneous* manner in which the model deals with these

---

[15]The model can be made dynamic by adding intertemporal constraints as Chambers and Charnes did with their linear programming model; D. Chambers and A. Charnes, "Intertemporal Analysis and Optimization of Bank Portfolios," *Management Science*, Vol. 7, July 1961. Formulating the model in a dynamic period-by-period optimization framework would allow the addition of new constraints. The customer relationship constraint, for example, could be restated as inequality (13.10a). An intertemporal QP analysis of assets was published with empirical results by Gerry A. Pogue, "An Intertemporal Model for Investment Management," *Journal of Bank Research*, Volume 1, Number 1, Spring 1970, pp. 17–34. This article is reprinted in *Elements of Investments*, 2nd edition, edited by H. K. Wu and A. J. Zakon, Holt, Rinehart and Winston Inc., 1977.

$$x_{bt} \leq x_{b,t-1}. \tag{13.10a}$$

Chen et al. have suggested how to include portfolio revision costs in a dynamic portfolio model: A. H. Y. Chen, F. C. Jen, and S. Zionts, "The Optimal Portfolio Revision Policy," *Journal of Business*, Vol. 44, No. 1, 1971, pp. 51–61.

[16]Students of banking may find that Chapter XIII glosses over too much banking detail. This was done to stress the portfolio aspects of the analysis. For more bank analysis and discussion, see the paper from which the example used in this chapter was taken: J. C. Francis, "Portfolio Analysis of Asset and Liability Management in Small-, Medium-, and Large-Sized Banks," *Journal of Monetary Economics*, August 1978. This article explains how the default risks associated with mortgage loans, business loans, and installment were brought into the variance–covariance matrix, and other important aspects of bank analysis.

variables. A third advantage is that the model optimizes; that is, the analysis yields efficient portfolios that tend to *maximize* both the *rate of return on equity* and the *owners' expected utility*. And finally, the model is a *microeconomic theory of the firm*. It is not the usual form of microeconomic theory because it deals with stochastic variables rather than a certainty model. Nevertheless, it is grounded in good utility foundations,[17] the model is amenable to useful comparative statics analysis, and it encompasses revenues and costs.

When empirical data are to be used, applying portfolio theory to a business firm that owned numerous categories of illiquid assets will be more difficult than for a bank. Most manufacturing companies, for example, own a long and heterogeneous list of illiquid assets. It is both costly and troublesome to appraise illiquid assets (that is, assets that are not actively traded in secondary markets) and to estimate single-period rates of return. Accounting data for estimating one-period returns from individual assets are virtually nonexistent. Overcoming this lack of readily available information will probably require (1) more meaningful accounting data, and (2) imputations based on various market-sensitive price indexes.[18] The period-by-period cost of liabilities would be easier to estimate than assets, since liabilities are usually denominated in dollar amounts, which are known. In any event, these problems will provide worthwhile goals for future research.[19]

---

[17]Assuming that bank owners have continuously positive but diminishing marginal utility of terminal one-period wealth, $U(w)' > 0$, $U(w)'' < 0$, implies that bank managers can increase the owners' expected utility by maximizing the bank's expected return in some preferred risk habitat, $U(r)' > 0$, $U(r)'' < 0$, in every period: E. F. Fama, "Multi-period Consumption–Investment Decisions," *American Economic Review*, March 1970, pp. 163–174. Since the modeled bank's rate of return on equity is the sum of rates of return on five assets and rates of interest on three liabilities, the central limit theorem suggests that returns on equity may be approximated by a normal distribution. Assuming that returns on equity are normally distributed implies that the variance of returns is an appropriate risk surrogate and Markowitz-efficient portfolios are desired,

$$E[U(r)] = f[E(r), \sigma(r)], \quad f_1 > 0, \quad f_2 < 0.$$

[18]If the accounting profession ever implements income-measurement procedures based on market values rather than book values, the analysis presented in this chapter would be much easier to administer to a wider range of firms. At the present time, however, the depreciation and depletion techniques, which can generate high unrealistic book values, undermine the use of most accounting data. The bank example was used because banking assets and liabilities are mostly monetary items that cannot be depreciated arbitrarily.

[19]This analysis should not be misconstrued to imply that a manufacturing firm that owns real assets should diversify by purchasing real assets that are unrelated to the firm's area of manufacturing. This analysis would not advocate the acquisition of such unproductive assets, because their expected return within the existing firm would be too low. Only complementary real assets and assets of good technology will be able to justify sufficiently high returns to enter into an existing manufacturing firm without diminishing the firm's (that is, the portfolio's) expected return.

## Appendix 13A
## Mathematical Shadow Price Analysis

To obtain efficient frontiers that allow evaluation of the shadow prices of the constraints, the bank analysis problem discussed in this chapter may be solved by minimizing a Lagrangian objective function:

$$\text{minimize } z = \text{var } (r_e) + \lambda_1 \left[ \sum_{j=1}^{8} x_j E(r_j) - E(r_e^*) \right] + \lambda_2 \left[ \sum_{j=1}^{8} x_j - 1.0 \right]$$

$$+ \lambda_3[x_c - 1.8] + \lambda_4[x_g - 2.9] + \lambda_5[x_h - 1.5]$$

$$+ \lambda_6[x_b - 3.3] + \lambda_7[x_d + 4.7] + \lambda_8[x_s + 2.3], \qquad (13A.1)$$

where the summations are over the eight balance sheet items. The objective function minimizes total risk, equation (13A.1), subject to eight Lagrangian constraints. The first constraint requires the bank to earn $E(r_e^*)$ return on equity. The second constraint is the balance sheet identity, equation (13.5). Constraints 3 through 8 constrain the solution to the weights of the average large bank given in Table 13.1 for cash, government bonds, home mortgages, business loans, demand deposits, and savings deposits. The problem was formulated in this way so that the costs of being an average bank instead of an efficient bank can be evaluated.

Partial derivatives are taken with respect to all the weights and Lagrangian multipliers to minimize the Lagrangian objective function, (13A.1).

$$\frac{\partial z}{\partial x_c} = 2x_c\sigma_{cc} + 2x_g\sigma_{gc} + 2x_h\sigma_{hc} + 2x_b\sigma_{bc} + 2x_l\sigma_{lc} + 2x_d\sigma_{dc}$$

$$+ 2x_s\sigma_{sc} + 2x_f\sigma_{fc} + \lambda_1 E(r_c) + \lambda_2 + \lambda_3 = 0$$

$$\frac{\partial z}{\partial x_g} = 2x_c\sigma_{cg} + 2x_g\sigma_{gg} + 2x_h\sigma_{hg} + 2x_b\sigma_{bg} + 2x_l\sigma_{lg} + 2x_d\sigma_{dg}$$

$$+ 2x_s\sigma_{sg} + 2x_f\sigma_{fg} + \lambda_1 E(r_g) + \lambda_2 + \lambda_4 = 0$$

$$\vdots$$

$$\frac{\partial z}{\partial x_s} = 2x_c\sigma_{cs} + 2x_g\sigma_{gs} + 2x_h\sigma_{hs} + 2x_b\sigma_{bs} + 2x_l\sigma_{ls} + 2x_d\sigma_{ds}$$

$$+ 2x_s\sigma_{ss} + 2x_f\sigma_{fs} + \lambda_1 E(r_s) + \lambda_2 + \lambda_8 = 0$$

$$\frac{\partial z}{\partial x_f} = 2x_c\sigma_{cf} + 2x_g\sigma_{gf} + 2x_h\sigma_{hf} + 2x_b\sigma_{bf} + 2x_l\sigma_{lf} + 2x_d\sigma_{df}$$

$$+ 2x_s\sigma_{sf} + 2x_f\sigma_{ff} + \lambda_1 E(r_f) + \lambda_2 = 0$$

$$\frac{\partial z}{\partial \lambda_1} = \sum_{j=1}^{8} x_j E(r_j) - E(r_e^*) = 0$$

$$\frac{\partial z}{\partial \lambda_2} = \sum_{j=1}^{8} x_j - 1.0 = 0$$

$$\frac{\partial z}{\partial \lambda_3} = x_c - 1.8 = 0$$

$$\frac{\partial z}{\partial \lambda_4} = x_g - 2.9 = 0$$

$$\frac{\partial z}{\partial \lambda_5} = x_h - 1.5 = 0$$

$$\frac{\partial z}{\partial \lambda_6} = x_b - 3.3 = 0$$

$$\frac{\partial z}{\partial \lambda_7} = x_d + 4.7 = 0$$

$$\frac{\partial z}{\partial \lambda_8} = x_s + 2.3 = 0.$$

The 12 partial derivatives above may be formed into a Jacobian matrix, as shown in Table 13A.1.

The matrix notation representation of the system of equations in Table 13A.1 is $MV = K$, where $K$ is the vector of constant terms, $V$ is the vector of eight $x$'s and eight $\lambda$'s, and $M$ is the 16 by 16 matrix of coefficients. The inverse of $M$ is used to solve for the vector $V$. Premultiplying both sides of the equation by $M^{-1}$ yields $M^{-1}MV = M^{-1}K$, which reduces to $V = M^{-1}K$, the vector of efficient portfolio weights.

The last six Lagrangian constraints could have been left off the objective function equation, (13A.1), to obtain an unconstrained efficient banking frontier. However, the constraints were appended to align all but two weights ($x_1$ and $x_f$ are not constrained) with the values of the average bank. This allows the shadow price of a Lagrangian constraint which is realistic to be evaluated.

Consider, say, the third Lagrangian constraint in the objective function, that cash equal 1.8 times equity. Multiplying the vector of constants, $K$, times the eleventh row of the inverse matrix, $M^{-1}$, yields the value of $\lambda_3$ shown in equation (13A.3) for a large bank.

$$\lambda_3 = 0.052E(r_e^*) - 9.6583. \tag{13A.3}$$

The third Lagrangian constraint is

$$\lambda_3 = \frac{-\partial \text{ var } (r_e)}{\partial x_c}.$$

This is the marginal risk from an incremental increase (decrease) in cash. At $E(r_e) = 20.0$ percent, the value of this shadow price is $\lambda_3 = -8.6183$. This means that at $E(r_e) = 20$ percent, an increase in $x_c$ would decrease

TABLE 13A.1  Jacobian Matrix

$$
\begin{bmatrix}
2\sigma_{cc} & 2\sigma_{cg} & 2\sigma_{ch} & 2\sigma_{cl} & 2\sigma_{cb} & 2\sigma_{cd} & 2\sigma_{cs} & 2\sigma_{cf} & E(r_c) & 1.0 & 1.0 & 0 & 0 & 0 & 0 & 0 \\
2\sigma_{gc} & 2\sigma_{gg} & 2\sigma_{gh} & 2\sigma_{gl} & 2\sigma_{gb} & 2\sigma_{gd} & 2\sigma_{gs} & 2\sigma_{gf} & E(r_g) & 1.0 & 0 & 1.0 & 0 & 0 & 0 & 0 \\
2\sigma_{hc} & 2\sigma_{hg} & 2\sigma_{hh} & 2\sigma_{hl} & 2\sigma_{hb} & 2\sigma_{hd} & 2\sigma_{hs} & 2\sigma_{hf} & E(r_h) & 1.0 & 0 & 0 & 1.0 & 0 & 0 & 0 \\
2\sigma_{lc} & 2\sigma_{lg} & 2\sigma_{lh} & 2\sigma_{ll} & 2\sigma_{lb} & 2\sigma_{ld} & 2\sigma_{ls} & 2\sigma_{lf} & E(r_l) & 1.0 & 0 & 0 & 0 & 0 & 0 & 0 \\
2\sigma_{bc} & 2\sigma_{bg} & 2\sigma_{bh} & 2\sigma_{bl} & 2\sigma_{bb} & 2\sigma_{bd} & 2\sigma_{bs} & 2\sigma_{bf} & E(r_b) & 1.0 & 0 & 0 & 0 & 1.0 & 0 & 0 \\
2\sigma_{dc} & 2\sigma_{dg} & 2\sigma_{dh} & 2\sigma_{dl} & 2\sigma_{db} & 2\sigma_{dd} & 2\sigma_{ds} & 2\sigma_{df} & E(r_d) & 1.0 & 0 & 0 & 0 & 0 & -1.0 & 0 \\
2\sigma_{sc} & 2\sigma_{sg} & 2\sigma_{sh} & 2\sigma_{sl} & 2\sigma_{sb} & 2\sigma_{sd} & 2\sigma_{ss} & 2\sigma_{sf} & E(r_s) & 1.0 & 0 & 0 & 0 & 0 & 0 & -1.0 \\
2\sigma_{fc} & 2\sigma_{fg} & 2\sigma_{fh} & 2\sigma_{fl} & 2\sigma_{fb} & 2\sigma_{fd} & 2\sigma_{fs} & 2\sigma_{ff} & E(r_f) & 1.0 & 0 & 0 & 0 & 0 & 0 & 0 \\
E(r_c) & E(r_g) & E(r_h) & E(r_l) & E(r_b) & E(r_d) & E(r_s) & E(r_f) & 0 & 0 & 0 & 0 & 0 & 0 & 0 & 0 \\
1.0 & 1.0 & 1.0 & 1.0 & 1.0 & 1.0 & 1.0 & 1.0 & 0 & 0 & 0 & 0 & 0 & 0 & 0 & 0 \\
1.0 & 0 & 0 & 0 & 0 & 0 & 0 & 0 & 0 & 0 & 0 & 0 & 0 & 0 & 0 & 0 \\
0 & 1.0 & 0 & 0 & 0 & 0 & 0 & 0 & 0 & 0 & 0 & 0 & 0 & 0 & 0 & 0 \\
0 & 0 & 1.0 & 0 & 0 & 0 & 0 & 0 & 0 & 0 & 0 & 0 & 0 & 0 & 0 & 0 \\
0 & 0 & 0 & 0 & 1.0 & 0 & 0 & 0 & 0 & 0 & 0 & 0 & 0 & 0 & 0 & 0 \\
0 & 0 & 0 & 0 & 0 & -1.0 & 0 & 0 & 0 & 0 & 0 & 0 & 0 & 0 & 0 & 0 \\
0 & 0 & 0 & 0 & 0 & 0 & -1.0 & 0 & 0 & 0 & 0 & 0 & 0 & 0 & 0 & 0
\end{bmatrix}
\begin{bmatrix}
x_c \\ x_g \\ x_h \\ x_l \\ x_b \\ x_d \\ x_s \\ x_f \\ \lambda_1 \\ \lambda_2 \\ \lambda_3 \\ \lambda_4 \\ \lambda_5 \\ \lambda_6 \\ \lambda_7 \\ \lambda_8
\end{bmatrix}
=
\begin{bmatrix}
0 \\ 0 \\ 0 \\ 0 \\ 0 \\ 0 \\ 0 \\ 0 \\ E(r_e^*) \\ 1.0 \\ 1.8 \\ 2.9 \\ 1.5 \\ 3.3 \\ 4.7 \\ 2.3
\end{bmatrix}
$$

315

var $(r_e)$ by 8.6183, *ceteris paribus*. This decrease in var $(r_e)$ converts to a decrease of about 2.94 in the standard deviation. Referring to Fig. 13.2, a decrease of 2.94 in risk implies a decrease in the average bank's return on equity of about two percentage points; this is the cost of additional liquidity.

### Appendix 13B
### Quadratic Programming Formulation
### for Analyzing Assets and Liabilities

The purpose of this appendix is to show how to formulate the type of quadratic programming (QP) problem associated with portfolio analysis of both assets and liabilities simultaneously (as discussed in Chapter XIII, for example). A more intricate QP formulation is required to include liabilities in the analysis than is necessary to analyze only assets.

Portfolio analysis problems that involve both assets and liabilities can be solved most expeditiously with a computer program to do quadratic programming (QP) because the QP algorithm can handle *inequality* constraints. The mathematical portfolio analysis techniques presented in Appendix 13A and also in the first three sections of Chapter VI can include *equality* constraints by using Lagrangian multipliers. However, the mathematical analysis cannot handle the inequality constraints which are essential for some problem formulations. See inequalities (13.3) and (13.4) for an example of the inequality constraints that were needed to analyze the bank problem explained in the chapter.

The root of the problem in formulating the QP is a contradiction between the following two facts:

Fact One: The weights of assets must be constrained to be nonnegative, $x_{\text{assets}} \geq 0$, while the weights of the liability items are defined to be nonpositive ($x_{\text{liability}} \leq 0$) in order to maintain the balance sheet identity expressed in equation (13.5).

Fact Two: The QP algorithm requires that all weights be nonnegative. That is, $x_i > 0$ for all $i$ regardless of whether the $i$th balance sheet item is an asset or a liability item.

This appendix will show how to include liabilities (defined as $x_i \leq 0$) and, at the same time, not violate the QP requirement that all weights be nonnegative ($x_i \geq 0$). The problem is solved by changing the signs on the liabilities coefficients appropriately. The key to solving this contradiction and obtaining solutions to the QP problem is to realize that for liabilities the weights themselves need not be negative in sign, only the *product* of liability weights and their multiplicative factors must be negative. The details of this formulation are explicated below.

### 13B.1 Reformulating the Portfolio's Average Return

The weighted average rate of return on equity for a portfolio containing $A$ assets and $L$ liabilities is defined in equation (13B.1).

$$E(r_e) = \sum_{i=1}^{A} x_i E(r_i) + \sum_{i=1}^{L} x_i(-1.0)E(r_i) \qquad (13B.1)$$

$$= \sum_{i=1}^{A=5} x_i E(r_i) - \sum_{i=1}^{L=3} x_i E(r_i), \qquad (13B.1a)$$

where $\sum_{i=1}^{A} x_i + \sum_{i=1}^{L} x_i = 1.0$. Note the negative unitary factor in the weighted-average rate of cost of the liabilities shown in equation (13B.1). This negative one causes the products of the liabilities weights times their expected rates of cost to be negative even though the liabilities weights are positive. This is all that is required to solve the QP problem. That is, the quantity $x_i E(r_i)$ must be negative for every liability and positive for every asset. Furthermore, the balance sheet identity must not be violated; it is shown as equation series (13B.2).

$$\sum_{i=1}^{A+L} x_i = 1.0 = x_e, \qquad (13B.2)$$

$$\sum_{i=1}^{A} x_i + \sum_{i=1}^{L} x_i = 1.0 = x_e, \qquad (13B.2a)$$

$$\sum_{i=1}^{A} x_i = \sum_{i=1}^{L} x_i + 1.0. \qquad (13B.2b)$$

Equation (13B.1a) is the weighted average rate of return on equity for the bank problem discussed in the chapter. The negative unitary factor from equation (13B.1) is handled implicitly in equation (13B.1a) by simply multiplying it through the summation on the liabilities. Thus, equations (13B.1) and (13B.1a) are mathematically equivalent.

Formulating a portfolio's variance–covariance matrix for risk analysis involving both assets and liabilities is more complex than formulating the portfolio's average return equation.

### 13B.2 Reformulating the Variance–Covariance Matrix

To add concreteness, this section will show how the 8 by 8 variance–covariance matrix for the bank problem discussed in the chapter was formulated for QP solution. The teaching points can be generalized by readers who comprehend this specific example.

The weighted-average variance of returns on equity for a portfolio of eight balance sheet items is defined in equations (13B.3), (13B.3a), and (13B.3b).

$$\text{var}(r_e) = \sum_{i=1}^{8} \sum_{j=1}^{8} x_i x_j \sigma_{ij} \tag{13B.3}$$

$$= X'cX, \tag{13B.3a}$$

where $X'$ is a $1 \times 8$ row vector of weights, $C$ is an $8 \times 8$ variance–covariance matrix, and $X$ is an $8 \times 1$ column vector. The compact matrix notation of equation (13B.3a) is expanded in Table 13B.1. The five asset and three liability bank analyzed in the chapter is represented by equation series (13B.3).

The first step in formulating a QP problem involving assets and liabilities is to write out the $n \times n$ variance–covariance matrix, $C$, and partition it as shown in Table 13B.1. The $8 \times 8$ covariance matrix is partitioned into four submatrices. The $5 \times 5$ submatrix of 5 assets covariances with other assets (including themselves, to include their variances) is denoted $C_{11}$. The $3 \times 3$ submatrix in the lower right-hand corner of the covariance matrix contains only liabilities and is represented by the symbol $C_{22}$. The two remaining submatrices are not square (that is, their number of rows and columns differ) and, more important, they contain only covariances of asset items with liability items. The $5 \times 3$ submatrix in the upper right-hand side is denoted $C_{12}$. Its mirror image, the $3 \times 5$ submatrix in the lower left-hand corner of the covariance matrix, is represented by the symbol $C_{21}$. These matrix relations are summarized below in matrix equation (13B.4).

$$C = \begin{bmatrix} C_{11} & C_{12} \\ C_{21} & C_{22} \end{bmatrix} \tag{13B.4}$$

Every weight in equation series (13B.3) must remain nonnegative in order to use the QP algorithm. Therefore, some elements in the covariance matrix which are associated with liabilities must have their signs changed in order to represent the financial economics of the problem realistically without violating the conditions required to use the essential QP algorithm. Stated simply, every element in the two submatrices containing the covariances between an asset and a liability item must have a negative value. Specifically, this means that every element in submatrices $C_{12}$ and $C_{21}$ must be a negative quantity (or zero, if that is appropriate). This is economically logical, because the returns flowing in from an asset item must covary negatively with the interest expenses flowing out to the owners of the firm's (or portfolio's) liabilities.

TABLE 13B.1   Variances and Covariances for an Eight-Item Balance Sheet, Equation (13B.3b)

$$\operatorname{var}(r_e) = \underbrace{\begin{bmatrix} x_c & x_g & x_h & x_l & x_b & x_d & x_s & x_f \end{bmatrix}}_{1 \times 8}$$

$$\underbrace{\left[\begin{array}{ccccc:ccc}
\sigma_{cc} & \sigma_{cg} & \sigma_{ch} & \sigma_{cl} & \sigma_{cb} & \sigma_{cd} & \sigma_{cs} & \sigma_{cf} \\
\sigma_{gc} & \sigma_{gg} & \sigma_{gh} & \sigma_{gl} & \sigma_{gb} & \sigma_{gd} & \sigma_{gs} & \sigma_{gf} \\
\sigma_{hc} & \sigma_{hg} & \sigma_{hh} & \sigma_{hl} & \sigma_{hb} & \sigma_{hd} & \sigma_{hs} & \sigma_{hf} \\
\sigma_{lc} & \sigma_{lg} & \sigma_{lh} & \sigma_{ll} & \sigma_{lb} & \sigma_{ld} & \sigma_{ls} & \sigma_{lf} \\
\sigma_{bc} & \sigma_{bg} & \sigma_{bh} & \sigma_{bl} & \sigma_{bb} & \sigma_{bd} & \sigma_{bs} & \sigma_{bf} \\
\hdashline
\sigma_{dc} & \sigma_{dg} & \sigma_{dh} & \sigma_{dl} & \sigma_{db} & \sigma_{dd} & \sigma_{ds} & \sigma_{df} \\
\sigma_{sc} & \sigma_{sg} & \sigma_{sh} & \sigma_{sl} & \sigma_{sb} & \sigma_{sd} & \sigma_{ss} & \sigma_{sf} \\
\sigma_{fc} & \sigma_{fg} & \sigma_{fh} & \sigma_{fl} & \sigma_{fb} & \sigma_{fd} & \sigma_{fs} & \sigma_{ff}
\end{array}\right]}_{8 \times 8}
\underbrace{\begin{bmatrix} x_c \\ x_g \\ x_h \\ x_l \\ x_b \\ x_d \\ x_s \\ x_f \end{bmatrix}}_{8 \times 1}$$

319

In contrast to submatrices $C_{12}$ and $C_{21}$, every element in submatrices $C_{11}$ and $C_{22}$ must be positive—this, too, is economically logical. The elements in submatrix $C_{11}$ should logically be positive because all the assets' inflows are positively correlated in the ex ante sense. (Only if an asset is unprofitable and ex post statistics are being used would a negative covariance enter submatrix $C_{11}$.) All elements in submatrix $C_{22}$ are also positive because (in addition to the fact that variances cannot be negative) the expense outflows associated with the various liabilities are all positively correlated (unless some creditor pays the portfolio to hold funds, an unlikely occurrence).

After the appropriate sign changes outlined above are completed, several related questions become relevant.

### 13B.3   Positive Semidefinite Considerations

All variance–covariance matrices are square and symmetric. And if the matrix has full rank (that is, the rank of the matrix equals the number of rows and/or columns) and contains only assets, it will also be a positive definite matrix. This is desirable because the QP algorithm can only handle problems with positive semidefinite matrices, and the positive definite form is a special case of the positive semidefinite matrix.

When working portfolio analysis problems with assets and liabilities and changing the signs of submatrices $C_{12}$ and $C_{21}$ in the variance–covariance matrix the question naturally arises about what these changes do to the QP solution. The answer to this question is simple matrix algebra. The sign changes to submatrices $C_{12}$ and $C_{21}$ are simply linear congruent transformations that do not alter the rank, symmetry, or positive semidefinite properties of the original variance–covariance matrix. Thus, the QP solution still exists and is unchanged by the sign-changing manipulations. Other problems may arise in formulating the QP, however.

### 13B.4   The Rank of the Covariance Matrix

If some row (column) of the variance–covariance matrix is linearly dependent on some other row (column), the rank of the matrix is less than the number of its rows or columns. In this case all but one of the dependent rows (columns) must be eliminated. Then the solution may proceed with a reduced matrix which has full rank.

In the bank problem of Chapter XIII, two rows and two columns of the $8 \times 8$ variance–covariance matrix were linearly dependent and had to be eliminated to solve the QP problem. Perusal of Table 13.2 shows that the variance of returns from cash was zero. And the variance of costs for demand deposits was zero, too. Thus, it appears that cash and demand deposits were not random variables, they are both constants. They could not be omitted from the analysis, however, because of their large financial proportions. Thus, the $8 \times 8$ covariance matrix had a rank of only 6 and may have to be reduced to solve the QP. There are two ways to solve the QP with a reduced covariance matrix and still have cash and/or demand deposits enter the solution. First, the reduced $6 \times 6$ covariance matrix can be solved while forcing cash and demand deposits into solution with constraints and also including any constant revenues and costs, respectively, in the portfolio's average return equation. Second, tiny positive values for the two items variances could be inserted in place of their zero variances and the QP could be solved with an $8 \times 8$ covariance matrix to obtain approximately optimal solutions.

In all QP computations a double-precision computer code is recommended. The cumulative errors can be substantial and lead to gross errors if only single-precision accuracy is employed.

## Selected References

Francis, J. C., "Portfolio Analysis of Asset and Liability Management in Small-, Medium- and Large-Sized Banks," *Journal of Monetary Economics*, April 1978.
The bank balance sheet analysis draws heavily from this paper. However, this paper delves into various aspects of banking analysis that were ignored in this chapter. Quadratic programming is used.

Parkin, Michael, "Discount House Portfolio and Debt Selection," *Review of Economic Studies*, October 1970, pp. 468–497.
Calculus is used to analyze the simple borrowing and investment portfolio management functions of a discount house. The analysis is in dollar dimensions and empirical tests support the results.

Pogue, G. A., "An Extension of the Markowitz Portfolio Selection Model to Include Variable Transactions Costs, Short Sales, Leverage Policies, and Taxes," *Journal of Finance*, December 1970, pp. 1005–1027.
A quadratic programming formulation to handle balance sheet analysis with allowances for brokerage commissions and taxes is suggested. Artificial variables are used to formulate the QP (in contrast to the Francis method).

Pyle, D. H., "On The Theory of Financial Intermediation," *Journal of Finance*, June 1971, pp. 737–747.
Calculus is used to analyze a bank with essentially one asset and one liability on its balance sheet. This paper explicates the nature of financial intermediation.

## Questions and Problems

1. Why should quadratic programming (QP) be used to analyze the variances and covariances for assets and liabilities rather than calculus? Could linear programming (LP) be used for risk–return analysis of a balance sheet as effectively as QP? Explain.

2. QP is a mathematical programming algorithm that minimizes a quadratic function subject to linear constraints. How can such a minimization procedure delineate portfolios that have the maximum rate of return at each level of risk?

3. Is it possible to determine how much return is lost and/or how much risk is associated with any given constraint imposed on a solution? (*Hint:* See Appendix 13A for a partial answer.)

4. Compare and contrast the calculus and the QP analysis of a balance sheet. What are the pros and cons of each type solution? (*Hint:* See Appendices 13A and 13B.)

5. Is there any truth to the statement that: "Liabilities are like negative assets"? Explain when this statement may or may not be true. If the signs of the risk and return statistics for some asset are reversed, will the calculus solution treat this asset as if it were a liability? Explain.

6. Will the level of the negative correlation coefficients between various asset and liability items on a balance sheet have any affect on which liabilities are optimal to finance a particular set of assets? Explain.

7. Do you expect that the optimal mix of liabilities to finance an efficient portfolio of low-risk assets will differ considerably from the optimal mix of liabilities to finance a portfolio of high-risk assets? Or will the optimal liability mix remain constant while only the debt/asset ratio (that is, the financial leverage) changes? Explain.

# Section Six

# NONSYMMETRIC DISTRIBUTIONS
# OF RETURNS

SECTION Six delves into an aspect of portfolio theory which has been expeditiously treated lightly in the preceding chapters—asymmetrical probability distributions. Three ways of dealing with this problem are explained. Chapter XIV suggests the various advantages of assuming security prices (or equivalently, the price relatives) are log-normally distributed. Markowitz's alternative risk surrogate, the semivariance, is analyzed in Chapter XV. Chapter XVI explains portfolio theory in three moments—skewness is explicitly brought into the analysis.

# NONSYMMETRIC DISTRIBUTIONS OF RETURNS

# Log-Normally Distributed Returns

If a market asset is purchased at a price of $p_0$ dollars and sold one period later for $p_1$ dollars, the noncompounded or discrete one-period rate of return from this asset is defined in equation (14.1).

$$r_1 = \frac{p_1 - p_0}{p_0}, \tag{14.1}$$

$$r_1 p_0 = p_1 - p_0,$$

$$p_0(1 + r_1) = p_1. \tag{14.1a}$$

Equation (14.1) was rewritten as equation (14.1a) to show that the discrete rate of return causes $p_0$ to grow to $p_1$ if $p_0$ is invested and *compounded once* during the investment period. If the interest rate is compounded more than once per period, $r_1$ in equation (14.1) is not the correct rate of return.

To continue the case above, assume that $p_{10}$ is invested at interest rate $r_{11}$ for one period and the interest rate was *compounded c times per period*; this case is represented by equations (14.2) through (14.2b). The symbol $n$ indicates the number of time periods.

$$p_{10}\left(1 + \frac{r_{11}}{c}\right)^{cn} = p_n \tag{14.2}$$

$$p_{10}\left[\left(1 + \frac{r_{11}}{c}\right)^{c/r_{11}}\right]^{r_{11}} = p_{11} \qquad \text{when } n = 1, \tag{14.2a}$$

$$p_{10}\left[\left(1 + \frac{1}{m}\right)^{m}\right]^{r_{11}} = p_{11} \qquad \text{where } m = c/r_{11}. \tag{14.2b}$$

327

If the cash flows in this second investment were identical to the cash flows in the first investment (that is, $p_0 = p_{10}$ and $p_1 = p_{11}$) and the lengths of time of the two investments were also indentical, then $r_{11} < r_1$ because of compounding $c$ times. The compounding of $c$ times per period (even though the periods are of equal length) allows the second investment to earn *interest on its own interest*; thus, a lower return ($r_{11} < r_1$) will yield as much terminal value, $p_1 = p_{11}$.

Finally, consider the extension of the two cases above when the interest is *continuously compounded*. In this case $c/r_{21} = m$ grows infinitely large and $1/m$ approaches zero, so equation (14.2b) may be rewritten equivalently as equation (14.3) for a single-period investment.

$$p_{20}e^{r_{21}} = p_{21}, \tag{14.3}$$

where

$$2.71828 = \lim_{m \to \infty} \left(1 + \frac{1}{m}\right)^m = e.$$

The three interest rates in equations (14.1), (14.2), and (14.3), denoted $r_1, r_{11}, r_{21}$, respectively, are all *approximately* equal.[1] But, the three rates are not exactly equal, $r_1 > r_{11} > r_{21}$. The rate decreases as $c$ increases. The easiest way to see the effects of continuous compounding is to take the natural (or naperian) logarithm, denoted ln, of equation (14.3) after it is rewritten as shown in equation (14.4). Dividing equation (14.3) by $p_{20}$ yields equation (14.4).

$$e^{r_{21}} = \frac{p_{21}}{p_{20}}. \tag{14.4}$$

Since the natural logarithm is the inverse of $e$, equation (14.4) may be equivalently rewritten as equation (14.4a).

$$r_{21} = \ln \frac{p_{21}}{p_{20}}. \tag{14.4a}$$

---

[1]In the interest of brevity and simplicity, the results for the $n$-period rate of return are not discussed here, although they follow directly. For example, if equation (14.1a) is generalized to the $n$-period case, it can be equivalently rewritten as equation (14.1b).

$$p_n = (1 + r_n)^n p_0, \tag{14.1b}$$

where $r_n$ is the compounded rate of return over $n$ periods. The continuous-time analog to equation (14.1a) is equation (14.3a). Of course, equations (14.3) and (14.3a) are identical when $n = 1$.

$$p_0 e^{rn} = p_n. \tag{14.3a}$$

Finally, the continuous-time $n$-period analogs to equations (14.4) and (14.4a) are equations (14.4') and (14.4a').

$$e^{rn} = \frac{p_n}{p_0} \tag{14.4'}$$

$$r = \frac{\ln (p_n/p_0)}{n} \tag{14.4a'}$$

To make the point clear, let $p_0 = p_{10} = p_{20} = \$100$, and let $p_1 = p_{11} = p_{21} = \$105$. According to equation (14.1), the \$100 had a one-period rate of return of $r_1 = 0.05 = 5.0$ percent. But, according to equation (14.4a), the one-period rate of return is $r_{21} = 0.04879 = 4.88$ percent. Continuous compounding is why the rate of return needed to make \$100 grow to \$105 in one period was less than 5.0 percent.

Henceforth, the convention of writing a dot over the rate of return is adopted to represent a continuously compounded rate of return. The general relationship between $r_1$ from equation (14.1) and $r_{21}$ from equation (14.4a) is shown in inequality (14.5).

$$\dot{r}_{21} \equiv \dot{r} \leq r_1. \tag{14.5}$$

### 14.1 Continuous-Time Versus Discrete-Time Models

The formula for the continuously compounded single-period rate of return may be written in several ways. For example, the logarithm of the price relative in equation (14.4a) may be rewritten equivalently as equation (14.4b) in terms of the link relative, $1 + r_t$, since $1 + r_t = p_t/p_{t-1}$ when dividends and interest are absent.

$$\dot{r}_t = \ln\left(\frac{p_t}{p_{t-1}}\right) = \ln(1 + r_t). \tag{14.4b}$$

Equation (14.4b) clearly shows the relationship between the noncompounded one-period rate of return, denoted $r_t$, and the continuously compounded return for the same investment, denoted $\dot{r}_t$. In studying stock price movements, researchers may study first differences, as shown in equation (14.4c), of daily stock price changes.[2] In any event, equation (14.4c) is another way to measure $\dot{r}_t$.

$$\dot{r}_t = \ln\left(\frac{p_t}{p_{t-1}}\right) = \ln(p_t) - \ln(p_{t-1}). \tag{14.4c}$$

Equation (14.4d) shows the logarithm of price plus cash dividend relative for a share of common stock's return.

$$\dot{r}_t = \ln\left(\frac{p_t + d_t}{p_{t-1}}\right). \tag{14.4d}$$

Equation (14.4d) is the continuous-time analog to the classic noncompounded (or discontinuous-time) single-period return shown in equation (1.1) on page 4.

---

[2]E. F. Fama, "The Behavior of Stock Market Prices," *Journal of Business*, Vol. 38, No. 1, 1965, pp. 34–105. Fama used equation (14.4c) of this study, as an example.

## TABLE 14.1 Finite-Time and Continuous-Time One-Period Returns Contrasted

| $r_t = (p_t/p_{t-1}) - 1.0$ | $\dot{r}_t = \ln (p_t/p_{t-1})$* | $\dot{r}_t - r_t$ |
|---|---|---|
| $-0.5 = -50.0\%$ | $-0.693 = -69.3\%$ | $0.193$ |
| $-0.4 = -40.0\%$ | $-0.510 = -51.0\%$ | $0.110$ |
| $-0.3 = -30.0\%$ | $-0.356 = -35.6\%$ | $0.056$ |
| $-0.2 = -20.0\%$ | $-0.223 = -22.3\%$ | $0.023$ |
| $-0.1 = -10.0\%$ | $-0.105 = -10.5\%$ | $0.005$ |
| $0$ | $0$ | $0$ |
| $0.1 = \quad 10.0\%$ | $0.095 = \quad 9.5\%$ | $-0.005$ |
| $0.2 = \quad 20.0\%$ | $0.182 = \quad 18.2\%$ | $-0.018$ |
| $0.3 = \quad 30.0\%$ | $0.262 = \quad 26.2\%$ | $-0.038$ |
| $0.4 = \quad 40.0\%$ | $0.336 = \quad 33.6\%$ | $-0.064$ |
| $0.5 = \quad 50.0\%$ | $0.405 = \quad 40.5\%$ | $-0.095$ |

*To see the relationship between $\dot{r}_t$ and the higher-order moments, the equation can be analyzed with a Taylor expansion.

$$\dot{r}_t = \ln (1 + r_t)$$
$$= r_t - \frac{r_t^2}{2} + \frac{r_t^3}{3} - \frac{r_t^4}{4} + \cdots + \frac{(-1)^{n-1}r_t^n}{n}.$$

The numerical differences between $\dot{r}_t$ and $r_t$ are small for returns with an absolute value of less than $0.25 = 25.0$ percent, as shown in Table 14.1. However, for large returns, the difference becomes increasingly large and the question arises: Which is the best measure of the rate of return? The main factors to consider in answering this question are (1) the mathematical economics, and (2) the econometrics. In terms of the mathematical economics, there are reasons to prefer the finitely compounded rate of return, and there are also reasons to prefer the continuously compounded return.

Several financial economists argue for using the continuous-time model for mathematical economics, for several reasons:

1. The continuous models are more amenable to solving multiperiod investment problems, where it is useful to use the geometric mean rate of return, because the logarithmic transformations expedite problem solving.

2. The Markowitz–Sharpe risk–return models are based on one-period returns, but they do not define the length of this "period." But by using continuously compounded returns, problems arising from the arbitrary length of time defined to be the relevant "period" are avoided because the compounding is continuous over all lengths of "periods."

3. It is easier to use calculus on continuous variables such as $\dot{r}_t$ than on the discretely compounded returns $r_t$ in some situations. The calculus can be used to obtain insights that discrete mathematics cannot.

4. The Markowitz–Sharpe models can be reformulated[3] and empirically

---

[3]E. J. Elton and M. J. Gruber, "Portfolio Theory When Investment Relatives Are Lognormally Distributed," *Journal of Finance*, June 1974.

tested in terms of continuous returns so that no major insights are lost, but some insights can be gained by using the continuous-time models.

This list of advantages to using $\dot{r}_t$ instead of $r_t$ is suggestive but not exhaustive. Merton has articulated the arguments in more detail elsewhere.[4] Of course, there are good reasons to resist continuous-time analysis.

Analysts who prefer to use the discrete-time model are also able to offer cogent arguments for their preference:

1. The pioneering models and studies about risk and return done by Markowitz, Sharpe, and others were all done with $r_t$ instead of $\dot{r}_t$ and it is more trouble than it is worth to try to change these original models to continuous time. That is, since the original models require less mathematical sophistication to use than continuous-time models, they should not be complicated (this is, of course, Occam's razor).

2. Market assets can only be traded at finite intervals, and thus continuous-time models are inappropriate and may even be misleading.

3. The $r_t$ definition of a one-period rate of return is intuitively more obvious than the $\dot{r}_t$ measure; furthermore, $r_t$ can be easily calculated while $\dot{r}_t$ requires a table of natural logarithms for evaluation.

4. Some of the multiperiod investment studies, utility analysis, and option pricing work that has been done with continuous-time variables could have been done more simply with finite-time models, and thus these studies represent arrogant displays of mathematical fetishes and poor scholarship.

The two preceding brief lists of arguments for using continuous time and for using discrete analysis are suggestive of polemics too complex to delve into here. Therefore, this discussion of which mode of analysis is better will move to firmer ground, where justifiable conclusions may be reached. In terms of econometric considerations, it seems fairly clear that $\dot{r}_t$ is superior to $r_t$, as explained next.

### 14.2  The Log-Normal Distribution

Empirical research strongly suggests that the one-period rates of return with finite compounding are from positively skewed probability distributions. One reason for such skewness is that the finitely compounded rates of return are bounded below at $-100.0$ percent—a look at equation (1.1) will quickly reveal the existance of this lower bound.

$$r_t = \frac{(p_{t+1} - p_t) + d_t}{p_t} \geq -1.0 = -100.0 \ \% \qquad (1.1)$$

---

[4]R. C. Merton, "Theory of Finance from the Perspective of Continuous Time," *Journal of Financial and Quantitative Analysis*, November 1975, pp. 659–674.

The random variable $r_t$ must be greater than $-100$ percent because it is impossible to lose more than 100 percent of one's investment. However, capital gains yielding rates of return in excess of 100 percent are not uncommon, and they skew the frequency distribution positively. Even though this skewness diminishes with the length of the differencing interval (that is, the "period" used), positive skewness is still found in returns measured over periods as short as a month for both individual stocks and mutual fund portfolios.[5]

When a probability distribution or a frequency distribution is positively skewed, its mean (that is, its mathematical expectation) is larger than its median, and its median is larger than its mode. But it is not known which of these three measures of central tendency investors use in forming their expectations of the central or most likely rate of return. As a result, both the mean and variance statistics on which portfolio theory is based may be biased. To see this possible bias, let $E(r)$ denote the mean return and let $M$ denote the mode (or median) rate of return. If investors perceive $M$ to be the central or most likely rate of return, so that they base their investment decisions on $M$ instead of $E(r)$, then the difference $[E(r) - M]$ measures bias. This bias affects the mean-squared error (MSE):

$$\text{MSE } (r) = E(r - M)^2 \tag{14.6}$$
$$= E\{[r - E(r)] - [M - E(r)]\}^2$$
$$= E\{[r - E(r)]^2\} + [M - E(r)]^2$$
$$= \text{var } (r) + [M - E(r)]^2 \tag{14.6a}$$
$$= \text{var } (r) + \text{bias}^2. \tag{14.6b}$$

Equations (14.6a) and (14.6b) show that the second statistical moment, var $(r)$, differs from the mean-squared errors around $M$. It is possible that skewness causes such bias by causing investors to focus on $M$ instead of $E(r)$.

It also can be shown that even if $E(r)$ is the measure of central tendency used by investors, skewness will nevertheless cause the alpha and beta statistics in the single-index market model, equation (4.4), to be biased and inconsistent.[6] The problem is that portfolio theory and ordinary least-squares (OLS) regression both consider only the first two statistical moments. As result, skewness causes biases that depreciate the value of portfolio theory and OLS regression statistics.

Luckily, the skewness can be reduced and even eliminated from many prob-

---

[5]J. C. Francis, "Skewness and Investors' Decisions," *Journal of Financial and Quantitative Analysis*, March 1975, pp. 163–172. Also see E. F. Fama, *Foundations of Finance* (New York: Basic Books, Inc., 1976), p. 37.

[6]Jan Kmenta, *Elements of Econometrics*, (New York: Macmillan Publishing Co., Inc., 1971), pp. 400–402.

ability distributions by transforming the finitely compounded rate of return from equation (1.1) to the continuously compounded rate of return, as shown in equation (14.4b).

$$\dot{r}_t = \ln\,(1 + r_t).\qquad\qquad (14.4\mathrm{b})$$

This logarithmic transformation "pulls in" the skewed positive tail of the distribution of $r$ and extends its truncated negative tail to minus infinity to create a more symmetrical (and hopefully more nearly normal) distribution, as shown in Fig. 14.1. The skewed distribution of finitely compounded returns is called a *log-normal distribution*; it has a mean of $E(r)$ and a standard deviation of $\sigma$ and is denoted $\Lambda(r\,|\,E(r),\sigma)$. The symmetric *normal distribution* of continuous-time returns has a mean of $E(\dot{r})$ and a standard deviation of $\dot{\sigma}$ and is denoted $N(\dot{r}\,|\,E(\dot{r}),\dot{\sigma})$.

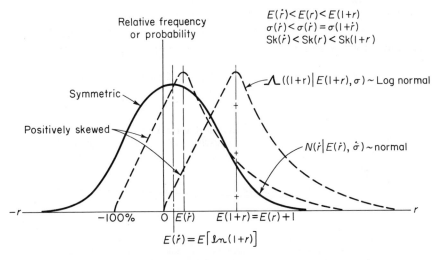

Figure 14.1. Relationships Between Normally Distributed $\dot{r} = \ln (1 + r)$ and Log-Normally Distributed $(1 + r)$ and the Distribution of One-Period Returns Compounded Finitely, $r$

Unity is added to the noncompounded time return to create a nonnegative link relative, $1 + r_t \geq 0$, because the logarithm of a negative number is undefined. The mathematical relationships between the log-normal and normal probability distributions, means, variance, coefficients of variation, and raw third and fourth statistical moments are shown in equations (14.7), (14.8), (14.9), (14.10), (14.11), and (14.12), respectively.[7]

---

[7] J. Aitchison and J. A. C. Brown, *The Lognormal Distribution*, (New York: Cambridge University Press, 1973), p. 8. This monograph stresses the use of the log-normal distribution in economic applications. However, portfolio analysis is not mentioned in the book.

$$P(r_0 \leq r) = \Lambda(r) = N[\ln (1 + r)] = P(\dot{r}_0 \leq \dot{r}), \qquad (14.7)$$

$$E(1 + r) = e^{E(\dot{r}) + 0.5\dot{\sigma}^2}, \qquad (14.8)$$

$$\text{var } (1 + r) = e^{2E(\dot{r}) + \dot{\sigma}^2}(e^{\dot{\sigma}^2} - 1) \qquad (14.9)$$

$$= [E(1 + r)]^2 c^2, \qquad (14.9a)$$

where

$$c^2 = \sqrt{e^{\dot{\sigma}^2} - 1} = (\text{coefficient of variation})^2, \qquad (14.10)$$

$$\text{Mom3 } (1 + r) = [E(1 + r)]^3(c^6 + 3c^4), \qquad (14.11)$$

$$\text{Mom4 } (1 + r) = [E(1 + r)]^4(c^{12} + 6c^{10} + 15c^8$$

$$+ 16c^6 + 3c^4), \qquad (14.12)$$

where Mom3 $(1 + r)$ denotes the third statistical moment and Mom4 $(1 + r)$ represents the fourth statistical moment.

Table 14.2 shows empirical statistics averaged over 100 mutual funds. The funds' returns were measured over the 108 months from January 1960 to December 1968 using monthly, quarterly, and annual differencing intervals.

TABLE 14.2　Statistics for $r$ and $\dot{r}$ Averaged Over Identical Samples of 100 Mutual Funds

| Statistic | Monthly | Quarterly | Annual |
|---|---|---|---|
| Noncompounded Returns, $r$ | | | |
| Mean, $E(1 + r) - 1$ | 0.0064 | 0.018 | 0.076 |
| Var $(1 + r) = $ var $(r)$ | 0.002 | 0.007 | 0.023 |
| Skewness† | 0.27* | 0.82 | 2.00 |
| Continuously Compounded Returns, $\dot{r} = \ln (1 + r)$ | | | |
| Mean, $E(\dot{r})$ | 0.0055 | 0.015 | 0.062 |
| Var $(\dot{r})$ | 0.002 | 0.007 | 0.022 |
| Skewness | 0.011 | 0.500 | 1.428 |

†The asterisk after a skewness statistic indicates that it is not significantly greater than zero at the 0.10 level of significance, using a skewness significance test published by E. S. Pearson, "A Further Development of the Tests of Normality," *Biometrika*, Vol. 22, pp. 239ff. The same test was published in two other sources: E. S. Pearson and H. O. Hartley, *Biometrika Tables for Statisticians*, Vol. I (Cambridge, England: Cambridge University Press, 1954), p. 183; and F. E. Croxton and D. J. Cowden, *Applied General Statistics*, (Englewood Cliffs, N.J.: Prentice-Hall, Inc., 1955), pp. 231, 720–721, 764.

The quarterly returns, denoted qr, were derived from monthly returns denoted mr as follows: $\text{qr} = [(1 + \text{mr}_1)(1 + \text{mr}_2)(1 + \text{mr}_3) - 1]$. The annual returns were derived similarly from four quarterly link relatives. The continuously compounded returns over each differencing interval were obtained by taking logarithms after the aforementioned link relatives were multiplied together to form quarterly and annual returns. Generally speaking, the empirical statistics confirm the relationships shown graphically in Fig. 14.1 and mathematically in equations (14.8), (14.9), (14.10), and (14.11). The distribution of $\dot{r}$ has less mean, variance, and, most important, less skewness than the distribution of $r$ for the same sample. Table 14.2 contains similar comparative statistics averaged over 600 NYSE stocks (from the CRSP tape) during the decade from 1962 to 1971 inclusive.[8]

The empirical statistics in Tables 14.2 and 14.3 tend to align with the mathematical relationships suggested in equations (14.7), (14.8), (14.9), (14.10), and (14.11). These statistics document the existence of positive skewness, on average. Transforming the noncompounded returns to continuously compounded returns greatly reduces the skewness, especially in the individual

TABLE 14.3   Statistics for $r$ and $\dot{r}$ Averaged Over Identical Samples of 600 Common Stocks

| Statistic | Monthly | Quarterly | Annual |
|---|---|---|---|
| Noncompounded Returns, $r$ | | | |
| Mean, $E(1 + r) - 1$ | 0.009 | 0.028 | 0.118 |
| Var $(1 + r) =$ var $(r)$ | 0.008 | 0.025 | 0.131 |
| Skewness | 0.738 | 0.793 | 1.852 |
| Continuously Compounded Returns, $\dot{r} = \ln (1 + r)$ | | | |
| Mean, $E(\dot{r})$ | 0.005 | 0.016 | 0.063 |
| Var $(\dot{r})$ | 0.007 | 0.024 | 0.089 |
| Skewness† | 0.195* | 0.011* | 0.955 |

†The asterisk after a skewness statistic indicates that it is not significantly greater than zero at the 0.10 level of significance, using a skewness significance test published by E. S. Pearson, "A Further Development of the Tests of Normality," *Biometrika*, Vol. 22, pp. 239ff. The same test was published in two other sources: E. S. Pearson and H. O. Hartley, *Biometrika Tables for Statisticians*, Vol. I (Cambridge, England: Cambridge University Press, 1954), p. 183; and F. E. Croxton and D. J. Cowden, *Applied General Statistics*, (Englewood Cliffs, N.J.: Prentice-Hall, Inc., 1955), pp. 231, 720–721, 764.

---

[8]The common stock sampling distributions of 600 observations for each statistic contained more sampling variance than did the mutual fund data; as a result, the common stock statistics are less efficient estimates. Nevertheless, all the relationships between the statistics for different differencing intervals are as suggested by the central limit theorem. That is, if $E(r_1)$ denotes the one-month expected return, then the three-month expected return is expected to be $E(r_3) = 3E(r_1)$. Likewise, if the variance of monthly returns is var $(r_1)$, then the quarterly variance is expected to be var $(r_3) = 3$ var $(r_1)$, and the variance of the annual returns should be var $(r_{12}) = 12$ var $(r_1)$ if the returns are serially independent (as suggested by the random walk model). The returns of many securities are not serially independent and thus their variances are proportional to the differencing interval. However, the returns of individual securities must be analyzed to discover the serial correlation that causes this result. Evidence which shows how the serial correlation affects the individual securities returns was published independently and reached similar conclusions: R. A. Schwartz and D. K. Whitcomb, "The Time-Variance Relationship: Evidence on the Autocorrelation in Common Stock Returns," *Journal of Finance*, March 1977, pp. 41–56.

common stocks. However, for returns calculated over differencing intervals of a quarter of a year or more, the skewness is still notably present.[9] This evidence suggests using continuously compounded returns to calculate betas and other risk statistics for empirical work. The more nearly symmetric continuously compounded returns will yield more efficient statistics than the noncompounded returns, *ceteris paribus*.[10] However, beta coefficients can be estimated with discrete rates of return and mathematically converted to the betas that would have been obtained if continuously compounded rates of return had been used by using the relationship derived by Lee.[11]

Some analysts have been opposed to using the continuously compounded returns because the portfolios theory (which was originally developed with noncompounded returns) may suffer distortions when the returns are transformed. This fear is ungrounded. The economics embodied in the risk–return capital market theory is not distorted by transforming the returns.[12]

### 14.3  Portfolio Analysis in Continuous Time

There is a similarity between the portfolios in $[\sigma, E(1 + r)]$ space and the portfolios in $[\dot{\sigma}, E(\dot{r})]$ space, as indicated by equations (14.8) and (14.9). The basic risk–return formulas for noncompounded price relatives or link relative are listed below.

The expected one-period price relative for asset $i$ is

$$E(1 + r_i) = \frac{1}{T} \sum_{t=1}^{T} (1 + r_{it}), \qquad (14.13)$$

---

[9]Regressions relating mean returns to the second and third moments are biased by the positive skewness that emerges when the longer differencing intervals are used to calculate returns. In the long run it is almost a self-fulfilling prophesy that securities with positively skewed annual returns will also experience better multiyear returns. This is demonstrated by J. C. Francis, "Skewness and Investors' Decisions," *Journal of Financial and Quantitative Analysis*, March 1975, pp. 163–172.

[10]These conclusions were reached by M. F. M. Osborne, "Brownian Motion in the Stock Market," reprinted on pages 100–128 of *The Random Character of Stock Market Prices*, edited by Paul Cootner (Cambridge, Mass.: The MIT Press, 1964). Much of the foundations for today's efficient markets literature may be found in Cootner's book of readings. Other papers published in Cootner's book which develop the log-normal distribution are: M. G. Kendall, "The Analysis of Economic Time-Series—Part I: Prices," *Journal of the Royal Statistical Society*, Vol. 96, Part I, 1953, pp. 11–25; and A. B. Moore, "Some Characteristics of Changes in Common Stock Prices" (an abstract of Moore's doctoral dissertation is published on pages 139–161 of Cootner's book of readings).

[11]Cheng-Few Lee, "On the Relationship Between Systematic Risk and the Investment Horizon," *Journal of Financial and Quantitative Analysis*, December 1976, pp. 803–815.

[12]Cheng-Few Lee has also shown how to test empirically to see if the logarithmic transformation is an appropriate method for removing skewness: "Functional Form, Skewness Effect and the Risk–Return Relationship," *Journal of Financial and Quantitative Analysis*, March 1977.

where $T$ different outcomes are all equally likely to occur, so that the quantity $1/T$ is like a probability, and $(p_{it}/p_{i,t-1}) = (1 + r_{it})$ denotes the noncompounded one-period price relative or link relative for time period $t$. The portfolio's expected link relative is defined in equation (14.14).

$$E(1 + r_p) = \sum_{i=1}^{n} x_i E(1 + r_i) \qquad \text{for } \sum_{i=1}^{n} x_i = 1.0, \qquad (14.14)$$

where $x_i$ denotes the weight of the $i$th item in the portfolio. The total variability of return for the $i$th individual asset is measured with equation (2.2a).

$$\sigma_i^2 = \frac{1}{T} \sum_{t=1}^{T} [r_{it} - E(r_i)]^2 = \frac{1}{T} \sum_{t=1}^{T} [(1 + r_{it}) - E(1 + r_i)]^2. \qquad (2.2a)$$

The portfolio's risk over $N$ assets is obtained using equations (2.4) and (2.9) to combine the individual assets' risks using the standard variance–covariance matrix. Figure 14.2 shows two elliptical opportunity sets of risky investments in $[\sigma, E(1 + r)]$ space and $[\dot{\sigma}, E(\dot{r})]$ space which were calculated for the same set of hypothetical investment opportunities. The efficient frontier in $[\dot{\sigma}, E(\dot{r})]$ space is derived below.

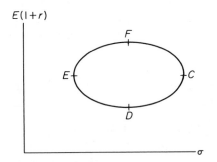

Figure 14.2A. Noncompounded Returns

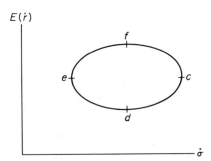

Figure 14.2B. Continuously Compounded Returns

Figure 14.2. Opportunity Sets in Risk-Return Space

A. Efficient Portfolios in $[\dot{\sigma}, E(\dot{r})]$ Space

Assuming that the continuously compounded rates of return are normally distributed allows these returns to be converted to the standard unit normal $z$ variable shown in equation (14.15).

$$z = \frac{\dot{r} - E(\dot{r})}{\dot{\sigma}}, \qquad (14.15)$$

where $z \sim N(0, 1) = N[E(z), \sigma_z]$. This conversion simplifies the derivation because the $z$ probability distribution is stable in $[z, f(z)]$ probability space and the statistical relationships are well known. These conventions imply that $\ln(1 + r) = E(\dot{r}) + z\dot{\sigma}$, and that the beginning wealth of $w_0$ is related to the end-of-period wealth of $w_1$, as shown in equation (14.16).

$$w_1 = w_0(1 + r) = w_0 e^{E(\dot{r}) + z\dot{\sigma}}. \qquad (14.16)$$

To maximize expected utility of terminal one-period wealth, the investor will maximize equation (14.17).

$$E[U(w_1)] = \int_{-\infty}^{+\infty} U[w_0(e^{E(r) + z\dot{\sigma}})] f(z) \, dz. \qquad (14.17)$$

Since $z = g[E(\dot{r}), \dot{\sigma}]$, as shown in equation (14.15), this implies that $E[U(w_1)] = f(z) = f\{g[E(\dot{r}), \dot{\sigma}]\}$. Verbally, this means that the portfolio owner's expected utility is a function of expected return, $E(\dot{r})$, and risk, $\dot{\sigma}$, measured in continuously compounded returns. The expected utility function, equation (14.17), is analyzed next to determine how risk and return affect expected utility.

The partial derivative of expected utility with respect to the expected return will show the effect of maximizing return in a given risk class. Using the chain rule to take the partial derivative of equation (14.17) yields equation (14.18).

$$\frac{\partial E[U(w_1)]}{\partial E(\dot{r})} = w_0 \int_{-\infty}^{+\infty} \frac{\partial U(w_1)}{\partial w_1} [e^{E(\dot{r}) + z\dot{\sigma}}] f(z) \, dz > 0. \qquad (14.18)$$

Equation (14.18) is positive since $\partial U(w_1)/\partial w_1$ is positive for investors who prefer more wealth to less wealth; the probabilities, $f(z)$, must be positive; and the number $e$ is positive, too. It can also be shown that the indifference map in $[\dot{\sigma}, E(\dot{r})]$ space is convex toward the $E(\dot{r})$ axis. All of this implies that risk-averse investors can maximize their expected utility (or their happiness from investing) by maximizing $E(\dot{r})$ in some $\dot{\sigma}$ risk class, or, conversely, minimizing $\dot{\sigma}$ at some level of $E(r)$.[13] Graphically speaking, this means that all the $[\dot{\sigma}, E(\dot{r})]$ portfolios in Fig. 14.2B along the curve through points efc may be efficient portfolios that maximize some risk-averse investors expected utility.

---

[13]This section draws heavily on E. J. Elton and M. J. Gruber, "Portfolio Theory When Investment Relatives Are Lognormally Distributed," *Journal of Finance*, September 1974, pp. 1265–1273. Readers who are interested in the log-normal distribution should consult the article for additional detail.

## B. The Correspondence Between $[\dot{\sigma}, E(\dot{r})$ and $[\sigma, E(r)]$ Portfolios

It is possible to show a one-to-one correspondence between the efficient portfolios in $[\sigma, E(1 + r)]$ space, shown in Fig. 14.2A, and the efficient portfolios in $[\dot{\sigma}, E(\dot{r})]$ space, shown in Fig. 14.2B. Equations (14.8) and (14.9) are the key to unraveling these portfolios' relationships. Consider the ratio of equation (14.9) and equation (14.8) squared, which is shown as the equation (14.19) series.

$$\frac{\sigma^2}{E(1+r)^2} = \frac{[e^{2E(\dot{r})+\dot{\sigma}^2}](e^{\dot{\sigma}^2}-1)}{[e^{E(\dot{r})+0.5\dot{\sigma}^2}]^2}. \tag{14.19}$$

Since $e^{2x+y} = (e^{x+0.5y})^2$, equation (14.19) can be rewritten:

$$\frac{\sigma^2}{E(1+r)^2} = \frac{[e^{(E(\dot{r})+0.5\dot{\sigma})^2}]^2(e^{\dot{\sigma}^2}-1)}{(e^{E(\dot{r})+0.5\dot{\sigma}^2})^2} \tag{14.19a}$$

$$= e^{\dot{\sigma}^2} - 1 \qquad \text{by cancellation.} \tag{14.19b}$$

By taking the square root of both sides of equation (14.19b) and rearranging, equation (14.19c) is obtained.

$$E(1+r) = \frac{\sigma}{\sqrt{e^{\dot{\sigma}^2}-1}} \tag{14.19c}$$

Equation (14.9c) represents a straight line from the origin in $[\sigma, E(1+r)]$ space which has a constant value of $\dot{\sigma}^2$ throughout its length. A family of such constant $\dot{\sigma}^2$ lines are illustrated in Fig. 14.3, to further analyze the investment opportunities in $[\sigma, E(1+r)]$ space from Fig. 14.2A.

Taking the logarithm of equation (14.8) and solving it for $E(r)$ yields equation (14.8a).

$$E(\dot{r}) = \ln[E(1+r)] - 0.5\dot{\sigma}^2, \tag{14.8a}$$

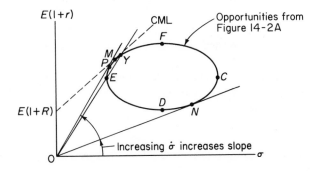

Figure 14.3. Analysis of $[\sigma, E(r)]$ Opportunities in Terms of $\dot{\sigma}$ and $E(\dot{r})$

Equation (14.8a) shows that for any given value of $\dot{\sigma}^2$, maximizing $E(\dot{r})$ is equivalent to maximizing $E(1 + r)$. This implies that moving out from the origin along any linear isoquant in Fig. 14.3 to the point on the opportunity set with the highest attainable value for either $E(1 + r)$ or $E(\dot{r})$ will trace out the unique $[\sigma, E(1 + r)]$ efficient portfolio which corresponds to one $[\dot{\sigma}, E(\dot{r})]$ efficient portfolio. For example, on the ray $OEY$ in Fig. 14.3, portfolio $Y$ has both the maximum $E(\dot{r})$ and the maximum $E(1 + r)$ along this isoquant. Tracing the maximum $E(\dot{r})$ portfolios at every value of $\dot{\sigma}$ in Fig. 14.3 reveals that the curve $PMYFCN$ is the $[\dot{\sigma}, E(\dot{r})]$ efficient frontier. The existence of this efficient frontier implies that var $(\dot{r})$ is a quantitative risk surrogate which may be used in place of the original var $(r) = $ var $(1 + r)$ Markowitz risk measure.

Several interesting observations may be drawn with respect to the $[\dot{\sigma}, E(\dot{r})]$ efficient frontier. First, note that efficient portfolio $f$ in Fig. 14.2B is the portfolio with the maximum expected return in the long run. That is, efficient portfolio $f$ has the maximum geometric mean rate of return, since $E[\ln (1 + r)] = E(\dot{r})$ is a geometric mean return. Second, note that the portion of the $[\sigma, E(1 + r)]$ efficient along the curve $EP$ in Fig. 14.3 is not $[\dot{\sigma}, E(\dot{r})]$ efficient. Other criteria have suggested that this lower portion of the traditional Markowitz-efficient portfolio is not desirable.[14] The $[\dot{\sigma}, E(\dot{r})]$ analysis tends to confirm the other conclusion that the minimum risk-efficient portfolios in $[\sigma, E(r)]$ space are undesirable. Finally, note that the market portfolio, denoted $M$ in Fig. 14.3, is a $[\dot{\sigma}, E(\dot{r})]$-efficient portfolio located in the low-risk portion of the efficient frontier.

### C. Computational Caveat

In the preceding section the $[\dot{\sigma}, E(\dot{r})]$-efficient frontier was delineated by first delineating the $[\sigma, E(1 + r)]$-efficient frontier. Then, the $[\dot{\sigma}, E(\dot{r})]$-efficient portfolios were found by using the relationships shown in equations (14.8) and (14.9). This indirect path to the $[\dot{\sigma}, E(\dot{r})]$-efficient frontier was employed because it is practically impossible to derive the $[\dot{\sigma}, E(\dot{r})]$-efficient frontier directly. That is, it is meaningless to calculate risk and return statistics by substituting $[\ln (1 + r)]$ in place of the noncompounded one-period returns in the expected return and variance formulas, equations (2.8) and (2.9). Since $[\ln (r_1) + \ln (r_2)] \neq [\ln (r_1 + r_2)]$, the summing processes involved in calculating the portfolio risk and return statistics will not lead to optimum (or even to unique) portfolios. Only by enumerating the infinite number of $[\dot{\sigma}, E(\dot{r})]$ portfolios would it be possible to find the efficient frontier in log space directly.

---

[14]See Section 16.1 in Chapter 16 regarding Baumol's expected gain–confidence limit criterion.

The most economical way to find the $[\dot{\sigma}, E(\dot{r})]$-efficient portfolios is to begin with one of the algorithms explained in Chapter VI and first derive the $[\sigma, E(1 + r)]$-efficient portfolios. Then equations (14.8) and (14.9) may be used to find the subset of the $[\sigma, E(1 + r)]$-efficient frontier which is also $[\dot{\sigma}, E(\dot{r})]$-efficient.

### 14.4  Conclusions

This chapter has shown how continuous-time rates of return obtained by transforming discrete-time returns can be used to reduce positive skewness in the probability distribution of discrete-time returns. More basically, the distribution of noncompounded returns becomes more positively skewed as the length of the differencing interval used to measure the returns increases. In contrast, the compounded returns maintained their normal distribution as the differencing interval was varied. It was shown how to extend portfolio analysis to the compounded returns and derive an efficient frontier in $[\dot{\sigma}, E(\dot{r})]$ space which is a subset of the $[\sigma, E(r)]$-efficient frontier.

Restating the efficient frontier in $[\dot{\sigma}, E(\dot{r})]$ space is worthwhile for several reasons. First, the $[\sigma, E(r)]$-efficient frontier contains some undesirable portfolios in its highest and lowest return sectors which are eliminated in the logarithmic transformation to the $[\dot{\sigma}, E(\dot{r})]$-efficient frontier. Second, the $[\sigma, E(r)]$-efficient frontier ignores the significant third moment. The $[\dot{\sigma}, E(\dot{r})]$ analysis, however, includes and eliminates the positive skewness of the discrete returns in deriving the continuous-time efficient frontier and is thus a superior decision-making process. Finally, the $[\dot{\sigma}, E(\dot{r})]$ analysis pinpoints the long-run wealth maximizing portfolio, whereas this maximum geometric mean return portfolio is not delineated by the $[\sigma, E(r)]$ analysis. The $[\dot{\sigma}, E(\dot{r})]$-efficient portfolio with the highest expected return is the optimal choice for investors wishing to maximize their terminal wealth.[15]

[15]E. J. Elton and M. J. Gruber, "On the Maximization of the Geometric Mean When Returns Are Lognormally Distributed," *Management Science*, December 1974, pp. 483–488.

## Selected References

Aitchison, J., and J. A. C. Brown, *The Lognormal Distribution: With Special Reference to Its Use in Economics*. Monograph 5 in Cambridge University's Applied Economics Series. Cambridge, England: Cambridge University Press, 1973.

This mathematical statistics book about the log-normal distribution contains important definitions, theorems, and examples of economics analysis applications. No examples of risk–return analysis are included, but the book is a valuable handbook for further research.

Elton, E. J., and M. J. Gruber, "Portfolio Theory When Investment Relatives are Lognormally Distributed," *Journal of Finance*, June 1974.

This paper uses algebra and statistics to show the interrelationship between the classic investment goals of maximizing terminal wealth (or, equivalently, the geometric mean return) and delineating the efficient frontier of investment portfolios when returns are log-normally distributed.

Osborne, M. F. M., "Brownian Motion in the Stock Market," *Operations Research*, Vol. 7, March–April 1959, pp. 145–173. Reprinted in *The Random Character of Stock Market Prices*, edited by Paul Cootner, The MIT Press, Cambridge, Mass., 1964.

This paper uses mathematical statistics to analyze the hypothesis that stock market returns are log-normally distributed. Some empirical data are examined. This paper showed the way for more recent studies using massive data.

## Questions and Problems

1. Consider the common rules below from the algebra of logarithms.

(a) The log of a product is the sum of the logs of the factors. More specifically, $\log (ab) = \log (a) + \log (b)$.

(b) The log of a number raised to an exponent equals the exponent times the log of the number, that is, $\log (a^b) = b \log (a)$.

(c) The log of the $n$th root of a product equals the sum of the logs of the factors in the product divided by $n$, for example, if $n = 3$, then $\log (\sqrt[3]{abc}) = \frac{1}{3}[\log (a) + \log (b) + \log (c)]$.

Can you think of a way to use each of these three rules from freshman college algebra to solve a finance problem that you may have to solve? Show examples of each and explain.

2. What are the lower and upper limits which the one-period noncompounded rate of return, $r_t$, may be expected to achieve in realistic financial applications? (*Hint:* The rate of return if you lose everything is the lower limit.) What are the lower and upper limits on the continuously compounded rate of return, $\dot{r}_t = \ln (1 + r_t)$, in realistic finance applications? Compare and contrast the ranges of the two one-period returns, $r_t$ and $\dot{r}_t$. Now can you explain why continuously compounded rates of return are less likely to be positively skewed than noncompounded rates of return?

3. Can logarithms be helpful in computing an investment's geometric mean rate of return? Explain.

4. Fundamental security analysts define the economic value of a share of stock as follows:

$$(\text{intrinsic value per share}) = (\text{earnings per share})$$
$$\times (\text{earnings multiplier}).$$

Can logarithms be useful in analyzing fundamental security analysis? How do you suspect the percentage changes in the three fundamental analysts' variables below are distributed? Explain why.

(a) Intrinsic value per share.

(b) Earnings per share.

(c) Earnings multiplier.

(*Hint:* See J. C. Francis, "Analysis of Equity Returns: A Survey with Extensions," *Journal of Economics and Business*, Spring-Summer 1977, Vol. 29, No. 3, pp. 181–192.)

5. The changes over time in a stock's price can be decomposed into smaller changes by using the following identity.

$$\frac{p_t}{p_1} \equiv \frac{p_t}{p_{t-1}} \frac{p_{t-1}}{p_{t-2}} \cdots \frac{p_3}{p_2} \frac{p_2}{p_1}.$$

Can you further decompose the identity above to facilitate the analysis of stock price changes?

6. Suppose that you took $n$ periods' prices for a security and calculated this asset's one-period rates of return two ways, compounded and noncompounded. Which series of returns will have the smaller expected return or average return? Why? Which series of returns will have the smaller variance of returns? Why? Which series will have less skewness? Why?

15151515151515151515151515151515151515151515151515151515151515151515
15151515151515151515151515151515151515151515151515151515151515151515
15151515151515151515151    15151    1515    515151515151    515151515151515151515
15151515151515151515    515    515151    151515151    5151515151515151515151515
151515151515151515151    1    1515151    51515151515    515151515151515151515151515
1515151515151515151515    5151515151    1515151    515151515151515151515151515
15151515151515151515151    151515151515    51515    5151515151515151515151515
1515151515151515151515    515151515151    151    .1515151515151515151515151515
15151515151515151515151    1    151515151515    5    515151515151515151515151515
1515151515151515151515    515    515151515151    15151515151515151515151515151515
15151515151515151515151    15151    151515151515    515151515151515151515151515151
15151515151515151515151515151515151515151515151515151515151515151515
15151515151515151515151515151515151515151515151515151515151515151515

# Semivariance Analysis

THE dictionary defines *risk* as being "the chance of injury, damage, or loss." Such financial losses could be equated with the disappointing outcomes in the left-hand tail of a probability distribution of one-period rates of return. Therefore, Markowitz reformulated his portfolio theory using only the disappointingly low returns to form a quantitative risk surrogate he called the *semivariance*.[1] The semivariance is calculated only with disappointingly low returns—the best investment outcomes are ignored. Surprisingly, however, when the probability distributions are symmetrically distributed (for example, normally), the implications of $[\sigma, E(r)]$ analysis are similar to the [semivariance, $E(r)$] results. In contrast, when the probability distributions are skewed, the results from using the semivariance diverges from the variance. This chapter presents the limited findings that are available about portfolio analysis with the semivariance.

## 15.1  Semivariance Defined

Letting the symbol $h$ stand for some constant reference point on the spectrum of possible one-period rates of return, defining $r_{it}^-$ to be a one-period rate of return from the $i$th asset in period $t$ which is less than the value of $h$ (that is, $r_{it}^- = r_{it}$ if $r_{it} < h$), and denoting the semivariance for the $i$th

---

[1]Harry M. Markowitz, *Portfolio Selection* (New York: John Wiley & Sons, Inc., 1959), Chap. 9.

asset as $s_i$ allows the semivariance to be defined various ways, as shown in equations (15.1), (15.1a), and (15.1b).

$$s_i = \frac{1}{N} \sum_{t=1}^{L} (r_{it}^- - h)^2 \tag{15.1}$$

$$= \frac{1}{N} \sum_{t=0}^{N} \{[\min (r_{it} - h), 0]\}^2, \tag{15.1a}$$

where $N$ represents the total number of returns and the symbol $L$ (presumably, $N \geq L$) represents the number of $r_{it}^-$ returns from asset $i$ (that is, low returns which are smaller than $h$). Or, in ex ante terms, equation (15.1b) defines the semivariance.[2]

$$s_i = E \{\min [(r_{it} - h), 0]\}^2. \tag{15.1b}$$

Equation (15.2) defines the semideviation, denoted $d_i$:

$$d_i = \sqrt{s_i}. \tag{15.2}$$

The riskless rate of return, $E(r_i)$, and zero are three commonly suggested values for $h$. Thus, the semivariance or the semideviation may measure the minimum acceptable rates of return for risky assets, $r_{it}^- = r_{it} < R$; or worse-than-expected returns, $r_{it}^- = r_{it} < E(r_i)$; or negative returns, $r_{it}^- = r_{it} < 0$. Or any arbitrary value of $h$ may be employed. Figure 15.1 illustrates the portion of an asset's probability distribution of single-period rates of return

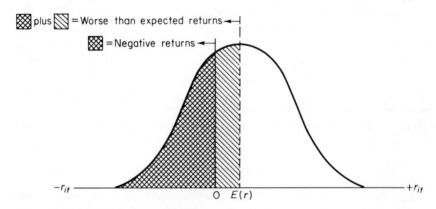

Figure 15.1. Probability Distribution Illustrating the Returns Used to Calculate Semivariance if $h$ Equals $E(r)$ or Zero

---

[2]For the continuous case, the semivariance is

$$s_i = \int_{-\infty}^{h} (r_i - h)^2 f(r_i)\, dr_i,$$

where $f(r_i)$ is a marginal probability distribution of returns for asset $i$.

which might be used to calculate its semivariance. Only the shaded left-hand portion of the distribution shown in Fig. 15.1 would be used in equation series (15.1) to calculate the semivariance.

Using the semivariance as a risk measure requires that the Markowitz efficient frontier be redefined to be:

1. Those assets (more specifically, the set of portfolios) that have the minimum semivariance (or semideviation) at each level of expected return, or conversely,
2. Those assets that have the maximum expected return at each level of risk (as measured by the semivariance or semideviation).

Figure 15.2 shows the Markowitz-efficient frontier in terms of the semideviation and expected return.

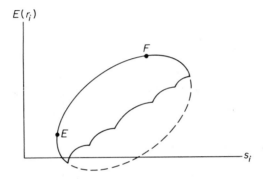

Figure 15.2. Efficient Frontier Is $[s, E(r)]$ Space

The type of single-period utility function that implies preference for $[s, E(r)]$ portfolios is analyzed in the following section.

### 15.2 Utility Theory

The more traditional Markowitz-efficient portfolios in $[\sigma, E(r)]$ space can be rationalized most easily in terms of the single-period utility-of-returns function shown in equation (15.3), if it is restricted to returns less than $(b/2c)$.

$$U(r) = br - cr^2 \qquad \text{for } r < b/2c. \tag{15.3}$$

The expected utility from this quadratic function is derived in equation series (15.4).

$$E[U(r)] = bE(r) - cE(r^2) \qquad \text{for } b > c > 0 \tag{15.4}$$
$$= bE(r) - c[E(r^2) + \text{var }(r)] \tag{15.4a}$$
$$= bE(r) - cE(r^2) - c \text{ var }(r) \tag{15.4b}$$
$$= f[E(r), \sigma], \qquad f_1 > 0, \quad f_2 < 0. \tag{15.4c}$$

The findings shown in equation series (15.4) were discussed in more detail in Chapter XI. They are summarized here merely to expedite comparison with the utility of semivariance analysis below.

Markowitz-efficient portfolios in $[s, E(r)]$ space can also be rationalized in terms of the single-period utility of returns function shown in equation (15.5).[3]

$$U(r) = br - c[\min{(r_{it} - h, 0)^2}] \qquad \text{for } c > 0. \tag{15.5}$$

Equation (15.5) is similar in some respects to the quadratic equation (15.3). Equation (15.5) is quadratic for returns below $h$ and linear in returns above $h$. Figure 15.3 compares the utility functions from equations (15.4) and (15.5) graphically.

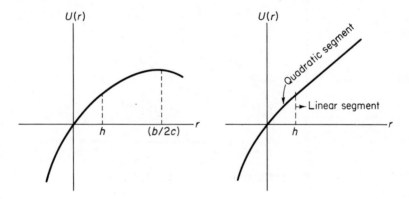

Figure 15.3. Comparison of Two Utility of Returns Functions

The expected value of equation (15.5) is analyzed in equation (15.6) series.

$$E[U(r)] = bE(r) - cE\{\min{[(r_{it} - c), 0]}\}^2 \tag{15.6}$$

$$= bE(r) - cs \tag{15.6a}$$

$$= g[E(r), s], \qquad g_1 > 0, \quad g_2 < 0, \tag{15.6b}$$

where

$$\frac{\partial E[U(r)]}{\partial E(r)} \equiv g_1 = b > 0, \tag{15.7}$$

$$\frac{\partial E[U(r)]}{\partial s} \equiv g_2 = -c < 0. \tag{15.8}$$

[3]J. C. T. Mao, "Models of Capital Budgeting, E-V Versus E-S," *Journal of Financial and Quantitative Analysis*, January 1970, pp. 657–675.

The effects that $E(r)$ and $s$ have on expected utility equation (15.6), as measured by partial derivatives (15.7) and (15.8), have the same signs that $E(r)$ and $\sigma$ have on expected utility in equations (15.4). This means that an investor's indifference curves in $[s, E(r)]$ space would be positively sloped and concave to the risk (measured on the $d$) axis. The numerical values of the semideviation and the standard-deviation risk measures would differ for almost all assets, $\sigma_i \neq s_i$. Nevertheless, the indifference maps in $[\sigma, E(r)]$ space and $[s, E(r)]$ could be similar.

It is difficult to assert generalities about investors' preferences for the efficient frontiers generated from a given group of assets if the efficient frontiers were done in terms of both $[\sigma, E(r)]$ and $[s, E(r)]$. If the utility function and the method of defining the efficient frontier were changed, it is most probable that the portfolio which maximized expected utility would change, too. However, cases may exist in which an investor with a given set of investment opportunities and a $f[\sigma, E(r)]$ expected utility function might select the same assets as another investor who had a $g[s, E(r)]$ expected utility function.[4]

Equations (15.6) and (15.7) and (15.8) rationalize the selection of Markowitz-efficient portfolios in $[s, E(r)]$ space to maximize expected utility. The following section discusses the derivation of the $[s, E(r)]$, or, equivalently, the $[d, E(r)]$-efficient frontier.

### 15.3 Portfolio Analysis with the Semivariance

The objective of portfolio analysis with the semivariance is to delineate the set of portfolios which have the minimum semivariance, denoted $s_p$, at each level of the portfolio's expected return, denoted $E(r_p)$, by varying the proportion of the $i$th investment, denoted $x_i$, in the portfolio without violating the balance sheet identity that the weights across all $n$ investments sum to unity.

The portfolio's expected return is simply the familiar weighted average return shown in equation (2.8).

$$E(r_p) = \sum_{i=1}^{N} x_i E(r_i). \tag{2.8}$$

The balance sheet identity which is always present in Markowitz portfolio analysis, equation (2.7), is

$$1.0 = \sum_{i=1}^{N} x_i. \tag{2.7}$$

---

[4]If the value of $h$ is identical to $E(r_i)$ and returns are symmetrically distributed, then $0.5\sigma_i^2 = s_i$ and the semivariance analysis yields the same results as the variance analysis: Markowitz, *Portfolio Selection*, p. 191.

The portfolio's semivariance, $s_p$, is defined in equation series (15.9).[5]

$$s_p = E\{\min [0, (r_p - h)]\}^2$$

$$= E\{\min [0, (\sum_{i=1}^{N} x_i r_i - h)]\}^2. \tag{15.9}$$

Hogan and Warren[6] have shown that quadratic programming can be used to delineate a convex set of $[s, E(r)]$-efficient portfolios under the following three conditions:

1. The variance of returns is finite.
2. The portfolio's semivariance, equation (15.9), is continuously differentiable in the weight decision variables ($x_i$ for all $i$).
3. The following first-order condition (namely, the gradient vector) is continuous in the weight decision variables.

$$\frac{\partial s_p}{\partial x_i} = 2E\{\min [0, (r_p - h)]\}.$$

These three conditions are met for many well-known probability distributions. So numerical solutions can be computed without problems, it appears.

Computation of the semivariance efficient frontiers does not revolve around a symmetric variance–covariance matrix, because the cosemivariance is not a symmetric statistic like the covariance. The cosemivariance is asymmetric (that is, $cs_{ij} \neq cs_{ji}$). Equation series (15.10) defines the cosemivariance, $cs_{ij}$, for a finite joint probability distribution of returns for the $i$th and $j$th assets.

$$cs_{ij} = E\{(r_{it} - h)\langle\min [0, (r_{jt} - h)]\rangle\} \tag{15.10}$$

$$= E\{(r_{it} - h)(r_{jt}^- - h)], \tag{15.10a}$$

where

$$r_{jt}^- = \begin{cases} r_{jt} & \text{if } r_{jt} < h \\ h & \text{if } r_{jt} \geq h. \end{cases}$$

Equations (15.10) and (15.10a) define the ex ante cosemivariance, while equations (15.10b) and (15.10c) define it in ex post terms.

$$cs_{ij} = \frac{1}{N} \sum_{t=1}^{L} \{(r_{it} - h)\langle\min [0, (r_{jt} - h)]\rangle\} \tag{15.10b}$$

$$= \frac{1}{N} \sum_{t=1}^{L} [(r_{it} - h)(r_{jt}^- - h)]. \tag{15.10c}$$

---

[5]For the continuous case, the portfolio's semivariance is defined as

$$s_p = \int_{-\infty}^{h} \{\min [0, (r_p - h)]\}^2 f(r_p) \, dr_p. \tag{15.9}$$

[6]W. W. Hogan and J. M. Warren, "Computation of the Efficient Boundary in the E-S Portfolio Selection Model," *Journal of Financial and Quantitative Analysis*, September 1972, p. 1883.

In words, the cosemivariance is the weighted average over all $N$ paired values of $r_{it}$ and $r_{jt}$ using only the paired values for which $r_{jt} < h$. The cosemivariance may be positive if the two series of returns, $r_{it}^-$ and $r_{jt}^-$, are positively correlated and some values of $r_{it}^-$ are not zero. The $cs_{ij}$ may be zero if $i$ and $j$ are independent, or if all the returns from the $i$th asset exceed the value of $h$. Finally, the $cs_{ij}$ can be negative if the returns $r_{it}^-$ and $r_{jt}^-$ move inversely and some values of $r_{it}^-$ are not zero. When $i = j$, the cosemivariance equals the semivariance, $cs_{ii} = s_i$. See Markowitz,[7] Hogan and Warren,[8] Ang,[9] and the references found therein for numerical examples of portfolio analysis with the semivariance.

The set of $[d, E(r)]$-efficient portfolios will be identical[10] to the set of $[\sigma, E(r)]$-efficient portfolios computed from the same investments if the following two conditions exist simultaneously:

1. The value of $h_i$ equals $E(r_i)$ for every probability distribution. That is, the first moment of each probability distribution is used as its own reference point in calculating the values of $(r_{it}^- - h_i)$ for $r_{it} < h_i = E(r_i)$.

2. All the probability distributions are perfectly symmetric, so that when the deviations from the mean are used the variances will differ from corresponding semivariances by a factor of 2.0.

There is some doubt about the second point, because the empirical skewness statistics in Tables 14.2 and 14.3 (pages 334–335) show that some skewness may exist. Some econometricians would argue that this skewness is sample-dependent and should be ignored because the unobservable skewness population parameters are zero. However, other econometricians point out that skewness cannot be whimsically ignored. Therefore, the question of whether to use the variance or the semivariance analysis must be considered.

Markowitz suggested the considerations of cost, convenience, familiarity, and the desirability of the portfolios as the criteria for selecting between the variance and the semivariance analysis.[11] However, with the advent of large high-speed digital computers, the first two considerations have paled into lesser significance. The third consideration, familiarity, is a temporary condition. A lack of familiarity with the semivariance can quickly be overcome by study. Therefore, the fourth consideration, the desirability of the portfolios, seems to be the crucial concern.

The desirability of the portfolios that can be obtained is of primary

[7]Markowitz, *Portfolio Selection*, Chap. 9.

[8]Hogan and Warren, "Computation of the Efficient Boundary in the E-S Portfolio Selection Model."

[9]J. S. Ang, "A Note on the E, SL Portfolio Selection Model," *Journal of Financial and Quantitative Analysis*, December 1975, pp. 849–857.

[10]Markowitz, *Portfolio Selection*, p. 191. See also T. J. Nantell and Barbara Price, "An Analytical Comparison of Variance and Semivariance Capital Market Theories," unpublished manuscript, 1977.

[11]Markowitz, *Portfolio Selection*, pp. 193–194.

importance in deciding whether or not to use the semivariance analysis. In this regard, various studies can be cited which suggest using the semi-variance.[12] However, if the probability distributions are sufficiently asymmetric to justify using the semivariance, it may be better to simply add skewness to the analysis and do portfolio analysis in three moments rather than use the semivariance. It may be advantageous to use three moments, because the semivariance ignores the information contained in the right-hand tails of the probability distributions. But portfolio analysis in three moments does not ignore any data points.

Portfolio analysis using the higher-order moments is examined in Chapter XVI. The next section of this chapter reviews the capital market theory implications of the semivariance analysis.

### 15.4  Capital Market Theory with the Semivariance

Hogan and Warren have shown that a capital market line in $[d, E(r)]$ space, denoted CMLd hereafter, can be derived.[13] Their derivation is similar to the mathematics in Appendix 8A and will not be reviewed here, to save space. Figure 15.4 illustrates the results graphically.

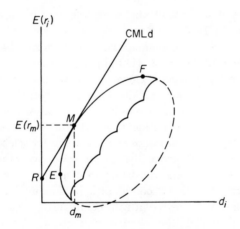

Figure 15.4.  CML in $[d, (Er)]$ Space

---

[12]A representative but not exhaustive list of references which consider various aspects about semivariance analysis include the following: J. P. Quirk and R. Saposnik, "Admissibility and Measurable Utility Functions," *Review of Economic Studies*, February 1962, pp. 140–146; R. O. Swalm, "Utility Theory Insights into Risk Taking," *Harvard Business Review*, November–December 1966, pp. 123–136; Mao, "Models of Capital Budgeting E-V Versus E-S."

[13]W. W. Hogan and J. M. Warren, "Toward the Development of an Equilibrium Capital-Market Model Based on Semivariance," *Journal of Financial and Quantitative Analysis*, January 1974, pp. 1–11.

The formula for the CMLd is shown in equation (15.11).

$$E(r_i) = R + \left[\frac{E(r_m) - R}{d_m}\right]d_i \qquad \text{the CMLd.} \qquad (15.11)$$

Equation (15.11) is an equilibrium portfolio pricing model in which the expected return from the $i$th dominant portfolio equals the riskless rate, $R$, plus a risk premium. This risk premium equals the product of the $i$th portfolio's semideviation, $d_i$, multiplied times the market price of risk, $[E(r_m) - R]/d_m$, in terms of the semideviation.

An asset pricing model for individual securities as well as portfolios which is analogous to the security market line (SML) in [cov $(r_i, r_m)$, $E(r_i)$] space is also implicit in semivariance analysis. The security market line in terms of the cosemivariance, denoted SMLcs, is defined by equation (15.12).

$$E(r_i) = h + \frac{E(r_m) - h}{s_m}cs_{im} \qquad \text{the SMLcs} \qquad (15.12)$$

$$= h + [E(r_m) - h]b_i^{cs} \qquad \text{the SMLb}^{cs}, \qquad (15.12a)$$

where $b_i^{cs} = (cs_{im}/s_m)$. The symbol $b_i^{cs}$ is the beta systematic risk coefficient associated with the $i$th asset's cosemivariance. Equations (15.12) and (15.12a) are depicted graphically in Fig. 15.5. The SMLcs and the SMLb$^{cs}$ are positive linear transformations of each other and are equivalent.[14] The

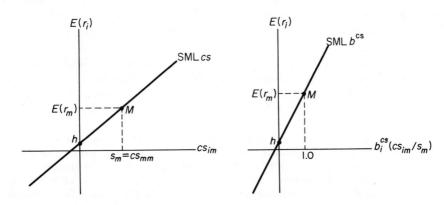

Figure 15.5A. The SMLcs          Figure 15.5B. The SMLb$^{cs}$

Figure 15.5. SML's from Semivariance Capital Market Theory

[14]Nantell and Price, "An Analytical Comparison of Variance and Semivariance Capital Market Theories." Nantell and Price show that the SMLb$_i^{cs}$ is identical to the classical SML derived by Sharpe when (1) returns are normally distributed, and (2) the riskless rate is used as the reference rate of return, that is, $h = R$.

systematic risk axis in Figs. 15.5A and 15.5B differ by the scale factor of $1/s_m$; otherwise, the two models are identical.[15]

All assets lying below the SMLcs and the SMLb$^{cs}$ are overpriced. Their expected returns are too low to adequately compensate investors for assuming the undiversifiable cosemivariance risk they entail. As a result, lack of demand for those assets lying below the SMLcs and SMLb$^{cs}$ should cause their market prices to fall and their expected returns to rise, as shown by the arrows in equation (15.13).

$$E(\overset{\uparrow}{r}) = \frac{E(\text{capital gain or loss} + \text{cash dividend})}{\downarrow \text{ purchase price}}. \qquad (15.13)$$

An opposite but symmetric line of reasoning will explain why those assets which plot above the SMLcs and SMLb$^{cs}$ are underpriced in relation to their systematic cosemivariance risk.

In general, the semivariance capital market theory implications are analogous to the mean–variance capital market theory of Chapter VIII.[16]

### 15.5  Conclusions About Semivariance Analysis

The semivariance is a quantitative risk surrogate which is similar to the variance. Similarly, the cosemivariance is analogous to the covariance of returns. However, it has not been possible to discern the superiority of one type of risk surrogate over another on behavioral grounds (1) because of their similarities, and (2) because risk aversion is personal, subjective, and therefore, impossible to measure definitively. As a result, financial analysts have done more economic research than behavioral research on the semivariance.

The economic implications of semivariance analysis are similar to those of the classical mean–variance theory. In fact, preliminary research suggests that there is a one-to-one correspondence between the efficient portfolios and asset prices implied by the different analyses based on the semivariance and

---

[15]Ali Jahankhani, "E-V and E-S Capital Asset Pricing Models: Some Empirical Tests," *Journal of Financial and Quantitative Analysis*, November 1976, pp. 513–528. Jahankhani has published empirical evidence which shows that the asset pricing implications of the capital market theory reformulated in terms of semivariance are similar to the classical $[\sigma, E(r)]$ capital market theory. These findings support the analysis of Nantell and Price (see footnote 14).

[16]Stone has written a monograph and a paper in which he shows that the semivariance, the standard deviation, the mean absolute deviation, utility theory, and other forms of risk analysis are special cases of a general three-parameter risk measure which he has devised. For a brief summary, see B. K. Stone, "A General Class of Three-Parameter Risk Measures," *Journal of Finance*, June 1973, pp. 675–685. The monograph by Stone is entitled *Risk, Return and Equilibrium: A General Single-Period Theory of Asset Selection and Capital Market Equilibrium* (Cambridge, Mass.: The MIT Press, 1970).

the variance if the probability distributions are symmetric. Since the empirical evidence that has been published (for example, see Chapter XIV) suggests that the discrete one-period returns calculated over short differencing intervals (of a month or less, for example) and the continuously compounded returns may be normally distributed, this has caused semivariance research to progress more slowly than research on the classic variance models.[17]

Additional research is needed to clarify the role of semivariance analysis. Mathematical analysis is needed to delineate differences between the analogous semivariance and variance economic models. Empirical research is needed to document the existence of asymmetric probability distributions of basic financial random variables which cannot be readily transformed into symmetrically distributed variables. Research is needed to compare the results of semivariance analysis with portfolio analysis models based on the first three moments (that is, mean–variance–skewness models). Portfolio analysis in three moments wastes less information than semivariance analysis, and thus may yield more optimal solutions in cases where the probability distributions are asymmetric.

### Appendix 15A
### Some Semivariance Mathematics

The purpose of this appendix is to present a few mathematical relationships that may be useful to portfolio analysts using the semivariance. Section 15A.1 shows that the semivariance can be stated as the sum of its related cosemivariances. Section 15A.2 compares and contrasts the variance–covariance matrix for a two-asset problem with the analogous semivariance sum.

### 15A.1 On the Sums of Cosemivariances

Equation (15A.1) shows that the semivariance of portfolio $p$ equals the weighted average of the $p$th asset's cosemivariance summed over $i = 1$, $2, \ldots, N$ assets.

$$s_p = \sum_{i=1}^{N} x_i c s_{ip}. \tag{15A.1}$$

Proof of equation (15A.1) is omitted to save space.[1]

---

[17]E. F. Fama, who proposed the Paretian distribution, later suggested using the normal distribution. See Chapters 1, 2, and 3 of Fama's book *Foundations of Finance* (New York: Basic Books, Inc., 1976).

[1]For a proof, see Appendix A of T. J. Nantell and Barbara Price, "An Analytical Comparison of Variance and Semivariance Capital Market Theories," unpublished manuscript, 1977.

## 15A.2  Decomposing Portfolio Variances and Semivariances

Equation (2.9) shows how a portfolio's variance can be decomposed into a weighted average of the variances and covariances over all assets in that portfolio for the case of returns which are finitely distributed. The equations below derive a similar relationship for returns that are continuously distributed.[2] Consider a two-asset portfolio with returns $r_{pt} = x_1 r_{1t} + x_2 r_{2t}$ which are distributed according to the joint probability distribution, denoted $f(r_1, r_2) = f(r_p)$, or, more briefly, $f_j$.

$$
\begin{aligned}
\sigma_p^2 &= \int_{-\infty}^{+\infty} (r_p - \bar{r}_p)^2 f(r_p) \, dr_p \\
&= \int_{-\infty}^{+\infty} (r_1 x_1 + x_2 r_2 - \bar{r}_p)^2 f(r_p) \, dr_p \\
&= \int_{-\infty}^{+\infty} \int_{-\infty}^{+\infty} (x_1 r_1 + x_2 r_2 - \bar{r}_p)^2 f_j(r_1, r_2) \, dr_2 \, dr_1 \\
&= \int_{-\infty}^{+\infty} \int_{-\infty}^{+\infty} [x_1(r_1 - \bar{r}_1) + x_2(r_2 - \bar{r}_2)]^2 f_j \, dr_2 \, dr_1 \\
&= \int_{-\infty}^{+\infty} \int_{-\infty}^{+\infty} [x_1^2(r_1 - \bar{r}_1)^2 + 2 x_1 x_2 (r_1 - \bar{r}_1)(r_2 - \bar{r}_2) \\
&\quad + x_2^2(r_2 - \bar{r}_2)]^2 f_j \, dr_2 \, dr_1 \\
&= x_1^2 \int_{-\infty}^{+\infty} \int_{-\infty}^{+\infty} (r_1 - \bar{r}_1)^2 f_j \, dr_2 \, dr_1 + x_2^2 \int_{-\infty}^{+\infty} \int_{-\infty}^{+\infty} (r_2 - \bar{r}_2)^2 f_j \, dr_2 \, dr_1 \\
&\quad + 2 x_1 x_2 \int_{-\infty}^{+\infty} \int_{-\infty}^{+\infty} (r_1 - \bar{r}_1)(r_2 - \bar{r}_2) f_j \, dr_2 \, dr_1 \\
&= x_1^2 \int_{-\infty}^{+\infty} (r_1 - \bar{r}_1)^2 f(r_1) \, dr_1 + x_2^2 \int_{-\infty}^{+\infty} (r_2 - \bar{r}_2)^2 f(r_2) \, dr_2 \\
&\quad + 2 x_1 x_2 \int_{-\infty}^{+\infty} \int_{-\infty}^{+\infty} (r_1 - \bar{r}_1)(r_2 - \bar{r}_2) f_j \, dr_2 \, dr_1 \\
&= x_1^2 \sigma_1^2 + x_2^2 \sigma_2^2 + 2 x_1 x_2 \operatorname{cov}(r_1 r_2).
\end{aligned}
\tag{15A.3}
$$

An analogous derivation of the semivariance for a two-asset portfolio is presented below for contrast.

$$
S_p = \int_{-\infty}^{h} (r_p - h)^2 f(r_p) \, dr_p
\tag{15A.4}
$$

$$
= \int_{-\infty}^{h} (x_1 r_1 + x_2 r_2 - h)^2 f(r_p) \, dr_p
\tag{15A.4a}
$$

---

[2]It is particularly useful to use integral calculus in semivariance work because the semivariance is defined over a well-defined segment of the probability distribution.

To insure $r_p < h$, define $x_1 r_1 + x_2 z = h$ and solve for $z = (h - x_1 r_1)/x_2$.

$$s_p = \int_{-\infty}^{+\infty} \int_{-\infty}^{z} (x_1 r_1 + x_2 r_2 - h)^2 f_j(r_1, r_2) \, dr_2 \, dr_1 \qquad (15A.4b)$$

$$= \int_{-\infty}^{+\infty} \int_{-\infty}^{z} [x_1(r_1 - h) + x_2(r_2 - h)]^2 f_j \, dr_2 \, dr_1$$

$$= \int_{-\infty}^{+\infty} \int_{-\infty}^{z} [x_1^2(r_1 - h)^2 + 2x_1 x_2(r_1 - h)(r_2 - h) + x_2^2(r_2 - h)^2] f_j \, dr_2 \, dr_1$$

$$= x_1^2 \int_{-\infty}^{+\infty} \int_{-\infty}^{z} (r_1 - h)^2 f_j \, dr_2 \, dr_1 + x_2^2 \int_{-\infty}^{+\infty} \int_{-\infty}^{z} (r_2 - h)^2 f_j \, dr_2 \, dr_1$$

$$+ 2x_1 x_2 \int_{-\infty}^{+\infty} \int_{-\infty}^{z} (r_1 - h)(r_2 - h) f_j \, dr_2 \, dr_1$$

$$= x_1^2 \int_{-\infty}^{+\infty} (r_1 - h)^2 f(r_1 | r_2 < z) \, dr_1 + x_2^2 \int_{-\infty}^{z} (r_2 - h)^2 f(r_2) \, dr_2$$

$$+ 2x_1 x_2 \int_{-\infty}^{+\infty} \int_{-\infty}^{z} (r_1 - h)(r_2 - h) f_j \, dr_2 \, dr_1$$

$$= a + b + c.$$

Since $a \neq \sigma_1^2$, $b \neq \sigma_2^2$, and $c \neq \mathrm{cov}\,(r_1, r_2)$, it follows that $s_p \neq \sigma_p^2$.

## Selected References

Hogan, W. W., and J. M. Warren, "Computation of the Efficient Boundary in the E-S Portfolio Selection Model," *Journal of Financial and Quantitative Analysis*, September 1972, pp. 1881–1896.

Calculus and mathematical programming are used to delineate the efficient frontier in terms of the semivariance.

Hogan, W. W., and J. M. Warren, "Toward the Development of an Equilibrium Capital Market Model Based on Semivariance," *Journal of Financial and Quantitative Analysis*, January 1974, pp. 1–11.

Differential calculus and finite probability theory are used to derive a security market line (SML) analog in terms of the cosemivariance.

Markowitz, Harry M., *Portfolio Selection*. Cowles Monograph 16. New York: John Wiley & Sons, Inc., 1959.

Chapter 9 of this classic monograph proposes the semivariance as an alternative risk measure to the variances. Algebra is used. See papes 288–296 regarding the utility theory implications of the semivariance.

## Questions and Problems

1. Look up the definition of the word "risk" in a dictionary. Does the dictionary definition of risk correspond closely to the variance of returns measure used throughout most of this book? Does the dictionary definition correspond more closely to the semivariance or the variance risk measure? Explain.

2. Compare and contrast the variance measure with the semivariance measure of risk with respect to the following points.

 (a) Familiarity.
 (b) Existence of mathematical statistical tools such as a sampling theory and significance tests.
 (c) Computational convenience and cost of implementation.
 (d) Desirability of the portfolios that are generated.

3. Use utility theory to compare and contrast the implications of $[\sigma, E(r)]$ portfolio analysis with the implications of $[s, E(r)]$ analysis. In your opinion, which form of economic behavior is more characteristic of individual investors? Of corporate investors?

4. Define skewness of returns from an investment. Does skewness effect your thinking about the variance and the semivariance risk measures? If it were known that all probability distributions were asymmetric, would that necessarily make either the variance or the semivariance a superior measure of risk? If the probability distributions of all (or even a significant minority of all) investments are skewed, is there another form of analysis (other than the variance or the semivariance analysis) available with which to explicitly analyze risky investments without ignoring any information? Explain.

5. What types of investments will appear more desirable in terms of $[s, E(r)]$ analysis than they would in terms of $[\sigma, E(r)]$ analysis if all aspects of the investments probability distributions were identical and only the methods of analyzing them differed? What types of highly desirable investments will not appear as being desirable in $[s, E(r)]$ analysis? In view of the inherent biases in the $[s, E(r)]$ and $[\sigma, E(r)]$ analysis, which seems most appropriate to use for allocating capital within a large corporation that does mineral (for example, oil well) exploration and development work? Within a large corporation that owns a chain of hundreds of supermarkets from coast to coast in the United States? Can you think of a capital-allocation model that might be more appropriate for both types of firms than either the $[\sigma, E(r)]$ or the $[s, E(r)]$ model of analysis?

6. Calculate the semivariance for a five-year investment that has had (or is expected to have in the future) the following five annual returns:

359

| Year | Year's Return | Market's Return |
|------|---------------|-----------------|
| 1 | 0.1 = −10.0% | 0.4 = 40.0% |
| 2 | 0.5 = 50.0% | 0.5 = 50.0% |
| 3 | −0.4 = −40.0% | −0.6 = −60.0% |
| 4 | 0 | 0.2 = 20.0% |
| 5 | −0.1 = −10.0% | 0 |

Assume that the riskless rate is $h = 20.0$ percent. Next, calculate the cosemivariance between this asset and the market. (*Hint:* See pages 188–189 of Markowitz, *Portfolio Selection,* for the semivariance calculations.)

7. Do you think the capital markets in the United States are more accurately represented by $[\sigma, E(r)]$ or $[s, E(r)]$ capital market theory? Explain why if you assume capital gains are taxed at half the ordinary income tax rate. What if capital gains were taxed as ordinary income? Does your answer depend on whether you assume that the securities markets are dominated by individual investors or professional money managers?

```
161616161616161616161616161616161616161616161616161616161616!616161616161616
1616161616161616161616161616161616161616161616161616161616161616161616161616
16161616161616161616    16161    161    1616161616161    161    16161616161616161616
1616161616161616161616    616    61616    616161616    6161    16161616161616161616
16161616161616161616161    1    1616161    161616161    16161    16161616161616161616
1616161616161616161616    616161616    6161616    616161    16161616161616161616
161616161616161616161    16161616161    16161    161616    16161616161616161616
1616161616161616161616    616161616    616    61616161    16161616161616161616
16161616161616161616161    1    161616161    1    161616161    16161616161616161616
1616161616161616161616    616    6161616161    616161616    16161616161616161616
161616161616161616161    16161    1616161616    1616161616    16161616161616161616
1616161616161616161616161616161616161616161616161616161616161616161616161616
1616161616161616161616161616161616161616161616161616161616161616161616161616
```

# Portfolio Theory in Three Moments

MARKOWITZ portfolio theory is based on the first two statistical moments, namely, the mean and variance. The mean and variance can adequately describe only certain symmetric distributions (for example, the normal and the uniform distributions). As a result, if probability distributions of returns are actually asymmetric, the classic two-parameter Markowitz analysis ignores information that is needed to make optimum investments (namely, maximize expected utility). The third- and perhaps even higher-order statistical moments should be included in the analysis.[1] This chapter reviews various aspects of portfolio theory when it is extended to include the third moment, a measure of a probability distribution's skewness.

### 16.1 Two Moments Can Be Inadequate

Consider the two probability distributions of returns shown in Fig. 16.1. Although these two distributions are different, they have the same means and variances. The positively skewed distribution in Fig. 16.1B is more desirable than the symmetric distribution however, because the skewed distribution has higher values for both its worst and best outcomes. The two parameter analysis would focus only on the first two moments, ignoring the desirable

---

[1] It is difficult to discern what the fourth statistical moment measures: I. Kaplansky, "A Common Error Concerning Kurtosis," *American Statistical Association Journal*, Vol. 40, June 1945, p. 259.

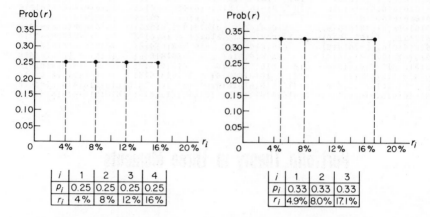

Figure 16.1A.  Symmetric Distribution

Figure 16.1B.  Positively Skewed Distribution

| Distribution | Symmetric | Skewed | Formula |
|---|---|---|---|
| Means | 10.0% | 10.0% | (2.1A) |
| Std. dev. | 9.0% | 9.0% | (2.3A) |
| Skewness | 0 | +.2 | — |
| Kurtosis | .41 | .49 | — |
| Lowest return | 4.0% | 4.9% | — |
| High return | 12.0% | 12.2% | — |

Figure 16.1. Two Different Probability Distributions with Identical Means and Variances

positive skewness and lesser "downside risk" and find the two distributions equally desirable. In such cases, the need to consider the third statistical moment is difficult to deny.[2] Other reasons unrelated to the probability distribution can also oblige the analyst to consider higher-order moments (namely, higher-order utility functions).

Equation (16.1) shows that the third *statistical moment*, denoted $M_3(r)$, is based on the first three *moments about the origin*, denoted $E(r)$, $E(r^2)$, and $E(r^3)$, for a probability distribution of returns.

$$M_3(r) = E[r - E(r)]^3$$

$$= E[r^3 - 3r^2 E(r) + 3r E(r)^2 - E(r)^3] \tag{16.1}$$

$$= E(r^3) - 3E(r^2)E(r) + 2E(r)^3 \tag{16.1a}$$

$$= f[E(r), E(r^2), E(r^3)]. \tag{16.1b}$$

---

[2]P. L. Cooley, "A Multidimensional Analysis of Institutional Investor Perception of Risk," *Journal of Finance*, Vol. No. 1, 1977, pp. 67–78.

It is informative to perform a similar type of analysis on the investor's utility of return function in order to see how these statistical moments effect utility in an uncertain world.

Equation (16.2) is a cubic utility of returns function, it is illustrated graphically in Fig. 16.2.

$$U(r) = a + br + cr^2 + dr^3. \tag{16.2}$$

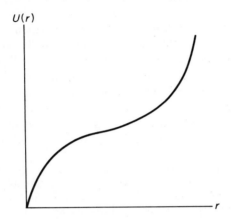

U(r)

r

Figure 16.2. Cubic Utility of Returns Functions*

*The shape and rationale for the cubic utility function are analyzed on pages 249–259 of Haim Levy and Marshall Sarnat, *Investment and Portfolio Analysis* (New York: John Wiley & Sons, Inc., 1972).

Taking the expectation of equation (16.2) yields *expected utility* equations (16.2a) and (16.2b).

$$E[U(r)] = a + bE(r) + cE(r^2) + dE(r^3) \tag{16.2a}$$

$$= g[E(r), E(r^2), E(r^3)]. \tag{16.2b}$$

Equations (16.2a) and (16.2b) show that the expected value of the cubic utility of returns function is derived from the first three *moments about the origin* from a probability distribution of returns. The fact that equations (16.1b) and (16.2b) are both functions of the same three moments about the origin is proof that maximizing a third-degree expected utility function requires that consideration be given to the third statistical moment (or skewness, which is the normalized third moment).

The results from equations (16.1) and (16.2) can be generalized to $n$-degree utility functions. That is, maximizing the expected utility from a utility function of degree $n$ requires that consideration be given to the first $n$ statistical moments.[3]

In addition to asymmetric probability distributions and higher-order utility functions, other reasons for considering the third statistical moment of the probability distribution exist.[4] These will not be discussed to save space. Instead, the next section reviews empirical evidence about whether or not the probability distributions are skewed or symmetric.

## 16.2   Empirical Evidence About Skewness

After the relevance of skewness in investment decisions is established, the next logical question is whether or not skewness actually exists. That is, if the probability distributions of investment returns are all symmetric, then skewness can be ignored. The question is empirical.

Table 16.1 shows mean returns, variances, and skewness statistics averaged over a decade of data from 600 NYSE common stocks.[5] The monthly price change plus cash dividend returns adjusted for changes in the unit of account are from the CRSP tape.[6] The cash dividends were included in the returns to

---

[3]Some writers have used a Taylor series expansion about the expectation to show that expected utility is a function of more than merely the first two statistical moments; for example, "The Fundamental Approximation Theorem of Portfolio Analysis in Terms of Means, Variances, and Higher Order Moments," by P. A. Samuelson, in Vol. III of *The Collected Scientific Papers of P. A. Samuelson*, edited by R. C. Merton (Cambridge, Mass.: The MIT Press, 1972), pp. 877–882. Otto Loistl has shown the fallacy of this in "The Erroneous Approximation of Expected Utility by Means of a Taylor Series Expansion: Analytic and Computational Results," *American Economic Review*, December 1976, pp. 904–910.

[4]Arditti has shown that a utility function which has positive but diminishing marginal utility and also exhibits nonincreasing absolute risk aversion in the Pratt–Arrow sense has a preference for positive skewness. See page 21 of Fred Arditti, "Risk and the Required Rate of Return on Equity," *Journal of Finance*, March 1967. It has also been suggested that a "clientele effect" causes investors to value skewness in certain investments more than others: R. W. McEnally, "A Note on the Behavior of High-Risk Common Stocks," *Journal of Finance*, March 1974.

[5]Skewness is defined as the normalized third statistical moment (that is, moment about the mean). The third moment about the mean is normalized by dividing it by the standard deviation cubed, as shown below, to obtain a dimensionless index number to measure lopsidedness.

$$\text{Skewness} = \text{Mom3}/(\text{cubed standard deviation})$$

Likewise, kurtosis is defined as the normalized fourth statistical moment (that is, moment about the mean).

$$\text{Kurtosis} = \text{Mom4}/(\text{squared variance})$$

See Mathematical Appendix G of *Investments: Analysis and Management*, 2nd edition, by J. C. Francis, McGraw-Hill Book Co., for a discussion which explains moments about the origin and moments about the mean, for readers with no background in these concepts.

[6]CRSP stands for Center for Research on Security Prices, at the University of Chicago. The Center sells daily and monthly returns recorded on magnetic computer tapes. The daily

TABLE 16.1  Empirical Estimates of the First Three Statistical Moments Averaged Over 600 NYSE Stocks, 1962–1971

| Statistic | Monthly | Quarterly | Annual |
|---|---|---|---|
| Mean, $[E(1 + r) - 1]$ | 0.009 | 0.028 | 0.118 |
| Var $(1 + r)$ = var $(r)$ | 0.008 | 0.025 | 0.131 |
| Skewness | 0.738 | 0.793 | 1.852 |

compensate for the well-known stock price dropoff, which occurs when the stock trades ex dividends—a source of white noise in the statistics. Equation (1.1) was used to calculate the monthly returns, denoted $mr_t$ for the $t$th month. The quarterly returns, denoted $qr$, were each calculated from three monthly returns ($mr_t$ for $t = 1, 2, 3$) by compounding the monthly link relative. The quantity $(1 + mr_t)$ denotes the $t$th month link relative, and the compounding was accomplished as shown below.

$$(1 + qr) = (1 + mr_1)(1 + mr_2)(1 + mr_3)$$
$$(p_3/p_0) = (p_1/p_0)(p_2/p_1)(p_3/p_2)$$

The annual returns, denoted $ar$, were similarly calculated by compounding as follows.

$$ar = (1 + qr_1)(1 + qr_2)(1 + qr_3)(1 + qr_4) - 1$$

The data used was from 1962–1971 inclusive.

Table 16.2 contains the first three statistical moments averaged over 126 mutual funds from 1960 through 1968 inclusive. The monthly returns included capital gain disbursements, unrecognized capital gains, and cash dividend and interest income.

TABLE 16.2  Empirical Estimates of the First Three Statistical Moments Averaged Over 126 Mutual Funds, 1960–1968

| Statistic | Monthly | Quarterly | Annual |
|---|---|---|---|
| Mean, $[E(1 + r) - 1]$ | 0.0064 | 0.018 | 0.076 |
| Var $(1 + r)$ = var $(r)$ | 0.002 | 0.007 | 0.023 |
| Skewness† | 0.27* | 0.82 | 2.00 |

†The asterisk after a skewness statistic indicates that it is not significantly greater than zero at the 0.10 level of significance, using a skewness significance test published by: E. S. Pearson, "A Further Development of the Tests of Normality," *Biometrika*, Vol. 22, pp. 239ff. The same test was published in two other sources: E. S. Pearson and H. O. Hartley, *Biometrika Tables for Statisticians*, Vol. I (Cambridge, England: Cambridge University Press, 1954, p. 183, and F. E. Croxton and D. J. Cowden, *Applied General Statistics* (Englewood Cliffs, N.J.: Prentice-Hall, Inc., 1955), pp. 231, 720–721, 764.

and monthly CRSP tapes contain periodic observations of all NYSE stocks from years of historical data. Returns with and without cash dividends are on the tape.

### 16.3 Moments Vary with the Differencing Interval

Perusal of the statistics in Tables 16.1 and 16.2 reveals that across the monthly, quarterly, and annual differencing intervals the sizes of the mean and variance tend to conform to the patterns shown in equations (16.3) and (16.4) over a sample period as long as a decade.[7]

$$E(r_i)_t^{t+1} = \frac{1}{T} E(r_i)_t^{t+T} \qquad (16.3)$$

$$\text{Var } (r_i)_t^{t+1} = \frac{1}{T} \text{ var } (r_i)_t^{t+T} \qquad (16.4)$$

$$_i\sigma_t^{t+1} = \sqrt{\left(\frac{1}{T}\right) \text{ var } (r_i)_t^{t+T}} \qquad (16.4a)$$

$$= \sqrt{\frac{1}{T}} \ _i\sigma_t^{t+T}. \qquad (16.4b)$$

Equation (16.3) shows that the average of expected returns over one period, from $t$ to $(t + 1)$, is $(1/T)$ times as large as the average return over $T$ periods, from $t$ to $(t + T)$. This proportional scaling may not be present over short sample periods that were dominated by a few bullish and bearish periods. However, over the long sample period from 1962 to 1971, the National Bureau of Economic Research recorded two periods of economic expansion punctuated by one recession, and even more "ups and downs" occurred in the stock markets. Over such a lengthy sample the long-run upward trend in stock prices (which has been documented by Lorie and Fisher,[8] Ibbotson and Sinquefield,[9] et al.) emerges and can be measured. Thus, over $T$ periods a stock's price will appreciate $T$ times more than it would in one average period.

The variance of stock returns also increases with the length of the differencing intervals over which the returns are measured, as shown in equation (16.4). The reason for this increase in the variance (or, equivalently,

---

[7]For an in-depth analysis of the effects on the statistical moments from the probability distributions of single-period rates of return which result from going from one-day to two-day, from daily to weekly, from weekly to monthly, from monthly to quarterly, and so on, differencing intervals, see Gabriel Hawawini, "On the Time-Behavior of Financial Parameters: An Investigation of the Intervaling Effect," unpublished Ph.D. dissertation, New York University, 1977. See also R. A. Schwartz and D. K. Whitcomb, "The Time–Variance Relationship: Evidence on Autocorrelation in Common Stock Returns," *Journal of Finance*, Vol. 22, No. 1, 1977, pp. 41–56.

[8]L. Fisher and J. H. Lorie, "Rates of Return on Investments in Common Stock," *Journal of Business*, Vol. 37, No. 1, 1964, pp. 1–21.

[9]R. G. Ibbotson and R. A. Sinquefield, "Stocks, Bonds, Bills and Inflation: Year-by-Year Historical Returns (1926–1974)," *Journal of Business*, Vol. 49, No. 1, 1976, pp. 11–47.

standard deviation) is simply that the variance of a series of large values exceeds the variance of a series of small values. For example, if a time-series of *independent* returns, denoted $r_1, r_2, r_3, \ldots, r_T$, is scaled upward by a constant factor of $k$ to become $kr_1, kr_2, \ldots, kr_T$, then the variance increases by $k^2$. Since the annual rates of price change are usually larger than quarterly changes, and, in turn, the quarterly returns typically exceed the monthly returns, the differences in their variances are thus explained.

The raw third statistical moment, denoted $M_3$, is defined in equation (16.5) for a series of returns.

$$M(r)_3 = E[r - E(r)]^3. \tag{16.5}$$

This third moment is increased by a factor of $k^3$ if the returns are all scaled upward by a factor of $k$, as shown in equations (16.6).

$$M(kr)_3 = E[kr - E(kr)]^3$$
$$= k^3 E[r - E(r)]^3 \tag{16.6}$$
$$= k^3 M(r)_3. \tag{16.6a}$$

Equation (16.6a) shows that the raw third statistical moment tends to increase with the differencing interval for the same reason that the variance does. However, the skewness is a pure index number which should remain invariant to scaling the basic random variable by a factor of $k$, as shown in equations (16.7).

$$\text{skew}(kr) = \frac{M(kr)_3}{[\text{var}(kr)]^{3/2}} \tag{16.7}$$

$$= \frac{k^3 M(r)_3}{[k^2 \, \text{var}(r)]^{3/2}} \tag{16.7a}$$

$$= \frac{k^3 M(r)_3}{k^3 \{[\text{var}(r)]\}^{3/2}} \tag{16.7b}$$

$$= \frac{M(r)_3}{[\text{var}(r)]^{3/2}} \tag{16.7c}$$

$$= \text{skew}(r). \tag{16.7d}$$

The invariance of skewness to scaling of the basic random variable, combined with its superior statistical efficiency, makes it a preferable statistic to the raw third statistical moment for empirical work.[10]

Inspection of the skewness statistics in Tables 16.1 and 16.2 reveals that they all average significantly greater than zero except the monthly returns

---

[10]If an outlying return causes the third moment to explode in value, the standard deviation cubed will also explode and their ratio (that is, the skewness) will remain unaffected by such explosive outliers.

from mutual funds. However, the average mutual fund's monthly returns are
positively skewed, albeit insignificantly at the 0.10 level. Looking beneath the
average statistics to the skewness statistics for individual funds reveals that
both significantly positive and significantly negative monthly skewness
statistics are present. Of course, all statistics can be sample dependent and/or
inefficient parameter estimators. But skewness is not prone to be an explosive
or inefficient statistic like the third statistical moment. The statistical efficiency of the skewness estimates, combined with supportive skewness statistics
from other periods, suggests that positive skewness may be present.[11] These
findings compel that more consideration be given to the first three statistical
moments.[12]

### 16.4  Portfolio Theory in Three Moments

W. H. Jean suggested how the first three statistical moments from market
assets' probability distributions might determine prices and expected
returns.[13] To represent this market situation graphically, Jean extended the
two-dimensional $[\sigma, E(r)]$ analysis to three-dimensional $[m(r)_3, \sigma, E(r)]$
space, where $m(r)_3$ represents the cube root of the third statistical moment of
returns.

Third-degree surfaces are essentially S-shaped. It is difficult to gen-
eralize in advance about what exact shape the set of risky investment
opportunities will assume. However, Jean has hypothesized that the convex

---

[11]When *continuously compounded* rates of return, denoted $\dot{r}_{it} = \ln(1 + r_{it})$ for the $i$th stock
in the $t$th time period are used, the amount of positive skewness is reduced. Using shorter
differencing intervals further reduces the positive skewness. However, the statistics for continuously compounded returns shown in Tables 14.2 and 14.3 show that the positive skewness
is only reduced and not eliminated by using monthly differencing intervals. Furthermore,
Fielitz reports positive skewness using continuously compounded daily returns: B. D. Fielitz,
"Further Results on Asymmetric Stable Distributions of Stock Price Changes," *Journal of
Financial and Quantitative Analysis*, March 1976, pp. 39–55. Fielitz's results make it difficult to
deny the presence of positive skewness.

[12]F. D. Arditti and Haim Levy, "Portfolio Efficiency Analysis in Three Moments: The
Multiperiod Case," *Journal of Finance*, June 1975, pp. 797–809. Arditti and Levy suggest a
portfolio analysis model which considers the first three moments. However, they assumed that
single-period (which they equate with one month) returns have zero skewness in deriving
their equation (8) from their equation (7). Their entire analysis rests on the assumption that
monthly returns are not skewed and that their equation (8) thus follows. However, the evidence in Tables 16.1 and 16.2 and the preceding footnote suggest that monthly returns are
skewed. Therefore, the Arditti and Levy analysis appears to be fallacious.

[13]The extension of the original mean–variance capital market theory to include the third
moment can be traced through the following literature: W. H. Jean, "The Extension of
Portfolio Analysis to Three or More Parameters," *Journal of Financial and Quantitative Analysis*,
January 1971, pp. 505–515; F. D. Arditti and H. Levy, "Distribution Moments and Equi-
librium: A Comment," *Journal of Financial and Quantitative Analysis*, January 1972; W. H. Jean,
"More on Multidimensional Portfolio Analysis," *Journal of Financial and Quantitative Analysis*,
June 1973, pp. 475–490.

hull shown in Fig. 16.3 represents the relevant subset of the total set of investment opportunities in $[m(r)_3, \sigma, E(r)]$ space. The dashed line traces the $[\sigma, E(r)]$ efficient frontier if all assets' returns are symmetrically distributed. The classic capital market line (CML) which exists in the absence of skewness extends from the riskless rate, denoted $R$, up through the uniquely desirable market portfolio, denoted $M$, in the $[\sigma, E(r)]$ plane. However, when non-symmetry is admitted to the analysis, the picture becomes more complicated.

Since every investor presumably has a different utility function, they all have *different* investment preferences in $[m(r)_3, \sigma, E(r)]$ space.[14] As a result, there is no uniquely desirable risk asset such as the market portfolio in the three-dimensional model—this is a major *source of vagueness* in the three-dimensional capital market theory.

The expected return, risk, and cube root of the third moment of returns for any risky portfolio, denoted $p$, which may be constructed from the $i$th risky asset, combined with borrowing or lending at the riskless rate, are defined in equations (16.8), (16.9) and (16.10b), respectively.

$$E(r_p) = R(1 - x_i) + E(r_i)x_i \qquad (16.8)$$

$$\sigma_p{}^2 = x_i^2\sigma_i^2 + (1 - x_i)^2\sigma_j^2 + 2(1 - x_i)x_i\sigma_{ij} \qquad (16.9)$$

$$= x_i^2\sigma_i^2 \qquad \text{since } \sigma_j = \sigma_{ij} = 0 \qquad \text{when asset } j \text{ is riskless} \qquad (16.9a)$$

$$m(r_p)_3 = \sqrt[3]{M(r_p)_3} \qquad (16.10)$$

$$= \sqrt[3]{M(r_i)_3 x_i^3} \qquad x_i \geq 0 \qquad (16.10a)$$

$$= m(r_i)_3 x_i \qquad x_i \geq 0. \qquad (16.10b)$$

Portfolio $p$'s risk and third moment are simple linear functions of the risk and symmetry of risky asset $i$, because the riskless asset has risk and skewness of zero, $\sigma_R = m(R)_3 = 0$, by definition of the riskless asset. Equations (16.8), (16.9), and (16.10b) form the skeleton of capital market theory in $[m(r)_3, \sigma, E(r)]$ space.

Equation (16.9), which shows the simple relation between $\sigma_p$ and $\sigma_i$, was derived on page 27. Equation (16.10b) is derived from the formula for the third moment of a portfolio of two assets.

$$m(r)_3 = \{x_i^3 M(r_i)_3 + 3x_i^2(1 - x_i)E[\{r_i - E(r_i)\}^2\{R - E(R)\}]$$
$$+ 3x_i(1 - x_i)^2 E[\{r_i - E(r_i)\}\{R - E(R)\}^2]$$
$$+ (1 - x_i)^3 M(R)_3\}^{1/3} \qquad (16.10)$$
$$= [x_i^3 M(r_i)_3]^{1/3} \qquad (16.10b)$$

---

[14]Research with stochastic dominance decision rules has developed techniques for eliminating a subset of the investments which are dominated. However, the stochastic dominance models cannot select a single most desirable investment opportunity, since they involve no utility function, either implicitly or explicitly. G. A. Whitmore, "Third Degree Stochastic Dominance," *American Economic Review*, June 1970. Also see Chapter 17 below.

since

$$M(R)_3 = E[\{R - E(R)\}^2] = E[\{(R - E(R)\}] = 0$$

for the riskless asset.

### 16.5  Three-Parameter Efficient Frontier

Figure 16.3 illustrates the location of the $i$th risky asset. The line from $R$ up through point $i$ to point $z$ graphically represents the expected return, risk, and cube root of the third moment of the portfolio possibilities which can be constructed from $i$ and $R$. Even if asset $i$ has the maximum return in its risk class (that is, $i$ is a Markowitz-efficient portfolio) for the value of its third moment, it will still not lie on the $[\sigma, E(r)]$ efficient frontier, as illustrated in the two-dimensional projection shown in Fig. 16.4.

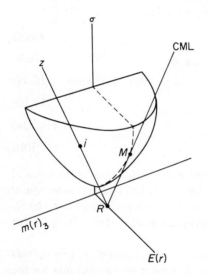

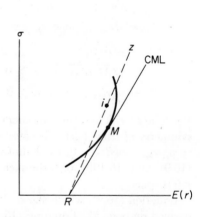

Figure 16.3. Investment Opportunities in $[m(r)_3, \sigma, E(r)]$ Space

Figure 16.4. Opportunities on Riz Are Dominated by the CML in $[\sigma, E(r)]$ Space

*Source:* W. H. Jean, "More on Multidimensional Portfolio Analysis," *Journal of Financial and Quantitative Analysis*, June 1973, Figs. II and III.

The line Riz and the CML shown in Figs. 16.3 and 16.4 are not the only investment opportunities. A line or ray from the riskless rate through *any point* in the set of risky investment opportunities shown in Fig. 16.3 represents a feasible investment possibility. As a result, the complete set of feasible investments in $[m(r)_3, \sigma, E(r)]$ space is shaped like a cone, with its tip at point $R$, as shown in Fig. 16.5. This cone envelopes the set of risky investments shown in Fig. 16.3. The cone extends infinitely far out from point $R$ if

borrowing and lending are presumed to be unrestricted. The cone of investment possibilities with borrowing and lending shown in Fig. 16.5 is termi-
nated to reflect the effects of margin requirements, credit restrictions, and
short selling limitations.

The surface of the cone in Fig. 16.5 is composed of an infinite number of
linear opportunity loci. Each of these lines is a CML analog in $[m(r)_3, \sigma, E(r)]$ space. However, when the CML analogs from Fig. 16.6 are projected
onto a two-dimensional $[\sigma, E(r)]$ surface, some of them will dominate the
CML, and some of them will be dominated by the CML, as shown in
Fig. 16.6.

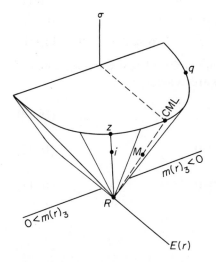

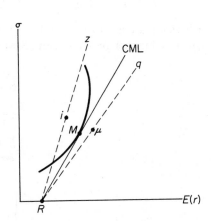

Figure 16.5. Cone of Investment Opportunities in $[m(r)_3, \sigma, E(r)]$ Space with Borrowing and Lending at $R$

Figure 16.6. CML Dominates Riz, and
Ruq Dominates the CML in $[\sigma, E(r)]$
Space

*Source:* W. H. Jean, "More on Multidimensional Portfolio Analysis," *Journal of Financial
and Quantitative Analysis,* June 1973, Fig. IV.

The line Riz from Figs. 16.3, 16.4, and 16.5 is dominated by the CML in
Fig. 16.6 (as it was in Fig. 16.4). Nevertheless, an investor who had positive
but diminishing marginal utility (that is, was greedy but risk-averse) might
prefer an investment on Riz over an investment on the CML if the opportunities on Riz were *skewed positively*. A positive cube root of the third moment
for the opportunities on the line Riz could more than compensate for the
lower expected returns on Riz relative to the CML. More simply, Riz offers
a long shot at a large return and could entice some investors away from the
opportunities on the CML which had higher average outcomes but less
exciting possibilities for large returns.

The line Ruq in Fig. 16.6 is a CML analog from the surface of the cone in

Fig. 16.5, but it dominates the CML in $[\sigma, E(r)]$ space. Opportunity lines such as Ruq can exist in a $[m(r)_3, \sigma, E(r)]$ equilibrium because the cube root of their third moments are negative. This negative skewness represents large probabilities of big losses. As a result, risk-averse investers will require higher expected returns at any given risk class to induce them to invest in the negatively skewed Ruq opportunities than the symmetrically distributed opportunities lying on the CML.

The wealth-seeking but risk-averse investor preferences revealed by the choices discussed in reference to Fig. 16.7 can be represented formally as follows:

$$U = f(\text{wealth}), f' > 0, f'' < 0 \tag{16.11}$$

$$U = g(\text{returns}), \qquad g' > 0, g'' < 0 \tag{16.11a}$$

$$E[U(r)] = h[m(r)_3, \sigma, E(r)], \qquad h_1 > 0, h_2 < 0, h_3 > 0, \tag{16.11b}$$

where equations (16.11a) and (16.11b) are positive linear transformations of (16.11). Further preference implications are as follows:

$$\frac{\partial m(r)_3}{\partial E(r)} \leq 0 \tag{16.12}$$

$$\frac{\partial m(r)_3}{\partial \sigma} \geq 0 \tag{16.13}$$

$$\frac{\partial E(r)}{\partial \sigma} \geq 0. \tag{16.14}$$

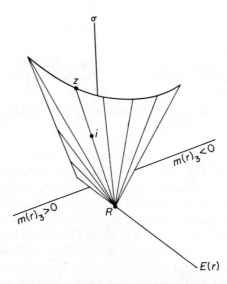

Figure 16.7. Efficient Frontier of Investments in $[m(r)^3, \sigma, E(r)]$ Space

*Source:* W. H. Jean, "More on Multidimensional Portfolio Analysis," *Journal of Financial and Quantitative Analysis*, June 1973, pp. 475–490, Fig. IV.

Convex utility surfaces posessing all the preferences shown in equations (16.11), (16.12), (16.13), and (16.14) can be generated from the logarithmic or power utility functions (that is, those possessing constant relative risk aversion, as discussed in Chapter XI). Thus, the analysis represents logical and realistic economic behavior.

Specifying the investors' utility functions as done in equations (16.11), (16.12), (16.13), and (16.14) allows the $[m(r)_3, \sigma, E(r)]$-efficient frontier to be delineated.[15] Efficient portfolios in three dimensions will be that portion of the cone in Fig. 16.5 with:

1. Maximum skewness for a given variance and a given rate of return.
2. Minimum variance for given levels of skewness and rate of return.
3. Maximum expected return for each level of skewness and variance.[16]

Figure 16.7 illustrates the subset of the surface of the cone of opportunities shown in Fig. 16.5, which comprises the efficient portfolios in $[m(r)_3, \sigma, E(r)]$ space. The $[m(r)_3, \sigma, E(r)]$ efficient portfolios are also [skewness, $\sigma, E(r)$] efficient since for any given values of $E(r)$ and $\sigma$, maximizing $m(r_3)$ is equivalent to maximizing skewness [namely, $M(r)_3/\sigma^3$]. Any point behind the efficient frontier is a dominated investment. Of course, what is an efficient investment in $[m(r)_3, \sigma, E(r)]$ space may be inefficient when moments above the third are considered.

The three-parameter portfolio theory illustrated above represents testable hypotheses. Some empirical tests of these hypothesized relationships between portfolios' returns are reviewed in the next section.

### 16.6 Econometric Skewness Tests for Portfolios

The partial derivative $\partial E(r_i)/\partial\text{skew}(r_i)$ defines the change in the expected return for the $i$th asset with respect to its skewness while holding all other things (namely, the risk) constant. Equation (16.15) is a cross-sectional econometric model which may be used to obtain empirical estimates of this partial derivative.

$$E(r_i) = a_0 + a_1\sigma_i^2 + a_2[\text{skew}(r_i)] + e_i, \qquad (16.15)$$

---

[15]Jean's multidimensional assets pricing models were mathematically developed through the series of articles listed below. Jean's work was then extended by Ingersoll and by Kraus and Litzenberger in articles which are also listed below. W. H. Jean, "The Extension of Portfolio Analysis to Three or More Parameters," *Journal of Financial and Quantitative Analysis*, January 1971, pp. 505–515; "More on Multidimensional Portfolio Analysis," *Journal of Finance and Quantitative Analysis*, June 1973, pp. 475–490; Jonathan Ingersoll, "Multidimensional Security Pricing," *Journal of Financial and Quantitative Analysis*, December 1975, pp. 785–798; Alan Kraus, and R. H. Litzenberger, "Skewness Preference and Valuation of Risk Assets," *Journal of Finance*, September 1976, pp. 1085–1100.

[16]Decreasing absolute risk aversion in the Pratt–Arrow sense (see Chapter XI) is necessary to generate skewness preference.

where $a_0$ is the regression intercept, $a_1 = [\partial E(r_i)/\partial \sigma_i^2]$ = a measure of the impact of the variance of returns on average returns, $a_2 = [\partial E(r_i)/\partial \text{skew}(r_i)]$ = the *ceteris paribus* impact of skewness on average return estimated across $i = 1, 2, \ldots, n$ different market assets, and $e_i$ is the portion of the $i$th assets' expected return which is left unexplained by the regression.

Since equation (16.15) is linear in three variables it represents a plane in the three dimensions of expected return, variance, and skewness, that is, $[E(r_i), \sigma_i^2, \text{skewness}_i]$. This three-dimensional model for determining the prices of portfolios can only be derived from an efficient frontier with infinite borrowing and lending, such as the one shown in Fig. 16.8. The three-dimensional CML analog in Fig. 16.8 is a plane from the riskless rate, $R$,

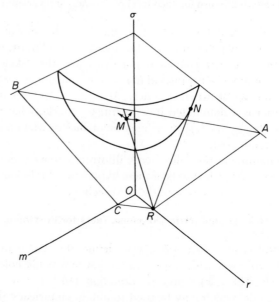

Figure 16.8. Three-Dimensional Efficient Frontier in $[m(r_p)_3, \sigma, \bar{r}]$ Space with Borrowing and Lending at Riskless Rate

*Source:* Carl Schweser, "A Comparison of Multidimensional Security Pricing Models," unpublished manuscript, 1977.

which is tangent to *one uniquely desirable market portfolio*, $M$. The four corners of this plane are points $R$, $A$, $B$, and $C$ in Fig. 16.8. Such a plane will only represent a market equilibrium if all *investors have identical preferences* in $[E(r_i), \sigma_i, m(r_p)_3]$ space, that is, identical utility functions. Although it is admittedly heroic to presume homogeneous preferences, the empirical estimates of equation (16.15) do furnish statistically significant evidence that lends support to such linear relationships.

Historical returns for 126 mutual funds from 1960 through 1968 inclusive were used to calculate each mutual fund's ex post arithmetic average return, $\bar{r}_i$, variance of returns, and skewness of returns. Ex ante equation (16.15) was reformulated as ex post equation (16.15a) by assuming that the past expectations were borne out [so that $E(r_i) = \bar{r}_i$, for example].

$$\bar{r}_i = a_0 + a_1\sigma_i^2 + a_2[\text{skew}(r_i)] + e_i. \qquad (16.15a)$$

Table 16.3 contains three different estimates of equation (16.15a) that were prepared using 108 monthly returns, 36 quarterly returns, and 9 annual returns to calculate the return, risk, and skewness statistics over the same nine-year sample.

TABLE 16.3   Regression Estimates of Equation (16.15a) for Monthly, Quarterly, and Annual Data from 1960 to 1968 Over 126 Mutual Funds

| Returns | $a_0(t_0)$ | $a_1(t_1)$ | $a_2(t_2)$ | $R^2$ | DW |
|---------|-----------|-----------|-----------|-------|-----|
| Monthly | 0.004(8.11) | 1.01(5.76) | 0.002(5.68) | 0.30 | 1.88 |
| Quarterly | 0.004(2.73) | 1.15(9.57) | 0.008(7.15) | 0.48 | 1.78 |
| Annual | 0.022(5.20) | 1.24(11.86) | 0.013(10.22) | 0.65 | 1.94 |

The statistics in Table 16.3 document the well-known risk–return trade-off. The $a_1$ coefficients are all positive and highly significant for the monthly, quarterly, and annual data. As suggested by the theoretical discussion related to equation (16.14), investors require higher average returns to induce them to invest in the riskier mutual funds. The three $a_2$ coefficients in Table 16.3 are also statistically significant, but their signs are puzzling.

Economic theory clearly suggests that investors should be willing to accept lower average returns in order to obtain investments with positively skewed returns, as indicated by equation (16.12). However, the signs of the three $a_2$ coefficients in Table 16.3 all have signs opposite that which economic logic suggests. These statistics may be the results of two possibilities. First, investors may simply have such poor skewness perceptions that skewness has no rational impact on their actual investment decisions. This may be true in spite of the fact that they may be willing to accept investments with average returns which are aligned inversely with skewness if they could appraise skewness correctly. Second, the regressions may be econometrically flawed. The econometrics are discussed next.

Every $t$-statistic in Table 16.3 is highly significant, and the adjusted coefficients of determination ($R^2$) all indicate that the regressions have good explanatory power. The three $a_0$ intercept are estimates of a riskless rate of interest. Multiplying the monthly intercept by 12 months suggests a riskless rate of ($0.004 \times 12 = 0.048 =$) 4.8 percent per year. The quarterly data imply a rate of 1.6 percent, and the annual inference is a riskless rate of 2.2 percent. These are fairly reasonable estimates which lend credibility to the other statistics. The Durbin–Watson (DW) statistics are all pleasantly near

2.0. This indicates that spatial correlation (that is, cross-sectional serial correlation) is not a source of inefficient statistics and also tends to indicate that the regression model has no specification errors.[17] However, the favorable Durbin–Watson statistics do not prove the regression is correctly specified—for example, the model may still be nonlinear.[18] Overall, though, the statistics shown in Table 16.3 appear to be free from econometric problems that would discredit the conclusion that the market has difficulty evaluating skewness.[19]

The regression model shown in equation (16.16) was estimated using annual data from mutual funds in two different studies.

$$\bar{r}_i = a_0 + a_1\sigma_i + a_2[M(r_i)_3] + e_i. \tag{16.16}$$

Equation (16.16) is similar to equation (16.15a) except that (16.16) uses the standard deviation of returns instead of the variance and the raw third moment instead of skewness. The results of this regression are interesting because they conflict with the results shown in Table 16.3. The statistics are shown in Table 16.4.

TABLE 16.4   Different Estimates of Equation (16.16) Using
Mutual Funds' Annual Returns

| Research | $a_0(t_0)$ | $a_1(t_1)$ | $a_2(t_2)$ | $R^2$ | Number of Funds |
|---|---|---|---|---|---|
| Arditti, 1954–68 | 0.045(4.45) | 0.57(8.26) | −7.05(−3.21) | 0.74 | 34 |
| L & S, 1946–67 | 7.20(16.2) | 0.019(9.9) | −0.000064(−8.4) | 0.86 | 58 |
| L & S, 1956–67 | 5.58(6.2) | 0.03(3.9) | Unknown (−0.08) | 0.65 | 86 |
| L & S, 1950–67 | 6.93(7.6) | 0.03(2.8) | −0.0012(−2.8) | 0.82 | 71 |
| L & S, 1943–67 | 13.69(22.16) | 0.02(16.20) | −0.0003(−8.5) | 0.94 | 51 |

*Source:* F. D. Arditti, "Another Look at Mutual Fund Performance," *Journal of Financial and Quantitative Analysis*, June 1971, pp. 909–912; H. Levy and M. Sarnat, *Investment and Portfolio Analysis* (New York: John Wiley & Sons, Inc., 1972), 246–257.

[17]M. Dutta, *Econometric Methods* (Cincinnati, Ohio: South-Western Publishing Co., 1975), pp. 108–109.

[18]Cheng-Few Lee, "Functional Form, Skewness Effect and the Risk–Return Relationship," *Journal of Financial and Quantitative Analysis*, March 1977, pp. 55–72.

[19]Many of the same data taken from the same sample periods were used in "Skewness and Investors' Decisions" by J. C. Francis, *Journal of Financial and Quantitative Analysis*, March 1975, pp. 163–172. The main difference between the results in this paper and the results in Table 16.3 can be attributed to the difference in their dependent variables—the geometric mean returns were used in the article and arithmetic average returns were employed for equation (16.15a). A negative reply to the article by Francis was published: F. D. Arditti, "Skewness and Investors' Decisions: A Reply," *Journal of Financial and Quantitative Analysis*, March 1975. Francis will provide on request a paper entitled, "Skewness and Investors Decisions: An Unpublished Rejoinder to Arditti." Essentially, the Francis reply to Arditti shows that Arditti's reply contained poor logic and econometric errors. Independent research supporting Francis has been published by Charles G. Martin, "Ridge Regression Estimates of the Ex Post Risk–Return Trade-off on Common Stocks," *Review of Business and Economic Research*, Spring 1978, Vol. XII, No. 3, pp. 1–15.

Arditti's and Levy and Sarnat's statistics in Table 16.4 indicate that the third moment had a significant inverse relation with mutual funds' average returns in four of the five sample periods. These findings tend to support the theoretical evidence about the relationship between the first three statistical moments. There are several possible reasons for the divergent skewness findings reported in Tables 16.3 and 16.4.

One conclusion that is fairly clear is that the skewness statistics are *sample-dependent*. This sample dependency may be because of the way third moments are calculated. Deviations from the mean are cubed and, as a result, one or a few large deviations can skew an otherwise symmetric distribution. More simply, the third moment is sensitive to outliers.

A second problem that would cause the regressions in Table 16.4 and/or 16.3 to be misspecified is the lack of a specific economic theory relationship. Since no logically derived economic model exists to be tested, it is not known whether skewness, or the raw third moment, or the cube root of the third moment, or what should be used to measure the effects on prices of lop-sidedness in the probability distribution. Furthermore, it is not known whether a linear or a curvilinear relationship should exist between the first three statistical moments. Only when a rigorously defined theoretical model which specifies these relationships is used can more definitive empirical tests be formulated. Until that time, researchers must merely "go fishing for answers" by estimating many differently specified regressions.

A third reason for the differences between the results in Tables 16.3 and 16.4 is the various lengths of the differencing intervals used to calculate the rates of return. The statistics in Table 16.1 and 16.2 show the tendency for skewness to increase directly with the differencing interval. As a result, skewness studies using returns calculated with sufficiently long differencing intervals and over sufficiently long sample periods seem more likely to relate the average return and skewness spuriously simply because more skewness exists with the longer periods.[20]

Multicollinearity is a fourth problem that may confound multiple[21] regressions such as the ones shown in Tables 16.3 and 16.4. Equation (16.1a) on page 362 shows that the third moment is partly a function of the first two moments about the origin. This gives a priori reason to suspect that the third moment may be correlated with the first two moments. In fact, the second and third moments are significantly correlated in some empirical samples. This interrelationship makes it difficult to econometrically separate (that is, partition) the effects of the second and third moments as they simultaneously interact to determine a market asset's price and expected return.

---

[20]"These and other possible problems are reviewed in J. C. Francis, "Skewness and Investors' Decisions," *Journal of Financial and Quantitative Analysis*, March 1975, pp. 163–172.

[21]Jan Kmenta, *Elements of Econometrics* (New York: Macmillan Publishing Co., Inc., 1971); see Section 3 of Chapter 10 regarding multicollinearity.

As a result of the four problems explained in the preceding paragraphs, the empirical statistics in Tables 16.3 and 16.4 do not *prove* anything. They only *suggest* avenues where further research is needed.

An additional reason to suspect the results in both Tables 16.3 and 16.4 is the possibility that they are erroneously formulated. More specifically, total skewness may be less relevant in the market than *systematic skewness*. Kraus and Litzenberger formulated an empirical test that used systematic skewness, for example, and found that it had a significant effect on common stock returns.[22] Thus, after the mean–variance–skewness efficient frontier is delineated and tested for *portfolios*, attention should be turned to the implications of such portfolio selection criteria for the prices of the *individual* market assets that make up these portfolios.[23]

### 16.7  Undiversifiable Risk and Undiversifiable Skewness

It is well known from the mean–variance portfolio theory that the owner of any existing portfolio, $p$, should evaluate the risk *increment* to the portfolio when considering including the $i$th risky asset. Equation (16.17) shows the formula for evaluating the risk of the revised portfolio, denoted $rp$.

$$\text{var}\,(r_{rp}) = x_p^2 \sigma_p^2 + x_i^2 \sigma_i^2 + 2 x_i x_p \sigma_{ip}, \qquad (16.17)$$

where $x_i + x_p = 1.0$. Taking the cross partial derivative of var $(r_{rp})$ with respect to the $i$th asset's weight and the old portfolio's weight yields the covariance term shown in equation (16.18).

$$\frac{\partial^2 \text{var}\,(r_{rp})}{\partial x_i \, \partial x_p} = 2 \sigma_{ip}. \qquad (16.18)$$

The covariance $\sigma_{ip}$ measures the increment the $i$th asset will add or detract to portfolio $rp$'s risk as measured by $\sigma_p$. The covariance $\sigma_{ip}$ is thus a measure of the undiversifiable risk increment. This covariance can be standardized by restating it as the $i$th asset's beta coefficient with respect to portfolio $p$, as shown in equation (16.19).

$$b_{ip} = \frac{\sigma_{ip}}{\sigma_p^2}. \qquad (16.19)$$

One of the insights from the mean–variance portfolio theory is that the systematic or undiversifiable risk which an individual security contributes to

---

[22]Alan Kraus and R. H. Litzenberger, "Skewness Preference and the Valuation of Risk Assets," *Journal of Finance*, September 1976, pp. 1084–1100.

[23]Cheng Few Lee deals with the problem of skewness effect in estimating the risk–return trade-off. See C. F. Lee and S. N. Chen, "Random Coefficient Capital Asset Pricing Model: A Theoretical Analysis and Empirical Investigation," unpublished manuscript, 1976.

a portfolio can be more relevant in determining that assets' expected return and price than its total risk. This is also true where skewness is concerned. Therefore, the systematic or undiversifiable portion of an asset's skewness is analyzed in the following paragraphs.

Equation (16.20) defines the third moment of the revised portfolio, denoted $M(r_{rp})_3$, if the $i$th asset is included in portfolio $p$.

$$M(r_{rp})_3 = x_i^3 M(r_i)_3 + 3x_i^2 x_p E[\{r_i - E(r_i)\}^2\{r_p - E(r_p)\}]$$
$$+ 3x_i x_p^2 E[\{r_i - E(r_i)\}\{r_p - E(r_p)\}^2] + x_p^3 M(r_p)_3. \quad (16.20)$$

Taking the cross partial derivative of $M(r_{rp})_3$ in order to evaluate the $i$th asset's increment to the revised portfolio's third moment yields equation (16.21).

$$\frac{\partial^2 M(r_{rp})}{\partial x_i \, \partial x_p} = 6x_i E(v_i^2 v_p) + 6x_p E(v_i v_p^2), \quad (16.21)$$

where $v_i = r_i - E(r_i)$ and $v_p = r_p - E(r_p)$. The term $E(v_i^2 v_p)$ in equation (16.21) will always have the same sign as $M(r_p)_3$ since the quantity $v_i^2$ is nonnegative. The sign of the term $E(v_i v_p^2)$ thus indicates whether including asset $i$ may increase, not change, or decrease the third moment of portfolio $p$.

The quantity $E(v_i v_p^2)$ gauges the skewness which the $i$th asset tends to bring to portfolio $p$. This quantity can be converted into an index number, to expedite cross-sectional comparisons by dividing $E(v_i v_p^2)$ by the third moment of portfolio $p$, as shown in equation (17.22).

$$\gamma_{ip} = \frac{E(v_i v_p^2)}{M(r_p)_3}. \quad (16.22)$$

The quantity $\gamma_{ip}$ is an index number comparing the contribution of the $i$th asset's skewness to the third moment of portfolio $p$. The sign of $\gamma_{ip}$ will be greater than, equal to, or less than unity depending on whether asset $i$ extends, does not change, or reduces the third moment of portfolio $rp$. Thus, $\gamma_{ip}$ is an index (somewhat like the beta coefficient) of the $i$th asset's systematic or undiversifiable skewness impact on portfolio $rp$. This gamma is additive, so that portfolio $rp$'s gamma with respect to the market portfolio equals the sum of its assets' gammas, $\gamma_{pm} = \Sigma_i x_i \gamma_{ip}$ and the market portfolio's gamma equals unity.

Although economic logic suggests that a market asset's total skewness or systematic skewness should be inversely related to its expected return [symbolically $\partial E(r)/\partial M(r)_3$], whether or not this is empirically true has not yet been discussed. In the final section of this chapter econometric estimates of the impact that systematic skewness has on the expected return of NYSE stocks is reviewed.

## 16.8  Empirical Evidence About Individual Assets' Prices

Kraus and Litzenberger (KL hereafter) derived a testable hypothesis for the common stocks which comprise portfolios rather than the portfolios themselves. KL showed that a security's risk premium should be positively related to its beta systematic risk, equation (16.19), and inversely related to its gamma systematic skewness, equation (16.22). They estimated equation (16.23) to test their hypothesis.

$$\bar{r}_i = a_0 + a_1 b_i + a_1 \gamma_i + e_i, \qquad (16.23)$$

where
$$\bar{r}_i = \frac{1}{T} \sum_{t=1}^{T} \frac{r_{it} - R_t}{R_t}$$

is the mean deflated risk premium for the $i$th asset group averaged over $T = 120$ months, $a_0$ is the regression intercept, $a_1$ and $a_2$ are regression slope coefficients, and $e_i$ is the unexplained residual for the $i$th asset group.

KL formed decile portfolios of NYSE stocks over 120-month periods from 1926 through 1969 based on rankings to minimize measurement errors for their variables. Then they measured $\bar{r}_i$ for their asset groupings over the 12-month periods that followed each 120-month period. They repeated this procedure for 414 different but overlapping sample periods by moving each sample forward one month for each month from January 1936 through June 1970 as they calculated their $\bar{r}_i$ and its associated systematic risk and skewness statistics. Then they ran 414 different cross-sectional regressions, one for each different sample period. Table 16.5 contains the regression statistics for equation (16.23) averaged over KL's 414 cross-sectional regressions from 414 different sample periods.[24]

The average $t$-statistics on the beta systematic risk and gamma systematic skewness coefficients in Table 16.5 are both significantly different from zero and have the signs suggested by economic theory. This piece of evidence suggests that, in fact, the market does correctly evaluate skewness in forming investment portfolios.

TABLE 16.5   Statistics Averaged Over 414 Estimates of Equation (16.23)

| $a_0(t_0)$ | $a_1(t_1)$ | $a_2(t_2)$ | $\bar{R}^2$ |
|---|---|---|---|
| $-0.11(0.32)$ | $1.12(2.23)$ | $-0.21(-1.19)$ | $0.45$ |

*Source:* A Kraus and R. H. Litzenberger, "Skewness Preference and the Valuation of Risk Assets," *Journal of Finance*, September 1976, Table II.

---

[24]This discussion abstracts from the theoretical derivation of KL's hypothesis and simplifies the explanation of their sampling methodology to save space. Interested readers should read the full KL study to appreciate the preparation that went into their analysis.

### 16.9 Some Concluding Remarks

The theoretical logic of portfolio analysis in three moments is undeniable. If skewness exists in either all or part of the probability distributions, this information should not be ignored. However, is difficult to measure skewness empirically, and thus to determine its importance in making investment decisions.

The empirical econometric evidence prepared by Kraus and Litzenberger (KL), for example, may have been different if continuously compounded rates of return had been used. The statistics in Tables 14.2 and 14.3 show that the continuously compounded returns are more symmetrically distributed than the noncompounded returns used in the KL study above. There is also the possibility that nonlinear functions would yield different conclusions. Thus, additional research is needed to confirm the KL conclusions about the effects of skewness on the returns demanded by investors.

The basic mean–variance–skewness theory of investments is better developed than the models to apply this theory. It is not clear whether monthly, quarterly, annual, or what differencing is appropriate. It is not known whether using continuously compounded rather than noncompounded returns will eliminate skewness as a significant consideration in evaluating investment decisions. Only when these and other practical problems are resolved will it be possible to develop more definitive empirical tests of the three-parameter portfolio theory.

## Selected References

Ingersoll, Jonathan, "Multidimensional Security Pricing," *Journal of Financial and Quantitative Analysis*, December 1975, pp. 785–798.
Calculus and mathematical statistics are used to develop a portfolio model in three moments.

Kraus, Alan and Litzenberger Robert, "Skewness Preference and Valuation of Risk Assets," *Journal of Finance*, September 1976, pp. 1085–1100.
Calculus, utility theory and econometrics are used to develop and test empirically a portfolio theory model for individual assets in three dimensions.

## Questions and Problems

1. If an investor is primarily concerned with principal maintenance and loss avoidance (for example, an elderly widow named Aunt Jane who is trying to stay out of the indigent elderly people's home) rather than getting rich, would this investor be better advised to use the two-dimensional mean–semivariance analysis or the three-parameter analysis? Explain.

2. Graph the type of utility of wealth (or returns) function which requires that the first three moments be considered to maximize expected utility, and write down an equation for this general class of utility function. What are the signs of the first three partial derivatives of this type of utility function with respect to wealth (or returns)? Interpret the signs of these partial derivatives in terms of their implications for human behavior. *Hint:* See Appendix 2 to Chapter 7 of H. Levy and M. Sarnat, *Investment and Portfolio Analysis* (New York: John Wiley & Sons, Inc., 1972).]

3. Find the expected utility of the following cubic utility function:

$$U(r) = ar + br^2 + cr^3, \qquad U'(r) > 0, \; U''(r) < 0.$$

Use the expected value operator to restate the expected utility in terms of the first three moments of the investment's probability distribution. If you had such a cubic utility function, what do you think the signs of your $a$, $b$, and $c$ coefficients would be? Explain.

4. Write verbal definitions with supplemental graphical illustrations to explain the first four statistical moments' meanings.

5. Compare and contrast moments about the origin with statistical moments.

6. It is sometimes said that the third statistical moment measures the "speculative aspect" of a probability distribution of investment returns. What does such a statement mean?

7. If an investor can borrow and lend at the riskless rate, $R$, what can be specified mathematically about the investor's most dominant investment opportunities in $[E(r), \text{var}(r), \text{skew}(r)]$ space? Derive the equations.

# Section Seven

# OTHER ISSUES

THE preceding 16 chapters explicated various phases and implications of portfolio analysis. Problems with the analysis were considered, but these critical discussions were limited in scope to whatever the relevant chapter's subject included. Chapter XVII concludes the book in a more nihilistic manner. A few basic problems that cast shadows over some major parts of portfolio theory are reviewed.

```
17171717171717171717171717171717171717171717171717171717171717171717171717171717
17171717171717171717171717171717171717171717171717171717171717171717171717171717
17171717171717171717     71717     717     7171717171717     717     717     717171717171717
171717171717171717171     171     17171     17171717171     1717     717     7171717171717171717
171717171717171717171717     7     7171717     717171717     71717     717     717171717171717
171717171717171717171     171717171     1717171     171717     717     7171717171717171717
171717171717171717171717     71717171717     71717     7171717     717     7171717171717171717
171717171717171717171     17171717171     171     17171717     717     717171717171717171717
17171717171717171717     7     71717171717     7     717171717     717     7171717171717171717
171717171717171717171     171     17171717171     1717171717     717     717171717171717171717
171717171717171717     71717     71717171717     71717171717     717     7171717171717171717
17171717171717171717171717171717171717171717171717171717171717171717171717171717
17171717171717171717171717171717171717171717171717171717171717171717171717171717
```

# Some Conclusions

Sɪɴᴄᴇ Markowitz first presented his basic portfolio analysis model in 1952, interest in the model has accelerated at an increasing rate. College curriculums have been redesigned to include more mathematics and computer science courses. Finance majors within the business schools have helped propel this increase in scientific rigor by studying and applying portfolio theory. Business managers have changed, also. There are an increasing number of influential people on Wall Street and elsewhere around the world's investment community who are working full time on various applications of portfolio theory.[1] These and other developments may be correctly viewed as positive improvements that have sprung from portfolio analysis. However, portfolio analysis is not completely free of blemishes. The analysis subsumes a few basic flaws which will be explained next.

### 17.1  Critic of $[\sigma, E(r)]$ Efficient Frontier

Some Markowitz-efficient portfolios are *not desirable investments*. Baumol's criterion for rejecting certain Markowitz-efficient portfolios is explained in this section. The Baumol criterion presumes that only the mean and variance of the portfolios' normally distributed rates of return are known.

---

[1]Charles Wells, "The Beta Revolution: Learning to Live with Risk," *Institutional Investor*, 1971.

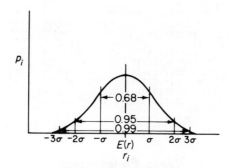

Figure 17.1. Unit Normal Probability Distribution

It has been shown that rates of return on securities are roughly normally distributed, as shown in Fig. 17.1.[2] In the elementary course in classical statistics it is shown that about 68 percent of the occurrences of a normally distributed random variable occur in the range $\pm 1$ standard deviation $(\sigma)$ from the mean. About 95 percent of the occurrences lie in the range $E(r) \pm 2\sigma$, and over 99 percent of the outcomes will be in the range $E(r) \pm 3\sigma$ for a normal distribution. These ranges and their probabilities are shown graphically in Fig. 17.1. Baumol has used such relationships to develop a selection criterion for efficient portfolios that limits consideration to a subset of the Markowitz efficient set.[3]

Baumol suggests using a lower confidence limit $(L)$ and $E(r)$ as a criterion in preference to Markowitz's $\sigma$ and $E$ criterion. He defines the lower confidence level $(L)$ as follows:

$$L = E(r_p) - (k)(\sigma),$$

---

[2]Some empirical studies have suggested that returns are only roughly normally distributed. Mandelbrot and Fama have shown they are distributed according to a stable Paretian distribution with parameters that cause the distribution to deviate from the normal. See Benoit Mandelbrot's, "The Variation of Certain Speculative Prices," *Journal of Business*, October 1963, pp. 394–419. Also see E. F. Fama, "The Behavior of Stock Prices," *Journal of Business*, January 1965, pp. 34–99. More recently, however, Fama has argued in favor of using the normal distribution. See Chapters 1, 2, and 3 of E. F. Fama, *The Foundations of Finance* (New York: Basic Books, Inc., 1976). Also, empirical evidence supporting the normal distribution exists: Randolph Westerfield, "Price Changes and Volume Relationships and the Distribution of Common Stock Price Changes," R. L. White Working Paper 6–73, 1973. Or see, R. Westerfield, "The Distribution of Common Stock Price Changes: An Application of Transactions Time and Subordinated Stochastic Models," *Journal of Financial and Quantitative Analysis*, December 1977, pp. 743–767; and see Westerfield's references for other sources of normality evidence, C. W. J. Granger and O. Morgenstern, *Predictability of Stock Market Prices*, Lexington, Mass., Heath Lexington Books, 1970.

[3]W. J. Baumol, "An Expected Gain-Confidence Limit Criterion for Portfolio Selection," *Management Science*, October 1963, pp. 174–182.

where $k$ is the maximum number of standard deviations below $E(r_p)$ which the portfolio owner can tolerate, $E(r_p)$ is expected return of the portfolio, and $\sigma$ is the standard deviation of returns for the portfolio. $k$ is selected by the investor or portfolio manager based on risk preferences—$k$ and $L$ vary inversely. For example, assuming that returns are normally distributed, if the investors are willing to accept a 0.025 chance that the portfolio's return is below $L$ [that is, $r_p < L = E(r) - k\sigma$], they should set $k = 2$. If less chance of a low return is desired, say $P\,[r_p < L = E(r) - k\sigma] = 0.005$, this may be achieved by setting $k = 3$.

The rationale for Baumol's criterion may be seen in terms of Fig. 17.2. The horizontal axis shows $E(r_p)$'s from the efficient set, the straight line from

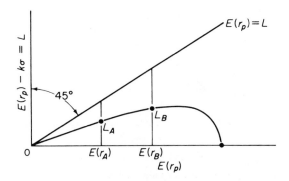

Figure 17.2. Baumol's $E(r)$, $L$ Criterion

the origin has a 45° slope, and the vertical axis measures the lower confidence limits for efficient portfolios. The curve $OL$ is the locus of $(E(r), L)$ pairs for portfolios in the efficient set. Portfolio $B$ with $E(r_B)$ offers both a higher expected return *and* a more desirable lower confidence limit ($L_B$) than any portfolio to the left of $B$. For example, $E(r_A) < E(r_B)$ and $L_A < L_B$; therefore, $A$ is completely dominated by $B$ according to Baumol's criterion. Thus, all portfolios to the left of $B$ should be eliminated according to Baumol. Baumol's criterion has an intuitive appeal—particularly to portfolio managers who cannot tolerate returns below $L$. The traditional Markowitz efficiency criterion would delineate both $A$ and $B$ as members of the efficient set. Baumol says[4]:

> The basic objection to the Markowitz criterion is that in the expression $L = E(r) - k\sigma$ an increasing $E(r)$ may more than counterbalance an increase in $\sigma$, so that despite greater variability in return from the portfolio with the

[4]Baumol, "An Expected Gain-Confidence Limit Criterion," p. 180.

larger $E(r_p)$, it may be considered relatively safe because the lower confidence limit $L$ is relatively high.

Baumol's suggestion limits the set of portfolios under consideration to a subset of the curve from $E$ to $F$ in Fig. 17.3. Baumol's criterion will limit consideration to only the upper portion of the efficient frontier, say, from $B$ to $F$. Baumol's suggestion is well taken; however, it has been shown to be of little value when the investor is willing to consider inclusion of a risk-free asset in his portfolio.[5]

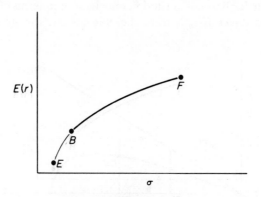

Figure 17.3. Efficient Frontier

One of the advantages of Baumol's criterion is that it requires only that the mean and variance statistics be estimated—this is a reasonable information requirement that can usually be fulfilled. As a result, the Baumol criteria can be valuable in practical applications. The stochastic dominance criteria for selecting investments is somewhat analogous to the Baumol criteria. But the stochastic dominance criterion requires more information—*every point on every asset's* probability distribution must be known. As a result of this severe information requirement, the stochastic dominance criteria is more difficult to use than Baumol's criterion. However, it is insightful to study stochastic dominance. With the use of certain simplifying assumptions, the analysis can be applied to actual investment problems.

### 17.2 The Stochastic Dominance Criteria

An investment selection criterion called the *first-degree stochastic dominance criterion* is a simple form of analysis which competes directly with Markowitz's portfolio analysis. This first-degree stochastic dominance selection utilizes

---

[5]See W. R. Russell and P. E. Smith, "A Comment on Baumol's $(E, L)$ Efficient Portfolios," *Management Science*, March 1966, pp. 619–621.

every bit of information in the probability distributions rather than simply focusing on the probability distribution's first two moments. As a result, stochastic dominance selection rules can occasionally yield portfolios which are more desirable than Markowitz-efficient portfolios. Figure 17.4 shows the probability distributions for three risky investments. Uniform probability distributions are used to expedite the explanation, but stochastic dominance rules apply to any probability distribution.

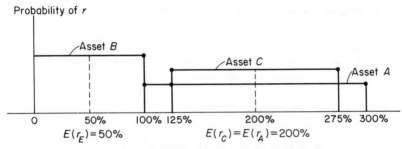

Uniform probability distributions for three assets

Figure 17.4. Uniform Probability Distributions for Three Assets Returns

According to the logic of first-degree stochastic dominance, *inefficient* portfolio $A$ is *more desirable* than efficient portfolio $B$, for example. This demonstrates that portfolio analysis which considers only the first two moments may waste some information that could be used to maximize investors' expected utility.

Probability distribution $A$ is said to *stochastically dominate* probability distribution $B$ if the cumulative probability of achieving any rate of return up to some specified level for distribution $A$ is less than or equal to that same cumulative probability for asset $B$, and, at least at one point, the less-than inequality holds.[6] In common sense terms this means that the chances of earning a low rate of return from asset $A$ are lower than the chances of earning a low return from asset $B$.[7]

---

[6]More rigorous mathematical statements are usually used to define stochastic dominance. Some writers distinguish between first-degree, second-degree, and third-degree stochastic dominance. In the interest of brevity, these distinctions are not developed here. For a more detailed critique of portfolio analysis, see J. P. Quirk and R. Saposnik, "Admissibility and Measurable Utility Functions," *Review of Economic Studies*, 1962. See also J. Hadar and W. R. Russell, "Rules for Ordering Uncertain Prospects," *American Economic Review*, Vol. 59, March 1969, pp. 25–34.

[7]The stochastic dominance model has been extended to include borrowing and lending at a riskless rate by H. Levy and Y. Kroll, "Stochastic Dominance with Riskless Assets," *Journal of Financial and Quantitative Analysis*, December 1976, pp. 743–778.

Figure 17.5 graphically depicts how portfolio $A$ stochastically dominates the efficient portfolio $B$ even though $A$ is an inefficient portfolio. For any given rate of return, the cumulative probability that asset $B$ earns up to that return is larger than the cumulative probability that $A$ earns up to that same return. This is easy to see, since portfolio $A$'s minimum return (that is, 100 percent) equals the maximum possible return from portfolio $B$.

The advantages of selecting investments with stochastic dominance criteria instead of risk–return criteria are:

1. Stochastic dominance orderings do not presume a certain form of probability distribution (namely, the normal distribution).

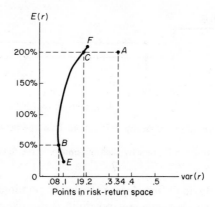

Figure 17.5A. Points in Risk-Return Space

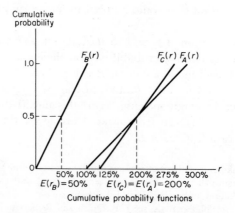

Figure 17.5B. Cumulative Probability Distributions*

Figure 17.5. Analysis of Three Risky Investment Assets

*The basis for the graphs are uniform probability distributions from $b$ to $c$. It is well known that the expected value of such distribution is $E(r) = (b + c)/2$; the variance $\sigma^2 = (c - b)^2/12$; and the cumulative probability of a return less than or equal to $r_0$ is $F(r_0) = (r_0 - b)/(c - b)$.

2. Fewer restrictions on the investor's utility function are implied by use of the stochastic dominance criteria.

3. Undesirable portfolios such as those on the lower section of the efficient frontier can be eliminated from further consideration.

4. The stochastic dominance selection criteria do not waste information about the probability distribution; *every* point is considered.

5. Investors with monotonically nondecreasing utility of wealth functions of any form will always obtain more expected utility from a stochastically dominant asset rather than a dominated one, but some Markowitz-efficient portfolios are not utility maximizers.

Although stochastic dominance selection rules are logically superior to other simpler selection criteria, their practical value is dubious since they require knowledge of *every point* on the probability distribution rather than, for example, merely the first two moments.[8] It requires rather heroic confidence to try to estimate *every* point on a probability distribution in this world on uncertainty and changing expectations. The cost of estimating the entire probability distribution exceeds the cost of estimating the first two moments, and this cost is probably not justified in terms of the additional benefits it could realistically be expected to yield. This is an empirical question that is not yet completely resolved. Simplifying assumptions (namely, assuming that probability distributions are all normal, for example) to expedite using stochastic dominance at reduced levels of cost can be exploited.[9]

Not only do certain parts of basic portfolio analysis (namely, the logic of the efficient frontier) lie open to some criticism, but some of the implications of portfolio theory can also be problematical. Trying to apply the single-period static equilibrium models from capital market theory to solve actual dynamic problems can be frustrating, as explained in Section 17.3.

### 17.3 Static Theory and Dynamic Changes

Capital market theory is a theory of static equilibrium. The dynamic disequilbria that actually occur are not delineated by the theory. Different market conditions must be analyzed by comparing different static equilibria; this is the well-known form of economic analysis called *comparative statics.*

---

[8]An easy-to-read survey of some of the stochastic dominance literature can be found in H. Levy and M. Sarnat, *Investment and Portfolio Analysis* (New York: John Wiley & Sons, Inc., 1972). R. B. Porter compares and contrasts stochastically dominant portfolios with Markowitz-efficient portfolios using empirical data in "An Empirical Comparison of Stochastic Dominance and Mean-Variance Portfolio Choice Criteria," *Journal of Financial and Quantitative Analysis*, September 1973.

[9]Jack Meyer has developed a new way to apply the stochastic dominance selection criteria which combines the Pratt-Arrow risk-aversion measures (see Chapter XI regarding Pratt-Arrow), "Further Applications of Stochastic Dominance to Mutual Fund Performance," *Journal of Financial and Quantitative Analysis*, June 1977, pp. 235–242.

Some of the problems that can arise in analyzing dynamic situations with a static theory are considered below.

In portfolio theory, total risk is measured by calculating the variance of the single-period returns, such as those defined in equation (17.1) for a common stock.

$$r_t = \frac{(P_{t+1} - P_t) + D_{t+1}}{P_t}. \qquad (17.1)$$

Thus, risk can be defined as shown in equation (17.2).

$$\text{var } (r_t) = \text{var}\left[\frac{(P_{t+1} - P_t) + D_{t+1}}{P_t}\right] = \left(\frac{1}{P_t}\right)^2 \text{var } (P_{t+1} + D_{t+1}), \quad (17.2)$$

where $P_{t+1}$ is the beginning of the period market price for period $t + 1$, $P_t$ is the $t$th period's beginning price—a constant for period $t$—and $D_{t+1}$ are dividends earned during period $t$ and received at the beginning of period $t + 1$.

The security market line (SML) assumes the risk of an individual security is "covariability of return" as measured by the covariance.

$$\text{cov } (r_i, r_j) = E\{[r_i - E(r_i)][r_j - E(r_j)]\}$$

$$= \frac{1}{P_{ti}} \cdot \frac{1}{P_{tj}} \cdot E\{[(P_{t+1} + D_{t+1}) - E(P_{t+1} + D_{t+1})]_i$$

$$\times [(P_{t+1} + D_{t+1}) - E(P_{t+1} + D_{t+1})]_j\}. \qquad (17.3)$$

Note that $P_t$, beginning price, is in both these risk surrogates. This is what constrains capital market theory to be a static model. Consider Figs. 17.6 and 17.7.

Assume that an underpriced security such as $U$ in Figs. 17.6 and 17.7 is observed over sequential time increments. Capital market theory says that $U$ is undervalued and will be in equilibrium at point $E$ after a temporary

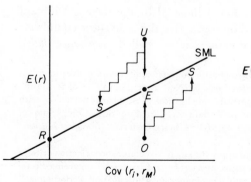

Figure 17.6. SML in a Dynamic Context

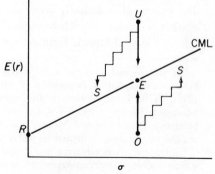

Figure 17.7. CML in a Dynamic Context

disequilibrium during which its price will rise. But when it is actually observed, each time period it will have a different beginning of period price $(P_t)$. Since $P_t$ will change each period as the security moves toward equilibrium, *the risk class of the security will also change each period*, although the distribution of $P_{t+1}$ and $D_{t+1}$ may not have changed. Thus, the time path for the security will follow the path like the ones ending at point $S$ if this static theory is used for dynamic analysis. A symmetrical but opposite argument will show why an overvalued security such as $O$ in Figs. 17.6 and 17.7 will increase its risk class as it moves toward equilibrium.

What is needed is a dynamic theory so that the market can be observed as it equilibrates. In a dynamic theory the securities would follow the time path to points like $E$ rather than to points like $S$ in Figs. 17.6 and 17.7. That is, the risk class of the security would be independent of the initial condition $P_t$.[10]

Until the model is adapted to dynamic analysis, capital market theory will not be able to deal with questions about the time paths of the variables. For example, consider the time derivative

$$\frac{dP}{dt} = f(D - S), \tag{17.4}$$

where $dP/dt$ is the change in price per time increment for some security; $f$ is some positive function that could be estimated with difference equations; $D$ is demand for a security and $S$ is supply, so $(D - S)$ represents excess demand for the security. Estimates of such time derivatives might be useful in estimating security prices if the security's risk class determined $f$ and would not change arbitrarily as the security moved toward equilibrium.[11]

Of course, many economic models are models that can only be used for comparative statics. Much rich analysis has come from some of these static models. However, the model would be more interesting if it were amenable to dynamics.[12]

---

[10]Sharpe refers to this problem in his footnote 17. W. F. Sharpe, "Capital Asset Price: A Theory of Market Equilibrium Under Conditions of Risk," *Journal of Finance*, September 1964, pp. 425–442.

[11]P. A. Samuelson, *Foundations of Economic Analysis* (New York: Atheneum Publishers, 1965), Chaps. 10 and 11. In an empirical study of Markowitz portfolio analysis that was conducted independently from Samuelson's theoretical work, Elton and Gruber found that unsystematic changes in a security's excess demand could result in spurious correlation coefficients (or covariances) which reduce the stability of the efficient frontiers generated with historical statistics. However, Elton and Gruber suggested methods of developing correlation coefficients which are more useful than the historical correlations which are inefficient statistics. See E. J. Elton and M. J. Gruber, "Estimating the Dependence Structure of Share Prices—Implications for Portfolio Selection," *Journal of Finance*, December 1973, Vol. XXVIII, No. 5, pp. 1203–1232.

[12]For another problem with portfolio theory, see N. Gonzales, R. Litzenberger, and J. Rolfo, "On Mean Variance Models of Capital Structure and the Absurdity of Their Predictions," *Journal of Financial and Quantitative Analysis*, June 1977, pp. 165–180.

## 17.4 Future Research

For financial researchers, portfolio analysis is probably the most promising model since present-value theory. As the capital budgeting models are expanded to consider risk and the interdependence of assets is recognized, the variance–covariance matrix may furnish the engine of analysis to consider these interrelationships. Many researchers foresee a merging of capital budgeting and portfolio analysis into a more general model for capital allocation.[13] Admittedly, it does seem paradoxical to use one model (capital budgeting) to allocate capital to physical assets while using another model (portfolio analysis) to allocate capital among financial assets. Certainly, the underlying principles of optimal capital allocation must not differ, depending on the type of asset considered.

Portfolio analysis has fostered a new approach to valuation theory and the cost of capital—capital market theory.[14] Capital market theory provides a macromodel that rationalizes the determination of security prices. The cost-of-capital dilemma will be solved only when a satisfactory security-valuation model is developed. Furthermore, it seems more logical to approach cost-of-capital determination externally to the firm through valuation theory before stepping inside the firm to see how the financial decision variables such as leverage affect the cost of capital. Thus, the future appears promising for financial analysts seeking to apply and/or extend portfolio theory in either academic or business uses. The problems reviewed in this chapter seem to be far outweighted by the analytical insights that can be gained from portfolio theory.

---

[13]J. Mossin, "Security Pricing and Investment Criteria in Competitive Markets," *American Economic Review*, Vol. 59, No. 5 1969, 749–756. See also J. C. Francis, "Portfolio Analysis of Asset and Liability Management in Small-, Medium-, and Large-Sized Banks," *Journal of Monetary Economics*, August 1978, Vol. 4, No. 3, pp. 459–480.

[14]R. S. Hamada, "Portfolio Analysis, Market Equilibrium and Corporation Finance," *Journal of Finance*, March 1969, pp. 13–33.

## Selected References

Levy, H., and M. Sarnat, *Investment and Portfolio Analysis*. New York: John Wiley & Sons, Inc., 1972.

This investments textbook compares and contrasts the mean–variance portfolio theory with the stochastic dominance theory of risk-asset selection. Some limited empirical tests are included which suggest the superiority of the stochastic dominance criteria.

Quirk, J. P., and R. Saposnik, "Admissibility and Measurable Utility Functions," *Review of Economic Studies*, October 1962.

Mathematical utility theory is analyzed to reveal some flaws in the portfolio theory.

## Questions and Problems

1. Consider the logical utility theory foundation that underlies the mean–variance portfolio theory. What basis for preferring efficient portfolios exists if the investor's utility function is completely undefined? Explain. (*Hint*: Consider stochastic dominance.)

2. Is it true that the returns on short-term U.S. Treasury bills are riskless rates? What about the difference between nominal and real rates of return? [*Hint*: See R. G. Ibbotson and R. A. Sinquefield, "Stocks, Bonds, Bills and Inflation: Year by Year Historical Returns (1926–74)," *Journal of Business*, Vol. 49, No. 1, 1976, pp. 11–47.]

3. Do you think that most investors know how to calculate a one-period rate of return? Do you think they could develop expected return and risk statistics to aid them in making investment decisions? Could they delineate an efficient frontier? If you responded negatively to any of these three questions, what is the value of portfolio theory?

4. If the probability distributions of returns are unstable intertemporally for a significant number of investments, what are the implications for portfolio analysis? For the capital market theory?

# Subject Index

# Name Index